YOU AND YOUR
AGING PARENT

You AND YOUR
Aging Parent

THE MODERN FAMILY'S GUIDE TO EMOTIONAL, PHYSICAL, AND FINANCIAL PROBLEMS

BARBARA SILVERSTONE
HELEN KANDEL HYMAN

With special contributions by
Charlotte Kirschner and Cathy Michaelson

SECOND REVISED EDITION

PANTHEON BOOKS

NEW YORK

Copyright © 1976, 1982, 1989, by Barbara Silverstone and Helen Kandel Hyman

All rights reserved under International and Pan-American Copyright Conventions.
Published in the United States by Pantheon Books, a division of Random House, Inc.,
New York, and simultaneously in Canada by Random House of Canada Limited,
Toronto.

Library of Congress Cataloging in Publication Data
Silverstone, Barbara, 1931–
You and your aging parent.
Includes bibliography and index.
1. Parents, Aged—United States—Family relationships.
2. Middle age—United States—Family relationships.
3. Old age assistance—United States.
4. Aged—Psychology.   I. Hyman, Helen.   II. Title.
HQ1064.U5S54   1981   362.8′2   81-47214
ISBN 0-394-52169-2   AACR2
ISBN 0-394-74948-0 (pbk.)

Grateful acknowledgment is made to the following for permission to reprint previously
published material:
The National Council on the Aging, Inc.: Excerpts from *The Myth and Reality of Aging
    in America*, a study for The National Council on the Aging, Inc. Copyright © 1975
    by Louis Harris and Associates, Inc.
New Directions Publishing Corporation and David Highman Associates Limited: Three
    lines from "Do Not Go Gentle Into That Good Night," from *Poems of Dylan Thomas*
    by Dylan Thomas. Copyright 1952 by Dylan Thomas. Reprinted by permission of
    New Directions Publishing Corporation. Rights in Canada and the open market ad-
    ministered by David Highman Associates Limited.
The New York Times: Excerpts from "Interview with Laurence Olivier," December 10,
    1975; "Like My Father . . . This Old Man to Take Care Of," by Will Durant, Novem-
    ber 6, 1975; and "Ma'am, The Door Is Being Jimmied," by William J. Dean, Novem-
    ber 8, 1975. Copyright © 1975 by The New York Times Company. Reprinted by
    permission.
Rosamond Fisher Weiss: Excerpt from *The Memoirs of Glückel of Hameln*, translated
    by Marvin Lowenthal (Schocken Books, 1977). Reprinted by permission.

Book Design by Ann Gold

Manufactured in the United States of America

Second Revised Edition

FOR OUR OWN CHILDREN
KAREN AND JULIA—LISA, DAVID, AND ALEX

AND OUR GRANDCHILDREN
CHARLIE AND BERNIE—DANIEL AND ANNA

First published in 1976, *You and Your Aging Parent* was one of the earliest books on old age written for the general public in order to offset the prevalent myth that "young people today don't care about their old relatives." Recognizing that there was, indeed, ongoing and often close involvement between the generations, our book focused on these relationships—their pleasures, their pains, and their search for solutions. The book was revised in 1982 and along with reporting on developments over a five-year period, pointed out that professionals, after acknowledging the crucial role played by families of the elderly, were showing a greater interest in family dynamics. The second edition, after reviewing how family members work together—or against—each other when an elderly relative needs help, included a new chapter with concrete, practical steps to help families reach solutions acceptable to everyone.

Why, then, a third edition thirteen years after the first? Old age remains pretty much the same. The relationships between the generations continue in 1989 much as they did in 1976. What difference have these thirteen years made? The most important difference is the growth in national awareness that the number of older men and women in our society is ever on the rise: 10 percent of the total population in 1976, 12 percent in 1982, and now well over 12 percent in 1989. Projections for the future when, as gerontologists like to point out, the baby-boom generation will arrive at Golden Pond, suggest that the over-sixty-five segment of the population will reach 25 percent early in the next century.

Along with this awareness has come a growing realization that the needs of these older Americans must be met. Some of them are being met, as the following chart shows.

YEARS OF RAPID GROWTH

	1974	1988
Population 65 and over	20,000,000 +	28,600,000
Membership in American Association of Retired Persons	7,000,000	30,000,000
Membership in Gerontological Society of America	3,800	7,000
Senior centers	1,200	9,000
Hospices	1	1,770
Alzheimer's Association chapters	0	177
Homemaker–home health services	Less than 5,000	15,000
Companies offering nursing home insurance	0	70

These last thirteen years have therefore brought new programs, new legislation, additional and expanded services, and increased appropriations. This current revision reviews related developments of the last five years: the Medicare Catastrophic Coverage Act of 1988, reverse mortgages, long-term health insurance, "elder law," care management—all of which affect the quality of life of the elderly and of their families, too. One such family with two sets of living parents, his and hers, reports on trying to deal with four different physical and emotional problems, each one requiring a different form of caregiving.

The traditional three-generation family, once rare, is almost routine these days, while the four-generation family no longer surprises anyone. Even the five-generation one is not uncommon, extending the family still further and presenting problems almost unknown in the past. Not unusual now are middle-aged couples with *two* generations of retirees ahead of them—parents in their sixties and seventies coping with their own aging while simultaneously trying to help *their* parents aged eighty, ninety, or even one hundred. The prevalence of divorce and remarriage has produced a proliferation of step-relationships—mother, father, sister, brother, son, daughter. It has also produced step-grandmothers and step-grandfathers.

Family caregivers formerly isolated with their own individual problems are now receiving public recognition for the central role they play in the lives of their elderly. Programs originally developed exclusively for the aged themselves are now being designed also to assist, extend, and relieve the ongoing care provided by one or more family members. The intent of these programs is also to help maintain older people in their own communities—preferably in their own homes—where, in general, they and their families want them to be.

Thirteen years have naturally brought many changes into our own personal lives. One of us has joined the ranks of the sixty-five-and-older, thereby becoming an "aging parent" herself. Both of us have become grandmothers and are now more than ever concerned with the quality of life for the young as well as for the old. Working to improve this quality for one end of the life-cycle in no way involves shortchanging the other or any of the weaker members of our society—the poor and the disabled.

There is a danger in our society of going to extremes. The youth culture of the 1960s was a good example. The intensity of focus on youth blinded everyone to the needs and accomplishments of other age groups. We do not suggest going to the other extreme and focusing with the same intensity on the old. Maybe it's asking for the moon to hope for generational equity, a middle course where every age has its rights and benefits and none thrives at the expense of the other.

Old age still has its own harsh realities—poverty, sickness, loneliness—but these are being faced and are beginning to be dealt with. We hope this encouraging trend will continue, but in these times of deficit and economic uncertainty predictions about the future are foolhardy. We therefore present this third edition of *You and Your Aging Parent* with a sense of hope mingled with a sense of realistic concern.

B.S. and H.K.H.
January 1989

ACKNOWLEDGMENTS

O ur appreciation fans out in so many different directions because so many people have helped us with all three editions of this book.

We are still indebted to all who contributed their support and technical help to the first edition when it was being written in 1976: to the families of the elderly whose expressed need stimulated us to undertake the book; to the Friends and Relatives of the Jewish Home and Hospital for Aged in New York City, and to Manuel Rodstein, M.D., Chief of Medical Services of that institution; to Dr. Ruth Weber, Professor of Social Work, University of Georgia; and to Judy Draper, who typed the original manuscript.

For this, the third edition, our special thanks go once again to Charlotte Kirschner, M.S.S.W., Director of the Geriatric Family Service, whose research contributions were essential to each of the three editions. Her special sensitivity to the problems and feelings of the elderly and their families helped in many ways to shape our presentation. We are also grateful to the Research and Community Services staff of the Benjamin Rose Institute in Cleveland, Ohio, and to Cathy Michaelson, Associate Director of the Lighthouse Center for Vision and Aging.

We continue to thank our husbands, psychoanalyst Stanley Silverstone and the late sociologist Herbert Hyman, not only because they gave us invaluable professional advice, guidance, and criticism, but also because they cheerfully endured the preparation of these editions, offering encouragement and enthusiasm all along the way.

CONTENTS

~~~~~~

YOU AND YOUR
AGING PARENT

1

INTRODUCTION

We always had Thanksgiving dinner at my parents' house: my brother and his family, my husband, and my children. Year after year it was always the same—the polished silver, the good china, the wonderful cooking smells. But last year something was different. My father's hands shook so he could barely carve the turkey. My mother looked frail, almost shrunken, at the other end of the table. Suddenly, for the first time, it hit me: my parents were getting old.

Mary Lewis was forty-five years old. Her father was eighty-two and her mother eighty. She knew their ages well. Hadn't she always celebrated their birthdays with them? But she'd never admitted that they were getting older with each celebration. It came to her as a shock.

• •

It was my mother's funeral, but I couldn't think about her at all. I kept watching my crippled father and thinking about him. What would happen to him now? Who would take care of him? Where would he live? How would we all manage?

Barry Richards was thirty-eight and his wife was pregnant again. Their apartment was barely big enough for another child, and they couldn't afford to move yet. There was no way Barry's father could live with them. But he certainly couldn't live alone. Where would he go now?

• •

I called my mother last night and I let the phone ring and ring, but she didn't answer. The same old panic started. Was she sick? Had she fallen and broken something? Was she unconscious? Maybe a heart attack? A stroke? I told myself she was probably out at the store—but I couldn't be sure. I'm never sure. I live five hundred miles away and I go through this every time she doesn't answer her phone. Why does she make it so hard for me?

Frances Black's mother insisted on staying on in her old house long after her husband's death, even though the neighborhood had changed and was no longer pleasant or even safe. She stubbornly refused repeated invitations to move in with Frances and her family or to move closer to them. So Frances worried constantly, phoned several times a week, and prayed each time that the phone would be answered. She continually felt guilty and inadequate. But that was nothing new—she'd felt that way most of her life. Somehow, Jerry, her younger brother, had always seemed to do everything right. He still did—even though Frances was the one who phoned regularly.

• •

Mary, Barry, and Frances are three separate people, living in different parts of the country, with different lifestyles, different careers, different incomes. They have never met, nor are they likely to. But if they were to meet, they would find they have one thing in common: they all belong to a special generation caught in the middle—men and women pulled in three directions, trying to rear their children, live their own lives, and help their aging parents—perhaps even their grandparents—at the same time. These sons and daughters, commonly referred to as the Sandwich Generation, need to have their title revised. Their sandwich is now, in many cases, a triple-decker.

This painful three-way pull is not experienced by everyone in the middle generation. Some people have no reason to feel conflicting loyalties if their parents remain active and self-sufficient into their seventies, eighties, and nineties. Many of the elderly take old age surprisingly easily. Far from needing help from younger relatives, vigorous old men and women are often the ones who do the helping, encouraging their children and grandchildren to turn to *them* in times of trouble. Recent research findings reveal that there is a great deal of exchange of "goods and services" between the generations—as much flowing from the older to the younger as vice versa.

Despite the popular image, to be old is not necessarily synonymous with being weak or helpless or finished. Old age can be a time of enjoyment, contentment, productivity—even creativity. Because of prevailing prejudices, younger generations are rarely aware that all kinds of people—writers, artists, politicians, musicians, philosophers, scientists, businessmen, craftsmen—often keep right on working for decades after their sixty-fifth birthday, sometimes making major contributions in their seventies, eighties, and nineties. The young tend to assume that life must be dreadful for the old, but the old themselves, who are experiencing old age firsthand, take a far less negative view of their own lives. As the columnist Russell Baker once wrote, "Wrinkles are just as natural a part of life as diaper rash and adolescent acne and a lot more comfortable, to boot."

A survey commissioned by the National Council on the Aging and conducted by survey expert Louis Harris as far back as 1974 dramatizes the gap between the feelings of the old and the younger generations. The sample of respondents sixty-five and older were asked about their own lives; the sample of respondents eighteen to sixty-four were asked their beliefs about the lives of old people. A few of the findings selected from the Harris tables are enough to illustrate how false are the prevailing assumptions (similar findings have been reported by subsequent studies).

	Percentage of aged reporting they themselves have a "very serious" problem of:	Percentage of those under 65 believing most people over 65 have a "very serious" problem of:
Not having enough friends	5	28
Not having enough to do	6	37
Not feeling needed	7	54
Loneliness	12	60
Not having enough money to live on	15	62
Poor health	21	51

These figures can be deceptive. It has been said that statistics are "people without tears." While life may have seemed easier for most older people than was generally assumed, there were substantial numbers for whom life was tragically difficult. Assuming the numbers are similar today, the 12 percent who feel lonely represent only a small minority of the total, but in a country with more than 28 million people over sixty-five, that small percentage translates into over 3 million lonely old people. The 21 percent who rate their problem of poor health as "very serious" translates into over 5 million ailing old people—one out of every five! Nor does it help much to read the statistics and find out that other people's parents are getting along pretty well if our own parents are getting along pretty badly. If we care about them at all, we usually want to do something to help them to get along better, and most of us don't know what to do. Few of us have even vague plans about how to proceed if the day ever comes when they cannot manage alone.

The statistics show us that the odds are in our favor—the day may never come. Many of us escape the problem completely. In the back of our minds we may think, "Why plan for something that may never happen—if we're lucky?" Our parents may not live to be old; they may never need help; or, if they do, they may turn to someone else in the family—not us. A brother or a sister may offer to take in both of them, or whichever is left alone, widowed or divorced. We can sidestep away. But there is always the possibility that the very problem we have refused to think about will one day descend on us, disturbing our lives, our emotions, and our finances.

Even the most careful planner is taking a gamble. Plans we make may be systematically foiled by the very unpredictable nature of the aging process. No one can sit back complacently in middle age and proclaim, "It's all set, I'm ready to take over when my parents need me," because except in certain special situations it is impossible to predict in advance what these parents will need and when.

Clare Fowler thought she was facing the future honestly and intelligently. She had begun thinking about it after her fiftieth birthday, when the younger of her two children got married. She knew that women usually outlive men in the United States—she had read the statistics, and in addition she was twelve years younger than her husband, who was already in his sixties. It seemed likely that she would be widowed at some point in the future; naturally, she hoped it would be the far future. Mr. Fowler was willing to discuss the likelihood with her, and they went over the financial picture. They both agreed that Mrs. Fowler should try to live an independent life and under no circumstances should live with either of the children. They even discussed some of their ideas with the children themselves, who—like most children—were not too eager to listen.

But things didn't go according to plan. Mrs. Fowler died suddenly of a stroke at the age of fifty-six, and her sixty-eight-year-old husband, who had never for a moment contemplated his own widowerhood, was left so emotionally helpless that he seemed incapable of living alone. To pull himself together he made his home "temporarily" with his son and daughter-in-law and their children. There he stayed for the next seventeen years, until he died at the age of eighty-five.

Just as the future is unpredictable, the aging process itself does not follow any uniform calendar. Parents of young children know what comes next in early childhood development. Within a reasonable period we know when our children will walk and talk, when their first teeth will come, when they'll be likely to start kindergarten or high school. We can anticipate some of the emotional stages: the negativism at two-and-a-half, the rebellion in adolescence.

The stages of growing old have no such predictable pattern. We can't look at our sixty-year-old parents and announce, "Okay, five years to go until you're over the hill." One man's father may be beginning to decline at sixty-five, it's true. But the next man's father may still be capably running his own life at eighty-five—and still trying to dominate his son's too, for that matter. We need only to look at the Armand Hammers, James Stewarts, Ronald Reagans, and George Burnses. One young woman of twenty-five whom we met recently is currently concerned, not about her mother or her grandmother, but about her great-grandmother. This nonagenarian adamantly lives alone in a somewhat isolated house, stoking her own coal furnace, warming water on her stove, and letting her well-heeled descendants agonize over her welfare—but from a distance.

Vigorous seniors are no longer a rarity. Many, less prominent though all wearing that rather meaningless identification tag "sixty-five-and-older," function just as well as their younger brothers and sisters still in their prime. Thanks to medical advances and widely followed regimes of healthy eating and regular exercise, millions of men and women are not only living longer but living healthier and stronger, playing tennis, running marathons, climbing mountains, starting new careers. Some gerontologists even suggest that the age range for middle age, formerly considered to be 35–55, be changed to 55–75, seventy-five being the point at which the term "old" may be more appropriately applied. This shift seems to be quite logical, particularly since professionals involved with the lower end of the life-cycle are suggesting that adolescence currently lasts until age thirty.

In addition to the irregular and unpredictable calendar of physical aging, emotional and personality problems intervene and confuse the picture. Failing eyesight or severe arthritis may be overcome by sheer will power and personal vitality by one elderly individual, who continues to live and function independently and even productively. By contrast, a similarly afflicted contemporary may retire quickly into invalidism and total dependency.

Until the 1970s, the later stages of life never received much attention either from professional experts or from the public at large. Society's interest was focused mainly on the earlier stages: infancy, youth, middle age. But old age is finally gaining some of the limelight and attracting long-overdue public attention. New scientific terms, coined in this century from the Greek *geron*, "old man," are now heard frequently: *geriatrics*, *gerontology*, *geropsychiatry*. (Our society was even accused not long ago of *gerontophobia*—fear of old age and old people.) Additional evidence of increasing interest in the whole subject of aging was the publication in 1975 of a book by an eminent veterinarian, Dr. George Whitney, *The Health and Happiness of Your Old Dog*.

The mounting concern about life in the later decades is well deserved. The elderly segment of the population has been steadily growing during the past century, increasing faster than any other age group. Moreover, within this elderly segment, the over-eighty-five group is increasing the fastest and will continue to do so according to projections.

	Over Seventy-five	Over Eighty-five
1977	8,853,000	2,040,000
2000	14,386,000	3,756,000
2035	26,178,000	6,854,000

At some point in the next century projections predict 1.2 million people over one hundred!

Average life expectancy—which was eighteen years in the days of ancient Greece, thirty-three in the year 1600, forty-two in the Civil War period, and forty-seven in 1900—is now over seventy-three. This dramatic change has taken place within the lifetime of the elderly still alive today. As Ronald Blythe points out in *The View in Winter*:

> *If a Renaissance . . . man could return, he would be as much astonished by the sight of two or three thousand septuagenarians and octogenarians lining a South Coast resort on a summer's day . . . as he would be by a television set. His was a world where it was the exception to go grey, to reach the menopause, to retire, to become senile. . . .*

The nearly 29 million men and women over sixty-five today represent over 12 percent of the population of the United States. The total population has increased threefold since 1900, but the ranks of the elderly have increased fivefold. By the year 2000, the older population is expected to reach 32 million. For the weight of its numbers alone, both present and future, that is a group to be reckoned with. The reckoning has been accelerating in recent years, although not nearly fast enough.

Over the twenty years from the first White House Conference on Aging in 1961 to the second in 1981, major efforts were made to improve the welfare of elderly Americans. The U.S. Senate Committee on Aging was established in 1961. The year 1965 saw the passage of the Older Americans Act and the creation, under the Department of Health, Education, and Welfare (now the Department of Health and Human Services), of a central federal office—the Administration on Aging. Legislators are constantly considering new bills to benefit the elderly, although not passing many, and this consideration is not without some amount of self-interest. The over-sixty-five segment of the population, far from being disengaged socially or politically, is a powerful and articulate interest group, likely to register its opinions at election time. Studies of voting patterns consistently show that the turnout at the polls is higher for older voters than for very young ones.

The rising interest in the elderly is not limited to legislative circles alone. Programs for the elderly are featured in the popular press. TV and documentary films are beginning to show the many faces of old age and are making the general public stop and think about the needs of the elderly. Professionals in public and private agencies are trying to meet these needs and provide more supportive services. Social planners are contemplating more comprehensive health services and suggesting second careers to make the retirement years more meaningful, less empty. Even the building and architectural fields are dreaming up new communities geared to the lives of older people. Thanks to the virtual explosion in its field, gerontology is expected to be one of the fastest-growing career opportunities for the next decade. A survey summarized in the *New York Times* in late 1988 reported that nine hundred programs in gerontology were offered in four hundred educational institutions—universities, colleges, and junior colleges.

Society is being forced to rethink those former prejudices and biases that led to the neglect of the needs of the aged. Many of their needs are still unmet today, but the elderly at last are beginning to demand their rights, speaking out for themselves at the polls and through their own political pressure groups such as the Gray Panthers, the National Council of Senior Citizens, and the American Association of Retired Persons.

During these recent years, as the elderly were coming forward to center stage, the nuclear family—mother, father, and children—has also been given the spotlight, although not such a sympathetic one. The nuclear family has been accused of living in selfish isolation as a tight, exclusive unit involved only in its own interests, its own problems, its own daily life. Admittedly, some families do fit this description and do deserve the accusation "Young people these days just don't care about their old parents." Such families are able to ignore the downhill slide of aging relatives, comfortably turning their backs on parents growing old on the other side of the country, five hundred miles away, or just across the park. A monthly or even an annual check, an occasional phone call, and birthday cards seem involvement enough.

But most families cannot so easily be written off as uninvolved and uncaring. They generally prefer separate homes. So do their elderly parents. But that does not mean that they prefer separate, independent lives. Far from it.

Most of these families continue some involvement—often a close one—with the parent generation. Of the nearly 29 million men and women over sixty-five, more than three-quarters have at least one living child. A series of surveys made over a twenty-year period with national samples of the elderly all report similar findings: older people and their children (at least one child) usually maintain ongoing contact with each other. Furthermore, despite the assumption that children these days grow up, move far away from their parents, and then do not visit much, the studies report that 85 percent of the elderly with living children have at least one child who lives less than one hour away and that 66 percent of the elderly respondents saw one of their children the very day they were interviewed or the day before; only 2 percent had not seen any of their children within the past year.

Many families are willing and eager to help when aging parents, even grandparents, are in trouble. These grown-up, usually middle-aged children, often over sixty-five themselves, may be motivated by a sense of responsibility, of duty, and of guilt; they are motivated just as often by genuine concern and love. But when elderly parents become more dependent and the problems of daily living multiply, their children soon discover that "love is not enough."

But if love is not enough, what else is there? Millions of sons and daughters are asking this question. These millions will increase steadily in the future as extended longevity creates a further abundance of three-, four-, and even five-generation families. The millions concerned about their aging parents can be found anywhere and everywhere. Their problems are not limited to any one geographical location, any one class. Some are only in their early thirties, others much older. Some may even be in their sixties already, concerned about their own futures while still trying to help their parents, their children, and perhaps their grandchildren as well. They have low, middle, and high incomes, because although money helps, it rarely provides the complete solution. Sons may be laborers, farmers, hardhats, blue-collar or white-collar workers; daughters may be housewives, office or factory workers, or career women. They are found in every ethnic group (with variations); they are urban, suburban, exurban, and rural. They are highly educated or barely educated. Today the Sandwich Generation—or the Triple-Decker—is talked about and analyzed and probed on TV panels and documentaries and on radio talk shows, as well as in seminars and conferences frequently titled "You and Your Aging Parent."

This book is addressed to that large and often unrecognized middle generation. It does not pretend to cover every situation or touch on every problem, but the authors hope that the chapters which follow will help the readers to think through their own personal situations more realistically and to begin to figure out more effective solutions to their own individual problems.

While many of the solutions can be found in the outside community if families know where and how to look, other solutions may be found much closer to home. Sons and daughters naturally must understand their parents' needs before they can help them, but they must also understand themselves and their own feelings. Their own emotions are likely to confuse the picture, and perhaps even prevent them from helping effectively.

This book is therefore divided into two parts, Part 1, "Taking Stock," presents an overall view of the range of problems which may complicate life for the elderly themselves and for their children: the emotions, conscious and unconscious, which color relationships between generations, the feelings between brothers and sisters which help or hinder when families try to work together.

The objective problems of the elderly themselves will be discussed: the "normal" losses of old age—physiological, psychological, and social— and the way some older people learn to compensate for these losses. Marriage in the later years will be examined, as well as widowhood and widowerhood, the possibilities of remarriage, and the continuing sexual life of the elderly—an issue raised frequently by professionals but often viewed with uneasiness or alarm by the younger generations. The equally difficult and often unmentionable subject of death and the period before death is included, a logical final step in the stocktaking process.

Part 2, "Taking Action," analyzes available solutions to the problems which have been raised in the earlier chapters. It considers first the ongoing relationships between children and elderly parents who are still managing independently. How much communication is necessary? How much is expected? How much visiting? Phoning? Is it possible to have too much communication? How can older people be encouraged to plan for future emergencies: disabling illness or accident? Supportive government programs and community services will be described—how to find them and how to pay for them, with particular stress on the ones which make it possible for older people to remain in their home communities. The question whether to institutionalize or not will be raised, and if this step is necessary, where to institutionalize, how to evaluate facilities, what they will cost, and who will pay for them. Ways to help a parent become a nursing home resident and ways to speed up the adjustment process once the move is made will be reviewed. Because the role of the family as the basic support system of the elderly has recently been receiving the recognition it has long deserved, Part 2 includes a chapter which describes how family members can work together to take more effective action.

A quick glimpse will be offered of the future and what it holds for those who will grow old in the years ahead. Will the now-unmet needs of today's elderly population be met more successfully then? What can we hope for? What can we do?

The Appendixes include directories of essential services and an overall guide to specialized agencies and services, public and private, across the nation, as well as a bibliography, checklists for evaluating services, and a short section on common diseases and symptoms of elderly people.

The pages that follow will not tell the whole story, because additional chapters are being written every year. A new character enters as each man and woman turns sixty-five. You may not recognize your own parents, but you are likely to recognize someone you know. A variety of answers will be suggested and many familiar questions raised. Among the most crucial are those asked recently by a young woman in her middle thirties:

> What's happened to me? I'm like the rope in a tug of war between my parents and my children. I always seem to be needed in two places at the same time and I'm never in the right one. When I'm with my parents I'm always asking myself, "What am I doing here? I ought to be with my children." And when I'm with my children I'm always asking myself, "What am I doing here? How can I leave my old parents alone so much?" It's awful to feel so guilty all the time. But do you know there's something even worse? It's that little voice inside my head that's always crying out, "What about me? When is there going to be time for me? Doesn't anybody care?"

I

TAKING
STOCK

2

FACING UP TO FEELINGS

Mary Graham was a devoted daughter—everyone said so. All her friends were amazed at the way she treated her old mother. . . . Such loving concern—such patient understanding! They knew that Mary phoned her mother every day, visited her several times a week, included her in every family activity, and never took a vacation without her. Her friends also knew that Mary's husband and children had learned to accept second place in her life years ago.

Mary herself knew that she had always done her best for her mother. Why did she always worry that her best was never good enough?

In times gone by, children who seemed loving and attentive to their parents were labeled "good" children, just as parents who seemed loving and attentive to their children were labeled "good" parents. The quality of the love and attention was not usually examined, nor the cost to the giver or the effect on the receiver. Things are no longer so black-and-white.

The behavior of family members toward one another is viewed today as a complex process governed by a wide range of feelings. In this context even traditionally "good" behavior is open to revaluation and tends to become suspect when carried to an extreme. "He gave up his life for his old mother" may have been considered the highest form of noble sacrifice several generations ago, but today such a sacrifice might be questioned. *Why* did he do that? Didn't he have a right to a life of his own, too? A sixty-year-old daughter still cowering in infantile submission before the rage of an autocratic ninety-year-old father may have symbolized the supreme example of "dutiful affection" to the Victorians, but current thinking would make us wonder about the deeper reasons behind such behavior.

It is important that sons and daughters take stock of their feelings about their aging parents if they want to find some comfort for themselves and be better able to help effectively.

Enough concrete obstacles can stand in the way when sons and daughters want to help. They may live too far away. They may have financial, health, career, or marital problems which legitimately prevent them from taking a supportive role in their parents' lives. But sometimes there are no such concrete obstacles—life may be going along quite smoothly—yet a daughter may be incapable of reaching out to her mother, and a son may wonder why his friends seem able to help their parents more than he can help his. Such children often excuse themselves by playing the "it's-easy-for-them" game:

"They have so much money—*it's easy for them* to help John's parents."

"With that big house—*it's easy for them* to find room for Mary's father."

"Jane doesn't have a job—*it's easy for her* to visit her mother every day."

"All their children are grown—*it's easy for them* to spend so much time at the nursing home."

All these statements have the same unspoken implication, "I would be just as good a son [or daughter] if only my life were different." But the unspoken implication would probably have greater validity if it substituted the words "If only my feelings were different." Unresolved or unrecognized feelings can affect a child's behavior toward a parent, blocking any attempts to be helpful. Those feelings can also serve as catalysts for unwise, inappropriate decisions that hinder rather than help to solve the older person's problems. Last, but equally important, unresolved feelings about parents can be very painful—sometimes really oppressive—for children. The well-being of both generations may improve once these feelings are understood, accepted, and acted on appropriately.

FEELINGS THAT SPARK
AN EMOTIONAL TUG OF WAR

It is self-evident that human beings are capable of experiencing and acting upon a wide range of feelings. Different people, different situations obviously arouse all sorts of different emotions. It is less self-evident that one single human being can experience an equally wide range of feelings toward another single human being. That is exactly what happens, however, when a substantial bond exists between any two people. A whole variety of different (and often conflicting) feelings can be aroused at different times. When people are important to us we love them when they please us, hate them when they disappoint us, resent them when they hurt us. Love is not a twenty-four-hour occupation, and there can always be time out even within the warmest relationships for moments of irritation, envy, frustration.

It might be easier if our feelings toward someone we love were more clear-cut and consistent, particularly when that person is old and perhaps helpless, but consistency and clarity are rare qualities denied to most of us.

All feelings do not have the same intensity. The minor annoyance we feel toward someone we love can easily be controlled, just as the occasional, though surprising, moments of affection we feel toward someone we dislike can also be tolerated. When contradictory feelings coexist with equally high intensity toward the same person, however, a painful conflict results. "I wish I didn't love my mother so much, then I could really hate her," a daughter cries in anguished frustration. She is deserving of sympathy for her emotional tug of war. Her struggle might be less painful if she realized that both the anger and the love she feels for her mother may be closely related and can sometimes last a lifetime. She might also be relieved to know that she is not alone and that many people are offended and angered most by someone they love best, although they may try to remain unaware of their less acceptable feelings toward their parents. When intense feelings are pushed out of our own awareness, they only rise again—sometimes in a disguised form. Once admitted and accepted, these feelings can more easily be placed in perspective and the person who bears them freed to behave more effectively.

Many of the feelings we have about our parents in their later years are the same old ones we always had about them. They were formed in childhood, and a pattern was established to be carried through life. The intensity and immediacy of these feelings may have changed somewhat as we grew into adulthood. By moving out of our parents' house we also moved away from daily contact and interaction. Emotional and physical distance provided a wide buffer zone. While our parents remain active and self-reliant, they live their own lives with greater or lesser involvement with ours. The relationship with them may be pleasant and gratifying, or frustrating and abrasive.

Old feelings from the past can rise up to plague us again when our parents get older, feebler, sicker, or poorer, and are in need of our help as we were once long ago in need of theirs. We can no longer so easily maintain an emotional distance, even when physically separated, and too easily fall back into old patterns, both the pleasant and the unpleasant ones: old affections may rise again, old wounds be reopened, old loyalties remembered, old debts revived, and old weaknesses exposed once more.

In addition to bringing old feelings into play again, our parents' aging—especially if they become dependent on us—may intensify feelings and attitudes which we have developed later because of experiences in our own separate adult lives. Some of these newer feelings, like the older ones, may seem unacceptable and we may prefer to ignore them. But ignoring them won't make them go away.

Because such a variety of feelings, some less comfortable than others, enter into the relationships between grown children and their aging parents, it may be helpful to examine a number of the most common ones: love, compassion, respect, tenderness, sadness, and then anger, hostility, shame, contempt, fear, jealousy, and sexual feelings. Finally, we shall turn to the most uncomfortable feeling of all—guilt—which is worn like the scarlet letter by so many children of the elderly today.

LOVE, COMPASSION, RESPECT, TENDERNESS, SADNESS

When some or all of these feelings are present in a relationship and are not too complicated by the simultaneous existence of powerful conflicting feelings, they serve as a vital source of support and strength for both generations. They provide comfort for the older one and enable the younger to reach out willingly to help. When these feelings have always existed between parents and children, they usually reflect a strong bond developed by a longstanding pattern of mutual caring.

While growing up, children look to those closest to them for models of behavior and tend to copy what they see. If both parents (or even one of them) show a young child love, care, unselfishness, and consideration, it is likely that the child as an adult will find it natural to show some of these feelings to his parents when they are old. Children who have never witnessed giving, reaching out, sharing, or tenderness in action often have no models to copy and never learn how to feel or show these emotions. Your parents' behavior to others, as well as to you, may have provided additional models. You may have seen them behave with respect and consideration to their own parents—your grandparents. Family traditions and patterns of behavior are often passed on from generation to generation.

But behavior is a complex process, and many other factors besides family tradition and models set in early childhood can influence the positive feelings we have toward our parents when they are old. Their treatment of us as children may have been far from tender and warm. We may have seen them as distant, cold, and punitive and thought them unfair and unreasonable while we were growing up. But later in life, when time, distance, and our own experience put a different perspective on past behavior, we may come to understand, as adults, what we could not understand as children: why our parents acted the way they did. Mistakes they made in the past may continue to rankle in the present, but the intensity of the resentment may be counteracted by a new respect we develop for the way they cope with life as old people. "He was a domineering tyrant when we were young," a son says of his father, "but how he's mellowed! He's great to be with now even though he's so sick— no complaints, no self-pity. I really admire the guy and I'll bet none of us do as well when we're his age." A daughter, raised in the Depression, remembers her deprived childhood: "We had to fight for everything we had. Mom and Dad seemed like misers—penny-pinchers. But now that I've got my own family, I can understand what they went through to raise five kids then. I'd do anything to make things easier for them now." Strong feelings of love, compassion, tenderness, respect are likely to be accompanied by sadness, as the younger generations realize that elderly parents are no longer the people they used to be and that death is coming closer every day.

INDIFFERENCE

Love, affection, respect, compassion, and concern can all exist simultaneously in any relationship between grown children and their aging parents. These emotions may all have equal intensity, or some may be stronger than others. It also may happen that one of these emotions may exist alone, without any of the others. A son may respect his parents and be concerned for them—and because of these feelings he may be extremely helpful to them—but he may never have loved them, liked them, or felt much real affection for either one; instead, he may have felt apathy and indifference. That lack of feeling may be quite painful, and he may experience considerable remorse because of it, but even so he may still feel responsible for their welfare and concerned about their problems. It is well to remember that while love and affection are often effective catalysts to a helping relationship, they are not essential.

LOVE MAY NOT BE ENOUGH

Although love and affection are important catalysts to a helping relationship, their usefulness may be diminished when they are not in partnership with concern and respect. A daughter's love and affection for her parents may spring from her own exaggerated dependency on them, which she did not outgrow when she left childhood. It may never occur to her to be concerned about their welfare, only that they should be concerned about hers. A son's love for his parents may be counteracted by his lack of respect for their behavior, their narrow-mindedness, or their bigotry. He may find it easier to love them from a distance.

FEAR AND ANXIETY

"She lies there like a fragile little doll—she couldn't lift a finger to hurt me. How can I still be scared to death she's going to be mad at me for something?" asked a middle-aged woman on one of her regular visits to her mother in a nursing home. She laughed as she spoke because she realized how ludicrous it seems to fear an eighty-pound, bedridden invalid. But she was serious, too. Some children live in fear of either or both of their parents even when these parents are weak, helpless, frail, or terminally ill. Children may be afraid of so many things—of disapproval, of losing love, of death, of the irrevocable loss of the older person, and also of losing out on an inheritance. Chronic, irrational fear or anxiety in relation to a parent is likely to have its roots in dimly remembered early childhood experiences. Small children are totally dependent on their parents; without them they feel stranded, abandoned, alone. The parents, being bigger and stronger, are also the ones who set the rules and enforce the dictates of society. Thus, a child can fear his parents on three counts: abandonment, loss of love, and punishment.

As children mature and learn to take care of themselves, that rather one-sided relationship disappears and feelings of affection and trust emerge as between close friends. A filial bond develops which surpasses the parent-child bond. Children who never resolve or shake off that close, dependent relationship may continue to suffer fearful or anxious feelings in relation to their parents in one form or another throughout life.

Older parents themselves are often responsible for reinforcing fearful feelings in their grown children, unconsciously or even deliberately continuing to nourish old childhood dependencies. Weak old men and fragile old women often somehow find the strength to retain command, directing their children's lives from wheelchairs and sickbeds. A son may champ at the bit, longing for freedom from a domineering mother while simultaneously suffering constant anxiety that he will do something to displease her, that she will leave him or disown him. A child may also grow up in fear that he will not live up to his parents' expectations for him in terms of career, worldly success, or material possessions. He may also be afraid he will never be the kind of person they want him to be—someone they approve of. His struggle to win approval may continue through his entire life, even when he is in his sixties and his parents are in their eighties. He may fear that he will be loved only when he measures up to their standards and that that time is unlikely to come. "I've got a good business going," a middle-aged man complains. "I put three kids through college, I'm president of our Rotary Club, but my father thinks I'm a failure—his only son was supposed to be a lawyer. And you know what? Whenever I'm with him I feel like a failure, too."

ANGER AND HOSTILITY

Large-scale upheavals and tragedies obviously have emotional impacts on children that often affect their future lives. Death or chronic illness of a mother or father, divorce, abandonment—such events can determine the kind of feelings children have for parents, feelings which can last a lifetime. "I hated my mother when she remarried" or "Our family fell apart after my father's business failed" or "My father walked out one day and left us alone." Such statements pinpoint causes and serve to explain the rise of hostile feelings. But even without such dramatic events, the development of angry feelings in childhood is often unavoidably stimulated through the early years of day-to-day family living.

Just as the comfortable feelings of love and tenderness, as well as the uncomfortable feelings of fear and anxiety, are associated with close ties, so, in many cases, are angry, hostile, and resentful ones. Those are often most intense between the persons most closely attached to each other. There are subtle differences between them. Anger is a transitory feeling, but if it becomes chronic it is usually referred to as hostility. Contempt describes the way a person feels toward someone he considers worthless or immoral. Children are likely to have moments, even longer periods, of all these uncomfortable emotions while growing up. Few relationships are free of them. But when occasional flare-ups become solidified into permanent attitudes, a complex relationship develops.

Oscar Wilde wrote in *The Picture of Dorian Gray*: "Children begin by loving their parents; as they grow older they like them; later they judge them; sometimes they forgive them." He implied that the judgments are not always so favorably resolved. Childhood may seem an eternity away as people grow older and many memories are left behind, both pleasant and unpleasant. But the feelings developed in that period are not so easily left behind; they tag along through life.

Once a resentful child begins to live his own adult life, he may forget how angry he used to be with his parents. But just as the helplessness and disabilities of their old age can awaken feelings of tenderness and compassion untapped for years, their new dependency can rekindle old feelings of anger and resentment long thought to be dead and buried. Buried—yes. Dead—never. Sons and daughters may remember all over again the way their parents neglected them as children, the way they punished them unfairly or too harshly, the way they scorned their abilities, belittled their accomplishments, and especially the way they favored another sibling. Forty years later we can still be angry and resentful about our parents' failures in the past. The fact that they are now old and frail may not diminish these feelings, particularly if they continue to behave in the infuriating manner we have disliked for so long. Our failure to help them now may be a form of unconscious retaliation: "You need *me* now. Where were *you* when I needed you?"

SEXUALITY

Most of us maintain two contradictory beliefs regarding our parents as sexual beings. We know rationally that we could only have been born as a result of their sexual union and that our brothers and sisters could never have been conceived in any other way. At the same time, it remains very difficult for most people even to tolerate the thought, or the mental image, of their parents as young adults engaged in sexual intimacy. How much more difficult this is to contemplate when parents are old! Many sons and daughters reject the idea completely, making the erroneous but comfortable assumption that sexual instincts vanish once the childbearing years are over.

The inability of grown children to admit that their elderly parents could have sexual needs has been traditionally reinforced by the attitudes of our society, which ridicules any suggestion of sexuality in the aged. Today these sexual needs are admitted and encouraged by some experts, but the subject is still taboo for much of the population.

SHAME

This uncomfortable feeling comes in several forms and with varying degrees of intensity. Everyone knows moments of shame; they come and go throughout life in response to an endless number of causes. For the sons and daughters of elderly parents, shame can sometimes be an ever-present feeling. The simplest and most common form of shame comes when children feel they do not do enough for their parents. Perhaps a son doesn't visit his parents enough; perhaps he is unable to give them financial help; perhaps he allows a brother, a sister, or even a stranger to provide solutions to problems he feels *he* should be handling himself. He may have his own reasons for behaving the way he does, but nevertheless he feels deep inside that if he were a better person he would be doing a better job. Sons and daughters who feel ashamed for those reasons have plenty of fellow sufferers.

A second form of shame is involved when sons and daughters are ashamed, not of themselves for their own failings, but of their parents for *their* failings. A self-made man may be ashamed of his poor, illiterate parents and keep them in the background because he does not want his world to know where he came from. An intellectual woman may be ashamed of her uneducated father, a sophisticated city-dweller of her small-town parents. A son may want to keep an alcoholic father hidden— like other family skeletons—in the closet. When we are ashamed of our parents it is usually because we fear that their shortcomings will reflect badly on us in the eyes of other people whose opinions we value: our friends, neighbors, colleagues, church groups, social clubs, employers, even in-laws.

A third level of shame is a combination of the first two: we may be ashamed of ourselves *because* we are ashamed of our parents. This is probably the most painful form of shame and the most difficult to cope with. It stirs up great emotional conflict in sons and daughters, prevents them from offering constructive help to their parents, and forces them to bear a continual and heavy burden of guilt.

SPECIAL REACTIONS TO AGING

While many of the feelings we have about our parents can be traced back to childhood sources, it is never too late to experience new ones. Successes and failures in adult life can also strongly affect the way we feel about our parents. Their plight itself or some new understanding of our own can stimulate unaccustomed feelings of love and compassion we never knew before. New stresses can produce angry or fearful reactions we would never have believed we were capable of feeling. While the intensity of some feelings persists unabated through life, the intensity of others can fade through the years, leaving room for new ones, although it is often difficult to figure out where the new ones come from. Men and women may seem quite puzzled by their changing feelings: "I used to get along so well with my parents; why are they driving me up the wall all of a sudden?" or "I don't have any patience with them anymore," or "I'd give anything to skip visiting Mother this week—I can't understand why she depresses me so much these days." Clues to the roots of these troubling feelings may be found in how the younger generation answers the following questions.

CAN YOU ACCEPT YOUR PARENTS' OLD AGE?

As old but active men and women begin to undergo mental and physical changes, their children can react with mixed emotions: shock (if there is sudden physical and mental deterioration), denial (if the deterioration is a slow slide downhill), anger, shame, fear, resentment, as well as the more expected feelings of sadness, sympathy, and concern. We may be surprised at our own reactions to our parents' decline and wonder how we could possibly be angry at them when we ought to be sympathetic. Yet anger is not as inappropriate as it may seem.

Most of us, as children, viewed our parents as immortal—strong enough to protect us forever. As we mature we learn we can take care of ourselves and in the process find out, with some regret, that our parents are not quite as perfect or infallible as we once thought. Somewhere inside us, however, remains a trace of the old conviction that our parents could still protect us if we needed them to, so that their physical and mental deterioration is shocking. On an intellectual level we keep telling ourselves, "It's understandable—they're getting old, they're fading." But on the gut level we can still be sad, frightened, resentful, as if they had broken a promise to us—a promise that was never actually made. Every time we see them we have to be reminded of their mortality—and our own. The deterioration of a vigorous mind—loss of comprehension, confusion, disorientation, loss of memory—can be even harder to accept than the deterioration of a vigorous body in those families where intellectual activities and verbal communication are particularly meaningful. Nothing can be more painful than the realization that a parent no longer understands us, or even recognizes us. Why should we be so surprised that the realization makes us angry or that we try to deny it?

DO YOU LIKE YOUR AGING PARENTS?

When this question is asked, it is rarely answered directly; rather, it is usually sidestepped. A typical reply might be, "My mother's pretty self-centered; she complains a lot and doesn't seem to appreciate anything I do for her. But she's *still* my mother." That, of course, does not answer the question, but most people find it almost impossible to admit that they really do not like one, or maybe both, of their parents. They may find it equally impossible to admit their dislike even to themselves.

It cannot be denied that, in addition to the infirmities and frailties brought on by age, some old people may also develop unpleasant personality traits that are hard for their children to take, and harder still to like. They may have been charming and appealing when they were young, but their charm may have vanished with the years. Or perhaps they never had either charm or appeal.

CAN YOU ACCEPT A DIFFERENT ROLE?

Although few old people return to "second childhood," which Shakespeare describes as the last in the seven ages of man, they frequently, because of increasing helplessness, need to depend on people who are stronger. When the family is young, the parent plays the independent, strong role and the child the dependent, weak one. When some parents age they may be willing to abdicate the power they once had, glad to pass it on to more capable hands. The "gift" may weigh heavily on some sons and daughters who prefer their old, familiar dependent roles. Others take the gift, use it well, but resent being forced to accept it. The acceptance in itself symbolizes the end of one longstanding relationship and the beginning of a new one.

A teacher in her forties described how shocked she felt one day when she heard herself speaking to her ailing mother in the cheery tones of the kindergarten: "Now, let's hurry up and finish this nice soup." Later she commented wryly, "I have three children at home and twenty in my class at school. I certainly don't need another one. What I need is a mother, and I'll never have one again." She knew that she and her mother had to an extent changed roles forever, and accompanying this new relationship were feelings of anger, resentment, fear, and sadness, all mixed up with love.

CAN YOU ACCEPT YOUR OWN AGING?

So far this chapter has focused on relationships between children and their elderly parents, and the feelings generated by these relationships. But another set of feelings can be aroused independently of interpersonal reactions: the feelings people have about old age in general, and their own old age and their own mortality. The behavior of children toward their elderly parents can be profoundly affected by these feelings. Many people are reluctant to talk about their old age and mortality; some even prefer not to think about either one. Until very recently, death and old age have been taboo subjects altogether, often denied until the zero hour.

Our attitudes vary, depending on whether we admire old people or secretly despise them, whether we feel older people deserve respect or consideration, whether we believe they can remain sexually or creatively active, whether we dread the day when we will be old or the day we will die. Not everyone can agree with the poet Walt Whitman:

> Youth, large, lusty, loving—
> Youth, full of grace, force, fascination.
> Do you know that old age may come after you
>   with equal grace, force and fascination?

The feelings we have about our own old age often have a direct bearing on how effectively we can help our parents during their old age, and how constructively we can plan for our own.

People who tend to have a positive attitude toward old age in general, including their own, are more likely to be able to reach out to their elderly parents with concern, compassion, and constructive support. If old age appears as a time to be dreaded—and many features of modern society would suggest to us that it is—then our parents' decline may seem very threatening. Their aging seems to toll the bells for our own aging and our inevitable death.

At the funeral of an eighty-five-year-old man, his gray-haired daughter was overheard saying sadly, "There goes our last umbrella." She explained later that she had always thought of the parent and grandparent generations as umbrellas, because even when umbrellas are broken and threadbare they can still give some form of protection and shelter from the elements. When her father, the last of the older generation, died, she mourned him because she felt, "Now we have no shelter left. There's nothing anymore between us and what lies ahead for us. We're next in line."

Being next in line, of course, means being next in line for death. If we cannot contemplate our own mortality, how can we contemplate our parents'? It can be really painful, yet every time we see them we are reminded of the very thing we'd prefer to avoid thinking about.

An interesting parallel can be drawn between the way people look at childhood and the way they look at old age. For many parents, one of the pleasures of watching their children grow involves the reawakening of childhood memories and the chance to relive the pleasures they knew when they were young. Similarly, as we watch our parents grow old we may see the shape of our own old age lying in wait for us. We may resent them because they force us to "pre-live" our own old age and death long before we need to. A Pakistani tale (similar versions of which are found in the folklore of other cultures, too) makes this point clearly:

An ancient grandmother lived with her daughter and her grandson in a small but comfortable house not far from the village. The old woman grew frail and feeble, her eyesight became dimmer every day, and she found it hard to remember where she'd put things and what people had asked her to do. Instead of being a help around the house she became a constant trial and irritation. She broke the plates and cups, lost the knives, put out the stove, and spilled the water. One day, exasperated because the older woman had broken another precious plate, the younger one gave some money to her son and told him, "Go to the village and buy your grandmother a wooden plate. At least we will have one thing in the house she cannot break."

The boy hesitated because he knew that wooden plates were only used by peasants and servants—not by fine ladies like his grandmother—but his mother insisted, so off he went. Some time later he returned, bringing not one but two wooden plates.

"I only asked you to buy one," his mother said to him sharply. "Didn't you listen to me?"

"Yes," said the boy. "But I bought the second one so there will be one for you when you get old."

ARE YOU OVERBURDENED?

Children who are beset by a multitude of demanding problems in their own lives—health, finances, career setbacks, children, grandchildren, even their own retirement worries—may be so drained that they cannot begin to shoulder their parents' problems as well. They may try to do their best, feel ashamed they are not doing better, and, more likely than not, resent the older generation for giving them additional burdens to bear. The following phone call dramatizes this situation—a conversation between a mother and daughter *including* the younger woman's unspoken thoughts:

DAUGHTER Hello, Mother. How are you? [*Don't let there be anything wrong today! I just can't take one more problem.*]

MOTHER (small shaky voice) I nearly died last night.

DAUGHTER (solicitously) Was your leg bad again? [*Oh, God! It's going to be one of those days again. I hope she doesn't keep me on all morning. I've got to get down to talk to Janie's teacher. Why is that child getting into so much trouble this year?*] Are you using the heating pad?

MOTHER The pain was like a knife. I said to Mrs. Forest this morning—

DAUGHTER (cutting in, a little impatiently) Didn't you take that new medicine Dr. Croner gave you? He said it would help.

MOTHER Don't talk to me about doctors! What do doctors care about an old person? It was a waste of my time going to him.

DAUGHTER But you said he was such a genius. [*A waste of whose time! Does she have any idea what I went through to take her to that doctor? I changed my whole week around; Janie missed her dentist appointment, I got a parking ticket, and Jack was furious. Jack's always furious these days.*]

MOTHER Mrs. Forest said he was a genius. Mrs. Forest cares about how I feel—she listens to me. You're so busy all the time—you don't really want to worry about me. You have your children and your husband to think about.

DAUGHTER (guilty but exasperated) Oh, Mother, stop saying things like that. [*Why does she always do this to me? I wonder if she'd care if she really knew what's going on with us now. One of these days I'll tell her; why shouldn't she know that Jack and I are fighting all the time and Janie's doing terribly in school and we have to borrow money to get the car fixed?*] You know how much I care about you!

It is never easy to take on another person's burden, even when things are going smoothly, but there are some periods in life when it's almost impossible. Ironically enough, it very often happens that older people begin to need more support just at the point when their children's lives are the most complicated and their responsibilities are heaviest. A middle-aged woman is likely to have to deal with her children's adolescent crises and her parents' geriatric ones just at the time she is going into the menopause herself. Her husband may be going through the same midlife crisis. A middle-aged man may struggle to provide money for his children's college tuition and his parents' necessary medical expenses just when he has been passed over for a long-awaited promotion—which he now realizes will never come. His wife, if she is working, may have similar financial pressures and career setbacks.

If, in establishing their life's priorities, sons and daughters have not been able to assign first—or even second or third—place to their parents, they may never forgive themselves. But if they try to shoulder their parents' burdens as well as their own, they may feel continually resentful and put-upon, wondering as the days go by, "When is there going to be time for me?" No matter which course they decide to take, they are likely to carry an additional burden: guilt.

AND FINALLY—GUILT!

Guilt has been left for last because it is usually the end result or the prime mover of many of the other uncomfortable feelings from past and present.

> John Wilson is ashamed of his parents. He feels ashamed of himself because he is ashamed of them and guilty because he is not helping them more. He then feels angry and resentful of them because he has to feel guilty and then anxious and fearful that some unknown punishment will be dealt out to him because of his anger.

Poor John. Because of one uncomfortable feeling, shame, he has to suffer the entire gamut of other uncomfortable ones. This is a frequent occurrence; rarely does one single emotion stand alone. The whole mixed bag of feelings is interrelated, one capable of setting off another. Guilt can evoke resentment, resentment more guilt, and guilt more fear—an endless, self-perpetuating cycle. Pity the unfortunate human being caught in the middle!

Guilt is a hidden or exposed emotion which signals to us our own sense of wrongdoing in words or deeds or even thoughts. It is often accompanied by lowered self-esteem and a wish for punishment. Conscious feelings of guilt are not the same as unconscious guilt, which may be manifested in a need for self-punishment.

> Phil had planned for some time to spend his only day off with his bedridden father. When the day came, it was so beautiful that he decided he had to go

fishing instead. On the way to the lake he got lost twice on what had always been a familiar route, dented his car when leaving the gas station, and, when he finally arrived at the lake, found he had left his fishing tackle at home. That night he slept fitfully and dreamed that his father had died.

In present-day thinking, guilt feelings are often attributed to personal neuroses or wishes not rooted in the real world around us. But guilt is not always so buried. It should not be forgotten that people can also feel very guilty for things they have actually done or not done: objective sins of commission or omission. In that respect, guilt means an acceptance of responsibility for action taken or action evaded and, within reasonable limits, can be a sign of emotional maturity. Our guilt may stem from the uncomfortable suspicion that we have not behaved responsibly to our parents, and then, the more guilt we feel, the more difficult we may find it to behave responsibly. Responsible behavior usually flows more easily when we understand not only our parents but also ourselves and our feelings toward them.

A fifty-year-old man put this understanding into action recently as he carefully inspected a well-known nursing home and discussed his situation with the administrator.

My mother and I have never had an easy or a pleasant relationship. She's always been a difficult, cold, resentful woman. I can't forget the way she treated me when I was young . . . and I only had superficial contacts with her when I grew up. But she needs someone to take care of her now, after her stroke. I certainly can't bring her to live with me and my family—none of us could take it. But she *is* old and she *is* my mother and I want her to be as comfortable and as protected as possible.

Such cool, objective understanding is rare. The guilty feelings of grown sons and daughters are so primed and ready these days that they can be set off by the most insignificant stimulus. A sentence, even a gesture or a shrug, from an old mother or father can easily do the trick. Some statements are heard so frequently that they are included in comedy routines because they strike home universally. "You young people run along and enjoy yourselves. I'm perfectly fine *alone* here by myself," or "I know how busy you are—I understand that you forgot to call me yesterday. Of course, I *did* worry." Shakespeare's King Lear pointed to the guilt of past, present, and probably future generations when he cried, "How sharper than a serpent's tooth it is to have a thankless child!"

Any discussion of guilt should include at least a reference to the guilt sons and daughters feel when they wish an elderly mother or father would die. Although not as universal as the "thankless-child syndrome," the "death wish" is felt more frequently than is admitted. Most people who feel it also consider it too terrible to admit, particularly if they are angry with their parents. The death wish comes in two forms: the more acceptable form is reserved for a parent who is terminally ill, in constant pain, with no chance of recovery. A daughter says in genuine sorrow, "I hope Mother dies soon. I can't stand to see her suffer anymore."

A less acceptable death wish is directed toward a parent who is not terminally ill but merely difficult or incapacitated, sapping the physical and emotional strength of the family. A son or daughter most closely involved may feel (but rarely admit), "I wish she would die and then I'd have some life for myself at last." There are many instances where both these wishes are understandable, but since it has traditionally been considered "wicked" to wish death to another person, particularly to a parent, these wishes usually involve some burden of guilt.

In addition to the specific guilt suffered by individuals, there may also be a pervasive guilt generated by the uneasy knowledge that we cannot provide for our elderly parents as they provided for us when we were young. We have a sense that we are welshing on a debt. But in present-day society, paying that debt is often impossible. Because of inadequate facilities within the family and inadequate services outside in the community, well-intentioned children may have to suffer the guilty burden "We are not caring for those who cared for us."

A fable of a father bird and his three fledglings seems to wrap up the subject. It appeared in a book written for her children by a widow in Germany in the year 1690. Glückel of Hameln's message still rings pretty clear in 1988.

We should, I say, put ourselves to great pains for our children, for on this the world is built, yet we must understand that if children did as much for their parents, the children would quickly tire of it.

A bird once set out to cross a windy sea with its three fledglings. The sea was so wide and the wind so strong, the father bird was forced to carry his young, one by one, in his strong claws. When he was half-way across with the first fledgling the wind turned into a gale, and he said, "My child, look how I am struggling and risking my life in your behalf. When you are grown up, will you do as much for me and provide for my old age?" The fledgling replied, "Only bring me to safety, and when you are old I shall do everything you ask of me." Whereat the father bird dropped his child into the sea, and it drowned, and he said, "So shall it be done to such a liar as you." Then the father bird returned to shore, set forth with his second fledgling, asked the same question, and receiving the same answer, drowned the second child with the cry, "You, too, are a liar." Finally he set out with the third fledgling, and when he asked the same question, the third and last fledgling replied, "My dear father, it is true you are struggling mightily and risking your life in my

*behalf, and I shall be wrong not to repay you when you are old, but I cannot
bind myself. This though I can promise: when I am grown up and have children
of my own, I shall do as much for them as you have done for me." Whereupon
the father bird said, "Well spoken, my child, and wisely; your life I will spare
and I will carry you to shore in safety."*

WHAT UNTOUCHABLE,
UNRESOLVED FEELINGS CAN PRODUCE

Earlier in this chapter we stressed that there is room for all kinds of
feelings in interpersonal relationships. Many people recognize this on an
intellectual level, but even so, they find it difficult to express or admit
feelings which have traditionally been considered immoral or "bad," tend-
ing to disavow unacceptable ones, pushing them out of awareness.

These feelings keep right on existing anyhow and struggling for expres-
sion. Lock them up and throw away the key—they'll still struggle to get
out. The struggle can distort our perception of ourselves and our relationships and make it difficult to arrive at appropriate decisions. It does
not necessarily follow, however, that every wrong decision is a result of
unresolved feelings. Plenty of mistakes can be made from simple ignorance, and sons and daughters admit these mistakes every day.

> "We thought John's father would love the country and being with us, but he
> just sits and looks out of the window. We forgot what a city person he is."
>
> • •
>
> "I made my mother give up the house much too soon after Father died. I
> didn't realize she needed more time."
>
> • •
>
> "We didn't know Medicare would cover some of Mother's expenses in a con-
> valescent home."

Errors can reflect lack of knowledge or know-how about an unfamiliar
situation. They can also reflect a family's inability to work together effectively. But well-meaning mistakes aside, it is important to explore
some of the typical pitfalls lying in wait when unresolved feelings direct
our relationships with our parents and the decisions we make with them.
Some of the most common ones are reviewed next.

WITHDRAWAL

Mel Brooks's "2,000-Year-Old Man" could always draw laughter from his
audience when he said, "I have 42,000 children and not one of them comes
to visit me." That statement strikes home to many listeners. Lack of

attention from children is a familiar parental complaint. Children avoid their parents for many reasons, and great numbers of them suffer only occasional twinges of guilt. But many want to be more attentive, and despite their conscious desire they find it difficult to visit, to phone, to write, and sometimes to keep in touch at all.

If, despite their claims that they *want* to be close and that they *try* to be, grown children find it almost impossible to keep satisfactory contact going, it may be that they are avoiding a confrontation which would arouse uncomfortable feelings they prefer to keep under wraps: anger, resentment, irritation, jealousy. They may wish they could behave differently and condemn themselves regularly—"What's the matter with me? Why can't I do better with them?"—and then withdraw still further.

OVERSOLICITOUSNESS AND DOMINATION

This pattern is at the opposite pole from withdrawal. Instead of removing themselves, children may come even closer, choosing a more acceptable type of involvement. By hovering over his parents, spending an abnormal amount of time with them, letting them become completely dependent on him before they need to be, a son may think he is acting out of love and devotion. This could be true, but it could also be *his* way of blocking out angry or guilty feelings.

Just as withdrawal may disguise fear, oversolicitous behavior may serve the same purpose. In that situation the fear lurking in the background may be fear of loss. It is not easy for an adult to accept the fact that he is still very emotionally dependent on his parents, that he has not grown up yet or proved to himself that he can stand alone. Such anxiety can be very painful, and he may attempt to palliate it by overprotective behavior which implies, "As long as I'm with them, nothing can happen to them," or conversely, "If I leave them alone for a minute, they may slip away from me."

FAULTFINDING

Sometimes there is a job we feel we should do, and we cannot manage to do it. Conscious of our own inadequacy, we may feel angry at ourselves and guilty. If we have to face the fact that we are shortchanging our parents, uncomfortable feelings may flow in still another direction. What a relief it may seem to blame, not our parents or ourselves, but a third party!

When someone else is shouldering the responsibility for our parents' welfare—other siblings, other relatives, favored housekeepers, or nursing homes—a little voice may keep reminding us that we are not doing our share. That voice can be successfully drowned out by an endless barrage of criticism of those who are doing *our* job for us. We may accuse these "stand-ins" of being inconsiderate, inefficient, and inept, and point out how they are not showing the right kind of care or concern. Certain criticisms, especially those of nursing homes, may be valid, and it is wise to keep a close, watchful eye on anyone who is providing for the welfare of the elderly. But if *nothing* is right—*no* way, *no*where—then could it be that deep down inside we feel that something is wrong with us?

People frequently distort the world around them in order to make themselves feel better. These games are popular with many sons and daughters. By placing the blame elsewhere, they give themselves the momentary comfort that they have removed the blame from themselves. The comfort provided by faultfinding is almost invariably offset by angry feelings from other family members and the paid or volunteer helpers the older people are depending on.

DENIAL

It is not uncommon for children to deny that their parents have problems or need help. Sometimes the denial is so successful that these children are able to disbelieve what is going on right in front of them. If they cannot accept weakness in themselves, they may deny the realistic symptoms of frailty in their aging parents. In Joseph Heller's recent book *Something Happened*, the hero, Bob Slocum, describes his behavior toward his mother:

> *My conversation to my mother, like my visits, was of no use to her. I pretended, by not speaking of it, for my sake as well as for hers (for my sake more than for hers), that she was not seriously ill and in a nursing home she hated, that she was not crippled and growing older and more crippled daily. I did not want her to know, as she did know (and I knew she knew), as she knew before I did, that she was dying, slowly, in stages, her organs failing and her faculties withering one by one. . . . I pretended she was perfect and said nothing to her about her condition until she finally died. I was no use to her.*

Children who need to deny longstanding sexual attachments to their parents may also deny, when a mother or a father grows old, that either one could still have sexual feelings or needs. That distortion of reality can make it very difficult for even the most devoted children to accept comfortably a widowed parent's remarriage or extramarital relationships.

Denial is also closely tied in with fear of losing parents. A daughter may feel that if she can ignore the warning symptoms of her mother's physical deterioration, perhaps they will go away. The most dangerous part of this kind of denial is that the older person may not get medical help until it is too late to do her or him any good. But even when doctors are consulted, denial leads many children to unrealistic hopes for miracles from the medical profession.

OUTMODED ROLE-PLAYING

Many a child discovers at a very early age that certain types of behavior produce enjoyable responses from his parents. Since these responses are so gratifying, he may repeat the behavior, and eventually it comes to be expected of him. Ironically, by assuming a role and playing it successfully, he may get trapped in it and fear that if he ever stepped out of it no one would value him any more—particularly his parents.

A role can be assumed by a child in order to get along in the family, but a role may also be assigned to a child. Listen to parents discussing their children with friends: "Jim's the dependable one," or "Jane's the emotional one," or "Fran's so easygoing," or "Susie's the clown." All these qualities may be found in these various children from time to time, but every child has more than one emotional color and will be in trouble if expected to function only according to one.

If roles are perpetuated as part of family fun and tradition, they are not necessarily harmful. A gentle family joke kept alive through the years may be a warm and tender reminder of past closeness. But if roles are perpetuated out of anxiety or fear—if a daughter feels she must cling to hers in order to remain acceptable to others—then she may find it hard to step outside it, be herself, and deal constructively with problems affecting her parents' lives and therefore her own. Thus, if she still clings to the outgrown role of being the "child" to her parents, she may see herself as still dependent on them when in reality they are the ones who now need to lean on her. Her behavior is therefore inappropriate to the real circumstances. On the other hand, she may cling to an old role of being "the dependable one" in the family, the child who always did the most for her parents. She may be afraid to give up this role and may make unreasonable demands on herself even when her brothers and sisters are perfectly willing to share the burdens involved in caring for their parents. This kind of self-martyrdom will be explored in the next chapter.

PROTRACTED ADOLESCENT REBELLION
AND BLIND OVERINVOLVEMENT

When grown-up people are still angry and rebellious toward their parents, it is legitimate to wonder if they ever as adolescents had a period of healthy rebellion which permitted them to mature successfully and assume separate adult roles.

There comes a time in the normal child's development when he needs to break away from close parental control, give his parents a hard time, disagree violently, try his own wings, make his own mistakes. Children need, in current adolescent lingo, to "do their own thing." This breakaway period has varying degrees of intensity, depending on the individual adolescent. The upheaval gradually quiets down, the struggle for independence becomes resolved, and eventually the stormy adolescent joins the adult world. But some children make rebellion a way of life. The skirmishes continue through the years, no decisive battle is won, and adult maturity remains elusive. A son who is still in constant conflict with his parents may also, in a perverse way, enjoy blaming them for preventing him from growing up. He may even project onto his parents tyrannical motives which he can rebel against. The anger he feels toward them may blind him to the fact that they are getting old and need him to grow up at last.

Those who never go through any adolescent rebellion at all are even more vulnerable. A child who has never been able to break away from one or both parents may never be able to see himself as a separate individual. The result, often masked as a loving, devoted relationship between parent and child, can in reality reach a point where the child cannot separate his feelings from those of his parents. This process may be particularly painful to bear, especially if the parents seriously deteriorate as they grow old. What a burden it can be for a son to live through his parents' old age with them and then have to face the same problems a second time when he gets old himself! Overinvolvement by a child can force an older person to be unhealthily stoic in order not to give his child pain, or a mother or father may be stimulated to more exhibitionist suffering by the knowledge that a child secretly enjoys being allowed to share the pain.

SCAPEGOATING

The burdens and problems of our own lives, as mentioned earlier, can lead to an unfortunate type of behavior toward our parents: the process of scapegoating. Human beings often find it difficult to face up to the real things that trouble them: illness, failing resources, marital problems, troubles with children or careers. It is sometimes convenient to blame a totally innocent source (or person) for these problems and unload anger and resentment on something or someone else. Even if the older person is not actually blamed for the problems, he may have to bear the emotional outbursts generated by them. A campaign of television commercials for a well-known headache remedy a few years ago centered around the scapegoating of an elderly relative by a younger one. The series included a line that became famous: "Motherrr—I'd rather do it myself." It ended with the gentle reminder, "Sure you have a headache, but don't take it out on her." Substitute the words *unfaithful husband, bankrupt business, frigid spouse, disturbed child, bad investment* for *headache,* and the possibilities for scapegoating are endless—in every family.

Scapegoating is not usually done deliberately. It is a very human type of behavior, but when carried to an extreme it can be very destructive to everyone, particularly to the elderly.

It's often difficult to understand our own feelings and our own behavior. Some people are able to discover insights for themselves and move ahead to work effectively on family problems. Others may find themselves in an emotional quandary, unable to mobilize themselves. Or they may over-react and behave inappropriately. These emotional quandaries can result from relationships with an aging parent in much the same way as they result from relationships with a husband, a wife, a child. Just as we may turn to a counselor or psychotherapist when in turmoil about our marriage or our children, we can find similar help with our mixed-up feelings about our aging parents. Many people find it helpful to talk to their family physician, priest, minister, or rabbi. Others prefer to consult mental-health professionals, who are sometimes able to clarify problems after only a few visits. (Ways to locate professional help are listed in Appendix A, pages 267–320.) It would be unrealistic to suggest that elderly parents and their grown children will live happily ever after even when their feelings toward each other are open and accepted. The best that can be hoped for is that problems will be faced directly and the most helpful solutions found—*under the circumstances* (see Chapter 10).

But the circumstances of old age are sometimes unhappy. Many old people carry into the later years the personal traits that colored their relationships in their earlier years: selfishness, greed, cruelty, bigotry, hostility. And even in the best relationships there will inevitably be pain and sadness. It is natural for children to feel these emotions when they watch their parents deteriorate and move every day closer to death.

There can be pleasure and comfort even in these final days. This can be a time for looking back and looking ahead. The younger generation has one last opportunity to relive family history with the older one and understand—perhaps for the first time—the continuity of the life-cycle.

Alex Haley's *Roots* and its television dramatization touched off a nationwide quest for answers to the questions "Who am I?" and "Where did I come from?" Younger generations, thought to be involved only with the here, the now, and the future, are turning back to the past to rediscover their own roots. Some look to elderly relatives as precious sources of soon-to-be-lost information and eagerly listen to old stories and older memories. There is a chance for enjoyment and peace of mind even in the midst of sadness. This reward eludes children who continue to struggle with unresolved, troubled feelings until their parents' death—and afterward.

Death ends a life . . . but it does not end a relationship which struggles on in the survivor's mind . . . towards some resolution which it never finds.

Robert Anderson, *I Never Sang for My Father*

3

THE FAMILY
MERRY-GO-ROUND

Martha Willis never fully recovered from the severe bout of flu she suffered in the winter before her seventy-fourth birthday. Although she stayed on in her own little house, she could no longer take care of it or herself alone even with the help of a homemaker who came in several times a week. Her oldest daughter, Sylvia, who lived closest and whose children were teenagers, took on the major responsibility for her mother's care. Eventually, Sylvia found she was spending more and more time in her mother's house and less and less in her own.

In the beginning everyone pitched in to help—her younger sisters, her husband, and her children—but as time went on Sylvia noticed that her sisters seemed less available, her husband less understanding, and her children more resentful, often accusing her of being more interested in Grandma than in them. Tensions built throughout the family and erupted frequently. In one typical week Sylvia screamed at her favorite sister over the phone, accusing her of "never doing anything for Mother." She had an ugly fight with her husband, who stormed out of the house and the next day forgot her birthday. In the same week her younger son was suspended from school for cutting classes and her older son had an asthma attack.

"Mother's the least of my worries," Sylvia complained bitterly to her friend. "Since she got sick the whole family's starting to fall apart."

Of the nation's more than 24 million citizens over sixty-five, too many have no families to care for them or about them. In sickness, in trouble, and in poverty they have to go it alone, and their very aloneness makes their situation even more tragic.

But millions of other elderly people are not alone. When their ability to manage independently seems threatened, plenty of relatives may be concerned, not only sons and daughters but sons- and daughters-in-law, brothers and sisters, stepchildren and foster children, nieces and nephews. Concerned friends and neighbors may also become involved. In times of serious crisis a few close relatives usually assume the real responsibility, but any number of others—all of whom have some connection with the older person *and* with each other—may be drawn into the act, offering help, suggestions, advice, criticism. Their offers can be constructive and valuable, or in some cases misguided and destructive.

It may seem to you, if your own mother is deteriorating, that it is impossible to find a solution satisfactory to everyone—to her, to you, and to others in the family. Some situations undeniably defy solution. But it may be a mistake to jump too quickly to the conclusion that your own situation is in that hopeless category. Just as your feelings about your mother may make it easy for you to help her or stand in the way, other relationships can similarly facilitate or block effective behavior: your feelings about your brothers and sisters, theirs about you, and everyone's feelings about your mother.

FAMILY HARMONY
OR FAMILY DISCORD

Throughout history countries have mobilized their efforts to deal with threats and disasters such as wars, famine, disease, rallying together with greater unity than ever. And so with families. A shared crisis—a father's stroke, a mother's blindness—can bring out the best in every member, drawing everyone closer together. At such times brothers and sisters may get to know one another again as adults and be gratified by the new relationships. Husbands and wives may find hidden strengths in each other and be pleasantly surprised by the discovery.

> "I got married and left home when my brother was a teenager. I never realized what a great person he'd turned into until I spent all that time at home when Mother was sick. We're real friends now."
>
> • •
>
> "Jennie was such a helpless crybaby when we were little—who'd believe she'd be the one we all depend on now that Dad needs so much care?"
>
> • •
>
> "I really *talked* to my brother when we visited my mother at the nursing home—we hadn't talked that way in twenty years."
>
> • •
>
> "Lizzie's sense of humor saved us. She could always make us laugh even when everything looked terrible."

• •

"My husband was always so quiet and unemotional. But he had what we needed when Mother got cancer. He was the one who kept things going—the rest of us just fell apart."

There are hidden benefits for everyone when the younger generations rally together to help the older ones. The elderly benefit if their relatives work together with them to find the best possible solutions to painful problems. The younger family members benefit if the crisis brings them all closer together again; old and valued relationships are often re-established, and new relationships may emerge, setting a pattern for the future.

But those benefits are enjoyed only in some families. The crisis that brings unity to one may lead to civil war in another, and the problems of the elderly may be further intensified by family conflict.

We tend to speak of families as homogeneous units. We refer to the Jones family and the Smith family and the Brown family as if each one had a single mind and personality: "Oh, you can't count on the Davidsons," or "The Katers are so generous," or "The Phillipses are loud." But every family is made up of a number of individuals and a variety of personalities, capabilities, needs, ambitions, and frustrations. In order to function as a unit, family members, even when they are adults, may develop a certain balance in their relationships.

Frequently the unifying force in such families is the older generation, which maintains the balance, perpetuating ties between children. Elderly parents often serve as the family news agency: "Mother told me about your promotion—we're thrilled," a sister may write to her brother, or "Father wrote to us about your car accident so I had to call," says another sister, using the long-distance phone for the first time in months.

When a sudden crisis reduces an independent old woman to helplessness, or a slow deterioration finally disables a formerly self-sufficient old man, the news agency closes down. Brothers and sisters are thrown together again and must deal with each other directly, without a parent as intermediary. They may once again need to function as a unit, as they have not done since childhood. The successful balance they may have achieved may be out of kilter. The family is forced to realign itself to absorb the changes.

Similar realignment may be necessary in marital relationships. A husband who has taken a back seat, staying carefully removed from his wife's family, may be forced by a crisis to take a more active role and contribute time, concern, advice, and even money. A wife who has managed a wary, though polite, involvement with her mother-in-law may eventually, because her husband needs her, be forced into an intimate, supportive relationship with a woman she never really liked.

IS YOUR SIBLING RIVALRY STILL SHOWING?

The roles children assume or are assigned in childhood influence their relationships not only with their parents but with their brothers, sisters, and other relatives as well. Some roles are accepted and admired by everyone and make for affectionate relationships which last a lifetime.

Many roles, however, while accepted or even encouraged by parents, are branded by others in the family as phony. A brother, aware of the admiration his sister always receives for being "the easygoing one," may always have been able to see through the role to her "real" self, which is actually fearful and manipulative. He may brand her as a fake and despise his parents for being so blind. "Don't pull that act with me," he may have said many times while they were growing up. "You'd like to stand up to Dad just the way I do, but you haven't got the guts!" Thirty years later he may still suspect her motives when she hovers anxiously over their ailing father.

A highly competitive group of brothers and sisters may continue to compete later in life, although not quite as directly with each other. But when their mother begins to age, they may resume open competition with each other over her welfare, particularly if she was the original source of their competitiveness. Each sibling may claim to be considering Mother's well-being, but the underlying motivation is winning out in a final family contest.

Sibling relationships can also be affected by the position held by each one in the family structure, and by the age differences between them. The oldest may have always been expected to shoulder the greater responsibility when everyone was young, and that expectation may continue when everyone is grown up. But the opposite may happen. The oldest may marry first and, by making an earlier separation, leave the younger ones to deal with problems that remain. The youngest, as "the baby" in the family, may be seen as the one who is let off scot-free, while more was expected of the older ones. Conversely, the youngest, being the last to leave, may be left holding the bag because everyone else has gone. The varieties and mixtures of old relationships between brothers and sisters are endless.

These relationships do change and shift through the years. You may be amazed, when your parents are old, to find yourself depending on the sister who was the most scatterbrained or the brother who was the most self-centered. Such switches may pleasantly surprise you, but you may be even more astonished to find out how few changes have taken place in all that time since childhood. What a shock to discover that your forty-year-old sister is just as selfish as ever, or that your sixty-year-old brother is still trying to boss everyone. Don't forget, they may be equally shocked that you haven't grown up much either. Even though you have all come together again to try to help Mother, she may be pushed aside while family history repeats itself all over again.

A particularly crucial childhood role—and one which often affects relationships years later—is the role of "the favorite."

When they are growing up, children often wonder about their parents' feelings, asking themselves, "Do they love *me* best?" or "Which one of us do they love best?" In some cases the favored relationship can be limited to one child and one parent: "Joey's always been closer to Mother but Dad loves me best." In other families the role of favorite is conferred on one child and then passed on to another, depending on the stage of development of each. That unstable state of affairs can lead to further tensions as children compete for the prize, never knowing exactly where they stand. Parents usually loudly deny having favorites and honestly believe they love *all* their children equally, but their behavior may reveal their true feelings. "Look, Ma, no hands!" a triumphant four-year-old may shout, balancing for the first time in his life on a two-wheel bicycle. If his mother's response to this dramatic accomplishment is merely, "Be careful! Don't scratch your brother's bike!" the four-year-old may wonder what further act of bravery he will have to perform in order to gain the maternal spotlight. He may keep trying all his life, hoping that one day he will do something to make his mother's face light up for him the way it does for his brother. Like eager scouts, less-favored sons and daughters often push themselves through life to do more and more good deeds, hoping for just that reward. But sad to say, no Brownie points are given out to middle-aged daughters and no merit badges to graying sons.

Favoritism is particularly hard to bear if the favorite seems to hold the crown for no valid reason. A ten-year-old sister (in second place) may wonder, "Why is it always Jennie? Why never me? Why can't they see how pretty and clever and kind I am?" Years later she may be asking the same questions: "Why do they always turn to her for advice—can't they see how greedy, cold, self-centered, and neurotic she is? Don't they realize how much better off they'd be if only they listened to me?"

Oversolicitous behavior toward old parents may mask the anger a grown child feels for having to take second place, but it may also be a way of saying, "Look how good I am to you. *Now* won't you love me best?" or "By God, I'm going to be your favorite child *just once* before you die!" Indifferent, uncaring behavior may also be a way of saying, "You always loved Jack the best—he got the most—now let *him* take care of you." An uncaring son may be accused by others of taking a back seat and not coming forward to help his parents when they are old and need him, but he may merely be continuing to stay in the exact place they assigned to him when he was young.

WHO'S IN CHARGE?

Your mother may have said over the years, "I will never be a burden to any of my children," but unless she has made some prior arrangements to cover all emergencies as she grows older, she may have no choice. She may be forced to turn to someone in her family for help. In families where there are several children, however, the big question is: *Who will that someone be?*

If you are the only daughter in the family, the chances are that it will be you, rather than one of your brothers. Experts in family relations feel that daughters (usually middle-aged) are more likely to take on the major responsibility for their parents' care. They and other female relatives are normally the ones who contact outside sources of support—family and community agencies—when they cannot cope with the responsibility alone. Even when their parents are getting along well and do not need help from anyone, daughters are usually thought of as keeping in closer touch than sons, who are more likely to become involved on special occasions or with major decisions and financial arrangements.

It could be argued that the behavior of daughters has been determined through the years because women have traditionally been at home and available, and also because housekeeping and nursing duties have always been seen as women's roles. According to gerontologist Elaine Brody, the term "alternatives to institutional care" is a euphemism for "daughters." It will not be known until the future whether this pattern will continue as more and more women become involved outside the home in careers, and domestic duties are shared to a greater extent by both sexes.

Business executives are becoming aware that many of their employees have ongoing responsibilities for elderly relatives. Now, with more women at all levels of the work force, the middle generations are often forced to be acrobats juggling child, career, and caregiving. These three Cs often add up to a fourth: conflict.

A 1985 survey of the Travelers Insurance Company in Connecticut identified 28 percent of the employees over thirty as caregivers who spent 10.2 hours a week on their elder-care responsibilities. Some of those hours were taken from their working time, causing loss of productivity for the company and therefore loss of dollars. A number of companies, ever mindful of the bottom line, have now begun programs offering their employees information about caregiving resources and how to find them.

THE CAREGIVER MAY BE CHOSEN

When there are two or more children in any family, one may be chosen by the parents to take care of them. Their preference may have always been known. One particular daughter (or son) may have always been called when problems arose, one who could always be counted on to answer any emergency, who keeps in touch on a regular, even a daily, basis. That relationship is often mutually gratifying and supportive to both generations over the years, with giving as well as receiving on each side. In the later years, when her parents have greater needs, that daughter may be willing, because of these strong mutual bonds of affection, to make sacrifices in her own life in order to make her parents' lives easier.

The child who is singled out by the parents as their main source of help may be the oldest, the youngest, the strongest, the weakest, the favorite, or the least favorite. One son (or daughter) may live close by, and that very proximity makes it natural for his parents to turn to him and his family. He may not even realize what is happening, but little by little he may assume more and more responsibility for his parents' welfare until one day he may wake up to realize he is the caregiver. If he is married, his wife will probably share the role with him to some extent at least. She may even bear the brunt of it. In other families, as one by one children grow up, get married, and move into their own lives, one particular child (usually a daughter but sometimes a son) may be expected to stay around, her plans for her own future constantly influenced by the thought, "I'm the only one left—I can't leave them now." The unmarried daughter, mainstay of her parents' old age, was seen more frequently in the past, but she has not gone completely out of style today. Her life may become a series of postponements. She may hope to travel, to work in a foreign country. She may consider marrying Joe or Frank or Tom, but only "after Mother gets well," or "when Mom and Dad sell the house and move south."

"I was always in the right place at the right time," an unmarried career woman explained. Specifically, her statement meant that whenever there was a crisis in her parents' lives she "happened" to be conveniently on the spot, while her brothers and sisters were conveniently (for them) miles away. After a number of years, everyone began to take it for granted that she would always be there and any plans for marriage or career advancement would always be indefinitely tabled. It never seemed to occur to the absent ones that they should disrupt their own lives and come home to help out. It *did* occur to their "dependable" sister as more and more years went by, but she was unable to extricate herself from a pattern everyone had allowed to develop—herself included.

The caregiver chosen by the elderly parents may not be their first or even second choice, but they may have no other one available. They may turn by default to the only son who is in good health, has a steady job, or has a wife they can tolerate (or who can tolerate them). Other brothers and sisters may determine the choice. Those who are married with children of their own may expect the childless couple to take the major responsibility. "I only wish I had as much time to spend with Mom as Mary does," a contented mother of three may say of her childless older sister. "But she's not tied down the way I am." Sister Mary may not agree that just because she is not tied down by children she should be tied down by Mom.

Being childless may, on the other hand, be a good excuse for avoiding responsibility. Brother Fred may say with genuine regret, "Phyllis and I would love to have Father live with us, but we're away so much—he'd be terribly lonely. Tom has all those kids at home anyhow, so Father's much better off with him." Brother Tom and his wife, already responsible for three children, become responsible for Father as well. The choice may seem logical and sensible, but neither brother may be completely happy, as Tom yearns for Fred's freedom and Fred envies Tom's closeness to their father.

A potentially explosive situation exists when parents divide their needs, accepting help and care from one child and advice and guidance from another.

"I spoke to Larry last night. He doesn't think Dr. Parker's doing a thing for your father's arthritis. He thinks we ought to go to Dr. Larribee over in Beechwood Center," Mrs. Fuller said to her daughter Kate.

"But you've always liked Dr. Parker. He's known Dad for years. And Beechwood Center's miles away," replied Kate, who always drove her father for his regular treatments. She tried not to show the resentment she always felt when her brother had one of his "great ideas."

"Larry wants us to try Dr. Larribee," continued her mother.

"Then let Larry drive. He lives around the corner from Beechwood," snapped Kate, knowing exactly what her mother's next words would be.

"Oh, Kate. You *know* how busy Larry is. Surely you want to do what's best for Father."

Of course Kate wanted to do what was best for Father. Didn't she always follow through whenever Larry had a great idea? She dutifully took her father to Dr. Larribee, driving the extra thirty miles to Beechwood Center and back, gritting her teeth and hissing at herself, "Here you go again—doing Larry's work for him!"

THE CAREGIVER MAY VOLUNTEER

The caregiver may ask for the job. A son may realize that he is in the best position to help; a daughter may feel she can take care of her parents as well as her children. When their parents begin to deteriorate, these volunteers are ready to help out or to take over completely. But sometimes they are ready too soon, and take control of their parents' lives long before this is necessary. "Premature volunteering" by one of their children may accelerate an older couple's decline and make them dependent long before they need to be. The volunteer may then be suspected of assuming control more to satisfy his own needs than out of concern for his parents. He may have been waiting all his life for just this opportunity.

The volunteer may be the child who has always felt least loved and hopes finally to gain recognition and approval from everyone. For this reward he may be willing to make painful sacrifices in his own personal life—in his relationships with his wife and children, and in his career.

The favorite may also volunteer. He may feel forced by his parents' expectation that he will return to them the concern they have always shown him, or he may volunteer out of guilt that he has received so much more than the other children in the family and feel obligated to make it up to everyone. Or he may always have had a lurking worry that he did not really deserve his favored position, that he was unworthy of it, that it was conferred on him by mistake, or that he would never live up to it. When his parents are old he finally has a chance to convince them and himself that they were right to favor him after all.

THE PSEUDO CAREGIVER

Occasionally, a son or daughter volunteers as caregiver but functions in name only, wearing the title but performing none of the duties. Like a good general or clever executive, he is able to delegate responsibility to the lower ranks. He may use phrases like "Just this once" when he asks someone to pinch-hit for him, as if asking for the first time. "You *will* call Mother every day while I'm on vacation, won't you?" a pseudo caregiver may say earnestly to his sister. She would be justified in replying, "What difference will it make if you *are* away? Don't I call her every day anyway?"

The child who acts as pseudo caregiver usually has his own motives: to establish himself firmly in first place in his parents' affections, to gain admiration from the outside world, or perhaps to inherit the most from his parents—even if they have very little to leave behind.

Brothers and sisters sometimes seem to conspire to help the pseudo caregiver retain the title, knowing that efforts to unseat him would be futile or would cause pain to the parent who needs to perpetuate the masquerade. "I'm the meat and potatoes in my parents' lives, but my brother's the champagne," a sister admitted honestly. "I'm around all the time, but I don't do anything exciting or dramatic—just the ordinary little everyday chores that everyone takes for granted. But he breezes in and whisks them off to the country for the day—brings them some special treat or takes them to a restaurant or a show. He breaks that awful monotony for them. They can live on one of his visits for weeks. They even look younger afterward. I can't do that for them. I guess they need both of us."

THE CAREGIVER AS MARTYR

Some aging parents place unreasonable demands on their caregivers. In many cases when other relatives are really unable to help or simply prefer to keep a safe distance away, the caregiver is genuinely overburdened and justified in feeling there is just too much for one person to handle. But caregivers, because of their own complex feelings toward their parents, often place unreasonable demands on themselves. They go overboard in their zeal, insist on carrying the entire responsibility single-handed, and discourage anyone else from sharing in it in any way. Brothers, sisters, and other relatives, initially willing and eager to help, will eventually back away when their offers are repeatedly rebuffed, at the same time resenting being rejected and shut out of the old people's lives. The caregivers may then complain bitterly to anyone who will listen about their heavy burdens and the selfishness of their families.

"I'm everyone's slave, doctor," complained Sally Horgan, explaining during her physical examination why she was overworked and rundown. "After I've cleaned and marketed for my own family, I have to go over and do the same thing at Mother's apartment. And Mother's lonely—she needs company—so I have to visit a little, too. It makes her feel better. I fix her a little supper and then I have to go home and cook for all of us. I'm usually too tired to eat."

"You're an only child, then, Mrs. Horgan?" asked the doctor.

"No, doctor. I have a brother and sister."

"They live far away?"

"No, doctor—they're right here in Maplewood."

"Can't they help you out a little with your mother?"

"They always leave everything to me."

"Do you ever ask them to help?"

"They never offer."

"Do you ever ask them?" repeated the doctor.

"No, doctor, I guess I don't."

The one in charge who does not ask for help, or rejects help when it is offered, ends up alone. The burdens become heavier as time goes on, and eventually the caregiver is likely to become the family martyr.

FRIEND OR ENEMY?

The caregiver may be seen as the most valued member of the family or the most hated. Brothers and sisters are often genuinely grateful to the one who performs a job they are unable or unwilling to do, and are often eager to do whatever they can to make the caregiver's life easier. The caregivers are often equally appreciative and report that the additional help they are given makes their responsibilities bearable. "There must be ESP in our family," one sister claims. "Whenever everything's about to get too much for me—almost before I know it myself—my brother and his wife take over for a few days. I'm always surprised after all these years that they keep on appearing just when I need them most." A sister in California tells her friends, "I always fly home to Philadelphia every summer to be with Father for a month. My brother and his family take care of him the entire year—they deserve a break. And anyhow I'm glad to know that I can spend some real time with Father every year."

The one in charge may be hated instead of loved by the rest of the family, for using the position to keep everyone apart. Aging parents can become pawns in family power struggles. They may be used to settle old debts and rivalries between siblings. A sister, always jealous of her brother, may deny him the thing he wants most: the chance to be close to their parents and share the final years with them. "Mary acts as if Father is her private property, as if *she's* the only one who cares about him," he might complain—justifiably—and then use every opportunity to draw his father over to *his* side. Poor Father, caught in the crossfire, is doubly threatened—by his own old age and by his own children.

THE CAREGIVER UNDER FIRE

In many families trouble may come from the most unexpected quarter: from the very child who seems the most remote from the parents, the least concerned, and the most willing to let everyone else take over. When plans have been put into action and seem to be working smoothly, an absent son or daughter may suddenly appear on the scene and imply to an elderly mother, "If I'd been around [or, if I'd been consulted] I'd never have let them do this to you." Mother, who may have been adapting pretty well to some new situation carefully worked out with the rest of the family, is likely to take several giant steps backward.

Well-run nursing homes, concerned with the future adjustment of a potential resident, know the value of consulting as many children as possible in the placement process. A daughter, making an application for her father, may find that the intake team discourages her unilateral decision and asks to see everyone else involved.

A brother or sister may disapprove of a plan, not because the plan itself is ill-advised, but because someone else thought of it first: "Bill would have approved of the nursing home if he'd selected it," or "Mary and John would have liked Mother's homemaker if they'd hired her."

Snipers and critics may not make real trouble, but they can be constant irritants. Rather than acknowledge how much responsibility the caregiver does shoulder, her siblings (and other relatives) may be quick to point out any omissions and mistakes. Aware that they aren't doing much for their parents themselves, they find it comforting to snipe at her.

> Older sister to younger sister: "Mother was so disappointed when you didn't visit on Thursday, Kim. She was in tears when I called." Kim visited Mother every day of the week—she just happened that week to miss Thursday.
>
> • •
>
> Younger brother to older sister: "How could you have let Dad gain so much weight since I was here at Christmas? Have you completely forgotten about his blood pressure?" Dad had lived with older sister for four years. She watched his diet carefully, cooking special salt-free, low-cholesterol dishes. But Dad cheated, and she couldn't watch him every minute.
>
> • •
>
> Younger sister to middle sister: "Aren't you *ever* going to get a new coat for Mother? She's been wearing that old rag for years. It makes me cry to see her looking so shabby." Middle sister did all Mother's shopping. She bought food, shoes, curtains, nightgowns, dresses, cosmetics, drugs. She just hadn't had time yet to look for a coat.

When the nursing home is the caregiver, sons and daughters who still feel they ought to have taken care of their old mother or father themselves may make themselves feel better by constantly criticizing the institution: the staff, the housekeeping, the food, the activities. They may think they feel better doing this, but their continual sniping will understandably antagonize the staff and may even permanently prevent their parent from settling down comfortably.

Caregivers must also defend themselves against well-intentioned relatives and onlookers, ready with unsolicited advice or criticism. Your mother's friends may gently but sadly intensify your own anxieties and conflicts by casual comments: how much worse she looks, how depressed she seems. They may ask if you *really* have confidence in her doctor, and remind you that she's alone too much, doesn't eat enough, doesn't get out enough. You may already know everything they tell you and be doing the best you can, but these reminders usually carry the implication that you aren't doing enough, and if they had the job to do they would do it much better.

A PERMANENT SPLIT
OR A CLOSER BOND?

"We've not seen each other since Mother died," a gray-haired matron answered sadly when asked about her older sister. "I guess we're not on speaking terms."

The wounds that are given and received during a parent's illness or period of dependency are sometimes so deep and painful that they can never be healed. Relationships between brothers and sisters can sometimes be permanently broken off. Often those wounds are only the final blows ending a relationship which has been distant or seething for years. The sister who has given up too great a part of her life caring for an elderly parent may, even when she is free of her burdens, never forgive her siblings for not sharing enough. A daughter burdened with remorse that she had never done enough for her father may, after his death, need to withdraw from the ones who did care for him. Siblings may resent the martyred caregiver who stood between them and their dying mother, making it impossible for them ever to resolve their feelings about her or to share her final days. Two brothers in Arthur Miller's play *The Price* voice their irreconcilable feelings toward each other while trying to dispose of their dead father's possessions:

> VICTOR You came for the old handshake, didn't you? The okay? And you end up with the respect, the career, the money and, best of all, the thing that nobody else can tell you so you can believe it—that you're one hell of a guy and never harmed anybody in your life! Well, you won't get that, not till I get mine!
>
> WALTER And you? You never had any hatred for me? Never a wish to see me destroyed? To destroy me, to destroy me with this saintly self-sacrifice, this mockery of sacrifice?

The split may be less dramatic, resulting more from apathy and attrition than from resentment. When the parent and the parental home go, the unifying force in the family often goes too, and there is no longer the same need for siblings to keep in touch with each other. One child may try to take over that central role. If the family had always gathered at Mother's for New Year's, sister Ellie may try to preserve this tradition. But her New Year's celebration may be a conscious effort on her part rather than the spontaneous gathering it had always been when Mother was alive. Sister Ellie may succeed and establish a new family pattern, preserving it for the next generation. But she may fail, and the new tradition may never take hold. Next year, brother Jack may say casually, "You won't mind if we're not there for New Year's, will you? We've got a chance to go south for the week. We'd never have accepted if Mother were still alive. But it doesn't make much difference now, does it?" This will be the first defection, and others are likely to follow. Despite Ellie's efforts, brothers and sisters and cousins and nieces and nephews will, in the future, probably meet each other only at weddings—or, more likely, only at funerals.

MONEY—
THE ROOT OF MANY EVILS

Money and material possessions—the abundance as well as the lack of both—very often provide the real underlying source of family dissension. Brothers and sisters have been competing over inheritances since the beginning of time. They are still doing it today, especially when their elderly parents have sizable estates to leave behind. But even when there is little money and only a few material possessions, these can still assume great symbolic worth. The struggle to win them may be out of all proportion to their value. "Mother's leaving me the silver candlesticks because I'm the oldest," or "I should get the candlesticks because I've done the most for Mother." "Doing" for Mother therefore is expected to pay off. But will this kind of "doing" really pay off for her?

Money can cause trouble when there is none. If Mother is barely scraping along on her small pension and Social Security checks, and her children are in a better financial position, who is going to contribute how much? Should they all contribute equal amounts? Or should the contributions be from each child according to his (or her) financial situation? Or from each child according to his (or her) emotional need? Will the contribution be given out of generosity or guilt? Will the gifts have strings attached? Will Mother have to subordinate her own wishes to the wishes of the biggest checkbook?

Money is therefore power: "I give Mother the most, therefore I have the right to decide what plans we should make for her." Does money ever buy that right? Many brothers and sisters say no.

Money can also be a substitute. A son who says "I send my father a monthly check" may feel he has thereby discharged his total filial responsibility. Does his monthly check balance out equally with his brother's weekly visit or his sister's daily phone call? They may feel that their contributions have greater value and no amount of money is a substitute for care and concern. Finally, money can be a contest. Competitive brothers and sisters who have money themselves may lavish luxuries on their elderly mother or father, not because either parent needs these gifts or even wants them, but to demonstrate which child has achieved the greatest worldly success.

> Jason Neville was a successful man who prized success in others. His three children competed with each other through childhood to win his approval, and each one became successful as an adult. They constantly reminded their father of their success by sending him lavish gifts as he grew older and was often in financial straits.
>
> When he was partially disabled by a stroke, they made arrangements for him to enter an expensive nursing home. The day he moved in, his daughter sent him an expensive bathrobe, his younger son provided a new radio, and his older son hired a limousine and driver to take the old man to the nursing home.
>
> Eighty-seven-year-old Mr. Neville arrived in style—and alone. It was a full week before any one of his three children thought it necessary to visit in person to see how their father was adjusting to his new situation.

WHAT ABOUT YOUR OWN FAMILY?

If you are involved with an ailing mother whose needs take up a lot of your time, your husband (or wife) and your children may give you great support, or resentment. They may share your problems, or add to them. Your conflicting loyalties may sometimes be unbearable.

HUSBANDS, WIVES, AND IN-LAWS

Husbands and wives react in a number of different ways when their in-laws need help. A husband may have no particular animosity toward his mother-in-law herself, but he may be jealous of anything or anyone who makes demands on his wife's time or concern. A wife who actively disliked her father-in-law from the beginning may be able to keep her feelings under wraps until he becomes helpless and needs something from her that she is unable to give. A mother may have made it clear through the years that she never approved of her daughter's husband. Can he be blamed for keeping his distance when she is old, or for resenting the amount of time his wife spends with her?

Your husband's (wife's) relationship with his own family also helps to determine how he behaves with yours. If he has always had a strong bond with his own parents, he may develop a positive one with his parents-in-law. A troubled relationship from the past, however, can affect his behavior in one of two opposite ways: he may, because of his conflicting feelings, be so neurotically tied to one or both of his parents that he has nothing left to spare for yours, or he may feel forced to separate from *all* parents—yours as well as his own—as if implying, "A plague on both your houses!"

Perhaps he came from an unloving family and hoped that your parents would make up for him all that he had missed in his childhood. He may come to resent them if they too let him down, fail to measure up to his expectations, and never become the parents he always wanted.

A son-in-law, as an outsider, may quickly size up the way his wife is treated by her family, and he may not like what he sees. She may have made her peace through the years and accepted the fact that her sister has always been the favorite, but her husband may never accept this. His feelings toward his wife's parents, therefore, may be determined by *their* feelings toward *her*. How can he feel close to people who do not appreciate the person he values? A daughter-in-law, wife of the unfavorite, may never forgive her parents-in-law because they have been so blind and never recognized her husband's superior worth. She may retaliate in two ways when they are old: either by withdrawing and trying to pull her husband with her, thereby adding to his problems, or by devoting herself overzealously to their needs. Her interest may be less in the welfare of the older people than in her continual desire to show up their favorite.

The wife of the favorite son (or husband of the favorite daughter) faces a different situation. She may have always known that her in-laws never considered her worthy of their son. She may always have to share him with them, or wage a constant and usually losing battle to win him away. When they are old and need to depend on him, she may sabotage his efforts to help them.

HOW DO YOUR CHILDREN FEEL?

An endless variety of relationships are possible between aging parents and children-in-law: supportive, affectionate, caring, hostile, antagonistic. An equal variety is possible between grandparents and grandchildren.

Even though many people like to cherish the rocking-chair and Whistler's Mother images of grandparents, this image was probably more appropriate in the past. Grandparents these days, far from being white-haired and frail, are often vigorous men and women in their forties and fifties still pursuing their own careers and interests. Many are actually relieved to be free of child-care responsibilities and not too eager to take on babysitting and domestic duties again. They may not even be comfortable in the role of grandparent and feel that it has been thrust on them too soon. Some may be pulled in a different direction, concerned about the welfare of their own parents, now great-grandparents in their seventies, eighties, and nineties. But even when grandparents are older, they may not behave according to the ideal image.

Bernice Neugarten and Karol Weinstein of the University of Chicago observed five major styles of grandparenting: the "distant figures," who have little contact with their grandchildren; the "fun-seekers," who play with and enjoy their grandchildren; the "surrogate parents," who take over when Mother works or is ill; the "formal" or traditional grandparents and finally, the grandparents who are "the reservoir of family wisdom." "Fun-seekers" and "distant figures" are more common among younger grandparents, while older ones (sixty-five and over) are more likely to follow the "formal" style.

The relationships that have developed over the years between the oldest and the youngest generation may determine how a grandchild will feel and behave toward a grandparent who is beginning to decline and needs help.

Occasionally, children see one particular grandparent as the person most important to them—more important than their parents. The relationship can be simpler, less pressured, less emotionally involved, and less conflicted than that between parent and child. A daughter may admit, "Mother's always driven me crazy, but Timmy won't hear a word against his grandma. He thinks she's great, and she is—to him!"

A granddaughter may depend on a loving grandfather, trust him, turn to him when she feels ill-used by the world, see him as a source of comfort, understanding, knowledge. He may have time to play with her when everyone else is too busy, time to tell stories, to make things, to go fishing, sightseeing, hiking. Grandfather, in turn, may thrive on this relationship, knowing he is still important in someone's eyes, delighting in the audience he has for his old stories that no one wants to listen to anymore. A sense of family history can be passed on from grandparent to grandchild, often skipping the middle generation. These close relationships have prompted some observers to refer to the old and young as "generation-gap allies." When such grandparents grow old and feeble, their grandchildren often share the family concern and try to do all they can to be supportive. Older grandchildren may even share caregiving responsibilities, chauffeuring, sitting, housekeeping, even nursing duties.

When several generations join together to help and comfort the oldest one, they usually comfort each other at the same time.

That closeness does not always develop. Your mother may never have been the ideal grandmother (or the ideal mother either), and when she needs help your children may not cooperate willingly. They may resent giving up their own interests and activities: "Why do we always have to go to Grandma's on Sunday?" or "Just because of Grandpa we have to miss out on our camping trip!" Some grandparents are seen as stern or punitive figures, always disapproving of something: language, lifestyle, dress, manners, or friends. The younger generation, in turn, sees the older one as interfering, old-fashioned, bigoted, or even physically distasteful: "I don't want to kiss Grandpa—he smells," or "All Grandma talks about is constipation."

Such problems can be intensified, even reinforced daily, when a grandparent lives in the same house with growing children. There is little opportunity to relieve the tension or to let off steam. You may hear yourself saying again and again, "Shhh, Grandma's sleeping," or "Turn that stereo down—you know Grandpa hates rock music." Your older children may ask resentfully, "How can I bring my friends home when Grandma's always there bugging everyone?" and solve their problems by staying away from home as much as possible.

Young children may feel jealous or abandoned when their mothers and fathers have to be out of the house all the time "taking care of poor old Grandma" if she is still living in her own home. Occasionally, children may become fearful, anxious, and bewildered when a sick older person lives in the same house with them. They may wonder what really is going on: "How sick is Grandpa?" and "Is he going to die?" One granddaughter, now grown up, remembers all the years her grandfather lived with her and her family; she also remembers standing at his door every morning on her way to school, listening carefully to make sure she could hear him breathing before she left the house.

THE GAMES
OLD PEOPLE PLAY

Your behavior toward your parents when they are old is determined by so many factors in your own personal history and your own current life. But your behavior is also determined by *their* behavior.

Older people are just as capable of playing games as younger people; in fact, they may become even more skillful over the years. Some children learn how to play the same games and win, but usually their parents come out on top because of long years of practice.

MANIPULATION

A mother who has always played games with her family will know from long experience exactly how to manipulate her children in order to get what she wants from them when she is old. She may know she can go only so far with one but that the tolerance of another is limitless. She may vary her strategy accordingly with each one.

> "She's a brave old girl," a son will say admiringly of his crippled mother. "She's going through hell, but she always manages to sound bright and chipper when I call."
>
> "And how often *do* you call?" his sister may snap back bitterly. "I talk to her every day, and the minute she hears my voice she sounds like the end of the world is here. I have to drop whatever I'm doing and rush over there to see what's wrong."

DENIAL OF INFIRMITIES

By pretending that they have no problems and refusing to admit that anything so terrible is going on, some disabled old people force their children into the same game.

> "Everyone tells me I ought to go into a home," says Millie Farkas pleasantly. "What do I need with a home? I'm doing fine here in my nice old apartment. I've got good children—we're a close family—they're happy to give a little help to their old mother once in a while."

Mrs. Farkas doesn't stop to define "a little help" or "once in a while." If she did, she'd have to revise her statement. She's not doing fine and her children know she's not. Jack stops by on his way to work most days to see that Ma has breakfast and doesn't burn herself making coffee. Francie usually comes in at lunchtime, brings groceries, and cleans up a little while she's there. Grandson Billy brings dinner over every evening before he goes to night school; his mother, Laurie, has cooked it. When Mrs. Farkas is ill, her three children take turns sleeping over at her house. By denying her incapacities she has made the lives of three adult families revolve around her needs.

EXAGGERATION OF INFIRMITIES

The rules of this game require older people to exploit their age, insist they cannot manage, play for sympathy, and demand attention. The elderly players use their physical infirmities to control everyone. Loud music, late parties, family arguments must be ended quickly if Grandpa has palpitations or Grandma has one of her dizzy spells. When no one is looking Grandpa doesn't hobble quite as painfully and can climb the stairs pretty well. Grandma can read the fine print of the TV schedule to find her favorite program even though she tells everyone, "My eyes are gone."

Eighty-one-year-old Grandpa Allen, living with his son, used his age as an excuse to avoid any activity he disliked. He would have liked to help his daughter-in-law around the house, but his legs weren't strong enough anymore. (He had always hated any form of housework.) "Make my excuses to the minister," he would say to the family on Sunday. "Tell him I can't manage to get to church anymore." (He had always hated church.) "Make my excuses to Aunt Cissie. Tell her those family gatherings of hers are too much for an old man." (He had always hated family gatherings *and* Aunt Cissie.)

But when his oldest friend moved back to town and suggested they go fishing, Grandpa packed his gear efficiently, rose at dawn one day and was off. His daughter-in-law stood at the window watching him leave and muttering to herself, "Okay, Grandpa—but don't play your games with me anymore."

SELF-BELITTLEMENT

The elderly themselves can contribute to society's generally negative attitude toward old age. An older woman may deliberately draw everyone's attention to the miseries old age has inflicted on her. "Look at these crippled hands!" or "Have you ever seen so many wrinkles?" or "I was beautiful once—would you ever believe it now?" She may reject herself before anyone else rejects her, answering all invitations, "Who wants an old woman like me along?" or "I'd only spoil your fun." The younger generation is then expected to respond to such statements, "Now, Mother, *of course* we want you to come, don't we, children?" The elderly may use self-belittlement to gain sympathy, to manipulate their children, but also to quiet their own anxieties about their deterioration.

THE MONEY GAME

Some older people use money as others use love, or the withdrawal of love, to control their families. They may try to buy attention, implying that certain behavior will be rewarded and other behavior will be penalized. Threats and promises which have price tags attached can keep entire families in line, bowing to the wishes of one frail old parent.

When old people play games with their children, it sometimes seems as if they always win. But their gamesmanship often backfires. It may create such resentment in their families that, when they really need help, everyone's judgment is so distorted that no one can function at all.

CAN OLD PATTERNS
BE REVERSED?

Family history can never be rewritten. Brothers and sisters cannot return to earlier days to heal old wounds. Husbands and wives cannot start married life all over again, this time loving their in-laws. The lifetime personalities of older people cannot be turned around either, nor can their old relationships with their various children. But attitudes and perspectives can be shifted slightly—problems approached in different ways may become easier to deal with.

Lack of communication often produces deadlocks. Families may not realize they are not communicating with each other—they may feel they are communicating too much. But sniping, complaining, recriminating is not communication. How can it be, when everyone is talking and no one is listening?

Learning to listen is one step toward gaining new insights. Willingness to try new approaches is another. There may be a certain amount of trial and error. The new approaches may not work at all, or it may take time before they work smoothly. You may feel uncomfortable with the new relationships that emerge; they may seem forced, artificial, unnatural. You may, from time to time, slip back into old patterns. But after a while the strains should begin to lessen; and in addition, by working together for the first time, you may all come up with solutions that never occurred to any one of you when you were searching alone. (Chapter 10 shows in more detail how families can get off the merry-go-round.)

4

WHAT HAVE THEY
GOT TO LOSE?

Frank Barrett lost a lot in the ten years after his retirement. As the cost of living rose, his income became barely adequate, arthritis prevented him from enjoying the active outdoor life he'd always loved, and finally, when he was seventy-four, his wife died. Even so, he still continued living his own life. His two married children who lived in the same city were devoted to him, and they did help. They shared his period of mourning with him, helped him to give up his house and move into a small, efficient apartment. They were relieved when they saw he was keeping himself busy. He visited his friends, although their numbers were dwindling. He sat in the park, worked at his hobbies, spoke to his children several times a week by phone, ate dinner with them frequently, and even babysat for his grandchildren occasionally. His children were proud of him—and of themselves—feeling that, all in all, their father's situation, if not happy, was at least pleasant and satisfactory.

But shortly after Frank's seventy-ninth birthday his children began to feel uneasy; they noticed little things at first. One day his daughter arrived and found the water running and overflowing the bathtub. Later that week she noticed that her father had forgotten to lock the door of his apartment. Then there were bigger things. A pot boiled over, extinguishing the flame, and escaping gas was filling the apartment when Frank's son arrived to pick him up one evening. Two days later his children were horrified at a long, nasty burn on their father's arm, but even more horrified that he didn't seem to remember where it came from—nor did it seem to bother him. He seemed increasingly confused and often forgot what day of the week it was, which meal he had just eaten, and what his children had told him yesterday. He began to be irritable when they corrected or contradicted him and defensive when they questioned him. The day he fell and broke his hip, his children had already come to the realization that their "satisfactory" situation was no longer workable. Even if their father managed to walk again, they could not let him live alone anymore. And so began their search for a safer, more protected kind of living. Then their real problems began.

F rank Barrett's story is being replayed by numbers of elderly people all over America and will be rerun even more frequently in the future as modern medicine prolongs life expectancy for additional thousands. Your parents and elderly relatives may be living out similar scenarios right now.

Their problems, like Frank Barrett's, although disturbing to everyone in the family, may be relatively simple and straightforward. You may know exactly what kinds of solutions to look for even though these solutions are often difficult to find. But things are not always so clear. Perhaps, instead, you are quite confused about what's happening to your parents. Perhaps you cannot put your finger on any one single difficulty, even though you are aware that *something* is wrong. They may seem weaker, more tired, less alert—or withdrawn, full of self-pity and complaints, dissatisfied with everything and everyone. But even though you know that things are not right, you may not have the slightest idea how to make them better. How can you find answers if you don't even understand the questions?

Just as you may find it helpful to consider all the various emotions involved in your relationship with your parents in order to answer the question "How do you really feel about them?" it can be equally important to consider all the various changes in their personal world in order to answer the question "What's really happening to them?" You may never have stopped to wonder how old age has affected their overall lives.

MISCONCEPTIONS
AND MISINFORMATION

Despite popular belief, most older people adjust quite well to the changes in their lives. Your parents may be in this adaptable majority. Old age of itself is not a problem. It is the final stage in the cycle of living. Like every stage, it has its share of pleasure and pain, but unfortunate misconceptions and stereotypes prevail, perhaps accounting for the existence of "ageism" in many places and the prejudices against old age and old people held by many Americans. The old are viewed generally as poor, lonely, useless, inactive, and sick. But the facts of aging, once they are known, can quickly prove these assumptions false. In the area of health, to take one example, although problems do mushroom during the later years, they are not nearly as universally incapacitating as many people suppose. Most men and women over sixty-five are healthy enough to carry on their normal activities—only 20 percent are not, and most of these are over age seventy-five. Less than 5 percent of the elderly are in institutions, nursing homes, or homes for the aged at any one time. Our elderly population averages less than fifteen days a year in bed because of ill-health, and even after sixty-five, illness and disability do not have to become chronic but can frequently be cured or at least arrested. So much for the idea that the old are sick. The aged themselves, in contrast to younger generations, give a far more optimistic report about old age, not only in matters of health but in other areas as well. Their views have been repeatedly confirmed by scientific surveys. After questioning a national sample of noninstitutionalized men and women over sixty-five, investigator Louis Harris, in *The Myth and Reality of Aging in America*, concluded that

> *while serious problems of not enough money, fear of crime, poor health, loneliness, inadequate medical care and getting where they want to go indeed exist among certain minorities of older people, they are by no means as pervasive as the public thinks. Nor should having a problem be confused with being a problem. . . . Such generalizations about the elderly as an economically and socially deprived group can do the old a disservice.*

The young, with most of life ahead of them, understandably have a different view of the future than the old, with most of life behind them. The present may be even more precious because the future is limited. While physical and emotional suffering are possible in every stage— childhood, adolescence, maturity, and middle age—except where fatal accident or terminal illness occurs there is "always a tomorrow." The ugly duckling becomes a swan, teenage acne usually vanishes, an ungratifying career can be changed, a bad marriage dissolved.

In old age there is a finality. It is the period that inevitably leads to the natural end of the life-cycle: death. The comforting clichés of previous ages are inappropriate now and sound emptier: "It'll be better in the morning," or "Things should be looking up next year," or "My time will come," or "When my ship comes in." Prosperity is *not* just around the corner. The only thing just around the corner is death. But death, the inevitable fact of life, is the only certainty in the final stage of the life-cycle. Everything else in old age is subject to chance variation and individual interpretation. Dr. Robert Butler, the well-known gerontologist, writes in his book *Why Survive? Being Old in America* that the elderly are *as diverse as people in other periods of life and their patterns of aging vary according to the range they show from health to sickness, from maturity to immaturity, activity to apathy, useful constructive participation to disinterest, from the prevailing stereotype of aging to rich forms of creativity. . . . Under suitable circumstances, the present remains very much alive and exciting to them; but they also turn to a review of their past, searching for purpose, reconciliation of relationships and resolution of conflicts and regrets. They may become self-centered or altruistic, angry or contrite, triumphant or depressed. . . .*

However, if any one word can sum up the varied catalogue of problems that do appear in old age, it is the word *loss*. A seventy-year-old woman may have had very little during a long and deprived life, but it's amazing how much she still has to lose as the years go by. Loss seems like a simple concept, but it often works in mysterious ways.

Children are usually quick to recognize obvious losses and to respond sympathetically to them. When Father is widowed, everyone expects him to mourn. If Mother's arthritis seriously cripples her, it's easy to see why her daily life is so difficult. But loss is not always so glaringly apparent. When a seventy-nine-year-old woman considers it a tragedy that she cannot drive anymore, her family may be quite impatient with her. "What's she making such a big deal about? Can't she understand we'll take her anyplace she needs to go? Why does she act as if the world's come to an end?" They may not even begin to realize that *her* world *has* come to an end because she has lost what she valued most: her ability to go her own way and her independence. When aging Michael Parker's canary died, he could not be comforted. "It's only a bird," his children kept repeating in disbelief. "He wasn't this bad when Mother and Aunt Ellen died." They were right that their father had been able to recover more easily from greater losses in the past, but they did not realize that his canary's loss may have been one loss too many. While he mourned for his pet, he may also have been mourning for Mother *and* Aunt Ellen *and* his childhood friends *and* his fishing companion *and* his eyesight *and* his good digestion—*and* his teeth.

Loss comes in so many different forms. It can be a single blow: the death of a spouse or a sudden stroke. Or it may be multiple: loss of work, combined with loss of social status, combined with loss of health, combined with loss of favorite activities. Your parents' ability to adapt to loss— single, double, multiple—is perhaps the key that determines whether they experience a satisfying old age, an unhappy one, or a totally dependent one.

IT'S A HIGH-RISK PERIOD

Despite the generally positive attitudes held by those who are experiencing old age firsthand, there is no denying that the years after sixty-five contain a considerable number of negative possibilities. More of the elderly suffer from chronic illness and disability than younger groups. Physical decline is often the underlying cause of other familiar problems of aging: mental illness, decrease in intellectual functioning, slowed-up reactions, and reductions in the gratifications and satisfactions of living. Even when the elderly are in relatively good health they have greater physical vulnerability, and that vulnerability may in turn affect many other aspects of their lives. The old definition of middle age as a time when "stairs become steeper, print becomes smaller, lights become dimmer, and people are always mumbling" is no longer a laughing matter for many of the elderly but stark reality.

If the potential losses of old age were merely physical they might be easier to deal with, but in our complex modern society, physical problems are usually interwoven with emotional and social ones. Throughout history men have been searching for the fountain of youth, but never with greater frenzy than in the period following World War II:

> Crabbed age and youth
> Cannot live together:
> Youth is full of pleasance,
> Age is full of care.

If these words were true in the sixteenth century when Shakespeare wrote them, how much truer they seem to ring today in the second half of the twentieth. The emphasis on being young, looking young, acting young, feeling young has grown more intense in this period and reached its peak in the youth culture of the 1960s and the famous slogans "Never trust anyone over thirty" and "Over the hill at forty." Your parents have been told so often by the media and the fashion industry that they are out of step with the world that it's not surprising when they seem to believe it, too.

The spotlight is shifting now and is no longer directed exclusively on youth, partly because the members of the youth culture are now middle-aged themselves. But there is still enough in our culture today to persuade older people that society's needs can be met only by the young and the middle-aged. Despite the fact that Congress abolished mandatory retirement in 1986, many older people are still made to feel that their usefulness is determined by the calendar and the clock rather than by their ability to function and produce efficiently. Some, however, retire at sixty-five or seventy with grace, ease, and perhaps relief.

Some people's parents are able to adjust without much trouble to the losses they suffer. Other parents cannot do the job alone. Whether they are then helped by you or someone else, it may be useful now to review the major areas of loss that can accompany old age, sometimes singly but more often in combination. Your parents may be experiencing one or more of those losses at this very moment.

LOSS OF PHYSICAL HEALTH

THE "NORMAL" CHANGES

If some genius in the medical profession were to discover a cure for all chronic and disabling disease, he would, of course, be removing some of the greatest problems that beset the elderly and would deserve worldwide gratitude and honor. But the process of aging would still keep right on, because some physical changes are inevitable. Fortunately or unfortunately, there is no built-in chronological timetable determining when these changes will begin, how fast they will take place, and how much damage they will do. Your father may show them early and your mother much later, or vice versa. There is tremendous individual variation, and no two people are likely to follow the same schedule. Some seem to show hardly any deterioration at all.

Each organ system of the body, including the brain, is made up of millions of cells, and each system loses cells with advancing age. We can even watch this process taking place, since it is visible in the progressive wrinkling, drying, and sagging of the skin. Another visible evidence is diminishing height. Some older people actually lose stature because of the flattening of one or more vertebrae, which leads to a forward bending of the upper spine.

Each of the sense organs suffers some loss. Although only a small percentage of the elderly have visual impairment, most experience vision changes; the lens of the eye loses elasticity, making it difficult to focus clearly. We have all seen older people trying with difficulty, when they come in from the dark, to recover from the glare of a brightly lit room. Many of us can remember the eighty-year-old poet Robert Frost, at John Kennedy's inauguration, trying to shield his script from the glare of the winter sun so he could manage to read the poem he had composed especially for the occasion. An older person's eyes may take eight or nine times longer to adapt to glare than a younger person's.

The ear suffers its own nerve and bone changes, and hearing loss is noticed first by many older people, particularly in the higher frequencies. Sensitivity of the taste buds becomes duller, making it difficult to discriminate among foods. Sensory changes, handicaps in themselves, are often particularly difficult for the elderly to cope with emotionally, since these losses can so radically affect the pleasures of their daily living.

Aging can also affect the nervous system and reduce sensitivity and perceptual abilities. You may have noticed a cut on your mother's hand or a large bruise on her leg and been surprised, even irritated, that she seemed unaware of it. Frank Barrett's children reacted that way to the burn on their father's arm. Reduction in pain response—its exact site unknown but lying somewhere in the brain—may make it harder for older people to perceive pain within themselves. Other familiar signals transmitted by the nervous system that formerly alerted them to the part of their body in trouble may no longer come through loud and clear. The doctor may tell you that your mother has "walking pneumonia" or has suffered a mild heart attack that went unnoticed some time back. You can't blame her for not taking care of herself. Blame her nervous system for sending out inadequate signals.

Osteoporosis, a condition in which the bones of the elderly skeleton become thinner and more brittle, makes older people, especially women, more susceptible to fractures. Think about the number of times you hear of an elderly relative or friend breaking a wrist, a shoulder, or an ankle, or spending months in the hospital recovering from a broken hip.

The body must adapt to other reductions: the excretory function of the kidneys diminishes, the speed of the conduction of nerve impulses slows, and there is a decrease in heart output, which does not necessarily imply that the heart is diseased. Decrease in muscle tissue may produce a decrease in strength, and lung capacity may be reduced, perhaps because the muscles no longer work efficiently. Digestive functions also slow down: the flow of saliva and gastric juices, the motion of the stomach, and the contractions of the intestines—factors leading to constipation.

There is also likely to be some alteration in the overall functioning of the nervous system, which plays an important role in coordinating the interaction between muscles, glands, and blood vessels. That may also account for a decline in muscle strength, and since so many acts of daily life depend on this three-way interaction, when all three do not function smoothly together older people may find simple, everyday activities affected: walking, sitting down, dressing, and housework. When the decline in vision, hearing, and reaction time is taken into account, it is not surprising that the elderly are more fearful of accidents and more cautious than younger people.

Perhaps the most devastating reduction of all is the depletion of the back-up reserves which determine the human body's ability to fight off or recuperate quickly from disease. Your father may take a week to recover from the same virus that you and your children threw off in twenty-four hours. How much longer, therefore, and more precarious is the recuperation period from a more serious illness!

The aging process that affects us all and accelerates after the age of sixty-five would seem inevitable and irreversible. And indeed it is, for most conditions. Yet what was yesterday a normal change of aging is today a treatable or untreatable disease, and tomorrow may be a curable condition. Alzheimer's disease and osteoporosis are cases in point; each of these diseases was once thought of as an inevitable condition of aging. The cure for Alzheimer's disease has not yet been found, but we do know that women who exercise regularly and drink adequate amounts of milk during their lifetime are less prone to develop osteoporosis. Geriatric research has far to go, but discoveries that separate the disease process from the normal aging process occur increasingly.

It is obvious that people are living longer and are in better physical shape than ever before. The need for continuing research is pressing, because, as the survival rate into the later decades increases, so do many chronic mental and physical disabilities.

THERE ARE COMPENSATIONS
AND SOMETIMES IMPROVEMENTS

Losses, even severe ones, are not always unbearable. Older people are often able to compensate in many ways, and the final stage of life has its special meanings. Your parents may have found this out for themselves already and discovered how to adapt. Many older people are very successful. Look at the partially blind who turn to large-type reading matter, "talking" records, or Braille—or the hearing-impaired who learn how to rely more exclusively on eyesight, the arthritics who search out more sedentary occupations to replace their formerly active ones. There are even those with mild memory loss who learn to keep a pad and pencil handy to jot down everything that needs to be remembered.

Normal memory loss should not be confused with overall mental decline or with diseases such as Alzheimer's disease (see Appendix C, page 326). Psychologists have found that while memory may decline with age, judgment often significantly improves, and the ability to comprehend what is seen also improves with experience. When rapid response is required, older people do not react as quickly as younger ones; they do not seem able to process as much information per time unit. But this slowdown is normal, and is not a sign of mental decline.

Some brain syndromes formerly considered irreversible and included in the catchall diagnosis "senility" are not necessarily chronic or hopeless. Reversible brain syndromes showing a variety of symptoms—confusion, disorientation, stupor, delirium, or hallucination—may result from any one of a number of causes: malnutrition, anemia, congestive heart failure, drugs, or infection, among others. If diagnosed quickly enough before too much damage is done, reversible brain syndromes can be treated successfully.

Surprisingly enough, some physical problems become less serious in old age: for example, duodenal ulcers seem to decrease in severity. High blood pressure and obesity are less threatening in the old, and cancer grows less rapidly in elderly bodies. Some older people have been found better able to survive acute heart attacks even though they may suffer as many such attacks as younger people.

Modern scientists have provided a variety of inventions to compensate for the losses of old age. For example, efforts continue to improve and refine hearing aids, those tiny, almost invisible instruments that can often improve hearing. Unfortunately, hearing-impaired older adults, who number at least one out of every four people over the age of sixty-five, frequently reject the hearing aid. Some complain of too much static, some are too impatient to learn to use the instrument, and some are just too vain to wear one.

Cataract surgery followed by lens replacement has been very successful in restoring and prolonging sight. For those whose visual impairment is not amenable to medication or surgery, low-vision services can sometimes help to restore visual functioning.

Orthopedic surgery has been increasingly successful during the past twenty years with total joint replacements to offset the devastating effects of crippling arthritis. Total hip and total knee replacements are now routine procedures, while replacement of other joints—ankle, wrist, shoulder—is under continuing study and evaluation.

The number of prosthetic appliances is endless—cane, walker, wheelchair. Although certain appliances were developed for a younger age group, a device developed for a paraplegic war veteran can be adapted perfectly well to the needs of an octogenarian partially paralyzed by a stroke.

Other important aids for disabled people have been developed by architects, engineers, and other specialists: barrier-free environmental designs, ramps, kneeling buses, wide doorways, low wall telephones, and even easily visible bright colors to provide cues for the visually impaired. Many more of these aids to the handicapped of all ages are in use in the community now, thanks in part to government regulations and in part to the architectural profession's developing awareness of the needs of the disabled.

Geriatric problems have never been given a number one priority rating in these professions any more than in society at large, but more attention has been given in recent years and more must be given in the future.

MANY PHYSICAL PROBLEMS *ARE* TREATABLE

It is important to keep in mind that many physical problems afflicting aging bodies can be treated; some are even reversible. Disease and illness must be separated from the inevitable changes, although undoubtedly those changes make the elderly more vulnerable and less resilient. Medical science is making great advances, and it is gratifying to know that some conditions once considered part of the inevitable process of aging can now be safely classified as diseases and therefore potentially responsive to treatment now or in the future.

Arteriosclerosis (hardening of the arteries), for example, was until recently considered part of the aging process because doctors found it more frequently in older people. It also seemed to become progressively more severe in particular individuals as the years went by. Today, however, it is seen as a complex metabolic disturbance and, thanks to advances in the management of hypertension and diabetes as predisposing causes, is subject to treatment and alleviation.

A few words of caution are necessary, however. If the condition has been present in various organs in an unrecognized form for a long period, it may have had time to produce irreversible damage. Furthermore, diseases in the elderly are often of multiple origin, and it can be difficult to recognize and treat each one. But it is somewhat reassuring to know that chronic disease, while not curable, may be controllable.

Admittedly, the threats of disability and death from long-term illness become greater in the older age group, despite medical advances, although the same threats are always present even in younger groups. The leading causes of disability in men and women over sixty-five are coronary heart disease, stroke, arthritis, hypertensive vascular disease, lung disease, accidents, diabetes, cancer, and diseases of the eye and ear. (For a more detailed description of these and other chronic diseases of the elderly, turn to Appendix C, pages 326–35.)

The list may sound like an overwhelming catalogue of catastrophe, but we must face the fact that illness and disability cannot be completely avoided with the passage of time, especially after the sixtieth birthday. But another side of the picture may be comforting. There is good evidence to indicate that with adequate medical care, relatively stable health can be maintained for years, even allowing the irreversible changes to take their toll, and elderly people can expect to function and carry on their normal schedules, some with more and others with less success. The statistics quoted earlier in this chapter bear out this expectation and are worth repeating: *Only about 20 percent of the elderly are physically incapable of continuing their normal activities.* That relatively small percentage, however, when translated into people, becomes nearly 6 million incapacitated men and women, a number equal to the total population of the state of Connecticut or the state of Washington.

WHY SOME FUNCTION BETTER THAN OTHERS

Except in severe situations, then, the physical losses of the elderly should not be considered insurmountable problems. They become problems when they interfere with an individual's ability to function, to live a somewhat "normal" life, and to carry on familiar routines.

Plenty of younger people go through life afflicted with one ailment or another, but rarely need to stop their activities except briefly. As a matter of fact, many mature and middle-aged people seem to carry their own special physical ailments as marks of distinction. Haven't you heard them announce almost with pride, "My allergies are terrible this month," or "My back's acting up again," or "I've got one of my migraines"? It's the same with the elderly. Most of this group should be able to function at least adequately, and many do, but some do not. The irreversible processes of aging or the associated diseases may well be compensated for by one elderly person while his neighbor, similarly afflicted, may be just barely getting along. Watch the progress of two patients recovering from the same long illness. One takes his medicine, follows the doctor's orders, and seeks out rehabilitative training, while his roommate gives up and retires into semi-invalidism without making even a halfhearted try.

Arthritis may have turned your friend's father into a crippled shut-in who hesitates to leave the house. Why is it that your own father, no less arthritic, moving a little more slowly than before and possibly needing a cane, still travels in the same circles he has always enjoyed? Your mother may refer to herself as "half-blind" and consider herself seriously incapacitated, while your colleague's mother, with equally deficient vision, tells the world that she's lucky her sight is holding up so well—and believes it, too.

To the despair of their children, many elderly people are unable to make satisfactory adjustments and seem unwilling to try; they almost perversely reject other people's suggestions. Listen to the conversations at the next social gathering you attend—cocktail party, sewing club, lodge meeting—it's almost predictable that you'll hear the same old familiar refrains: "Mother's a diabetic but she won't stick to her diet," or "John's mom won't consider a cataract operation," or "Father's got a walker but he's never tried to use it," or "We bought Ginny's dad a hearing aid but he's never worn it once."

Certain losses may be more difficult to bear for individual, personal reasons. A vain woman may be able to compensate for impaired hearing, but she may be totally devastated by her wrinkled skin, which another woman might accept as a natural, although unwelcome, fact of life. Your parents' feelings, attitudes, psychological make-up, and personalities are often the factors determining whether or not physical losses are seen as overwhelming problems.

LOSS OF SOCIAL CONTACTS

Just as cell loss inevitably takes place in your parents' bodies, almost as inevitably do social losses occur in their world, particularly in the later years. Patterns of living, working, communicating, socializing, built up over all the earlier stages of their lives, often break down completely or at least are harder to maintain. The universe of the very old tends to become a smaller, more confined place, less crowded with familiar faces: friends, relatives, co-workers. As widowing takes its toll, husbands are left without wives and wives without husbands.

There are always exceptions: because of some unusual event or accomplishment of their own, or the rise to prominence of a son or daughter, men and women in their seventies or eighties may find their horizons expanding and discover new faces, new experiences, and even new geographical locations. That is not the norm, however, at least for older persons today. In general their social world is a shrinking planet. The situation may be less confining for today's better educated, health-conscious middle-aged, who will be tomorrow's old. Their social world may be a different one, with wider horizons.

Here again, as with physical loss, the variation among the elderly is tremendous—and mysterious. For some, the social losses can be devastating. For others the impact is not unbearable—they may have always been self-sufficient. Severe physical impairment and financial privation can produce the greatest social hardships, but your parents' ability to accept their social losses depends (as it did with their physical losses) on a number of factors: their own personalities developed over a lifetime, the stability of their marriage, their relationship with their children, their roots in their community, the plans made in earlier years for their retirement period, and their own attitudes toward age and even death.

CHANGES IN HUMAN RELATIONSHIPS

Physical problems are difficult enough to cope with, but the social problems that result from severe physical decline can be additional traumas. If your father has been immobilized by arthritis or paralyzed by a stroke, if he is confined to bed or just confined to the house, if he can no longer board a bus or take a walk by himself, or if he cannot go out with you in your car, then his world will become no larger than his own apartment or house. It may even be no larger than his own room, if he is bedridden. Then, in addition to the physical pain he is suffering, he will also suffer the pain of social isolation. Your mother, if she is alive and healthy, will inevitably share some of this isolation. Because of *his* incapacity, *her* life will also become more limited. A constant stream of relatives and friends can help to bring the world to the housebound. A few concerned neighbors who drop in regularly can prevent social isolation. For the less fortunate, with no relatives and friends nearby, social isolation can be relieved only by planned visits from social workers and nurses, priests, ministers, and rabbis, and occasional impromptu contacts with the mailman, the newspaper boy, neighborhood children, and dogs that may drop by.

Social isolation also occurs when older persons can no longer communicate easily with the world around them because of impaired vision or hearing. Here again, the more physically active partner suffers some of the same isolation. When familiar social patterns, formerly shared by both husband and wife, are lost for one, they are often lost for both.

But social isolation comes not only from physical causes. It can come from the death of close family members—husband, sister, brother—or friends. Even more tragic for the elderly is when death strikes younger generations: children, nieces, nephews, grandchildren. When those ties which have been so close for so long have been broken, how can they ever be replaced? Many old people do form new friendships, but some very old people live long enough to see the disappearance of their entire generation and every close relative and friend they have known. There may be no one left in the world to call them by their first names. The only human voices they ever hear may be those of the grocer, the doctor, the minister, and the disembodied voices coming from radio and TV.

CHANGES IN ENVIRONMENT

Social isolation may also result from changes in familiar patterns. Ours is a mobile society; friends and children (even loving and devoted ones) may move far away for jobs or a preferred style of living. Thousands of miles may separate parents from children, friends from friends, although relationships can still remain close even when no longer face-to-face. The telephone, the tape recorder, and the video camera can keep contacts amazingly alive. Friendly neighborhoods change, too. They become more built up, less cared for, less residential. Familiar faces disappear from the streets and are replaced by unfamiliar ones. Favorite stores where shopping was a comfortable, even a sociable process, change hands and merchandise and cause bewilderment in elderly customers. Mr. Malatsky's little delicatessen on the corner may have been replaced by a new modern supermarket, but for your elderly mother nothing will replace Mr. Malatsky. Many children try arguing, shouting, pleading, in vain attempts to dislodge elderly parents or a widowed father or mother from an apartment or a house situated in a neighborhood that is rundown and unsafe. "It was good enough for your father and me for forty years. It was good enough for you as a boy. It's good enough for me now," is a typical response, and nothing short of abduction or a crowbar will budge the speaker.

Because they risk being mugged, robbed, or beaten if they are alone on the streets, older city-dwellers often fear to go out at all. They become shut-ins or limit their outings to certain "safe" times of day. "I rush to be home every day at four-thirty P.M. My son calls me to see that I'm home," is a typical statement from an aging urban resident. Being inside, however, is not necessarily much safer than being outside. One elderly woman interviewed by a *New York Times* reporter about crime in her neighborhood described the system she had invented to burglar-proof her apartment:

> *I now have my valuables, if there's anything a little valuable which I haven't got much of anymore, hidden away in a place where nobody will look. My television I have covered up with blankets and a pillow. It looks like a daybed. Or I put it in the bathtub with a load of clothes on it. I do it every morning. It's like a baby—I put it to bed.*
>
> *When my son came in he said, "Where in the name of God did you put the television I gave you?" I said, "It's there." "Where?" "It's in the bathtub." He said, "I didn't see it." I said, "You weren't supposed to."*

To the despair of their children, elderly parents often cling to familiar walls even though an alien country lies right outside their front door.

LOSS OF FAMILIAR ROLES

The elderly cannot escape undergoing some changes in their customary roles, in all the various patterns of behavior that accompany an individual's numerous positions or statuses in life—behavior that others expect from him and he expects from himself.

In the course of a lifetime, people assume a multitude of roles. They take on the role of parent, breadwinner, homemaker, spouse, church member, athlete—even black sheep. But then, as individuals age in our society, they lose or voluntarily give up a number of their earlier roles—in extreme cases, all of them. Here again there is variation. Some roles are given up easily; others are more painful to lose. Older people no longer fulfill a parenting role unless they live with their children and grandchildren, and even then they may have to take on a less direct role and are rarely encouraged to interfere. The role of meddler is not usually acceptable. With retirement age, the breadwinning role is given up. Eking out a small pension as babysitter or watchman does not replace the prestige of the role of breadwinner.

In other times and other societies, the elderly who no longer were able to perform their former roles could turn to auxiliary ones and continue to be, as well as feel, useful and needed in their communities. Among the polar Eskimos, old couples helped in summer to store the winter's supply of bird meat; old women too feeble to travel stayed indoors doing household chores and repairing clothing. They tanned leather, chewing it to make it soft. Elderly men made seal spears and nets. There is a shortage of meaningful auxiliary roles for the elderly in our society. "Older persons are our great unutilized source of labor," writes Malcolm Cowley in *The View from 80*. "A growing weakness in American society is that it regards the old as consumers but not producers, as mouths but not hands."

The one role left for many older people is the role of householder. "My own place," whether a house or an apartment, can symbolize the last rampart, and it can become crucially important to defend it. That may be one reason why older people so often refuse to leave familiar neighborhoods and are far less likely to move than younger Americans. Even the final role of householder is removed when the elderly need to enter a home for the aged or an institution. Here they can only fill a dependent role: the role of patient or resident is rarely satisfying.

Many do make successful adjustments to their role loss. Some actually thrive on being relieved of burdensome demands and find greater contentment in the final years than in the previous ones. "I'm an old lady and glad of it!" insisted one active grandmother on her eightieth birthday. "I don't have to prove anything to anyone anymore. No more competing, no more pretending—I can just be myself now." Those who are still working at first or second careers and retain some job identification usually suffer less, and some who find it painful to lose the parent role may derive compensatory satisfaction—sometimes even greater satisfaction—

from the role of grandparent. Some older people maintain their sexual identities, their male and female roles, through a continuing active sexual life. But even taking these successful examples into account, loss of an important role can be a painful blow to the self-regard and emotional well-being of some of the elderly population.

LOSS OF FINANCIAL SECURITY

One of the most heartening developments over the recent years is the great improvement in the financial picture of older people. There has been a dramatic decline in poverty. In 1959, 33.2 percent of men and women over sixty-five fell below the poverty line. In 1986, only 12.6 percent of this group were poor. Social Security, Medicare, and some improvement in pension systems are largely responsible for this welcome change. Despite this improvement, 3.5 million men and women still live below the poverty line, and another 2.3 million rank as "near-poor" with incomes just above the poverty level, making a total of 5.8 million poor or near-poor older people.

Even though there is greater financial security for the elderly these days than in the past, this should not suggest that those over sixty-five are affluent. Many have to live on diminished resources, while the threat of medical expenses and long-term nursing home care are ever-present, haunting concerns. For those who live on fixed incomes, the fear of inflation is not an irrational anxiety.

In other times and places the elderly could expect that the struggles and labors of their earlier years would be rewarded in their later years by comfort and security. "I shall cherish your old age with plenty of venison and you shall live easy," was the customary assurance of an Iroquois son to his father. Even poor Job, afflicted for so long by trial and tribulation, could relax when he became old!

> So the lord blessed the latter end of Job more than his beginning: for he had fourteen thousand sheep, and six thousand camels, and a thousand yoke of oxen and a thousand she asses.

There are many growing old in America today who cannot expect such comfort and security ahead. Too many learn that to grow old is to grow poor.

The purpose of the Social Security Act, passed in 1935 as part of President Franklin Roosevelt's New Deal, was to guarantee basic economic security to older Americans. In the words of Supreme Court Justice Benjamin Cardozo, "The hope behind this statute is to save men and women from the rigors of the poorhouse as well as from the haunting fear that such a lot awaits them when journey's end is near."

Although Social Security has gone a long way toward relieving the economic plight of the elderly, today, more than fifty years after the act was passed, the "haunting fear of poverty", and poverty itself, are a daily reality for too many. In 1986 some 12.4 percent of those over sixty-five lived at or below the poverty threshold, defined by the government in 1988 as $5,770 annually for a single person and $7,730 for a couple. This represents a considerable decrease from a decade earlier, when one-fourth of those over sixty-five could be classified as poor. But during the same period of time the number of those in the "near-poor" category has increased, so the picture still remains bleak for too many.

Retirement is almost inevitable for most people. Overnight their incomes are severely reduced. The postretirement income for millions of retirees consists only of their monthly Social Security benefits, which in December 1987 averaged $513, the exact amount depending on how much they had paid in prior to retirement, supplemented for some by pensions which are not much higher. Alone or even in combination these amounts rarely approximate a retired person's former income. In addition, increases in Social Security payments and pension checks cannot keep up with the present inflationary spiral.

For lack of other sources of income, those over sixty-five are forced to augment inadequate incomes by using savings built up with struggle over the years, or they may turn to their children or fall back on public assistance. Many still reject this solution because of the stigma that they feel is carried with it, and they scrape along on a subhuman level. "Somebody's cat is eating well," said the cashier to the little old lady piling up cans of cat food on the check-out counter. "I'm the cat," she replied.

A retired mechanic probably once could feel somewhat secure as his nest egg piled up in his savings account, but now he watches with dread as the inflationary spiral turns a tidy sum into an insignificant pittance. In the face of today's cost of living, a few thousand dollars in the bank will not provide warmth and comfort for many winters.

For some mysterious reason government economic experts seem to think that older people have fewer needs than younger ones. The Bureau of Labor Statistics has worked out a series of sample budgets for a variety of families, and all of these budgets reflect the assumption that older people need less for clothing, home furnishings, travel, even for their pets. Whether the old need to spend as much on clothing, travel, entertainment, or furniture as the young is open to argument, but there is no argument about the fact that the old have greater medical expenses. The nation's per capita health costs for those over sixty-five in 1984 ran $4,200, showing a 13 percent annual growth rate since 1977, when the cost was

$1,745. Those over sixty-five spend on the average three times as much for prescribed medicine alone as those under sixty-five. The Medicare and Medicaid programs administered under the Social Security Act cover many health costs, but there are significant loopholes in both programs, so that extreme financial burdens often fall on the very people these programs were established to protect. Costs that are not covered by Medicare must be shouldered by the individual and his private insurance, if he is fortunate enough to have any. Out-of-pocket drug expenses for elderly individuals amounted to about $300 in 1988—a threefold increase over 1980.

Earlier in this chapter we mentioned that some people seem able to compensate better than others for the variety of losses experienced in old age. It is not always easy to explain these different reactions, but in light of diminished finances they are more understandable. An older person living on a small Social Security check and a small pension may desperately need orthopedic appliances to compensate for progressive arthritis, but he simply does not have the financial ability to purchase them. If compensatory devices are not provided under Medicare, they might as well not exist. The financial limitations of life are among the most severe obstacles blocking elderly people from compensating for the problems of aging.

Financial insecurity and money problems do not vanish above the poverty level. Fear of reduced income may realistically haunt even middle-income elderly couples and individuals who have substantial assets, a car, an unmortgaged house, and many personal possessions collected over a lifetime. When regular salaries and incomes stop coming in, healthy seventy-year-olds with thousands of dollars' worth of assets are not unrealistic when they worry, "When this is gone, what will happen to me?"

Financial curtailment, if not financial hardship, is a fact of life with most elderly people, except in the small highest-income groups. When so many of the elderly are living below the poverty line, it may seem difficult to sympathize with the comfortable elderly matron who bemoans the loss of her servants, her trips to Europe, and her country home. But they are real losses in her life, and she may have great difficulty adjusting to them. Her emotional health may be threatened, if not her physical existence or her daily bread. Furthermore, money in our society represents not only purchasing power but social power as well. It brings prestige, respect, control of others. It may also provide for immortality. Some older people are reluctant to spend their money or see it dwindle away, because they hope to leave legacies to younger family members. If they have no money to leave, they fear they will not be remembered after they die.

Financial insecurity—whether absolute, as in the poverty levels, relative, as in the more affluent levels of society, or even imagined, as among the wealthy—can produce severe emotional consequences which make it even more difficult for older men and women to achieve satisfactory adjustments.

LOSS OF INDEPENDENCE
AND POWER

The combination of some or all of the losses described in the previous sections—loss of physical health, familiar roles, social contacts, and financial security—can precipitate two other losses which have particular meaning in our society: the losses of independence and power, qualities which are highly regarded personal assets today, particularly for men. The loss of either or both can be a stunning blow to an older person's self-esteem.

Increased dependency is forced willy-nilly on the severely disabled elderly. They must accept help, which can pose severe problems for the disabled and for close family members who must care for them. Severe problems are also created for the larger society, which is expected to provide medical, nursing, and protective care. Increased dependency can affect all the invalid's social relationships. The disabled ones may overreact to their needs and become too dependent and too demanding. They may try to deny their dependence or mask its magnitude by "showing who's boss" and ruling their relatives, wives, and children, curtailing everyone else's freedom and independence. We've all heard these relatives commenting helplessly from time to time, "We try to do everything Mother wants, but it never seems to be enough!"

Conversely, the disabled ones may try vehemently to deny their dependency by insisting, in the face of all handicaps, "I can manage perfectly well," and refusing the willing offers of help essential to maintaining health. Independence can be admirable, but when carried too far can lead to trouble. The loss of financial security, especially if it is severe, also contributes to the loss of independence. Many older people are just about able to scrape along on Social Security benefits even when these are supplemented by meager pensions. They must live from check to check, each month's activities determined by carefully allocated dollars and cents rather than by personal preferences and inclinations.

You may be financially able, willing, and eager to provide additional funds for your parents. You may insist on doing so. But when forced to accept money from their children, many older people feel that they are surrendering in return much of their independence, so the extra income may prove to be at best only a mixed blessing. Your monthly check may be a sweet and loving gesture on your part, but it may be received as somewhat bitter medicine by your parents, who had grown accustomed through their lives to earning their own money, paying their own way, feeding and educating their families—and taking care of *you.*

If the day finally comes when an older person finds it impossible to manage on his own, financially or physically, and must accept institutional living, the greatest sacrifice he may have to make is the final portion of his independence. Institutionalization, by its very nature, seems to symbolize that ultimate loss and probably explains why so many older people prefer inadequate, isolated living conditions to the protective care of even the best institutions.

A sense of control over one's life—autonomy—is considered such an essential positive value that many forward-looking professionals are currently searching for ways to maintain this feeling among their residents within the institutional framework.

Groups of older persons are increasingly powerful in our society because of their reawakened awareness of their own numbers and power at the polls. Their voices are being heard through groups like the Gray Panthers and the American Association of Retired Persons(AARP). Far less powerful are the ill and impaired old, including those in nursing homes. For these elderly persons, the loss of independence and power is striking.

LOSS OF MENTAL STABILITY
AND FUNCTIONAL ABILITY

You may have noticed that the discussion of each of the areas of loss examined in the preceding pages ends with the mention of the psychological ramifications: the effects on the emotional well-being, the ego, the self-esteem of the elderly. Psychological problems resulting from losses, as well as those triggered by other threats, real or imaginary, are often the most difficult to handle. In dealing with your own parents you may have already discovered that their psychological problems place the heaviest demands on your own emotional resources. Physical incapacity can present enough problems; these become even more difficult to deal with when they are accompanied by increased dependency, financial hardship, and social isolation. The physical picture grows more complex when psychological problems are added. Those problems can be very perplexing for the children of the elderly, especially when the emotions of both generations become intertwined. It is not unusual for a family to report that an elderly relative has undergone a real personality change: "He's not the same person he used to be," or "I just don't know my mother anymore." Surprisingly enough, some personality changes are for the better, although many, admittedly, are for the worse.

As your parents begin to age, psychological difficulties may appear for the first time, developing in direct response to their physical and social losses. But those psychological difficulties may also be continuations of lifelong emotional problems which, successfully held in check at earlier times, become intensified in old age, and therefore more difficult to control.

WHAT ARE THE PSYCHOLOGICAL PROBLEMS?

They include a familiar list—depression, anxiety, hypochondriasis, psychosomatic disorders, alcoholism, unwarranted suspiciousness, and sometimes severe neurotic and psychotic reactions. There's nothing really new or special in this list. These are the psychological problems of all ages—the young as well as the old—but statistics reveal that some appear with greater frequency in the population sixty-five and over. This greater frequency occurs in part because of the higher incidence of depression among the elderly, and also because of the organic brain disorders of the elderly which produce their own special symptoms, including disorientation, loss of memory, confusion, and wandering.

There is no doubt that psychological problems are closely related to the physiological losses of aging. But physiological damage to the brain or sense organs is only one cause. All the areas of loss, as well as other stressful changes confronting the older person which have been discussed earlier, can individually or in combination trigger psychological problems.

It is always important to remember that all older people do not necessarily react in the same way to the same loss. What is stressful to one may not be stressful to another. Some also have a far greater capacity to withstand stress, although the elderly in general are less equipped physiologically to handle stress than younger people. Old people do not come naked into old age—they bring with them the accumulated experiences of a lifetime. It is generally believed that if people have developed the capacity to deal successfully with change and difficulty at earlier stages of life, they will more easily face the insults and injuries of old age. Rich experiences and resourceful capacities accumulated throughout life can be priceless treasures to draw on in later years. Studies in which old people have been followed from earlier ages to later ones have shown this continuity. The same loss which is devastating to some becomes for others a new challenge to face and overcome.

Certain patterned psychological responses to loss are commonly seen in older persons and, while upsetting to relatives and difficult to deal with, must be accepted as within the normal range. Other types of behavior are so extreme that they must be considered pathological.

"NORMAL" REACTIONS TO LOSS

It is completely normal to react to loss emotionally. The emotions your parents feel in their old age are no different from childhood emotions, young-adult emotions, and middle-aged emotions. The infant faces loss when giving up the close, dependent relationship with its mother; the adolescent when breaking away from parental authority; the middle-aged adult when facing the loss of youth. The elderly react with the very same emotions to the physiological and social losses accompanying old age as well as to the indignities and neglect imposed by society. The latter are particularly hard for some older men who find the experience of helplessness especially painful. Since losses appear with greater variety and frequency in old age than in any other stage of life, anxiety and depression, fear, anger, and guilt can be anticipated. They are normal, even appropriate, emotions. You would certainly be surprised if an older person who had suffered a severe loss did *not* seem to be sad or angry—if he did *not* grieve. More damage can be caused when the mourning process is circumvented. "We shouldn't leave Mother alone today—she'll only sit and think about Dad," may be an understandable, well-meant, loving reaction from concerned children shortly after a father's funeral. Yet perhaps that's just the very thing Mother *needs* to do for a while before she's ready to do anything else. Oversolicitous relatives can sometimes cause as much harm as neglectful ones. Mourning plays an essential part in making a healthy adjustment to the loss of a beloved person. It helps those who mourn to work through their grief and redirect their energies to new interests in life.

Anxiety and fear play equally useful roles. There's nothing abnormal about an older person's fears for his future—he's got every right to be afraid, within reason. If a person's eyesight is failing, it is perfectly realistic for him to wonder how he will manage for himself and to feel a diffuse sense of foreboding. It's also realistic for someone who has already had one heart attack to be concerned about his health or even to fear approaching death.

Anger is also to be expected as a normal emotional reaction to loss. When you've suffered an injury or an insult, what's wrong with being angry? After all, anger is an emotion of retribution, a way of striking back at whatever has caused an injury. Just as a young child gets angry at the hammer with which he has smashed his own finger, an older person may get angry at the gods or fate or whatever he believes may have caused a particular loss. Your father may even direct his anger at you, for lack of a better target, and feel guilty as a result. There's no need to be alarmed when your parents exhibit fear, anxiety, grief, or anger. They are not pleasant emotions—no one claims they are—but they may be necessary, even therapeutic, at certain periods. Your parents should not have to feel guilty if they show those emotions, nor should you feel guilty yourself. There is room for those feelings in the total context of life.

Older people, like younger ones, develop special behavior patterns which help them to ward off anxiety, depression, or a fear of uncontrollable rage. These behavior patterns are important to their own sense of survival. They may be within a "normal range," although you may, on occasion, find them bewildering, frustrating, even infuriating. It is important to note that these patterns of behavior are used by all ages, although the old may rely on some of them more than the young.

One of the most potentially effective behavior patterns employed by the elderly, yet misunderstood by their families, is *living in the past*. As death approaches, many older people spend much time reminiscing— going through a life-review. Remembrance of things past can be a painful process, but it can also be comforting. It can provide meaningful significance to the final years and help to reduce fear and anxiety. Living in the past is often mistakenly seen as a symptom of brain damage: "What's the matter with Father? He can remember the name of his first-grade teacher, but he can't remember his neighbor's name or whether he's had lunch or not!" At best the tendency to live in the past is viewed as unnecessary nostalgia—an unfortunate disengagement from the present—or as self-preoccupation. You may despair that your parents always seize every opportunity to discuss their past life with you or with anyone else who will listen, but it may be an indication of health rather than a sign of deterioration. If this does not seem to be merely meaningless repetition but rather something that gives them pleasure, peps them up, or possibly even rejuvenates them, it should be encouraged, not stifled.

Some older people, while not seriously depressed, do not bounce back from a period of mourning and are never again ready to contemplate new directions. Mourning can become a lifestyle, best described as *preparatory mourning*. It can be seen as a protective pattern of behavior and is often reflected in a morbid interest in death, fascination with obituaries, and a preoccupation with funerals—even those of strangers. All of us know people who, even in the prime of life, turn first to the death notices of the daily paper. Some older people find this their favorite section.

One testy seventy-year-old used to horrify his grandchildren at the breakfast table by chuckling cheerfully as he scanned the obituary page of the newspaper every morning: "Well, I see another old friend of mine has made headlines today!" Preparatory mourning can be seen in the widow who refused to discard her black clothes years after her husband's death. She still mourns for the past, but also for her future losses. Preparatory mourning is exhibited in the gloomy interpretation of all events, even happy ones, including the activities of younger family members: "She's a lovely child. I do hope she doesn't inherit her grandmother's weak heart!" or "What a beautiful day—there are sure to be lots of accidents on the highway!"

"Old Mr. Jones is really showing his age these days, isn't he?" commented Mr. Smith to his daughter. Mr. Smith himself is eighty years old, bent with arthritis, walking with a cane, and increasingly hard of hearing. Yet he is only able to notice the signs of aging in others, not in himself. His own old age and impending death are not conscious realities to him. He uses *denial*—a common defense—to ward off facing his own advancing years and the painful feelings accompanying this advance. Denial, used in moderation, is a necessary and useful mechanism for maintaining a sense of stability and equilibrium. If it is carried too far, however, it can become hazardous. The elderly may deny pain and physical symptoms until they are beyond help; they may deny dependency, deafness, blindness, and confusion, thereby jeopardizing their safety. Denial need not be limited to physical symptoms or sensory losses and may be used in relation to other losses as well. A seventy-five-year-old widow seemed to take the drastic reduction in her finances after her husband's death with remarkable good will—or so her children thought, until they discovered that she had simply denied her financial problems and continued to spend her dwindling capital and to use her charge accounts as if there had been no change. Denial is not uncommon, nor is it dangerous in itself. Only if it interferes with reality and prevents sound decisions can it legitimately be considered a serious problem.

You may sense that your father is becoming increasingly suspicious as he grows older. That is quite possible. *Mistrustful behavior* is sometimes used by the elderly. Some forms of this behavior stem from an unconscious process and arise when the elderly project their own uneasy feelings elsewhere—away from themselves. Having unconsciously attributed these uneasy feelings to other people, they then may be consciously fearful of these people. Mistrustfulness which has no visible roots can be bewildering and upsetting to families and may, if carried to extremes, be considered a mental illness.

Some mistrustful behavior can be more easily understood and clearly grounded in reality. It may be realistic and self-protective. A frail old man can be at the mercy of other people who are stronger. He may become a prime target for abuse and exploitation. Caution and suspicion may be the only weapons he has with which to protect himself. Sometimes the elderly are not mistrustful enough!

Other forms of mistrustful behavior, although unwarranted, are rooted somewhere in reality and stem from the anxiety aging men and women feel as independence slips away from them. Once able to care for themselves independently, but now increasingly dependent on someone else, they begin to wonder if that "someone" is really doing right by them. They feel they must watch out for their own interests or "someone" will take advantage of them: cheat them, rob them, hurt them. You may find it quite painful when that suspected "someone" turns out to be you. The concerned child who is trying hardest to help may accidentally become the target for mistrust and the focus for the anger which can accompany it.

Stubbornness and *avoidance of change* are two particularly successful and related adaptive patterns of behavior used by the elderly. Both are likely to be extremely frustrating to children, close friends, and other relatives. "I can't budge him!" is a familiar cry from a long-suffering son or daughter trying in vain to help an aging father. "He won't listen," "won't move," "won't see a doctor," "won't watch his diet." Stubbornness is also used as a magical solution to fight the forces which disrupt life, and it's remarkable how strongly a frail one-hundred-pound old woman is able to resist the combined weight of hundreds of pounds of concerned relatives. So many changes and losses are forced on the elderly as the years go by that they may often try to control their lives in such a way that they can avoid change whenever possible. To that end a whole way of life may be developed. When your parents insist on remaining in a familiar house, apartment, or neighborhood, even though they agree with you that the neighborhood is changed, the house is too big for them, and the apartment is too isolated, they are obviously avoiding change, although you may see this as stubbornness.

A pattern of avoidance can also operate more subtly. It can explain fear of travel—fear of even leaving the house—or refusal to consider new activities, meet new people, or try new doctors or new medicines, even though they know the old ones are not doing them much good. Avoidance of change and stubbornness can often be used by the elderly as a kind of protective armor that wards off the changes well-meaning children or relatives would like to impose.

Mr. Thompson always thought of taxis as extravagant, and he had lived frugally all his life. But it was unsafe for him to walk home alone at night. His children begged him to take taxis, but he refused to pay for that extravagance or let his children indulge in it. He could not allow himself to change the frugal habits of a lifetime. He found it easier to risk the danger.

• •

Mrs. Gross became a quasi shut-in. She went out only for occasional emergencies. Her children made superhuman efforts to dislodge her, urging her to "come to dinner," or "come to the movies," or "come for a drive." "It's for your own good," they insisted. But she turned down all invitations. She was, however, very sociable, always delighted to have visitors and to serve light meals very hospitably. Mrs. Gross did not ask her children for help and was contented with her life.

Admittedly there are cases where parents do act out of spite, refusing to change a lifestyle that disturbs their children *just because* it does disturb them. They may find this a successful way to produce guilt among those closest to them. By clinging to a disturbing pattern they seem to say, "See how miserable my life is!"

Closely connected with avoidance of change is a passionate, although often inappropriate, *worship of independence.* Many older people see independence as another weapon with which to protect themselves from outside interference. To the horror of family, friends, and social agencies, aging men and women may reject safe and protective surroundings and endure drab furnished rooms, inadequate nourishment, and irregular health care in order to preserve that treasured state. It is painful to accept the fact that when independence is weighed against protected living in a child's home, independence often wins. But painful as that is, relatives should understand that when such a value is given to independence, its loss could trigger a devastating emotional reaction.

Overdoing it is a very common defense among the elderly against depression, anxiety, and other painful conditions. "When in trouble, keep busy" is the rule they appear to be following.

> John Parker, after his retirement, had adapted to a fairly leisurely and involved way of life. That included a little volunteer work, puttering around the house, visiting his cronies. But most of his time was spent with his wife in a variety of shared pursuits, particularly traveling. After she died from a cerebral hemorrhage, John Parker threw himself into his volunteer activities, running for office as the head of the local senior citizens' club, spending many hours on his activities, and seeming to relish it. Keeping busy was good medicine in John's case—it warded off painful depression and gave him the leeway he needed to work slowly through his grief over the death of his wife. But his children were undoubtedly concerned that by "overdoing it" he was jeopardizing his health.

You may feel that your mother has become a slave to routine, that she wants everything to be "just so," that every move—coming in, going out, dressing, eating, going to bed—seems to involve a whole series of regular steps. She's probably involved in *ritualistic behavior.* Some people behave as if repetitious ritual has the magic power to ward off evil and the threat of future loss. That kind of behavior also helps the handicapped to compensate for sensory and memory losses and thereby bolster their command of their environment. So even though you tap your foot impatiently as your mother spends ten minutes putting out these lights and putting on those, and checking the windows, the gas on the stove, the jewel box, and the refrigerator before she is able to put on her sweater and go out for a walk, remind yourself that she's not necessarily losing her grip but rather reinforcing her sense of security.

EXTREME REACTIONS

Behavior patterns and feelings, "normal" when kept within limits, become serious when they go out of bounds and interfere with your parents' overall ability to function. Someone who is still mourning after more than a year, and showing no signs of recovery, may be suffering from a depressive reaction. Someone who is continuously anxious about his health, even though a competent doctor has pronounced him in fine shape, may have a psychiatric problem. Someone who gets angry for an inordinate amount of time and, even worse, directs his anger broadside at anyone in his path—engaging in verbal, even physical, violence—is certainly showing an emotional problem. Grief, anger, anxiety—all normal emotions—can lead to severe difficulties which may require psychiatric attention when they are unremitting and intense. Other severe problems, such as Alzheimer's disease, may develop independently of these intense reactions to loss and stress. To a significant degree, however, these reactions play an important role in the mental disturbances of older persons. Here are several of the more common ones.

DEPRESSION

As a mental disorder depression is quite different from the temporary moods almost everyone experiences from time to time, moods which we describe by saying, "I feel so depressed today." The symptoms of a real depression go beyond "blue" feelings and are not always obvious. Prolonged periods of insomnia, fatigue, lack of appetite, agitation, or various psychosomatic ailments may all be indications of depression, although the correct diagnosis is often overlooked.

So-called depressive reactions in later life often can be related to earlier experiences. A person who lost a great deal as a child, or has never worked through the conflicts of childhood satisfactorily, may suffer periods of depression repeatedly throughout the life-cycle. Depression, mild or severe, may return when there is a reminder of early childhood trauma—the loss or rejection of a parent, illness, deprivation. The onslaughts of aging can be such grim reminders of earlier losses that they can trigger acute depressive states. Depression can also be an extension of unresolved mourning. Extreme depression is one of the causes of the high rate of suicide among the elderly, particularly among elderly men.

Severe chronic depression is also thought to be related to physiological causes, which may be amenable to medication. Not infrequently it is mistaken for dementia, since the presenting symptoms of depression can include difficulty in cognitive functioning.

Depression can mask other conflicts: severe guilt, shame, or unacceptable anger. If a person cannot accept these feelings he may turn them inward, bringing on an apparent state of depression. Loss normally produces some depression and anger, but if a person in any way feels responsible for the loss he has suffered, he may suffer as well the painful feelings of guilt and shame. That is especially true when death comes to someone who has been very dependent, very troublesome, or very unloving. The partner who survives may feel all the more guilty. (The same kind of depression may afflict grown children when a difficult, troublesome parent dies.)

HYPOCHONDRIASIS

A neurotic reaction, hypochondriasis is an excessive concern with health accompanied by unfounded physical complaints. In mild forms hypochondriasis can be acceptable, even useful. Older people should be encouraged to take care of their health. However, when carried to an extreme and turned into an all-consuming activity, this type of behavior can be a major problem. Hypochondriasis has a number of meanings. Some professionals say that older people tend to withdraw their interest from the world around them and, in preparing for death, turn their interest inward—to their bodies. Others say, conversely, that the world of the elderly becomes so limited that, lacking other interests, they focus on themselves. Hypochondriasis, as a form of behavior, can be an excellent attention-getting device for someone who feels neglected or left out, as the elderly often do, or it may be part of an individual's life history. Hypochondriacs are found in every age group, and young hypochondriacs are likely to grow into old hypochondriacs. This behavior is sometimes used to identify with a lost loved one, or as a means of self-punishment. Whatever the cause, intense bodily preoccupation can prevent otherwise normal, healthy older people from living satisfying lives. In addition, it can rub off and interfere with the normal living of everyone close to them.

PSYCHOTIC REACTIONS

When people lose contact with the world around them, psychotic reactions may occur. They may see, hear, or think things which have no basis in reality. Overanxious, depressed, and angry feelings can precipitate psychotic reactions, which can also result from severe impairment to the sense organs and the brain. Loss of hearing can affect mental stability;

the deaf often turn to their own inner world for sensory clues. Unable to hear what is going on around them, they invent explanations. Furthermore, brain impairment can interfere with an older person's ability to process information from the real world, thereby setting off or compounding a psychotic reaction. Paranoid states are a type of psychotic disorder involving delusional thinking and false beliefs of persecution and victimization.

DEMENTIA

Last but not least in the mental disorders suffered by older adults are the dementias, the best-known and most prevalent of which is Alzheimer's disease. Best estimates suggest that as many as 15 percent of the over-sixty-five population are afflicted by dementia, a devastating condition in which there is marked deterioration of intellectual performance. As with other age-related disorders, dementia occurs with far greater frequency among the very old; 20 percent of the over-eighty population are afflicted by this disorder. In all, over 4 million Americans suffer from dementia. Health economists estimated in 1985 that there was an $88 billion loss due to Alzheimer's disease and related dementias.

The specific problems experienced by persons with dementia always include gradual loss of memory and usually of problem-solving ability and other aspects of abstract thinking. Other related symptoms include disorientation in time and space, personality changes, difficulty in communicating, word-finding, and learning, decreased attention span, and impaired judgment.

In the early stages of dementia, symptoms may resemble those of other psychological conditions discussed previously. As the disease progresses, however, the changes become more marked and the older person may begin to need twenty-four-hour-a-day care. In addition to the severe impact of advanced dementia on intellectual functioning, personality changes can be particularly difficult for family and other caregivers. Depression, paranoia, and agitation are common symptoms.

Alzheimer's disease is the major cause of dementia, accounting alone for over 50 to 60 percent of the cases examined on autopsy, and in combination with other conditions, another 20 percent. Strokes and a number of other conditions account for the remaining cases. (See Appendix C, pages 326–35, for descriptions of symptoms and pathological changes.)

There is no known cure or treatment for the symptoms of Alzheimer's disease, although research has increased dramatically in the past decade and much more is known about the pathological changes that occur in the brain. This is bad news for the large majority of older persons whose dementia is caused by Alzheimer's disease. As we have stressed, however, the symptoms of dementia may also be due to other conditions, some of which are treatable. Included here are depressive reactions, malnutrition, drug toxicity, and anemia.

Therefore, when the symptoms of dementia present themselves, the need for a thorough medical examination is imperative. The diagnosis of an irreversible condition such as Alzheimer's disease can be made only by a process of elimination—by ruling out other causes of dementia—and can be confirmed only by brain biopsy or autopsy.

The good news for families of persons with Alzheimer's disease, or AD, is the dramatic growth in the past decade of public awareness of the condition, its devastating effects on the family, and the extraordinary demands it places on the long-term care system. Contributing to this public awareness and growing concern has been the advocacy of the Alzheimer's Disease and Related Disorders Association, a national organization composed mainly of the families of persons with AD. This association and its 177 chapters in forty-six states are providing essential information and counseling for families as well as support groups. The motto of the association is "Someone to stand by you."

There is little question that one of the greatest losses that can be experienced by elderly persons is in their ability to function intellectually and to keep in touch with the world around them. Just as devastating for some older persons is loss of sight, hearing, home, money, or independence.

For family members, the losses brought about by Alzheimer's disease are probably the most devastating and most feared, since the total dependency of the persons in advanced stages of the disease and the changes in their personality place great physical and emotional burdens on the family.

INDIRECT PSYCHOLOGICAL PROBLEMS

Psychological reactions among the elderly are not always expressed in extreme emotional states or difficult behavior. Like the brain and nervous system, other organ systems depleted by cellular loss and tissue change can show physiological breakdown as a result of psychological stress. Anxiety in particular has been shown to be related to cardiovascular difficulties. All the various systems of the body—the neurological, the cardiovascular, the gastrointestinal—depleted by age, may no longer have the backup reserves to withstand headlong attacks from the emotions.

No one can deny that there is a broad array of losses which may be incurred in old age—losses which often multiply and interact. It is essential to be aware of them. Equally essential to keep in mind, though, is that 80 percent of the over-eighty population do *not* suffer from dementia; the majority function fairly independently and could function better if aware of *what can be done*. The family is an important resource in seeing that *something is done*. Old age is full of endless possibilities—long-suffering acceptance, dreary monotony, grim misery, high tragedy—as well as deep satisfaction, unexpected gratification, serenity, and even fun.

5

MARRIAGE, WIDOWHOOD, REMARRIAGE, AND SEX

> *Like my father, I've learned that the love we have in our youth is superficial compared to the love that an old man has for his old wife. "My old gray-haired wife," my father used to call my mother. And I can still remember her saying as she passed the food around the table on their 50th anniversary, "I thank God for giving me this old man to take care of."*
>
> Interview with philosopher Will Durant,
> *New York Times*, November 6, 1975

Will Durant was celebrating his ninetieth birthday on the day of this interview. He himself had been married to his wife, Ariel, for more than sixty-two years. The public responds with delight to such stories of marital longevity and contentment. Pictures in magazines and newspapers of a white-haired couple cutting the cake on their golden anniversary are sure to arouse pleasant emotions. No words are necessary—those pictures evoke images of love, tenderness, fidelity, companionship, and mutual support. In some cases these images are true. In others they are not.

For better or for worse, old age affects not only each husband and wife individually but also their life together—their partnership.

The institution of marriage has been examined, probed, and analyzed by scholars, professionals, and the clergy. Much attention has been focused on marital problems in the early and middle years, but little of that scrutiny has been turned on marriage in the later years. Part of this neglect in the past may have been because of the lower life expectancy.

Few marriages continued intact with both partners alive in their seventies and eighties.

But there are many of these durable marriages today. There will be even more in the future. In 1955 there were 6.9 million men and women over sixty-five still living with their spouses; in 1970 the number increased to 9.4 million, and in 1986 to 14 million. (The figures include remarriages as well as the original ones.) The growth of the population in general, as well as current extended life-expectancy, accounts for the dramatic rise in recent years.

MARITAL ADJUSTMENT
IN THE RETIREMENT YEARS

After thirty or forty years of life together, it would seem that two people would have come to know each other as intimately as possible and, assuming that the marriage has been a relatively stable one, there would be few surprises left. But there may be plenty of surprises in the postretirement period, the greatest one probably being that they do not know each other quite so well after all.

In the middle years—particularly if there are children in the family, but even when there are not—husbands and wives usually function independently of each other much of the time, even in the closest of relationships. When they both work, each one goes off every day to a separate place. Even if they share all household tasks equally, they are physically in each other's presence only in the evenings, on weekends, and on holidays. When the husband is the sole breadwinner and his wife cares for home and children, there are also many hours of separation. The two may thoroughly enjoy the time they do spend together, yearn for more, steal occasional weekends away, and resent the stresses of life which prevent them from being together more often. But the fact remains that their hours together are limited.

In the postretirement years, their hours together are limitless. Unless they have prepared themselves in advance with activities and routines to share together or ones which will take them in different directions for some time at least, they may face each other twenty-four hours a day, seven days a week, Saturdays, Sundays, and holidays. Like children on rainy afternoons they may say, "There's no place to go. There's nothing to do."

When both husband and wife have had careers, each one at some point past sixty may have to develop a new, different (sometimes even more rewarding) lifestyle for the retirement years. But the housewife and mother whose children are launched by the time she is in her early fifties or younger usually faces her midlife crisis—sometimes known as the empty-nest syndrome—much earlier. She may face her menopause at the same time. Her husband, still in his mid-fifties and probably still in mid-career, may remind her, with understanding and compassion (or possibly with irritation and exasperation), that she has always wanted to "eat dinner at a civilized time," or "go back to school," or sell real estate, volunteer at the hospital, spend time at a club, go into politics. He may even wonder how she can be depressed when she finally has the time to do all the things she always complained she had no time for. She may go ahead and do any one of these things, or instead devote herself to domestic routines, gardening, close involvement with children or grandchildren. During the next ten or fifteen years, while her husband is still actively involved in his own work, she may establish a very satisfactory way of life for herself. But suddenly one day, after the gold watch has been presented and the farewell dinner for her husband is over, she may find she suddenly has a constant companion sharing or possibly interfering with that new way of life.

She may watch her husband go through some of the same confusion and uncertainty she herself had known years before and may say to him as he had said to her long ago (also with understanding or exasperation), "You always wanted to go fishing," or do more carpentry; take up golf, painting, sculpture; learn a foreign language; work in a settlement house. Many men—sometimes joined by their wives—do develop new interests by enrolling in adult education classes or university courses. But often the same activities which, in their working days, seemed to promise relaxation and satisfaction now lose their appeal for the retirees and appear more as idle puttering and meaningless time-filling.

Sweden, which prides itself on its elaborate network of social and economic care that covers its entire population from birth to death, provides its elderly population with great financial security. Yet the government, recognizing the psychological hazards of retirement, is trying to set up a system in which workers can move into retirement slowly, tapering off their working hours between the ages of sixty and seventy so that when they stop working completely, they will have made their adjustment to a new lifestyle.

The United States has no such tapering-off period, but many men and women prepare themselves by thinking through alternative patterns for the future and developing compromises that will satisfy both partners in a marriage. Such advance preparation is usually the best insurance against the apathy, depression, anger, and interpersonal conflict that lie in wait for many couples.

Despite the fact that the mandatory retirement age has been abolished, there is no indication that everyone stays on the job to the bitter end.

Even when sixty-five was the great dividing line, there was a growing trend toward early retirement. That trend continues, and has shown no sign of slowing down. Perhaps more realistic and thoughtful planning is involved when retirement is a matter of personal choice rather than mandatory policy.

Retirement can hardly be considered a complete shock. Except for the self-employed, retirement is a fact of life. Every worker knows it lies ahead, yet many react to the inevitable with anger and surprise. Your parents may not have planned ahead—or perhaps their plans do not work out as expected. Your father may seem to go downhill after his retirement.

The breadwinner (usually the husband) often feels that by losing his job he also loses his valued role and therefore his prestige, purpose, and self-respect. He may feel aimless, rejected, cast aside, excluded, forgotten, and often reacts with depression, anger, resentment. If he directs those emotions toward the person who is closest to him—his wife—a great strain will be placed on their marriage. You may notice that your parents disagree and bicker as never before. Some newly retired men age dramatically in the first years of inactivity or go through a period of depression—fertile ground, according to some experts, for premature disease and deterioration.

Personalities may clash as they have not done since the early days of marriage. Tastes and interests may be in constant opposition. Your father may want to make the most of his new freedom: to adventure, see the world, rent a camper and gypsy for six months, or sell the house and move away. Your mother may be thoroughly content in the new life she has built for herself and reluctant to leave it, or her children or grandchildren.

Conversely, your mother may be the one with the wanderlust. She may have been waiting all these years for a chance to "live a little." She may be constantly frustrated by your father's preference for a quiet life and resent his inclination to putter around the house, watch TV, lick the wounds caused by his retirement. She may appeal to you in desperation to "help him snap out of it."

After all those years of knowing how to spend weekends and holidays together, a retired couple may seem virtual strangers to each other on weekdays. "Is that what you eat for lunch?" a husband asks his wife as she spoons out cottage cheese. Married for nearly forty years, he may not have the slightest idea of what goes on in his house for eight hours every weekday. "I never knew your father was such a busybody," your mother may sigh to you. "He's into everything I do. He's forever asking me what I'm doing, why I'm doing it, and then telling me how to do it better. I don't have a minute's privacy. Who does he think has been taking care of this house all these years, I'd like to know?" She may complain on a regular basis that he intrudes on her kaffeeklatsches with her friends, insists on buying the groceries, and monitors all her conversations. "The next time he says to me, 'What in God's name do you and Flora have to yak about every day?' I'm going to throw the phone at him."

You may find yourself drawn into their disagreements and be tempted to take sides, either with the parent you are most closely attached to or with the one who seems to be most ill-used. If your father is withdrawn and apathetic, you may criticize him for giving your mother so little pleasure: "He's burying her alive! He doesn't want to do anything himself and he won't let her do anything either." Or you may take his side against her: "Why can't she let him alone? He's worked hard all his life. Doesn't he deserve a little peace now?"

Instead of taking sides with either, you may be critical of both of them and quick to tell them all the mistakes they are making and what they ought to do instead. You may even come up with a variety of wonderful ideas which appeal to you tremendously but might not give them the slightest satisfaction. If, instead of pushing your own solutions, you are able to show some concern, patience, interest, and understanding, they will probably in time work out their *own* solutions—in their *own* way.

Some couples, confused and disturbed by their unaccustomed incompatibility, turn not to their children but to friends, ministers, doctors, and other professionals. "Imagine me—at sixty-seven—going to a marriage counselor!" a retired salesman said sheepishly, at the same time admitting that he and his wife really needed someone to help them smooth out the fraying edges of their forty-four-year marriage. Not infrequently, couples, finding life in the later stages as difficult as in the earlier stages, are turning to professional help. Marriage counselors report what many couples find out for themselves in time: that if a marriage has strong bonds and a firm foundation, it is likely to weather the postretirement crisis and come out intact. Any marriage which has lasted more than forty years has undoubtedly weathered its share of crises in the past.

IN SICKNESS AND IN HEALTH—FOR RICHER, FOR POORER

In addition to adjusting to the changes in daily life produced by retirement itself, many older couples may also have to adjust at some point to each other's failing health and the dwindling of their joint financial assets. The famous words of the wedding ceremony are really put to the test when husbands and wives live on together into their seventies, eighties, and nineties. Poverty and ill-health may come separately or in combination, since the more frequent or chronic the physical disability, the more money must be spent on medical expenses.

Reasonable, well-thought-out plans for retirement can be disrupted overnight by the sudden illness of one partner or by the gradual decline of both. Your mother and father may have developed an enjoyable pattern of living, pursuing some activities independently and sharing others, but what if your father has a stroke or a heart attack, or crippling arthritis? He may need constant care. The new life the two have made together may come to an end, yet another pattern has to be developed. Your mother may be ready and able to care for your father, but at the same time, whether she admits it or not, she may resent being so tied down. The strain may affect their relationship with each other.

Illness can also reverse longstanding behavior patterns. A wife who has always been dependent and submissive may find herself forced to take control when her invalid husband can no longer run the show. If a domineering wife is incapacitated, she may, for the first time in her married life, have to turn to her henpecked husband, expecting him to manage everything *and* take care of her. Frequently those formerly submissive spouses rather enjoy their newfound power and flourish, despite the burdens they have to assume. They may even turn the tables completely, becoming dictatorial and autocratic, to the amazement of their children, their friends, and their relatives.

Dwindling financial resources, inadequate pensions, Social Security checks which cannot keep up with the nation's rising inflation rate, or heavy medical expenses: all can strain marital relationships, particularly in marriages where money—or the lack of it—has always been a source of conflict. An elderly couple may have to give up their home because of increased rents, higher taxes, or rising maintenance costs, and cramped quarters may contribute to irritation. If they are able to hang on where they have always lived, there may be no money at all for entertainment, relief from monotony, or occasional escapes from each other. Medical expenses may erode their food budget; their health, emotional as well as physical, may deteriorate from inadequate nutrition.

Couples who were always in greatest conflict when life was easier may be drawn closer together by the harsh problems of ill-health or poverty. Their days are devoted to fighting off the enemy at their gates, concentrating their energies, husbanding their resources, and caring for each other with greater determination than ever.

THE FINAL YEARS

As they get older and physically less active, some couples become even more closely involved with each other, zealously watching over each other's health, protecting each other from excitement, sparing each other exertion. At the pace they establish for themselves they may read, walk, market, do the housework, watch TV, listen to music, garden, take their medicine—always together. Relatives and friends may report with admiration, sometimes mixed with irritation, "They don't really need anyone else. They're only interested in each other," or "They think alike, they talk alike, they even look alike."

If the elderly wife in such couples ages more rapidly or is more seriously incapacitated than her husband, he may try to assume full responsibility for her care. The wife may respond in the same way to her invalid husband. A parent-child relationship can develop; if it has always been present in the marriage, it may become more intense.

These relationships can become so totally interdependent that in time they can tolerate no separation at all. Not infrequently, the death of one spouse is followed within a short time by the death of the other, who may have seemed in comparatively good health. One doctor reports that he was obliged to place a ninety-four-year-old man in intensive care after a severe stroke even though his eighty-nine-year-old wife begged to be allowed to take care of him at home. Two days after her husband was hospitalized, she died of a heart attack.

The family may be understandably concerned when an elderly relative insists on nursing her bedridden husband. Everyone may try to persuade her to institutionalize him or hire a nurse, saying, "You've got a right to live, too." But that may be the only way she wants to live. One seventy-seven-year-old wife, persuaded against her will by her children to place her paralyzed husband in an excellent nursing home, agonized constantly that he was not getting the right care: "They don't shave him the way he likes," or "They always forget the pillow he needs under his legs," or "He'll starve with that slop they feed him." She could not enjoy a minute of her new freedom. "But, Ma," her children kept saying, "he's better off in the home. You would have killed yourself if you'd gone on any longer." She had only one answer: "I should have died trying."

When the stronger partner in a marriage dies, the weaker one is often incapable of continuing alone. Such dependent survivors have few options open to them and must either live with a child or accept some form of institutional life.

DISCORD IN
THE "GOLDEN YEARS"

Your parents may not have such an exclusive relationship. Instead of turning to each other they may turn to you, trying to involve you and their other children in their conflicts. Hearing them fighting or complaining about each other may make you very uncomfortable. You may remember that they fought all the time you were growing up, but somehow you may have expected all this to stop as they grew old together. The answer to the question "How can they still be fighting, at their age?" is "Why should they stop now?"

> *For forty-seven years they had been married. How deep back the stubborn gnarled roots of the quarrel reach, no one could say—but only now, when tending to the needs of others no longer shackled them together, the roots swelled up visible, split the earth between them, and the tearing shook even to the children, long since grown.*
> Tillie Olsen, *Tell Me a Riddle*

There is no reason to expect tempers and personality clashes to fade away with the years. Occasional conflict is to be expected in any close relationship. It can provide a catharsis, a release. Conflict may even arise for the first time in the later years, as couples struggle to cope with the stresses and difficulties caused by their aging. When there is a strong bond between husband and wife at any age, periodic quarrels can serve to cement rather than destroy a relationship. But some couples—perhaps your parents—make quarreling a way of life.

A young child is often terribly upset when his parents fight, particularly if they carry on directly in front of him. Even if they try to keep their conflicts private, he can be just as upset knowing that something terrible is going on in the house. Years later he may be upset all over again when they attack each other and may need to withdraw for his own protection. "I'm nearly fifty, but I still get that old sick feeling in the pit of my stomach when I hear Mom and Dad fighting," a daughter admitted to her mother's doctor, trying to explain why she visited her parents so rarely.

A successful writer claims that he invariably falls asleep at the theater when the scene onstage involves a marital battle. As a child he had always used sleep to escape hearing the thing he hated most: his parents fighting. They are in their eighties now and still at war. Their son visits them, although infrequently, and after he visits he usually goes home and sleeps.

Some stressful marriages which have held together during the middle years "for the sake of the children" feel free to break up when the family is launched. Couples separate, divorce, start afresh with new partners at fifty, sixty, even over seventy. A recent study reports that although the absolute numbers are small—about 30,000 a year—the percentage of couples over sixty getting divorced is two-and-a-half times as great in 1988 as it was in 1983. This figure is expected to continue to rise. The American Association of Retired Persons even publishes a how-to pamphlet entitled *Divorce After 50*. Some couples feel that it's never too late to separate. In Marian Thurm's short story "Sounds," an elderly mother says to her daughter, "It's over, thank God," as her husband in his early seventies drives off to meet his young bride-to-be. "It went on forever, didn't it, like a bad movie you can barely manage to sit through, but it's finally over."

Margaret Mead, the famed anthropologist, would not have been surprised at the rising divorce rate among older couples. She claimed that we have an antiquated idea about marriage lasting forever. When life expectancy was forty-five and couples vowed "Till death do us part," death parted them pretty quickly. In Mead's opinion, that's why marriage lasted forever: everyone was dead. Since couples now stay alive much longer, there is more time for them to outgrow each other or to develop "irreconcilable differences," or to find new and more stimulating relationships.

By contrast, other seemingly shaky pairs, while using their children as the rationale for staying together, remain intact permanently because of their dependence on each other. Despite constant threats through the years to separate, they never follow through, to the surprise of their children, who report, "We grew up expecting our parents to get divorced—we almost still expect it now—but they're still together and still at each other's throats."

> The Vaughans' marriage had always been a battleground. No one had heard Philip Vaughan refer to his wife by name for years—only as "that woman." Even when they grew older their conflicts continued, and they frequently spent long periods of time refusing to speak to each other. In their later years they often communicated to each other by making long-distance calls to their daughter, Edna, who had moved far away from her parents. "Tell your father to see a doctor about that cough of his," Mrs. Vaughan would say to her daughter, who could hear her father coughing in the background. Edna, in New Hampshire, would then speak to her father when he got on the phone in Iowa and urge him to see a doctor. In reply her father would shout, "Tell 'that woman' to stop worrying about my health all the time."

At least the Vaughans, despite their bickering, managed to keep a close watch over each other's physical well-being, but other couples may remain so wrapped up in their conflict that they no longer communicate about anything else. Each one may keep quiet about a disturbing physical symptom, refusing to admit to the other that something hurts somewhere. Thus they may keep their fears to themselves until it is too late.

Children, friends, and relatives even go so far as to recommend divorce or separation to an elderly couple who battle on a daily basis. An outsider may not realize that along with all the anger there are also strong bonds holding the two old people together, and that beneath the conflict they may be deeply attached to each other.

Seventy-nine-year-old Mavis Wood had been threatening to leave her husband, who was a year older, for most of the six decades of their marriage. In her mid-seventies her threats were somewhat idle, since she was confined to a wheelchair and dependent on his help. When a double room became available in a nearby nursing home, their children, tired of being drawn into their conflicts, urged their parents to move in. Jack Wood was reluctant for one reason only: "She'll leave me when she has someone else to take care of her." But he was persuaded, and the two moved in carrying their conflicts with them. Now they involved the nursing-home staff as well as their children.

After some time, the staff, tired of the situation and convinced that the two would be better off separated, offered to move Mrs. Wood to another room. When the move was made, she was delighted: "You never believed I'd ever leave him, did you? Well, I did!" she gloated to everyone. Her children and the staff were relieved at the peaceful period which followed, but their relief was short-lived. Within four days Mrs. Wood was back in her old room with her husband once again, ready and eager to resume their old combative relationship once more.

WIDOWHOOD

A marriage may remain intact, in harmony or in conflict, for forty, fifty, or sixty years, but sooner or later it will inevitably be broken by death. Unless they die together in a plane crash or other disaster, one partner will have to face life without the other for some period of time. Of all the losses which must be faced in old age, the loss of a partner is often the most cruel and disruptive loss of all.

In most cases the wife will survive her husband. According to current statistics women can expect to live seven years longer than men. Since women tend to marry men older rather than younger than themselves, the likelihood that they will survive their husbands is even greater. In 1986, 13.7 percent of the men over sixty-five were widowers while 50.5 percent of the women were widows.

In addition to the grief and upheaval caused by the loss of their husbands, numbers of elderly widows living alone (along with other elderly single women) face dire financial privation. Some 30 to 40 percent fall below the poverty line.

Because most wives are aware of the strong possibility that they will outlive their husbands, some go through a kind of "preparatory widowhood" in the later years, talking to their children about what lies ahead, thinking through specific plans, working out budgets, or concentrating their efforts on protecting their husbands' health and well-being. Even if they prefer not to think about the future, they cannot avoid the fleeting thought "Am I next?" as more and more of their friends become widows. Husbands, by contrast, are generally not prepared for the possibility that, despite the statistics, they may be the ones who survive, and give little or no thought to the idea that one day they, too, could be alone. Widowers may be even more shocked and helpless than widows in the initial stages.

But prepared or not—even if death follows a long period of illness, even if it is expected, almost hoped for—the loss of a partner is almost always a devastating occurrence followed by some period of grief and disruption. Mourning usually involves a number of emotional reactions— numbness, apathy, longing, sorrow, remorse, and guilt—as well as physical symptoms of weight loss, insomnia, irritability, and fatigue. But there is a great variation, depending on the individual, in the intensity of the emotional and physical reactions and their duration. It may be hard for you to predict in advance just how your own mother or father will react.

When a surviving husband has always been particularly dependent on his dead wife (or vice versa), it is understandable that he will feel utterly lost without her. But dependency in marriage is often a very subtle process. You may have always thought that your father was a very independent, self-sufficient, dominant type who ran everyone's life. Why should he seem so shattered by your mother's death? It is worth remembering that the most independent of husbands may, underneath, be very emotionally tied to their wives and dependent on them, although heaven forbid they should ever admit it! You may not believe your father could ever feel dependent on anyone—he may not even believe it about himself. The realization may only dawn on the day he is widowed, and his reaction may shock everyone.

On the other hand, you may have always underestimated the strength of your surviving parent. Although your mother may have seemed docile and passive, inner reserves you never saw before may surface when your father dies. You may have a sneaking suspicion after a while that she actually seems somewhat relieved, which may seem quite surprising and inappropriate under the circumstances. But once the funeral is over and the mourning period is past, some widows and widowers experience an unexpected sense of freedom rising above their feelings of loss. If a dead husband has been truly dominating, a kind of parental figure, his wife may be quite relieved to be free of his control. She may need some time before she can reactivate her rusty old self-sufficiency, but she may surprise everyone, including herself, by her ability to think and act as an independent person.

A similar sense of freedom may be felt by widows and widowers who have spent long years caring for physically or emotionally dependent spouses. A husband who felt duty-bound to care for his invalid wife, who never could bring himself to gain his freedom by institutionalizing her, will be freed by her death—and not through any deliberate act of his own. He may then find he still has time to make use of his new freedom, although for many it comes too late.

If relief seems to be an unexpected emotion, you may be just as surprised if one of your parents reacts to the loss of the other with calm tranquility. Some widows and widowers, after a short time, reflect this quality in the midst of sadness. They seem able to pick up their lives and carry on, even start afresh if there is still time.

DISRUPTION IS TO BE EXPECTED

Widowhood for elderly men and women almost invariably involves disruption, which may last longer than the grief itself. An elderly widow is no longer anyone's wife, anyone's companion, anyone's sex partner (for the time at least). She has no one to care for or to run a house for except herself. With no one to cook for, she may not bother to cook at all and may become further weakened by malnutrition. She may have to change her level of living completely because of reduced income. If her husband has always been the handyman, finance officer, and business executive in the marriage, she will have to grapple with these unfamiliar roles. Widowers face similar disruptions in habitual patterns of daily life.

If the couple's social life has always been carried on together, that, too, will be disrupted temporarily—or permanently. Widows and widowers often report that they don't "fit in" anymore, that they are no longer as comfortable or as welcome in their old social niches, although widowers are more likely than widows to be sought out and included by friends. A widow often senses (rightly or wrongly) that her old friends are uncomfortable with her grief, that they feel depressed around her, or that she has become a fifth wheel in couple-oriented activities. Widows are more likely than widowers to discover that if they do not drive or can no longer afford accustomed forms of entertainment, their social life begins to fade away. Older widows have one compensation denied to younger ones: since it is unusual to be widowed early, young widows often feel out of step with their married contemporaries, while older widows, because of their numbers, can often find kindred spirits among their contemporaries. A steady diet of female companionship may not be completely satisfying for most, but for some widows it beats loneliness.

Loneliness itself is not a simple feeling and can mean different things to different people. When your widowed mother tells you she is lonely, you may not understand exactly *how* she is lonely. Helen Lopata, in *Widowhood in an American City*, reported that the widows she interviewed defined their loneliness in a variety of ways: some were lonely because they missed everything about their dead husbands; others were lonely for companionship, for someone to organize their days around, for escorts, for someone to love or to be loved by, for someone to share activities with. Widows and widowers have to learn how to live with their own individual variety of loneliness.

In recent years, subjects that formerly were not discussed openly have been dissected minutely in the press and on TV and radio talk shows— even in television dramas, movies, and theater. Old taboos have melted. Buzzwords abound and are used—and misused—broadside and authoritatively. There is a danger of nonprofessionals becoming parlor psychiatrists after exposure to a battery of pop-psych. The public has been bombarded with a similar battery of material on aging and widowhood. Friends and relatives may flaunt their newfound expertise even when not asked for advice.

"I heard Dr. Simonov say just yesterday on TV that mourning should only last a year. Jack's been dead two years. You better start making a new life for yourself"—words of a so-called friend to a widow.

If your parents do not conform to patterns you have heard experts put forth, this does not mean there is anything wrong with your mother or your father. Experts discuss overall patterns—there's always room for individual differences. Your mother may hear a different drummer and follow a different star. Statistics (remember "people without tears" on page 5) may indeed show that widows and widowers make bearable adjustments within the first year or so. But your father may need to stick with his own timetable.

Unless totally dependent on others because of ill-health or prolonged depression, your widowed mother (or father) is likely to adjust eventually to the disruption in her life and develop a new pattern which may go on for many years. Things will never be the same for her again. Life will certainly be different; it will probably be bearable; and it may—in some cases—even be better.

WHEN MOURNING GOES OUT OF BOUNDS

While shock, pain, depression are not only normal emotions during the mourning period, but actually necessary ones which make it possible for survivors to work through their grief and eventually resume life again, some widows and widowers never recover.

Prolonged mourning was more obvious in the past, when the process was more ritualized. Some widows refused to give up their "widow's weeds" and lived on, shrouded in black, never letting themselves or the world forget their loss. Although less visible, prolonged mourning is not unknown today.

While experts agree that the survivor of a marriage is more susceptible to physical and mental illness in the early days of widowhood—a higher rate of suicide is reported in this period—they also report that the intensity of these emotions and physical symptoms normally eases with time. Those who remain in a state of perpetual grief may have conflicting feelings about their dead partners or have been known to have had depressive episodes in the past. What seems to their families to be a state of perpetual mourning may actually be a state of severe depression set off, but not caused by, the bereavement itself. Simple remedies which help to ease normal grief will not work. Some form of professional help may be needed.

Queen Victoria gave the world a classic example of prolonged mourning. Victoria, as queen of England, was one of the most powerful figures of her time. No one could possibly say she did not have enough to keep her busy. Yet in 1861, after the death of her husband, Prince Albert, she retired, at the age of forty-two, into seclusion at Windsor Castle. For three years she never appeared in public, and she did not open Parliament again—an annual duty for British monarchs—until 1866. Even though she lived another forty years after her husband's death, she never let her country forget her loss. The poet Rudyard Kipling suffered permanent royal disfavor when he dared refer to his queen as "the widow at Windsor."

THE DEATH OF A PARENT: THE EFFECT ON YOU

The previous discussion has focused on your parent's reactions to his or her widowhood, but your own personal ones cannot be ignored. When your father dies, you may feel some responsibility to help his widow (your mother or your stepmother) recover from her loss. But you may have a hard time behaving in a cool, level-headed way yourself, because her loss is yours as well. She has lost a husband, it's true, but you've lost a father.

If your father is widowed, he mourns for a wife while you mourn for a mother. When sympathy goes in two directions, when the older generation is able to acknowledge that the younger one is suffering too, it is easier for everyone. But that does not always happen. A mother may complain to everyone, "Carol carries on so! You'd think she'd lost a husband. Can't she think what it's like for me?" But Carol may tell a different story: "Mother acts as if she's the only one who misses Dad. Doesn't she remember that I loved him, too?"

Even if both generations recognize each other's grief, they may mourn in different ways. Your mother may turn to religion after your father's death, taking her comfort in ritual and prayer, visiting the cemetery, lighting candles, wearing black. None of these rituals may be at all helpful to you—they may even seem distasteful. Many families are in disagreement about the entire mourning process, starting with the funeral itself. Some members may want a lavish ceremony, a constant stream of condolences, and find comfort when the world seems to share and witness their grief. Others can mourn only in privacy. If you find no comfort in the rituals that comfort your mother, there is no reason why you should be forced to do everything her way—but no reason, either, to prevent her from taking comfort where she finds it.

You may be so shattered by your own grief after your mother's death that you find it painful at first to talk about her at all, even to mention her name. Your father may need to talk about her all the time. For your own sanity you may need to withdraw a little and let others do the listening.

A particularly painful situation exists when a son or a daughter has had a stronger bond with the parent who has died and greater conflict with the surviving one. If you had an especially close feeling for your father, his death may be devastating to you and you may find it almost impossible to comfort your mother. You may even resent her for still being alive while he is dead, and also for never—in your opinion—treating him well enough or appreciating him enough during his lifetime.

Although it has always been customary to speak well of the dead, children are frequently amazed at the way the surviving parent manages to remember the dead one. Widows and widowers often seem to find comfort in idealizing relationships that were actually far from satisfying and are quite skillful at rewriting their own marital histories. Relatives may listen in disbelief as a widow describes her dead husband as "the gentlest soul on earth," when everyone knows he was tyrannical and demanding. A widowed father may remember his wife as "selfless and saintlike" after her death, when in reality she had been self-centered and hot-tempered. Families at such times quickly come to believe Sigmund Freud's comment: "Consideration for the dead, who after all no longer need it, is more important to us than the truth."

WHAT YOU CAN DO TO HELP

Your involvement when one of your parents is widowed depends on your mutual relationship, your desire to help, how many other people are available, and where you live. Obviously, if you live far away you will not be able to do much more than return for the funeral (or possibly during a final illness) and help out with the arrangements and initial problems. You may be able to continue to help from a distance by keeping in touch by phone and visiting more frequently, especially in the early period.

It is important to keep in mind that mourners go through many different stages on their way to recovery, and some of those stages may be difficult to deal with. Your mother may be full of self-pity at one time and anger at another. She may withdraw from you and your siblings this week, and accuse you of neglecting her next week. Those stages may be surprising and burdensome, but they are likely to pass.

The mourning process does not necessarily proceed in a straight line—improving steadily from the deepest distress to reasonable normalcy. The mourner may well take one step back for every two steps forward. Innocent, seemingly insignificant reminders may precipitate setbacks—a song, a picture, a bit of "your father's favorite cake," the smell of "your mother's favorite flower." Anniversaries—and not only the obvious annual ones—may trigger temporary relapses. One daughter was puzzled because her father always seemed lower in spirits at the end of the week than at the beginning. Eventually it dawned on her that her father dreaded Thursdays because he became a widower on a Thursday.

Mourning takes time, and since older people are likely to move more slowly in all situations, they cannot be rushed through their grief or accept changes before they are ready. "We can't let Mother stay here alone. Everything here reminds her of Dad. We'll have to sell the house" may seem like a logical conclusion, but Mother may be worse off and her recovery permanently jeopardized if her home is sold out from under her and she is bundled off to a strange environment. Familiar surroundings as well as familiar faces are very comforting, although temporary changes of scene can be helpful.

When elderly widows or widowers are initially helpless and bewildered because of their grief, children may be tempted to rush in with impetuous invitations. "Come live with us—you can't live alone here," may seem like a kind solution at the moment, but unless it has been considered carefully from all angles in advance, it may turn out to be far from kind for anyone. Your mother, persuaded to become dependent on you before she has given herself a chance to test her self-reliance, may forfeit her independence forever, while you and your family may come to resent the unnecessary and uncomfortable adjustments you have to make in your own lives.

The elderly themselves, in an attempt to escape their grief, may be the ones who rush into impetuous decisions. They may ask or demand to live with you. A widow may decide to sell her house and move into a one-room apartment or a hotel. Once the move is made, she may regret it. A widower, thinking he cannot face a winter alone in a cold climate, may pick himself up with little notice and move to a warm place where he knows no one. You may be able to forestall radical moves that could boomerang in the future by agreeing with the idea in principle but suggesting alternative approaches. "I can see why you don't want to stay here alone, Dad, but why sell the house? Why not rent it this winter and see how you like living in Arizona? If you don't like it there, you'll always have a place to come back to."

Even if a widowed mother does not seem to need anything from her children, it is usually helpful for her to know they can be depended on. Dependability and availability are important; so are sympathetic listening and genuine concern. It is equally important to help widowed parents build up their self-confidence and to encourage them to take their first independent steps. Your first instinctive reaction to your widowed mother may be to protect her in every way. "Don't worry about a thing, Ma, we'll take care of everything" may be a well-intentioned offer but may only make her more dependent than ever. A more effective approach would be to reassure her that she is perfectly capable of taking care of herself but that you're ready to back her up when she needs you.

On occasion widowed parents who no longer have partners to share their lives focus all their attention—and their demands—on one particular child. A daughter may be expected by her father to take the place of her dead mother, or a son to replace his dead father. (Children themselves sometimes try to assume these roles, and are hurt and angry when their attempts are rejected and their parents prefer to be self-reliant.) The only way to prevent those expectations from taking hold is to set firm boundaries from the beginning: "No, Mother, I can't spend Saturdays working in the garden with you like Dad used to do. You know I coach Jim's Little League team on Saturdays. But we'll be over to see you after church on Sunday as usual." Or: "No, Father, I can't get over every day. You know how much I have to do at home. But don't forget you're spending the weekend with us." The situation is more difficult to handle when the requests are less specific. It is harder to set boundaries when your mother wants you to be responsive to her emotional needs just as your father always was. It is equally hard to reply to broad, unspecific complaints like, "I feel blue," "My life's so empty," "Why am I living?" Trying to counteract these statements with encouraging upbeat sermons is likely to be a waste of breath. Here again a concrete, specific reply given with an understanding tone may be more helpful: "I know you're lonely and it's hard for you, but Aunt Flo's coming back next week and we've all got tickets for the ice show. How about going out to dinner first?"

REMARRIAGE

Older men and women, widowed or divorced, may remarry, even in their eighties. It will be impossible for anyone to predict after your father dies just *what* your mother will do. You can't be sure and neither can she. A categorical *never* can be said only in cases where individual survivors are seriously incapacitated. Widows and widowers often swear during the mourning period that they will never marry again. Their children usually believe them, often finding the mere idea inconceivable. You may share this view. Yet your widowed mother may surprise herself—and you, too.

The chances of remarriage are obviously greater for older widowers than for widows, because single women over seventy-five outnumber men of the same age 3 to 1. The field, therefore, is wide open for the widower, and his selection is not limited to women in his own age group. His new wife could be ten, twenty, thirty, forty years younger than he is. Women, because of social mores, are less likely to marry men who are much younger. Winston Churchill's mother, Jennie, was a famous exception. After she was widowed she had two more husbands, both younger than her own sons. Such exceptions seem to be on the increase today, although they usually cause quite a furor.

Some older widows and widowers are unable to contemplate marrying again because they feel it is somehow improper, undignified, or frowned on by society. Their children frequently agree and voice even greater opposition, adding a new concern of their own: money. When a father remarries, who will inherit from him? His children or his widow? If he marries a younger woman, he may have children with her. Who will be his heirs? His first set of children or his second? Or will the inheritance be less for everyone because it has to be shared? Prenuptial agreements are sometimes made by an elderly pair to reassure the children on both sides that their "rightful" inheritances will not be lost.

You may approve in principle of the idea of remarriage for older people but find it appalling when your own father remarries. Your reasons for thinking it is ill-advised, in his particular situation, may seem to be valid. His new wife may be after his money; she may be from a different background, have different interests, less education. Her health may be poor, and you may be concerned that he will have to take care of her or possibly that you will have to take care of both of them. But actually, if you are completely honest with yourself, you may admit that these are not your real reasons for opposing his marriage. You may be against it because you feel it is disloyal to your mother. It may be too painful to you to think of another woman taking your mother's place in your father's life, using her things, sleeping in her bed. You may be jealous that your father prefers another woman and is not content to depend on you. Finally, you also may feel that remarriage at his age makes him look ridiculous—and therefore makes you look ridiculous, too.

But unless elderly men or women are seriously disturbed and not responsible for their actions, their children might be better advised to consider the consequences of opposing a remarriage. A son who seriously opposes his mother's marriage is telling her that she is better off living with her loneliness than with someone *he* considers inappropriate. Is she really better off? Can he be sure?

Although you initially opposed the idea, once your widowed parent has remarried it may become easier for you to accept. The closeness you once had may be gone, however. The new remoteness you feel may be obvious if you refer to the woman your father has married as "my father's wife" rather than as "my stepmother." Many children are never reconciled and continue to feel hurt and resentful because a father treats his new wife better than he ever treated them or their mother, or a mother seems to show more affection for her new husband than she ever showed for their father.

Although remarriage after the death of a spouse, particularly soon after, may appear to children and close friends as disloyalty to the memory of the dead man or woman, it actually may be the reverse. Some experts claim that when there has been a good, solid, mutually gratifying relationship in a marriage, there will inevitably be pain and grief after one partner dies, but the survivor will eventually be freer to start life again and even to contemplate marriage again. A widow or a widower whose former married life has been gratifying may want "more of the same" and hope to continue, in a new marriage, patterns enjoyed in the old one.

When the marriage has been difficult, conflicted, and unsatisfying, with elements of dependency, anger, and resentment, the death of one will not wipe out those emotions for the survivor. The grief that follows may be intense and as conflicted as the marriage itself. Those conflicts may prevent the survivor from making a new life or a commitment to marriage again. Even though the marriage was generally happy, a widow may reject remarriage if her husband had been ill for a long time before his death and she had carried the major burden of his nursing care. Or conversely, if her widowhood came suddenly with no warning, she may say, "I never will go through that again," when the subject of remarriage comes up.

A woman (or man) remarries late in life for a variety of reasons: for companionship, for financial security, to share common interests, to have someone who cares about her or someone she can care about, to satisfy sexual needs.

Elderly widows and widowers, even those who have all these needs, may fail to remarry for many reasons: fear of making a mistake, family opposition, lack of desire to resume marital responsibilities, and lack of opportunity. But they may find alternative ways to satisfy their needs. Just as young people are turning to more unconventional lifestyles, so may their grandparents: group marriages, shared living arrangements, communes, and homosexual or lesbian relationships. Their financial situation frequently makes marriage economically unwise, and they may decide to live together without legal ties in order to protect their assets. This situation is uncomfortable for many elderly men and women but is forced on them by Social Security regulations, which provide lesser benefits to married couples than to single individual recipients (see Chapter 7).

Such unconventional living arrangements, difficult enough for the elderly themselves to accept, may be hair-raising for their sons and daughters, who may already be having a hard time accepting the unusual lifestyles of their children. Consider the discomfort of the conservative middle-aged citizen who is forced by current mores to refer to "the girl my son is living with" or "the boy who shares my daughter's apartment" at a social gathering. How much greater his discomfort will be if, in addition, he has to include "my father's girlfriend" and "my mother's boyfriend"! He may prefer to withdraw from both generations.

SEX AFTER SIXTY-FIVE—
MYTH VERSUS REALITY

Many children like to ignore the fact that sex plays a part in their parents' lives at any age. That possibility can be ignored even more easily when their parents are old because of the prevailing assumptions that sex is not possible, necessary, or nice in the later years, and furthermore, that it can be hazardous to the health! You yourself may never have given a conscious thought to your parents' sex life or have discussed your own with them, and may accept the belief passed on through the centuries that while the other appetites last indefinitely and must be satisfied, sexual appetites die young.

> *You cannot call it love, for at your age*
> *The hey-day in the blood is tame . . .*

said Hamlet to his mother, Queen Gertrude. He could not understand why she married with such "indecent haste" after his father's death, and denied that a woman of her age could be motivated by love or passion. Yet Gertrude's age was probably less than forty-five.

It's easy enough to smile at Hamlet's naïveté, to point out that knowledge of human biology was very limited in Shakespeare's time, and to say that things are different now in our own liberated century. But are things really so different?

> A young doctor, graduate of a famous medical school and with advanced training in a great teaching hospital, recently cautioned his patient, Mary Walters, against continuing to use The Pill because of her high blood pressure. When Mary objected, reluctant to give up the convenience and security of The Pill, he reviewed the dangers again and added kindly, "At your age, Mrs. Walters, is it really *so* important?" Mary Walters was forty-eight—echoes of Hamlet four hundred years later!

Popular attitudes, supported by some members of the medical profession, are not so radically different today, despite the advances in scientific knowledge. The facts concerning sex and the later years continue to be distorted by old myths and false assumptions.

Many young adults are proud to be liberated from the sexual inhibitions of Victorianism and puritanism. Well informed about all aspects of sex, they discuss with ease the pros and cons of contraceptive devices, open marriage, group sex, gay liberation, and abortion. Yet that same uninhibited, "well-informed" group may also still believe that a woman's libido vanishes after the menopause and that impotence lies in wait for middle-aged men.

Plenty of aging men and women, of course, know from personal experience that these myths are false. Their own continuing sexual activity is all the proof they need. But plenty of others share the beliefs of the younger generation. If they feel any sexual drives or suffer any sexual difficulties, they often worry that something is the matter with them, hesitating to seek advice about their anxieties for fear of looking foolish. In addition, they are constantly reminded by the media that to be old is to be undesirable—another way of saying *sexless*.

Any example of passion and sexual potency still surviving in the later years is considered unusual enough or "abnormal" enough to be news-worthy: the marriage of a seventy-nine-year-old man and a thirty-year-old woman, fatherhood at eighty, an affair between an older woman and a younger man, or a crime of passion.

> *Paris November 29, 1975 (Reuters)—An 80-year-old man, Charles Bouchet, who served 27 years in the Devil's Island penal colony for manslaughter, was under close guard today, charged with having stabbed to death a rival of his own age for the love of a woman in a Paris home for pensioners.*

Such stories should make people question their old assumptions, but public response is most likely to be, "Oh, yes, but these are the exceptions."

Modern studies of human sexuality have shown that sexual activity among the elderly is far from unusual. Nearly thirty years ago Alfred Kinsey's first studies showed that while the frequency of intercourse declines steadily among men through the years, the majority continue some pattern of sexual activity. A number of men are sexually inactive at seventy, but a greater number still have intercourse with some regularity at the same age or older. (Kinsey's sample included one seventy-year-old whose ejaculations were still averaging more than seven a week, and a man of eighty-eight who had intercourse with his ninety-year-old wife anywhere from once a week to once a month.) Kinsey also reported that the sexual capacities of women show little change with aging.

Present-day researchers confirm Kinsey's earlier findings. Their studies show that men and women can, and often do, remain sexually active at sixty, seventy, eighty, and beyond, and furthermore, that older couples who maintain sexually gratifying lives are usually continuing the pattern of a lifetime. Sex may be less frequent, possibly less intense, but just as meaningful in their old age as it was when they were young, perhaps even more satisfying. Similarly, single men and women—widowed, divorced, separated, never married—who have always been sexually active are likely to seek out sexual relationships when they are old, although partners are increasingly difficult to find as the years go by. (Kinsey found that among previously married women masturbation became more important with age, possibly as the only available sexual outlet.) Far from dying out with age, sexual feelings, if they have been strong and satisfied through the years, may be intensified when an elderly man or woman is alone and lonely.

Sexual patterns of behavior may start early and continue late but only be considered socially acceptable in the earlier years. A young man who sows wild oats at twenty may be admired and envied, but he would be branded a roué at fifty and a "dirty old man" at seventy for the same behavior. "Mother, you were flirting with the butcher!" a daughter may say reprovingly, but the white-haired old lady may merely shrug off the reproof: "I can't change old habits at my age."

Eyebrows are usually raised when an elderly man marries a younger woman. People are quick to assume that she married him for his money, or for security, or for social position, or because she needs a father, and that he needs someone to take care of him. But their assumptions may easily be wrong.

> Friends and relatives were happy when old Phil Richter married his fifty-year-old housekeeper a short time after he was widowed. "How nice for him," they said. "He was so lonely. Now he'll have companionship at least." They were quite upset some time later to learn that the marriage had not worked out and that the newlyweds had separated. Rumors circulated that the trouble was caused by sexual incompatibility. "Of course," everyone quickly assumed, "she was too young for him—not sixty yet. She still needed a physical relationship. Poor old man—how sad—he probably couldn't satisfy her."
>
> Those closest to old Mr. Richter knew that the situation was reversed. The younger woman had always found sex distasteful and was glad to marry for companionship, convinced that nothing more would be expected from her. Mr. Richter had other ideas. He had maintained a high level of sexual activity all his life, not only with his wife, until she died, but with a series of mistresses as well. Now in his eighties and widowed, he needed companionship, but he needed a sexual partner, too, and expected to find it in the younger woman he married.

Age, therefore, is not a barrier to healthy, ongoing sexual activity. The barriers come rather from physical disability, mental disturbance, longstanding sexual maladjustments, and—more frequently—lack of an appealing or willing sexual partner.

THE ELDERLY MAY BE MISINFORMED, TOO

Scientific research has broken down many of the myths that have surrounded the subject of sex and the elderly, but many older people still do not fully understand the changes taking place in their own bodies as they age. Temporary setbacks in their sexual performance may quickly revive the old myths. Their anxiety may then make temporary setbacks permanent. A woman may know intellectually that her libido will not be affected after the menopause even though her ovaries stop functioning, but she may not be aware of other possible changes: thinning of the vaginal walls, and decrease in elasticity and lubrication, resulting in painful intercourse. Those conditions can usually be treated, but unless she gets good medical advice she may decide by herself that her sex life is over.

A man may be concerned that his sexual potency will be gone after prostate surgery or may worry merely because his reactions are slower, and because it takes him longer to achieve an erection and an orgasm. He may be anxious that he is becoming impotent, and his very anxiety may make the impotence a reality—a self-fulfilling prophecy. Many problems, not necessarily related to age, can cause periods of impotence in younger as well as older men, such as drinking, fatigue, worry, fear of failure, or boredom. Careful physicians are often able to pinpoint the problems, suggest ways to overcome them, and reassure elderly patients that impotence is not necessarily permanent. But sexual failure seems so shameful to many men that they are reluctant to admit the problem. If they decide to consult a doctor they are often told, "Don't worry about it—it's to be expected at your age!"

Modern medical thinking has exploded another old myth: that sex is hazardous to the health of older people. Many doctors are convinced that the opposite is true, even for the elderly with heart conditions and arthritis, and that sexual activity can actually be therapeutic in reducing tension, heightening morale, and maintaining a sense of well-being. Nursing home rules until recently required the segregation of the sexes, or permitted only married couples to share a room. But today some of the more concerned institutions, realizing the importance of sex to the adjustment of elderly residents, are making it possible for unmarried couples to have privacy together. This innovation, while producing great happiness for the residents concerned, often produces even greater consternation among their children.

WHAT WILL THE CHILDREN SAY?

Laurence Olivier, in an interview in the *New York Times*, discussed a new play, *The Seagull*, and its author, the late British playwright Ben Travers:

> *Travers is well into his 90's. It's a very naughty play indeed. He discovered sex very late in life. He was thrilled by it and quite ashamed of the play. He put it in a drawer. He didn't want to shock his children, all of whom were over 60. We persuaded him that they would be able to take it.*

Perhaps Ben Travers's children were able to "take it," but children are not always so open-minded. They may accept a widowed father's remarriage to the elderly woman who was their mother's best friend, or a mother's remarriage to a kindly old man everyone loves. If sex is considered at all in these marriages, everyone may like to assume that the elderly couples maintain separate bedrooms or at least separate beds.

But what if you cannot make any such comfortable assumptions in your own father's situation—or your mother's? What if the behavior of one or the other makes it perfectly clear that a sexual relationship is going on? A special set of feelings may be aroused and suddenly, although you firmly believe that sex is normal and appropriate for other people's fathers and mothers, it may now seem highly inappropriate for your own. You may try to prevent what you feel is an "unwise" marriage or break up a relationship that does not seem "right." You and others in the family may insist that "he is making a fool of himself," or that "she doesn't know what she's doing." You may even consider that your elderly parent is becoming mentally impaired. It is dangerous to jump to such conclusions. Although older people who are seriously deteriorated mentally or physically may lose the defenses they once had which inhibited inappropriate sexual acts, you may have a hard time deciding if your father's behavior is *truly* inappropriate or if it just *seems* inappropriate to you and simply makes you uncomfortable or ashamed. Perhaps you want your father's or your mother's affections to be exclusively yours and are jealous when someone else comes between you. Perhaps you cannot bear to see your once very proper parent, who cautioned you against sexual display, exhibiting open sexuality.

When children feel ashamed or jealous of an elderly parent's sexual relationship that is appropriate and gratifying to the parent, it is the children's problem and not the parent's. The children may deal with their problem by learning to accept the relationship or by staying away from it as much as possible. Worrying, "What will the children say?" may make older men and women hesitant to remarry and also prevent them from establishing new relationships, forcing them to settle instead for unnecessary loneliness and sexual abstinence.

6

FACING THE FINAL CRISIS

*"He is certainly of an age to die." The sadness of the old; their banishment.
. . . I too made use of this cliché and that when I was referring to my mother.
I did not understand that one might sincerely weep for a relative, a grandfather
aged seventy or more. If I met a woman of fifty overcome with sadness because
she had just lost her mother, I thought her neurotic: we are all mortal; at
eighty you are old enough to be one of the dead. . . . But it is not true . . . the
knowledge that because of her age my mother's life must soon come to an end
did not lessen the horrible surprise.*

Simone de Beauvoir, *A Very Easy Death*

The death of an elderly mother or father inevitably touches the children who are left behind, whether they are just grown up, middle-aged, or nearing old age themselves. Even if it is expected because of a hopeless illness, even if it is welcomed as an end to suffering, even if there is remoteness or estrangement between the generations, the death of a parent cannot be a casual event.

Any review of life in the later years must therefore include a consideration of death. Death becomes more and more of a reality with every passing year. Its closeness touches not only those who are about to die but also those who love them and will survive them.

According to the laws of nature, the younger generation will survive the older one. But the process is not necessarily without pain. A son expects to survive his father but also expects to mourn him and to feel some amount of sadness, regret, loneliness. He may also realistically expect to feel a certain sense of relief when the burden of caring for an invalid is lifted, particularly if the invalid has been difficult, demanding, or suffering. Many children respond in just these ways when their parents die. Others surprise themselves and wonder why they respond with more painful emotions: inconsolable grief, anger, fear, guilt, and a sense of abandonment when someone who has been old, sick, helpless, and no longer able to enjoy life finally dies.

Painful reactions should not be so surprising. Parents are crucial figures in our lives when we are children. If they live on into their seventies, eighties, and nineties, they may continue as integral parts of our adult lives, too; we and they may even grow old together. When a mother dies at eighty, her children at fifty or sixty may learn for the first time the meaning of life without her. Each one of us has only one mother or father to lose, and when either or both die, some part of us dies with them.

Our personal being is in some way, to a greater or lesser extent, diminished. A strong force linking us to our past is gone. As our parents' lives end, an eventful chapter in our own life history ends, too. It may not have been a particularly good chapter for us, but it is finished and can never be revised or rewritten. There will never be an opportunity again for reconciliation, for explanation, for understanding, or for saying things left unsaid for years: "I'm grateful," "I'm sorry," "I love you."

Psychologist Clark E. Moustakas, in *Loneliness*, describes the thoughts of a son watching his dying mother:

> *This was my mother; and the word "mother" brings on a flow of feeling and past experiences and years of living together, loving together, and hating, too. The fighting and conflicts do not seem important anymore, the arguments and intense pains and emotions that clouded the relationship have evaporated. This was my mother, and I realize the uniqueness of our relationship. It was not an impersonal fact of someone having cancer and dying, but it was a basic relationship that can never be repeated, a piece of eternity, never to be the same anymore.*

A story, fact or fiction, was repeated recently about a sixty-year-old man who, when asked to indicate on an insurance form whether he was married, widowed, or divorced, wrote in the appropriate space "orphan." While this word did not describe his marital state, it did describe the state of his feelings. Many of us have a similar feeling, if only for a fleeting moment, and the old fear of abandonment is remembered from childhood. As long as our parents live we are always somebody's child, no matter how old we are. Whenever they die, we are orphans for life.

Most of us are unprepared for this feeling. If we sense it in advance we are likely to laugh at it and ourselves for being ridiculous. We certainly are not likely to discuss it with our parents who are close to death, yet undoubtedly they must know something about it—after all, they have probably been orphaned, too.

THE CONSPIRACY OF SILENCE

As a matter of fact, we are likely to talk to them about very little that relates to their death, and more likely to stop them from bringing up the subject. Families with deep religious faith may be able to deal with death more directly, to talk about it and what comes after, but the subject of death—like sex, only more so—has been generally taboo in modern society. Freud discussed that taboo in his essay "Obscure Thoughts on War and Death":

> . . . *we were of course prepared to maintain that death was the necessary outcome of life, that everyone owes nature a death and must expect to pay the debt—in short, that death was natural, undeniable and unavoidable. In reality, however, we were accustomed to behave as if it were otherwise. We showed an unmistakable tendency to put death on one side, to eliminate it from life.*

For some, not only the subject but also the word is taboo. Euphemisms are used instead: "passed on," "gone," "departed," "lost," "at rest." Not wanting to be reminded of the inevitable, people find it safer to avoid the topic; if they talk about it at all, they tend to do so in general, impersonal terms with no names attached. A wall of silence, therefore, can grow up between those who are about to die and those who care about them most. That silence can deprive both sides of help, comfort, and support just at the time when those elements are needed most. In *I Knock at the Door*, Sean O'Casey writes of a dying old man:

> *And here he was now reclining in a big horse-hair covered armchair, shrinking from something that everyone thought of, but no one ever mentioned.*

The same taboo which makes it difficult for us to discuss death with the dying makes us uncomfortable with mourners. "What can I say?" you may have asked every time you sat down to write a condolence note or went to visit friends in mourning. A few conventional, stilted words of sympathy—and then on to pleasanter, safer topics. The subject uppermost in everyone's mind is the subject that is hardest to bring up. Children, as Freud himself noticed, uninhibited as yet by social taboos, often spontaneously break the conspiracy of silence and refer point-blank to the thing that terrifies them.

When Frank and Eleanor Thorne returned with their two children after a three-year assignment in Japan, their homecoming was a sad one. Eleanor's father, who had always lived with them, had died at eighty-two while they were all overseas. He had been extremely close to his daughter, his son-in-law, and his grandchildren, and they were all acutely aware of his absence when they came back to the house he had shared with them for so long.

Friends who dropped in to welcome the family were also aware of the pain of the homecoming and were determined to be helpful. A succession of visitors came and went, each one full of bright chatter and careful to avoid any reference to the missing person. The Thornes were surprised at first when no one mentioned Grandpa—they would have liked to talk about him—but they decided it would put a damper on their friends' efforts to be cheerful, so they kept silent, too.

At the end of the day a small boy arrived with his parents, surveyed the piles of luggage scattered all over the house, spotted a giant duffel bag standing upright in the corner, studied it with fascination, and then, to the horror of his mother, asked in a shrill voice, "Is *that* where they keep the grandfather?" The silence was broken.

Man has orbited in space, harnessed nuclear power, and walked on the moon, but death remains undiscovered territory, terrifying in its mystery. The motto observed by many is, "When terrified—hide." So they try to hide in silence, but that does not always provide real shelter. Without a word being spoken, our parents' aging forces us to acknowledge the fact that we are trying to ignore. Their increasing frailty, their whitening hair, their fading vision, their advancing birthdays can be daily reminders of their mortality and, by extension, our own. No wonder many of us react with anger and impatience if, on top of those visible reminders, they want to *talk* about dying, too. They are likely to find themselves cut off before they have a chance to begin:

ELDERLY PARENT I'm not going to be around forever.
SON/DAUGHTER Nonsense! You'll outlive all of us! [The subject is closed.]

ELDERLY PARENT When I'm gone . . .
SON/DAUGHTER Oh, Mother, stop talking that way. [The subject is closed.]

ELDERLY PARENT I've had a good life, but I . . .
SON/DAUGHTER Don't act as if it's over. You've got years to go. [The subject is closed.]

These are all direct references to death, but some older people make more indirect allusions which sensitive sons and daughters are quick to catch and resent.

Bernard Hill's father always had his affairs in order. "His drawers are all neat and tidy," Bernard reported. "He's always reminding me where his papers are and which keys fit which locks. He used to be like this when we were kids before we went off on a trip. He always seems packed for a trip these days and ready to go. Whenever I visit him I feel like I ought to say goodbye. I hate it."

•   •

Everytime there was a sale—sheets or underwear or stockings or towels—Meg Corwin always asked her mother whether she needed anything. Her mother invariably answered, "No, I have enough to last me." Meg always groaned when she heard this. "Why does she have to keep on reminding me all the time that she's going to die?"

SOME PEOPLE NEED
TO TALK ABOUT DEATH

If death were not so taboo, if it could be talked about more freely, those direct and indirect references might stimulate rather than abort discussion. The discussions would not be likely to go on indefinitely, or to monopolize all conversation. The elderly are not usually preoccupied with thoughts of death every minute. Thoughts and fears come and go. When they come, it can be comforting and reassuring to voice them occasionally. Not much is required of the listener except listening and a few words: "I know," or "I understand," or "I remember, too."

Your father may be looking for a chance to talk to someone about himself—to reminisce about what his life has meant to him, what certain people have meant to him. He may wonder what he has meant to others—to you. He may want to talk about his accomplishments, mistakes, regrets—or perhaps his fears not only of death but of the process of dying. He may hope to be reassured that he will not die alone or be in pain. He may also want reassurance that he will be remembered, that he will be able to leave some kind of legacy behind for future generations.

He may want to discuss his will and the distribution of his material things, his feelings about funerals and burials. His concerns may be not only for himself but also for those he will leave behind, people he worries about: you, or your mother, or your brother, or a grandchild. He may not expect to find answers to all his questions, but talking about them can be therapeutic if only there is a willing listener.

Children frequently look back on lost opportunities after a parent has died and wonder why they did not listen more, both for their parent's benefit and for their own. After his father died, John O'Brien said regretfully:

I'd get pretty bored when Pop rambled on about the old days and what happened before I was born. But he always seemed to catch me when I was busy—I'll admit I hardly ever listened. But I wish I had. Who is there left now to tell me the name of the town in Ireland where my great-grandfather is buried? Who remembers Aunt Tessie's mother's maiden name? Why should I care about such silly little unimportant things? But I do. And he'll never know I do.

Direct and indirect references to death are often ignored, but sometimes the subject never comes up at all; there seems no way to open it. You may feel you would like to talk to your mother when you realize she is failing and may sense that it would help her to talk to someone, but both of you may be uncomfortable and uncertain how to begin. There may be awkwardness and reticence on each side. It's easy enough to say to her, "Listen—before you take off for California is there anything we should go over together, anything you need me to do for you?" It's harder to speak so freely when she is not going to California but is going to die. Much, therefore, is likely to be left unsaid by both of you.

> *Do not go gentle into that good night,*
> *Old age should burn and rave at close of day;*
> *Rage, rage against the dying of the light.*

So wrote the Welsh poet Dylan Thomas, opening one of the best-known contemporary poems about death. According to those who knew him, Thomas wrote those words for his dying father but never could bring himself to read them to him because of the great reticence in their relationship. The poem has been read by countless strangers instead of by the one dying man for whom it was written.

The conspiracy of silence has generally included not only the relatives of the dying but the healing professions as well: physicians, scientists, and technicians, who by training are more concerned with fighting death than with helping their patients to meet it more easily. Their professional life is dedicated to avoiding, preventing, or at least postponing death and to developing life-preserving procedures: antibiotic therapy, chemotherapy, transfusions, infusions, transplants, and life-sustaining machines. By machine, lungs can now be kept breathing, hearts kept pumping, kidneys kept functioning. In the past, human organs had no such miraculous support systems, and without them greater numbers of people died, and died younger. The only possible benefit offered the dying then was that more of them died at home in a familiar atmosphere with people who loved them nearby.

The patient dying in the hospital today is in an alien environment made more alien if he has to be surrounded by strange tubes, bright lights, machines, and monitors—with teams of experts and skilled technicians, all strangers, concentrating their efforts on preventing death. While so much necessary intensity is concentrated on physical needs, there is a danger that the dying patient as a person may be forgotten, his other needs brushed aside.

Intensive-care procedures often save lives, and those whose lives have been saved are thankful, but some speak later about the sense of personal isolation they experienced. They could hear voices, but the voices did not usually talk to them; they were touched by gentle, capable hands, but the hands, busy with tubes and wires, usually transmitted impersonal messages. After surviving a critical illness, the recuperating patient is able to resume human contacts again, but many of the elderly remain isolated until death.

BREAKING THE SILENCE

The conspiracy of silence is not pervasive as it once was. Among certain groups of people death is currently being discussed openly and examined freely. It is the subject of books, articles, seminars, institutes, workshops, and public lectures. Concern for those who are about to die is coming not only from physicians but also from psychiatrists, social workers, philosophers, scientists, and theologians. Popular books, magazine features, and TV programs are making the general public aware that more can be offered to the critically ill than medical procedures alone to make the process of dying easier and less painful.

Thanatology, the study of death, is an emerging field of science, its name derived from *thanatos*, the Greek word for "death." Particular concern has been focused by the growing number of professionals in this new field on the emotional needs of those who are nearing death. Dr. Elisabeth Kübler-Ross, a psychiatrist, best known to the general public for her book *On Death and Dying*, observed after years of close contact with numbers of terminally ill patients that they usually go through a series of emotional stages—denial, isolation, anger, bargaining, and depression—before they finally accept the fact of their own death. Some may not have time to work through all these stages, and many have difficulty working through them alone without the help of someone who understands and who cares: a relative, a friend, a professional. In some hospitals and nursing homes today staff members are given special training to make them more responsive to the needs of the dying and to the feelings of the dying person's family.

A more all-encompassing type of care is provided by hospice programs, established originally in England for the sole purpose of offering comfort to the dying and their families. Modern hospice care began in 1967 when St. Christopher's Hospice opened its doors in London. This new approach for treating the terminally ill soon spread across the Atlantic, and the first hospice in the United States was established in 1974. Today—fifteen years later—there are 1,700 hospices located in fifty states. Of these, 800 are sponsored by hospitals, 600 are independent, and 300 are affiliated with home-health agencies.

Some hospices operate with a full team of physicians, nurses, psychiatrists, and social workers as well as homemakers and specially trained volunteers. Others are not so fully staffed, but all hospice workers are trained not to cure but to comfort the dying and to help sustain them and their families. The hospice goal is to alleviate the pain and other problems caused by the illness itself or by side effects of medication. Most hospice care is provided in the home by professionals and volunteers on a daily or occasional basis, according to the individual patient's needs, but some hospice services are located in hospitals and in nursing homes. The location is not important, since the hospice is not a place but rather a system of care that offers physical, emotional, and practical support to the terminally ill. It also recognizes and tries to ease the strains imposed on caregivers and family members who have to endure weeks, even months, of rigorous daily and nightly routines—bathing, feeding, toileting, medicating, lifting. The stress of such routines can drain the energies of the strongest and most willing caregiver. Hospice care—a night off, a weekend off, even an hour off, provided by a hospice volunteer—can give caregivers a chance to recharge their batteries and start in again. Many hospices provide counseling for family members after the death of a relative they have cared for so constantly.

Medicare and private insurance help to cover some of the cost of hospice services. A copy of *Hospice Benefits Under Medicare* is available in most local Social Security offices. Information about the location of hospices nationwide can be found by phoning the National Cancer Institute's information line, 800-4-CANCER.

It has been generally assumed that the elderly fear death less and face it with greater equanimity than the young. This may be true for many old people. They undoubtedly have had plenty of experience with death. Most of them are forced by their advancing age to acknowledge their own mortality, and their awareness is constantly reawakened as, one by one, close friends and relatives die. But even though they may fear death less, this does not mean that they are not afraid. Many are fearful until the end and never reconciled, continuing, in Dylan Thomas's words, to "rage, rage against the dying of the light." Kübler-Ross is convinced that most dying people go through the same stages, perhaps with some variation in the intensity and duration of each phase, regardless of age. The old may even begin to work through these stages prior to the period when they are actually dying, beginning in some cases when they have endured too many losses, when they become seriously incapacitated, or when they must enter an institution. Sons, daughters, and close relatives of the elderly may go through parallel emotional stages before they, too, can accept irrevocable separation.

TELLING THE
TRUTH TO THE DYING

Those who have been working closely with the dying are convinced that frankness and honesty about their physical condition is usually essential before patients and their families can begin to work through the stages of dying. A dying man has the same right to know, whether he dies at forty or at eighty. While that may be the best approach in most cases, there are always exceptions. It may be necessary to take a somewhat more cautious approach with the elderly who are confused or mentally disturbed, and there will always be some older people—just as there are younger ones—who do not want to hear the truth, rejecting it and denying it when it is offered to them. There obviously can be more than one approach to death, and truth should not be forced on anyone; neither should it be denied to those who ask for it or are willing to receive it.

You may think, as many loving children do, that you are protecting your mother, whether she is at home or in a hospital or institution, when you urge her doctor not to tell her the facts about her physical condition. You may honestly believe it is kinder to lie to her. But how kind can it be to keep her completely in the dark about what's wrong with her? How can she understand why she feels so terrible? How can she explain her aches and pains? How can she accept her limitations? Nothing is more confusing to an older person—or a younger one—than to sense that something is seriously wrong and then to be told by everyone that it's nothing, just a minor problem that should go away soon. Yet relatives and doctors have been equally timid about being honest, not realizing that uncertainty, confusion, anxiety, and distrust are usually much more damaging than the simple truth.

When Lily Simmons, a nursing-home patient, complained of abdominal pains at eighty-two, her physician in consultation with her family decided not to tell her the diagnosis they had made—carcinoma of the stomach—but told her instead that she had an allergic condition. That did not really satisfy Mrs.

Simmons, a bright, alert woman, since it did not explain the severity of her pain or her sense of foreboding.

One day, as she was signing some Medicare papers, she noticed that the diagnosis of her condition—carcinoma of the stomach—was filled in on the form. She went immediately to the nurse on the floor to ask the meaning of the word, and when she was told it meant cancer she demanded that the nurse tell her the truth. At first she was angry and resentful of both the doctors and her family, but eventually she understood their motivation. During the next weeks she went through a variety of emotions similar to the stages described by Kübler-Ross, but in time she began to reconcile herself to her condition. Since her cancer progressed slowly, because of her advanced age, she found herself once more taking an interest in the world around her and decided there were things she could still enjoy before she died. Until the last months, which came several years later, she remained quite actively involved in life around her.

Although it is important that your mother understand the truth about her condition and its implications, it is not necessary to go into great detail or to keep referring to it continually. Once she knows what's going on she can begin to prepare herself, ask questions, raise her fears, and receive reassurance. She may wonder how much pain and discomfort lie ahead and how these can be alleviated. It is not necessary, either, to tell her she is dying in so many words, because she may not be dying at the point the diagnosis is made. Her cancer may be inoperable and it may cause her death one day, or her heart condition may be serious and her next attack may kill her, but she may surprise everyone. There are all kinds of terminal illnesses, and many make slower progress in elderly bodies than in younger ones. Cancer may be detected in an eighty-year-old man, but he may die of a massive stroke before his cancer has had a chance to do much damage.

Professionals are reluctant to pinpoint months and years. The dramatic "death sentences" so popular in drama and fiction—"You have three months to live" or "one year at the most"—are less likely in real-life situations today. The future is unpredictable even for the elderly. There is evidence to suggest that those who are about to die can sometimes, in some mysterious way, postpone their death in order to remain alive for some particular occasion or until some particular piece of work is finished. It is not uncommon to hear families report, "Mother was determined to live until Billy came home from Vietnam," or "Father wanted to see Mary and Jack get married," or "He managed to stay alive until he finished his book." One indomitable grandmother has kept alive through a series of goals. As soon as one was reached, she had a new one to aim at. Now over ninety, she is determined to see a great-grandchild. So far none has yet been conceived.

Just as there are disease factors governing death, so social and psychological factors play important roles. Statisticians, demographers, and social-psychologists have documented the existence of a phenomenon which they have termed the "death dip," in which the death rate among certain groups of people drops prior to a special occasion and rises shortly afterward. A recent study reported in the *British Medical Journal* suggested that, among the elderly, an approaching birthday can be a motivation for survival since research showed that fewer older people died in the two months before their birthday. An earlier study of more than three hundred famous Americans, whose birthdays were of national significance, revealed the same pattern.

The death dip has also been noticed prior to less personal occasions, such as Thanksgiving and other holidays. In two separate studies of big cities with large Jewish populations, a death dip was documented among Jews in the period immediately preceding Yom Kippur, the most solemn day in the Jewish calendar.

Thomas Jefferson, at eighty-three, and John Adams, at ninety-one, both died on the Fourth of July, 1826, the fiftieth anniversary of their country and of the signing of the Declaration of Independence, which they had both shared in drafting. The words of the doctor who was with him document the fact that Jefferson was aware of the significance of the date until the end.

About seven o'clock of the evening of Thursday, he [Jefferson] awoke, and seeing me staying at his bedside exclaimed, "Oh, Doctor, are you still there?" in a voice, however, that was husky and indistinct. He then asked, "Is it the Fourth?" to which I replied, "It soon will be." These were the last words I heard him utter.
Merrill Peterson, *Thomas Jefferson and the New Nation*

SHOULD LIFE BE PROLONGED?

That question has been asked over and over again. Many people would give the old familiar answers: "Life must go on," or "While there's life there's hope." But is there hope for the hopeless? Must life go on in any condition? The right to die is a controversial issue, becoming even more pressuring in the recent period as more and more life-sustaining procedures keep alive men and women—old and young—who would have died fifty years ago. But there is a great difference between "being kept alive" and "living." It is possible through "heroic measures" to prolong life, but it is much more difficult to assess the value of the life that is being prolonged.

The controversy over the right to die has been making front-page news recently with dramatic cases involving young and hopelessly ill people, but the controversy has been ongoing, although less publicized, over the old and hopelessly ill. It is possible to prolong the life of a seventy-five-year-old man in a coma for months. It is possible to keep an elderly woman alive even though a stroke has condemned her to a vegetative existence. It is possible to extend life for someone over eighty with one operation after another, each one causing additional suffering. But is life worth prolonging under these conditions?

Opinion today is divided about the right to die. Some deny that right, abiding by religious teachings and secular law or because they believe that life itself must be valued regardless of its condition. Others are convinced that life without meaning and dignity has little value. The controversy is not new. As long ago as the sixteenth century, in England, Sir Thomas More, sometimes called the "Father of Euthanasia," wrote in his *Utopia*:

> If the disease be not only incurable, but also full of continual pain and anguish, then the priests and magistrate exhort the man that . . . he will determine with himself no longer to cherish that pestilent and painful disease. . . . And in so doing they tell him he shall do wisely, seeing by his death he shall lose no happiness, but end his torture. . . . They that be thus convinced finish their lives willingly, either by fasting, or else they are released by an opiate in their sleep without any feeling of death. But cause none such to die against his will.

Euthanasia for the aged was not uncommon in certain primitive cultures. Some peoples, because of the rigors of their life—particularly in nomadic tribes—were forced to abandon their very old who were helpless and ill, leaving them alone to starve or freeze to death. Some Eskimo groups left their aged to die on ice floes. But other groups found euthanasia more humane than abandonment. As one Chukchee, a reindeer-herding nomad of Siberia, put it:

> Why should not the old woman die? Aged and feeble, weary of life and a burden to herself and to others, she no longer desired to encumber the earth, and claimed of him who owned nearest relationship the friendly stroke which should let out her scanty remnant of existence.

Leo Simmons, *The Role of the Aged in Primitive Societies*

Today even those who believe in the right to die are not unanimous in their feelings about it. There are the advocates of "active euthanasia," the ending of life for the hopelessly ill and disabled, and the advocates of "passive euthanasia," the withdrawal of all life-saving medications and interventions without which life cannot go on. Whatever the logic and reason in either approach, one crucial question remains unanswered: "If such decisions are to be made, who will make them?" Who will decide what condition is hopeless? Who will decide when life is no longer meaningful? Will it be the relatives of the dying—those with the closest emotional ties? Or will it be the doctors—those with the best medical judgment? Such power over life and death may be too great to be entrusted to any single person or group of people, who might use it irresponsibly or for personal gain. Dr. Robert Butler suggests that a panel of experts be established—including not only physicians but also psychiatrists, social workers, and legal advisers, as well as family members—to judge each individual case.

Many older people feel that they themselves are the only ones who should have the power over their own lives, and many are careful to let their feelings be known clearly in advance. Some discuss their desires with their families, exacting promises that no "heroic measures" be taken on their behalf. Others feel safer when they put everything in writing; just as they specify certain funeral arrangements or bequeath their bodies for medical research, in the same way they may leave written instructions about their desire to die with dignity or sign a "living will." One such document is addressed "To my family, my physician, my lawyer, my clergyman. To any medical facility in whose care I happen to be. To any individual who may become responsible for my health, welfare, or affairs." The document states:

> *If the situation should arise in which there is no reasonable expectation of my recovery from physical or mental disability, I request that I be allowed to die and not be kept alive by artificial means or "heroic measures." I do not fear death itself as much as the indignities of deterioration, dependence and hopeless pain. I, therefore, ask that medication be mercifully administered to me to alleviate suffering even though this may hasten the moment of death.*

By 1972, thousands of copies of the living will had been distributed by the Euthanasia Educational Council. By 1988, the number distributed was in the millions. Concern for Dying and several other organizations are supporting the individual's right to die, and distribute their own living wills. These documents have legal status in thirty-eight states and the District of Columbia.

Occasionally the elderly are not content to put their trust in others, and they make their own decisions on when and how to die, choosing to end their lives by suicide. The public—as well as philosophers, scholars, and theologians—usually responds with shock to the act of suicide, which goes against most religious and moral teaching. Yet in 1975, seventy-eight-year-old Dr. Henry P. Van Dusen, a world-famous theologian, and his wife committed suicide together. Ill for several years and knowing they would both soon become completely dependent on others, they felt there would be little meaning or dignity in the life ahead for them. In the letter they left behind, the Van Dusens wrote: "Nowadays it is difficult to die. We feel this way we are taking will become more usual and acceptable as the years pass. Of course, the thought of our children and our grandchildren makes us sad, but we still feel this is the best way and the right way to go." In commenting on their suicide in the *Saturday Review*, editor Norman Cousins asked, "What moral or religious purpose is celebrated by the annihilation of the human spirit in the triumphant act of keeping the body alive? Why are so many people more readily appalled by an unnatural form of dying than by an unnatural form of living?"

A TIME FOR
EMOTIONAL DARING

Elisabeth Kübler-Ross, in *Questions and Answers on Death and Dying*, described her answer to the question "How do you, if you do, protect yourself emotionally in your relationships with terminally ill patients?" Her reply was, "I dare to get emotionally involved with them. This saves me the trouble of using half my energy to cover up my feelings." The conspiracy of silence about death, the awkwardness so many feel about it, their discomfort, often makes those most closely involved with the dying do just that—waste their energy covering up their feelings, the very feelings which could provide so much comfort and support.

But sometimes there is little opportunity for this closeness. Babies in the past were born at home, with fathers and close relatives hovering nearby. The dying died in the same environment. Birth and death were events not to be experienced alone but to be shared. In that intimate atmosphere emotions could be shared, too—the painful as well as the joyous ones. Birth and death in this century have moved out of the home into institutions. The moves were essential in order to provide the greatest protection for the new lives and the old ones. But in this highly efficient and highly sterile atmosphere, strangers may usher in life and usher it out, while those with the deepest personal ties can feel like trespassers. There is a growing trend—encouraged by some doctors, nurses, and hospitals, and by young parents themselves—to reinstate the family in the process of birth. In some hospitals fathers are allowed to be with their wives during deliveries so that the ones most intimately involved can share the first minutes of life. The same kind of closeness could be allowed during the last minutes of life. But this is not always possible, as one middle-aged son discovered:

Ellis Martin was very fond of his friend Tom's father and quite shaken when he heard the elderly man had an inoperable brain tumor. But Ellis learned a lot from watching the family during this period. He described it this way: "When they learned that nothing more could be done for Tom's father in the hospital, they—his wife and his children—decided to bring him home to die— to the house by the lake which he had inherited from his own father. This was what he wanted, and they knew it. I thought it would be terribly hard to visit him, but it wasn't—even when he got much sicker. He lay there in his room, looking out over the lake which he had always loved, and he could hear his family in other parts of the house—his wife, his children, his grandchildren— preparing meals, playing games, talking to each other. He could hear laughter and music. They didn't hover over him, but they didn't leave him alone much either. Every once in a while someone would stop by his room to talk a little, to read, or just to sit quietly with him. Even the littlest children came. I thought then, 'What a wonderful way to die, with your whole life around you— past, present, and future.' I hoped my father could die this way, too.

"But he didn't. My father had a massive heart attack when he was eighty-three and we had to rush him to the hospital. They did everything they could to save him. We were there with him, but there was no place for us. We were only allowed to see him for a few minutes at a time—never long enough to say much. We didn't know what to say anyhow. We were in the waiting room when somebody came out and told us he was dead. I wonder if he knew we weren't with him when he died—and that he was dying alone."

II

TAKING
ACTION

7

HELPING—WHEN THEY CAN MANAGE INDEPENDENTLY

Marian Franklin—seventy-two, widowed, somewhat arthritic, and mildly diabetic—continued to live in her old neighborhood that had gone dangerously downhill. Her children, comfortably settled in pleasant suburbs, were frantic. They worried when their mother went out alone and worried when she stayed home alone. They complained that she "exhausted" herself with volunteer work at her church and were upset every fall when she went apple-picking at a friend's orchard. She kept telling them that she was fine, steadily refused their offers of help, and rejected their repeated invitations that she make her home with one of them. She was reasonably content with her life.

Eventually, her children found the opportunity they needed when an elderly woman was brutally mugged in the lobby of Mrs. Franklin's building. All the other tenants were fearful and understandably upset, including Mrs. Franklin herself, and therefore her children were able to persuade her that she was unsafe in her apartment. Within a short time they helped her move out to live with her younger son in a room they redecorated especially for her. They were delighted that they were finally able to "give Mother a good life," but wondered why she didn't seem to enjoy it the way they expected she would. She was somewhat bewildered during the move, remained apathetic and uninvolved in her new surroundings and physically frail. Everyone was heartbroken when she died of pneumonia less than a year later. They all continued to believe that they could have prolonged her life if only they had insisted she make the move earlier.

I t could be said that Mrs. Franklin was fortunate. She had loving children, eager and able to help her as she grew older. Many old mothers and fathers would envy her. It could also be said that she was unfortunate, because those loving children were unable to understand the kind of help she needed. With the best of intentions, they weakened rather than supported her.

"Help" sounds like a simple four-letter word, but many steps are involved in the helping process, and being ready and willing to help is only the first. A second step is knowing the right kind of help to give. Many well-meaning children take the first step easily but never are able to take the second, or else they fail in the process.

Help for the elderly can be undermined by the younger generations because of ignorance, lack of understanding, or total misunderstanding. In many instances they jump to false conclusions about what is best. Too little listening is done, too little attention paid to the desires and inclinations of the older person. Too little time is taken to understand him and to evaluate the adaptation he is making to his old age and its accompanying losses. Understanding in and of itself can be helpful. But understanding can go further and produce a realistic assessment of what kind of help—and how much—an elderly person actually needs in order to get along. (See Chapter 10.)

Although the term "elderly" is used to describe the sector of the population sixty-five and over, that sector is far from homogeneous. Using age sixty-five to mark the onset of old age is something of an anachronism today and serves little purpose except for determining the customary age for Social Security payments and pension checks. Sixty-five is a hangover from the 1880s when the German chancellor Otto von Bismarck had to set an age for pension benefits. He took the average life-expectancy figure—then 43—and added 50 percent more years to arrive at the figure 65. If the same formula were used today, old age would begin at 112. The tag "sixty-five and over" makes things simpler from the point of view of legislation, but in the process one label is pinned on a very diverse group of people. "Sixty-five-and-over" may cover a thirty-year time span. In addition to the tremendous diversity among the elderly as a group, aging men and women as individuals may go through many different stages. A more accurate approach, taken by some experts, would be to think of the elderly as three separate groups: the young-old (up to seventy-four), the middle-aged-old (seventy-five to eighty-five), and the old-old (eighty-five and over). Your father may live one kind of life at sixty-five, another at seventy-five, another at eighty-five, and still another at ninety-five. His needs will change accordingly. The young are inclined to forget the diversity, and to forget that needs of older people are determined not by chronological age but by the ability to manage independently.

In the next chapters we shall consider the help and understanding likely to be supportive to the elderly at strategic points along the dependency scale, ranging from the totally independent to the totally dependent:

- Older people who can manage alone and know it
- Older people who can manage alone but think they can't
- Older people who cannot manage alone

The members of each of these three categories have all suffered, in varying degrees, the losses and stresses of aging. Many are able to make successful adaptations and find at least some compensations. Others give up without a struggle. The elderly are capable of an amazing assortment of adaptations, and their capacities can be strengthened by the effective support of their children or weakened by their children's well-meaning interference—although in some instances, where parents are particularly determined, children have no effect at all.

"I'M OKAY"—THOSE WHO CAN MANAGE AND KNOW IT

Because the plight of the elderly who cannot manage is so heartrending and tragic, it is easy to forget that a large proportion of older people adapt to aging fairly successfully. A surprising number take the cumulative losses of old age in their stride, are somewhat content with their lot, and would be justifiably offended if anyone were to suggest that they were not competent to handle their own daily routines by themselves: cooking, cleaning, dressing, shopping. In addition, they feel perfectly able to take care of their own finances, entertainment, and health. They still consider themselves functioning members of society, perfectly capable of making their own decisions and deciding what is best for themselves—by themselves.

When it comes to needing help, those capable older individuals usually know when they need it, how much they need, and what kind. They can be quite definitely outspoken when they do not need any help at all. A self-reliant octogenarian has a real sense of pride and personal dignity; he may even delight in flaunting his age and letting the world know he's not finished yet. An energetic older couple may insist on roughing it on camping vacations and take pleasure in disregarding the anxious pleas of younger relatives that they vacation instead in a safe and comfortable motel.

If your parents fall into that enviable group, the best approach to take is to give them quiet support. Let them know that you accept, even admire, the lifestyle they have chosen for themselves. Jumping in with unsolicited advice or offering unwanted help may only rock the valuable equilibrium they have established, or create bad feelings. A good rule to follow here would be to let it be known that you are willing to discuss things with them and that you are willing to help if they want you to help. Even though they don't want to be dependent, they probably like to know that you are dependable. Lewis Carroll made this point in *Alice's Adventures in Wonderland*:

> *"You are old, Father William," the young man said,*
> *"And your hair has become very white;*
> *And yet you incessantly stand on your head—*
> *Do you think, at your age, it is right?"*

Father William was not asking for anyone's help to stand on his head; he managed successfully by himself. His feat may have been unusual, but if he could still perform it, how could it possibly be considered wrong? If your parents have established a way of life they feel works for *them*, it would be foolish to try to impose a different lifestyle just because *you* feel it is more appropriate.

It is easy enough to take this live-and-let-live philosophy when your parents adopt a way of life that is socially acceptable, or even admirable. It is no hardship to encourage your parents when they have found a satisfying life in a retirement village and are in a safe, comfortable environment with plenty of congenial companionship. It is even easier to applaud an elderly relative who views old age as a time of renewed vigor, creativity, vitality, and curiosity. There are numbers of remarkable old people who chart new courses for their lives after seventy and experience a kind of rebirth. Stories appear frequently in the press of seventy- or eighty-year-olds who have just completed the requirements for a high school diploma, a college degree, or even a graduate degree. It is not unusual today for a retired businessman to start a new and successful business venture at a time of life when many of his contemporaries are in wheelchairs. Those admirable examples are endlessly pleasing and reassuring to the younger generation, who can say to themselves, "That's what I'll be like when I'm old." The world loves a "wonderful old man" or a "fabulous old lady."

Quiet support for those lifestyles comes naturally. But what about the elderly who also get along completely independently but in less acceptable, less socially approved ways? It may well happen that your parents develop a lifestyle in their seventies or eighties that satisfies them perfectly well but that you find terrifying, unsatisfactory, or embarrassing. What if you fear for their safety (as did Mrs. Franklin's children), despise their hobbies, disapprove of their friends, or look down on their interests? What if your father still pursues an active sex life and your mother talks about her dates and going dancing? A live-and-let-live philosophy may not be so easy then. But if your father's lifestyle seems to be working for him, although it makes you uncomfortable, you may have to keep reminding yourself that it's his life and not yours. It does not matter that you would *prefer* him to live differently, nor what the neighbors say to your face or behind your back. If he is able to take command of his own destiny, he deserves a willing go-ahead.

Parents of adolescents or young adults often face a similar dilemma. One family decides that the older son will be a doctor, or a lawyer, or an accountant. But that son may have different ambitions for himself. Parents may wring their hands when an artist daughter paints—and starves—in a garret. "This is no life for her," they cry. But this may be just the life that stimulates and excites their daughter.

And so with older parents. It may be embarrassing to admit that your mother is obsessed by some offbeat spiritual cult, that she swears by an astrologer, that she accepts money for babysitting, mending, or ironing (even though you'd be willing to double that income for her), that she hurries off to pick fruit at harvest time. But as long as she is able to manage her own daily routine, and as long as she chooses to live this way, it is better to forget your embarrassment. No one would suggest that you have to follow your mother's spiritual leader or abide by her astrologer's prediction, but don't try to make radical changes. Enough changes will have to be made when she can no longer manage to live so independently. A well-meaning but interfering daughter might do well to ask herself before she tries to redirect her father's life, "I'm asking him to give up everything he's always known, but what am I offering him instead?"

Children court trouble for themselves not only when they try to interfere with a lifestyle that works well for their parents, but also when they try to modify behavior patterns which their parents find useful. These patterns, related to the defensive behavior discussed in Chapter 4, may be worrisome, infuriating, depressing, and irritating to the young, but can be very supportive for the old, helping to offset the strong emotional reactions brought on by the losses of aging. They may enable your parents to maintain some measure of equilibrium. If a certain behavior pattern works well, like it or not, there is no reason to interfere with it. If it does not work well (if your mother uses denial to ignore a dangerous physical symptom), then some interference may be necessary.

THE PSEUDO-HELPLESS—THOSE WHO
CAN MANAGE BUT THINK THEY CAN'T

In contrast to the resolute, independent elderly, who insist on managing their own lives, stands another group of their contemporaries, who present a totally different set of problems to their children.

While your friend down the street worries about his independent mother who won't let him take over any part of her life, you may have the opposite situation to cope with. Your mother may be in relatively good health, enjoying relatively solid finances and relatively pleasant living conditions. She may be managing perfectly well. But the problem is, you can't convince her that she is doing fine. Unable to adapt to the losses of aging, she shows increasing self-pity and inordinate anxiety, while demanding unreasonable amounts of time from you and your family. Sometimes this behavior is short-lived, following a time of crisis, but it may become chronic.

The elderly who feel they cannot live through their old age by themselves often tyrannize their children. Chapter 3 described how one particular child may be chosen or may assume the role of "Mother's support," sometimes becoming a martyr to Mother's old age. Many of the pseudo-helpless elderly like to claim that they can manage, but the minute the focus of attention is drawn away from them, they will cry for help. They often have a sixth sense of the exact moment when the child they depend on is particularly involved elsewhere.

John Farnetti's mother managed quite well some of the time but could turn helpless overnight, particularly when her only son and his family were about to leave on a trip, when a new baby was about to arrive, or when a particularly important business deal was pending. John could always expect at every crisis in his life that the phone would ring (usually late at night) and he would hear his mother's voice saying faintly, "You're going to be very upset with me." This was the dreaded but familiar opener: the overture to a new crisis that would demand John's immediate attention. He was expected to let his personal affairs simmer on a back burner while he made an emergency trip to another state to settle his mother's problem. It must be admitted that John allowed his mother to run his life and his family's.

The elderly who engage in this type of behavior do so for many reasons. One is fear or anxiety due to lack of understanding or knowledge. Some people do not understand the normal aging process. Ignorance leads them to exaggerate the danger of each physical symptom. Given greater understanding, they may be able to take their physical losses with greater equanimity and revert to less demanding behavior. In some cases, when logical explanations and reassurance are given by a child, a nurse, a doctor, or a social worker, anxiety can be allayed and episodes of panic prevented.

Reassurance and understanding do no good at all to others in the pseudo-helpless group, who make self-pity their way of life, exploiting their old age and their incapabilities in order to gain an inappropriate amount of time and attention.

> Eighty-year-old Jack Forbes was obsessed with his failing hearing and had been for years. His daughter, who had been helpful and sympathetic for a whole decade, was relieved when he finally agreed to a hearing aid, but she could not enjoy peace for long. Within the next few months, when his hearing improved, he began to complain of intestinal pain and sinus trouble. By moving on to new symptoms, he could regain the attention he lost when his hearing improved.

If life histories were to be taken of pseudo-helpless older persons, it would most likely become clear that they had always been dependent or self-centered. Old age merely provides the golden opportunity to exploit these needs more openly. Helpless behavior may also be a continuation of guilt-invoking behavior, which a parent may have used throughout life with various family members. The old ploy "I brought you up and now you leave me out in the cold" is a favorite and familiar type of guilt-producer, as is the commentary "One mother can take care of ten children, but ten children cannot take care of one mother." Such simple statements can activate ulcer-type pains and depression in quite sturdy children.

These statements, admittedly, are often rooted in reality, and many children deserve such accusations, but the words are just as frequently used as ammunition against the most devoted children, who keep asking themselves, "What more can I do?"

WHEN TO SAY NO

Just as unreasonable demands on the part of young children, teenagers, and adults can and should be turned down, there is no reason to give in to unreasonable demands from your parents. That is especially true if the demands add severe and unnecessary burdens to your life. The resulting bitterness, tension, and resentment that build up may make you completely ineffective when your parents legitimately need your help at some future time. Some children, who have never learned to say no firmly, find their only solution lies in cutting loose completely and disappearing from their parents' lives, a potentially guilt-producing act in itself. There is no reason to grit your teeth, penalize your children, or wreck your digestion while trying to satisfy your mother's unreasonable demands. Your pulse will be steadier, your intestines quieter, if you can learn to say no. Once you've said it, you may be surprised to see that it is often accepted with relative equanimity and little argument. Your mother may be relieved to know where you stand and exactly what she can expect of you. She also may catch a supportive message which tells her, "We will not treat you like a baby, because you aren't a baby. You are not help-less—you're doing all right on your own." There may be initial bitterness, but if you can live through this period, the ground rules for living will be firmly established for everyone.

"I CAN'T SAY NO"

You may not want to say no to your parents in their old age even if their demands are somewhat unreasonable and they are really getting along well. You may feel they deserve to be indulged, telling yourself that they worked hard all their lives and deserve to be pampered. But it would be a good idea to think things through less sentimentally and consider the long-range effects on yourself and the rest of the family. You could also consider the debilitating effect on your parents themselves when you allow them to be prematurely and unnecessarily dependent on you. A greater gift to them might really be to say no to unreasonable demands and refuse to allow yourself to become a partner in behavior which makes them grow old prematurely.

You may be equally reluctant to say no because you are inhibited by all sorts of unresolved conflicts. Guilt, shame, anxiety, anger always seem to get in your way, so you say yes rather than having to cope with these unpleasant emotions directly.

If you find it impossible to say no directly, it may help to make a quick run-through of the consequences to your life if you say yes.

How can I say no when Mother suddenly announces she wants to spend the summer with us?

If I say yes and let her come, we'll have to give up the camping trip to Canada which we've been planning and saving for all year. Jenny won't be able to have her best friend spend August with us because there won't be enough beds. The dog will have to be boarded because Mother's allergic. And I'll have to give up coaching the softball team because Mother hates it if I'm out at night.

After looking at the results of giving in to Mother, a better question to ask yourself might be, "How can I say yes?"

.   .

How can I say no when my father says he doesn't want to live alone in the big house anymore? But he won't give it up and he wants us to give up *our* apartment and move in with him.

If I say yes it will mean that Jim will have to commute an hour longer to his job, the kids will have to change schools, I'll be tied down with extra housework, I'll have to give up my hospital work, and I'll have to cook two sets of meals because of Dad's low-fat diet.

How can you say yes?

.   .

How can I say no to Mother when she begs to come to live with me? She's afraid to live alone even though she's managing quite well.

If I say yes we'll both go under. Mother is eighty-five and I'm nearly sixty. I'm having enough problems of my own. If she comes to live with me I'll never be able to take care of both of us.

Saying no to Mother will be kinder to her and to yourself.

.   .

Saying no doesn't mean that the subject is closed and that the desires of the older generation are ignored. A different approach can be taken: "I'm sorry, Mother [or Father], I know things are hard for you now, but your idea just won't work. Let's try to figure out a different way that's better for all of us." By rejecting the unreasonable demands of the pseudo-helpless, the younger generation need not always be accused of callousness, selfishness, or indifference. The firm *no* can ultimately be the greatest blessing to both generations.

PREPARE FOR THE DAY
WHEN THEY CAN'T MANAGE

Whether your parents can manage and know it, or can manage but *think* they can't, there is no guarantee that the situation will continue. The time to look into the future is while they are still living independently; it's also the time to explore what will happen if and when their independence runs out.

Some of the blows of old age are beyond all remedy, and no amount of advance planning can soften them. But many can be averted completely or made easier to bear. Preventive care is probably one of the most important and most neglected areas of help for older people. That may be why so many of us are caught unprepared when a crisis occurs in our parents' lives.

It's great to be able to boast with pride about a parent's independence, good health, and varied activities. It's wonderful to be able to say, as some fifty-year-old sons and daughters can, "Mother's eighty but she looks sixty-five and does everything for herself. Last year she traveled to Europe alone." The strong possibility is that this eighty-year-old woman will run into difficulty before she's finished unless a massive stroke, a fatal heart attack, or a plane crash makes it possible for her to die with her boots on.

Serious difficulties may lie ahead for even the most active parents, because tragic gaps exist in the support society provides. The sad results of insufficient advance planning are seen over and over again in hospital emergency rooms or in substandard nursing homes where families literally have to "dump" elderly relatives who can no longer manage. Such a tragedy might have been avoided if someone had given any advance thought to what would happen to them. The family usually feels the greatest sense of failure when problems occur because of lack of planning, but the older person who has not thought ahead himself should share the blame. Careful anticipation of future crises by all concerned can offset the shock, grief, disruption, and guilt which accompany them. When it comes to planning for old age, a stitch in time saves more than the proverbial nine—it can save whole families.

Ideally, planning should start in young adulthood, although few young people make any such moves other than entering a pension plan. Certainly, planning should begin by the middle years. But it is never really too late to begin, and if your parents are in their sixties now, they may still have quite a future ahead of them. According to U.S. Bureau of the Census figures, men who have reached the age of 65 can expect to live another 14.6 years to age 79.6 on the average, while women can expect to go on another 18.3 years to 83.6.

Perhaps the most effective help you can give your parents while they are still independent is preventive help: planning along with them to avoid tragedy in the future. Although easier said than done, the best way to initiate planning is in the context of open, respectful, relaxed discussion. Some parents bring up the subject spontaneously with their children or with one particular child whom they consider—sometimes mistakenly— to be the most levelheaded or caring. They want to talk about what they will do if they become sick, if their money runs out, or when one of them dies. They may just want to talk and have someone listen, or they may ask for help, suggestions, guidance. Some middle-aged children, however, are not receptive to these overtures because of their own feelings about death and dying.

Others will play their cards closer to the chest, clinging to secretiveness about their resources and about any thoughts they have for the future, becoming angry and insulted if you insinuate there could be trouble ahead. Of course, underneath the anger may lie their own fear, which they cannot face. Some will close any discussion about the future with the flat statement, "Don't worry about me. I'll be gone soon enough." Or they may loudly deny that their health could ever fail them.

Emma Dexter at seventy-seven was admired by her younger relatives and friends. Widowed and still living alone in her comfortable apartment, she dined out, went to the theater and concerts, traveled, and continued to work as a volunteer in her favorite hospital. It dawned on her suddenly that some of her younger colleagues avoided discussing any subject with her that was related to old age, even the tragic problems of some of the elderly patients—sensitive that they might be personally upsetting to her. As soon as she realized this, Emma quickly reassured them at a coffee break.

"Don't worry about my feelings," she said. "Old age isn't a touchy subject with me. I never believed I'd enjoy it as much as I do. I love talking about it—even the problems I have. Ask me anything you want."

"Are you sure, Emma?" asked a young volunteer tentatively.

"Of course," she replied.

"Well, then, I've often wondered when one of these awful stroke cases come in—does it worry you? Do you think about yourself and what could happen to you?" the younger woman said.

"*That*," replied Emma, turning on her heel and walking out of the room, "is a subject I never think about."

Your parents may share Emma's feelings, and if they have any plans for their old age tucked away in the back of their minds, they may refuse to talk about them. Their feelings should be respected and they should not be forced too suddenly into a discussion of the future. But the subject need not be dropped completely. You deserve to know what they are thinking, particularly if you are likely to figure in their plans, and you may be able to open up the touchy subject by making casual references to it from time to time.

When the casual approach does not serve to open a real discussion of your parents' plans, or their anxieties about the future, a more direct approach may be necessary. One man approached his father by saying, "Dad, Jean and I have been doing a lot of thinking about you and Mother. You're doing fine now and we hope things stay this way, but you never talk to us about what you'll do if either of you gets sick. We'd like to know what you're thinking and what you'd like us to do."

If nothing works and your parents steadily refuse to share their plans with you or even to plan at all, you can do some planning on your own, so that you will be ready with some reasonable alternatives when a sudden crisis descends.

Future planning for your parents should focus on three major areas of their lives: their health, their social world (including the big question "Should they live with you?"), and—what may be the most crucial area of the three—their finances.

HEALTH CARE PLANNING

Even if they seem to be in excellent health, all aging individuals should have frequent regular medical checkups. A seemingly healthy seventy-year-old may have an undetected condition which can lead to a catastrophic illness or further physical deterioration. Early detection and early treatment can prevent some conditions from progressing further. Once the symptoms become obvious, it may be too late to reverse the disease. Incipient diabetes and high blood pressure, for instance, can be brought under control if they are detected early. They do not need to become fatal or incapacitating.

Some basic health education is essential for everyone. Many people, old and young alike, are unaware of the danger signals of cancer or the symptoms of a heart attack. Health education includes nutritional guidance. Medical studies repeatedly show that poor nutrition is the cause of many problems formerly attributed to the aging process. Since older people living alone tend to eat only the foods that they like and that are cheap and easy to prepare, eventual deterioration may come as much from inadequate diet as from age. They may hardly eat at all if they have no one to eat with. When they become seriously ill and are hospitalized, they often not only recover from their illness during their stay but also regain much of their former vitality. The balanced diet offered by hospital dieticians can often reverse the process of deterioration in the very patients who frequently complain loudly, "The food here is so terrible I wouldn't give it to a dog!"

Basic instruction in bodily care and personal safety is equally essential. The importance of regular exercise, tailored to each individual's personal capacities, should be stressed, as well as regular attention to teeth, gums, hair, and nails. (Nail care is particularly important for diabetics.) Some discussion of sexual matters should be included. Safety measures should be emphasized: handrails and grabrails in the bathroom to prevent slipping, unwaxed floors, special clothing (elimination of tight garters, knee socks, and corsets), and an awareness of the adverse effects of alcohol and tobacco. New developments in optical and hearing aids should be pointed out. Older people need to be cautioned on the use and abuse of drugs—prescription and nonprescription—and taught how to recognize side effects. Ideally, the elderly should be convinced that they do not have to accept what was once considered "normal" aging, that even if they cannot stop the aging process completely, they have the power to stem the tide and are in control of their own bodies—except in cases of disease, accident, and trauma. Following instructions on bodily care and safety may not make older people live longer, but surely it will help them to live better and feel more youthful. Dr. T. Franklin Williams, director of the National Institute on Aging, claims that "the trick is to die young as late as possible."

Focusing on the whole range of health and hygienic needs can be of double benefit to the elderly. They will understand something about preventive medicine and at the same time understand more clearly just what is happening to their bodies as they grow older. Emotional preparedness can often forestall or minimize the anxiety and depression that accompany serious physical losses. You may recoil from discussing their possible physical deterioration with your parents, fearful that such ominous predictions will depress them. (You may also recoil because these predictions depress *you* and make you anxious about *your* own future.) Rather than producing negative reactions, however, a full and thorough knowledge of possible afflictions of old age can have the opposite result for the elderly. Fear of the unknown can be more frightening. Open discussion also works against denial and the childish game many old people play: "If I don't think about it [some alarming symptom], it will go away." Many young people play the same game, but with the elderly, "it" is not likely to go away and is likely to get worse. Denial prevents care and cure and leads to further deterioration.

Any discussion of future health care has to touch on the dreaded subject of catastrophic illness and physical incapacity. Either situation will make it impossible for the older person to care for himself. That is the most painful area to open up, and some parents cannot face it at all. Your mother may be touching on the subject when she talks to you about how she will live "after Father is gone." But she may not be able to move further ahead and discuss what could happen if she has a stroke "that paralyzes me." The younger generation may be equally reluctant to contemplate these possibilities. One parent may open up the discussion, only to be turned aside by the child: "When the time comes that I can't walk anymore," a severely crippled mother may begin, and then be quickly interrupted by her daughter with, "Oh, Mother, don't talk that way. It's not going to happen."

Her mother may have done a lot of thinking about the future. She may have some strong feelings about her preferences and really want to voice them. These preferences should be explored whenever possible. Some older people decide that a good nursing home will be the best solution. They may turn to their children for help in finding a suitable one. (Chapter 9 deals with nursing home selection.)

Others, who dread the idea of nursing homes, admit that they hope to remain right where they are. An investigation of how much outside care is available in a given community could be reassuring and establish whether this hope is realistic. (Chapter 8 reviews community services.) Your parents may imply they hope to move in with you or other relatives or a special friend. If you already know that such moves will be impossible, make it clear as soon as you can and then move on quickly to alternative plans. Promises that can't possibly be kept should be avoided, as should deathbed promises. Unless you have considered the possibility carefully, instead of just emotionally, you may rue the day that you promised your dying mother, "Of course, I'll bring Dad to live with us," or, "I promise never to put you in a nursing home." Deathbed promises can produce the same chain of disastrous consequences as the question "How can I say no?" They can put a stranglehold on the living. When such promises are broken a son (or daughter) may be accused of bad faith by the rest of the family and by a more severe judge: himself.

Nothing is lost by anticipating future problems and making a tentative plan of action. Like insurance that may never need to be used, the plans are comforting to have in reserve. They may never need to be activated if your parents are spared disabling illness, but if disaster does come, you will not have to go through the additional insult of being caught unprepared, floundering helplessly, and having to resort to makeshift, unsatisfactory solutions.

Once you have opened up the whole painful subject of possible deterioration with your parents, you also have an opportunity to help them consider what will happen if, eventually, they have to give up some of the activities they enjoy the most. The active sixty-five-year-old who still spends hours on the tennis court may need to review other outlets which do not require such physical stamina. Similarly, progressive arthritis may be a painful blow to a woman who is known for her fine embroidery. Failing eyesight may disrupt the life of the book-lover, and loss of hearing end hours of contented listening for the music-lover.

Much more is known today about the activities that can be undertaken successfully by handicapped older people, and the elderly are continually contradicting the old adage "You can't teach an old dog new tricks." Sixty-, seventy-, and even eighty-year-olds are proving it is not necessarily ever too late to take up a musical instrument, a paintbrush, yoga, meditation, sculpture, indoor gardening, or creative writing. An instructor in a correspondence school for writers reports that many of her students are sixty-five and older, and some in their eighties—and that the senior group are just as productive and eager as their junior classmates. Senior citizen centers in the community often provide a variety of activities.

Now is also the time for your parents to investigate—by themselves or with your help—organizations which actively promote the welfare of the elderly: the Gray Panthers, the American Association of Retired Persons (AARP), and the National Council of Senior Citizens. (See Appendix A, pages 316–20.) Opportunities for paid or volunteer work may be found through government programs or groups like Retired Seniors Volunteer Program (RSVP). There is a lot of time to be filled in the later decades, even when energy is limited, and finding gratifying activities can have a positive effect on the total health and well-being of the elderly.

SOCIAL PREPAREDNESS

The future well-being of the elderly is also greatly dependent on the social supports they will be able to rely on. Advance planning should also consider whether continuing contacts will be possible with friends, family, and other meaningful groups or individuals. Who will be around in the future for your parents to turn to for affection and companionship, as well as for help with chores, transportation, and small emergencies? How accessible is their housing to church or temple and community recreational activities? Would moving to a different location provide greater safety and easier social contacts? These questions about social supports are often tied in with health and financial problems. If physically disabled or financially strapped, the elderly may not be able to visit friends easily or have friends visit them. Furthermore, if they live far from medical services, it may one day cost too much in physical and financial terms to get essential medical care.

Although it may be clear to you that one day your parents will have to move, you may have a hard time convincing them. They may refuse to listen when you point out that their friends are slowly vanishing, that their neighborhood is going downhill, that the house is really too big for them, or that they may not always be able to maintain it. Their home may mean so much to them that they cannot contemplate living anywhere else. Some old people willingly suffer social isolation, loneliness, serious inconvenience, and unsafe conditions in order to stay right where they are. Although you may find more appropriate, safer places for them to live right in their own community, even around the corner, they may keep on insisting that there's no place like home for them. (Special housing for the elderly is discussed in Chapter 8.)

Even if they are willing to give up their home, they may have a hard time deciding where to go. Moving is not always advisable, and any move, particularly a distant one, should be weighed carefully. You may be able to point out potential difficulties they had not considered: a retirement community several thousand miles away may make sense for the immediate moment when your parents are "young-old," but what of the more remote future when they become "old-old"? What if they become incapacitated far away and need your help? What if they need a nursing home and there is none convenient in their new location? What if you want to bring them back again from two thousand miles away to be near you, and they have lost their residency rights in your state and may no longer be eligible for certain services?

Before your parents make a move to a distant place, or even to a new location nearby, one that would isolate them from familiar social activities or necessary health facilities, it is important to voice your reservations in advance. "It's your move," you might say pleasantly, "and I'm not going to stop you. But remember, if you're way out there I can't promise I'll be able to drive you as many places as I do now—and you'll hardly ever be able to see Aunt May and Uncle George."

SHOULD THEY LIVE WITH YOU?

Even though a negative answer can be legitimately given, this question can provoke stabs of guilt in even the most resilient children. Somewhere way back, many of us formed the erroneous but unshakable belief that yes, indeed, aging parents *should* live with us—and that there is something lacking in us if we don't make it possible. In Lou Meyer's short story "Live a Little," published in the *New Yorker* in 1980, the narrator describes meeting Abrams, an outspoken elderly resident in his mother's nursing home:

> There are tears in Abrams's eyes as he turns to me. "How is it, young man, that your poor mother, a veritable jewel among women, is spending her remaining years living here in the Home? Wasn't there a small place for her in your house? Under the sink? On the piano? In a dresser drawer?"

Many of us can laugh at Abrams's words, but accompanying the laughter may be a sigh or a small prick of guilt. It can be painful when you have to admit that you cannot ask your mother or father to live with you. You may have quite legitimate reasons, such as insufficient living space, ill-health, or no settled home, or simply longstanding personality clashes—"She'd drive me crazy in a minute," or "My marriage wouldn't take it." But how much more painful it is to take such a giant step, invite your mother to live with you, and then find out later that it just plain does not work. It may make you feel better to try living together, even though you fail, so you can comfort yourself later by saying, "Well, I did my best," but what a price you may have to pay later in terms of your subsequent relationship with her and the responsibility you feel for having disrupted her life!

If you are feeling that you ought to ask your mother to live with you, even though you are reluctant to, it might be of some comfort to know that other people share that reluctance. National surveys consistently show that the majority of adults in the United States, young and old alike, think it is a bad idea for elderly parents and their children to live together. Only about 14 percent live with sons, daughters, or other close relatives. It might be reasonable to assume that the strongest opposition to such living arrangements comes from the younger generation, but it is not true; the surveys show that the older the individuals, the less likely they are to favor living with their children. Older people particularly do not want to be burdens.

Rather than asking a parent to live with them permanently, some children think a part-time invitation is the best solution: "Mother lives with us in the summer, and then she goes to my brother Bill until New Year's. She's at Jeannie's all spring. We've decided that's the best arrangement for all of us." It may well be a good arrangement for the children, but what about Mother? Older people usually function best with stable roots and less change. Mother, in that case, must have felt she was on the road all the time. A more permanently satisfactory situation could have been worked out by her three children.

Two- and three-generation families living in one household occur for a number of reasons:

- A parent is widowed (or divorced) and, although physically independent, is emotionally dependent and too fearful or helpless to live alone.
- A parent, physically incapacitated and incapable of living alone, wants to be cared for by a child rather than by strangers or in a nursing home.
- Parents and children decide to pool their finances so that both generations can live more comfortably, or they may live together because they get along well and choose to have a combined household.
- An older but somewhat active parent escapes a lonely life by living with a child but at the same time fills a useful function, such as that of babysitter or housekeeper, freeing the child (usually the daughter

or daughter-in-law) of many household chores and making it possible for her to pursue a career or a special talent.

Many parents, aware of the pitfalls or reluctant to give up their independence, state flatly long before the issue comes up that they will "never, under any circumstances," live with any of their children. Some parents even mean it. Ironically enough, it is often the children of those very parents who press the invitations most strongly. But even if your mother hints subtly, asks directly, or even pleads to live with you, sentiment should not dictate your decision. Instead, try to avoid emotion and base your choice on cold, careful analysis of your own situation, the wishes of the rest of your immediate family, and the history of your past relationships with her. Consider these questions:

1. How does your husband (or your wife) feel? (This is perhaps the most important.)
2. What kind of financial arrangements are being considered?
3. What kind of living space will there be for everyone? (Cramped quarters can wreck the best relationships.)
4. Will she depend completely on you and your family for companionship and entertainment? What about other friends, relatives, contemporaries? What about recreational and religious needs?
5. Can you *really, honestly* expect to live comfortably together? Do your personalities clash? How have previous visits gone? How often, during these visits, did you (or your wife or husband) have a migraine headache or an ulcer flare-up?
6. When she visited you in the past, did you always count the days until she left?
7. Can she take a back seat in the running of the household and the rearing of the children? Of course, promises can be made, but will they be kept?
8. Would she by temperament, education, or social experience feel continually out of place in your home? With your friends?
9. Will you be able to provide ongoing, accessible, competent medical care?
10. Do you treasure your privacy?
11. Would it be wise to uproot her from her familiar surroundings? Her friends? Her church? Her doctor?

These questions make up a rigorous test and should be taken by both generations. If you and your mother manage to pass it well—and that can happen—you have a good chance of creating a successful two- or three-generation family. If you fail the test, it is better to know it before you find yourself tied into a situation that is unworkable for everyone. All these questions can be faced and pondered before any crisis strikes and one of your parents suddenly needs a new place to live. Do not move into the future on the basis of unspoken or poorly considered assumptions.

Kathleen Graham lived comfortably with her husband until his death. She was left financially well off and remained healthy enough to keep her own apartment, but it was generally assumed by her children and relatives that she would move in with her only daughter if she ever became incapacitated. At least, that was assumed by her three sons. Julie, the daughter, by remaining silent, seemed to share the family assumption. In reality, Julie was far from eager for the move, and her husband and children were equally against it. Whenever she visited, Mrs. Graham usually managed to tangle with her son-in-law and upset her grandchildren. To complicate things, Mrs. Graham had a hidden competitive relationship with her daughter which made it difficult for Julie to accept comfortably her role as mother and wife.

But Julie kept quiet out of her sense of duty, her guilt, and her concern over what everyone else would say. No alternative plans were made, therefore, and when Mrs. Graham suffered a paralytic stroke, she was brought to live in Julie's house after she had made a partial recovery. Her presence caused all the problems that Julie had anticipated and feared previously, as well as new problems resulting from her mother's illness. Eventually, with bitter, guilty feelings, Mrs. Graham had to be resettled in an excellent nearby nursing home. The old lady felt betrayed as long as she lived, and Julie never completely recovered from her feeling of failure.

SHOULD THEY LIVE WITH OTHERS?

Those unfamiliar with the problems of old age automatically assume that when elderly parents begin to lose their independence there are only two choices for them. If they can no longer live alone, they must either live with a child or enter a nursing home. That assumption is wrong. There are other options. Special housing for the elderly—admittedly in short supply—is available in many parts of the country. Sponsored by church organizations, community groups, private investors, and sometimes established with government funds, these facilities admit the well and "independent" elderly and provide them with easy-to-care-for living units. Some of these also offer meals, housekeeping services, and recreational activities. Most important, perhaps, is the fact that they provide safety, companionship, and in some instances assurances of care in the case of illness and disability. These facilities are sometimes referred to as retirement communities or congregate housing. (See "Special Housing with Special Care," Chapter 8, page 202.)

Some older persons choose not to live in housing that includes only their own age group. They prefer to live near old and young alike. Yet a move may still be wise for them for reasons of safety, accessibility to services, social stimulation, and ease of housekeeping.

All pros and cons should be weighed when considering any move. After finding a perfect retirement community near your own home, have you stopped to wonder whether the place will be equally perfect for your parents if it forces them to relocate from their familiar community? The director of a retirement complex in a large Midwestern university town reported that the majority of their residents made quick adjustments. The poorest adjustments were made by those who had moved from a different state in order to be close to a son or a daughter. Having left homes, friends, and longstanding routines far behind, they had nothing familiar in their new situation except their children. Their children replaced one burden of long-distance worrying about their parents' welfare with a different burden—worrying about their parents' morale around the corner.

FINANCIAL PREPAREDNESS

Money can be a touchy subject, even in the closest of families. Men are often unwilling to discuss their finances even with their wives. Widows may be equally secretive with their children. There are still people who claim, proudly or smugly, "We don't discuss money in our family." That may have been another sign of good breeding in Victorian days, but now, one hundred years later, it can be a prelude to disaster.

The elderly may be secretive if they feel—and sometimes they are right—that their children are always trying to find out what inheritance can be expected. They also may be secretive if they are ashamed they have so little. But your parents may be willing to explore their financial future with you. There is no need to imply that you question their ability to manage intelligently, but you may be able to point out pitfalls ahead that they have not considered, or benefits that are due them which they had not heard about. Some older people are fully aware of the economic realities, but others may not realize that an ever-increasing proportion of their limited income will have to be devoted to health needs as time goes on, or be fully aware of the rate of inflation and the limitations of a fixed income steadily decreasing in buying power. It is also important to consider how they will be able to cope with the cost of a serious illness, and to find out exactly how much of the cost will be covered by insurance.

If they are unwilling to discuss the dollars and cents of their own personal income and assets, you may find it helpful to inform yourself about the variety of financial supports available at present for the elderly in America. Once you know what these supports are—the range of their payments, who is eligible for them, and how they are administered—you may have a more realistic understanding of your parents' current and future financial situation. But always remember that what you learn today may be changed tomorrow. The entire financial picture for the elderly is in a state of flux. Costs and benefits change from one year to the next. It is hoped that benefits will continue to change for the better, but there is always the danger that cutbacks will be made if economic conditions worsen. In 1986, 54 percent of those sixty-five or older were dependent exclusively on retirement benefits: Social Security, and public and private pensions. Some 17 percent continued to earn money by working, 26 percent had income from assets, 8 percent received public assistance, and 3 percent drew veterans' benefits; 3 percent had outside sources of support, such as contributions from their families.

SOCIAL SECURITY

You may feel somewhat reassured if your parents tell you that they are receiving money both from Social Security and from pension funds. But even though the intent of the Social Security Administration, when it was established in 1935, was to provide ongoing financial security for Americans after retirement, inflation has turned that dream into a pipe dream for many. Pension checks and Social Security checks, even in combination, cannot keep up with rising prices. The dollars and cents on most monthly checks confirm this story. Your father's Social Security check from age sixty-five onward depends on his average earnings over a period of years prior to his retirement. During that time both he and his employer were contributing equal amounts to the Social Security trust fund. If he retired before he was sixty-five (this is permitted after age sixty-two), his checks are reduced accordingly. If he delayed retirement until after sixty-five, his benefits are slightly higher.

If your mother is still alive and has been working, she is entitled to her own Social Security. If she did not work and make independent contributions, she then qualifies as your father's dependent and collects an amount equal to half his check. In other words, two people are entitled to one-and-a-half payments. If a wife who has worked finds that Social Security benefits she would receive as her husband's dependent are higher than her own benefits would be, she may choose to be considered his dependent. This means, however, that she forefeits all contributions that she and her employer have made to the Social Security fund. (The same is true for a husband who chooses to be considered his working wife's dependent.)

If your father keeps on working after retirement, he is allowed, as of 1988, to earn up to $8,800 annually without affecting his benefits if he retires at age sixty-five, but only up to $6,120 annually if he retires between ages sixty-two and sixty-five. These limits are exclusive of non-work sources of income: dividends, interest, or pension payments. If your father's earnings go over the limits, $1.00 is deducted from his Social Security check for every $2.00 he earns over $8,800 (or $6,120 if under sixty-five). He will receive full benefits in any month in which he does not earn more than $700 (sixty-five) or $510 (under sixty-five). If he takes seasonal employment, therefore, he is not penalized in the months he is not working unless his annual total exceeds the limit. One small note of comfort: at age seventy-two he will be permitted to return to full-time employment without any reduction in his benefits—*if* he lives that long, *if* he is healthy enough, and *if* anyone will give him a job.

What does all that mean in cold cash? Not very much today, unfortunately. The *maximum* monthly retirement benefit paid to a retired worker who turned sixty-five by December 1987 was $953.88. However, the *average* benefits paid after December 1987 was $513 to a single worker.

The moment your mother is widowed, her financial situation almost automatically goes downhill unless she has independent assets. If your father died before retirement age, having accumulated but never collected any of his Social Security benefits, your mother can collect 100 percent as his dependent when she reaches sixty-five. If she is already collecting her own benefits, she has a choice: she can either continue independently or collect as your father's widow, whichever amount is higher. She cannot collect both. If your father had already been collecting before he died, according to a formula which takes into account the length of time he had been collecting, your mother's benefits will be reduced.

If your mother has been collecting her own benefits and decides to remarry, her checks will not be affected. But if she has been collecting as your father's widow, she again has two choices: she can collect as your dead father's dependent, receiving half his benefits but losing her widow's status—which probably provided a larger amount—or she can collect as the dependent wife of her second husband. She will obviously choose the system which pays better. But she may decide to choose neither and turn down a second marriage because it costs too much and she cannot afford the luxury. Unwilling to lose her widow's benefits, she may instead set up extramarital housekeeping with the man she would like to marry and, by pooling resources with him, gain a somewhat greater state of financial security. Such a decision is particularly hard on conventional, self-respecting older people, but according to current Social Security regulations, no matter which way the pie is sliced, women who did not work come out receiving the smaller share. Any confusion that you or your parents feel about their benefits, entitlements, or eligibility can usually be cleared up by a phone call or a visit to your local Social Security office, listed in the telephone directory under U.S. Government, Department of Health and Human Services, Social Security Administration. A staff member should be able to answer your questions and also to supply you with a variety of free pamphlets explaining the workings of Social Security.

SOCIAL SECURITY IN THE FUTURE

There is much apprehension about the future bankruptcy of the Social Security system. Admittedly it is overburdened now partly because of inflation and the need to increase benefits according to rising living costs, and partly because the median age of the population is shifting upward. The architects of the system established in 1935 expected that funds contributed by the workers of America, the employers, and the self-employed would go toward supporting the retired, over-sixty-five segment of the population as well as younger people who were disabled. But in those days the ratio of old to young was much lower. This ratio has been steadily increasing over the years. In 1950, for every retired person collecting benefits, there were 7.5 workers. In 1979 there were 5.4, and in 1986 there were 5. By the year 2000, there may be only 2. Legislators are debating a variety of different solutions to shore up the threatened system, including raising the age at which benefits may begin. While drastic revisions may be made in the future, the chances are minimal that these will affect any retired person already receiving Social Security benefits.

PENSIONS

Unless your parents have other assets, the only way they can get along reasonably well is if they have Social Security and adequate pension benefits. (Many pensions are far from adequate.) A variety of retirement systems do provide reasonable incomes for retired personnel: the Federal Retirement System, the Teachers Insurance and Annuity Association, veterans' pensions, and many union and company plans. There are also a number of private pension plans for self-employed men and women.

But many workers arrive at retirement age with no pensions at all or find when they near age sixty-five that the pensions they had been counting on vanish before they can reap the benefits. The faithful worker is not always rewarded when he retires. An assistant secretary of the Department of Labor testified at a congressional hearing in 1969: "If you remain in good health and stay with the same company until you are sixty-five, and if the company is still in business, and if your department has not been abolished and if you have not been laid off for too long a period, and if there is enough money in the fund, and if that money has been prudently managed, you will get a pension" (Thomas R. Donahue, quoted in the *Washington Post,* November 24, 1970). The statement is still true today nearly twenty years later. Factories and plants may close down, leaving employees near retirement and unprotected. Pension rights may be lost if any elderly worker is laid off, retires too soon, or transfers to another job. The money such workers have paid into a pension fund may be forfeited. Pension reform legislation was introduced with the Employee Retirement Income Security Act of 1974, popularly known as the Pension Reform Act, which established an Office of Employee Benefits Security under the Department of Labor to investigate questions and complaints from individuals about their pension rights.

Social Security was never intended to serve as the total financial support of elderly Americans. It was expected that it would be supplemented by other sources of retirement income—private savings and private pensions. These three sources of income are referred to in other countries— Switzerland and West Germany, for example—as the three pillars of retirement income. But many of the elderly in the United States are supported by one pillar only: Social Security. This explains why too many live at, below, or near the poverty line. There has been no broad coverage of the non-retired population with adequate pension plans. Those not covered or covered inadequately have had no opportunity to prepare for retirement. How to increase participation in retirement programs is a major challenge facing policymakers today who are working to improve the financial security of future retirees.

SUPPLEMENTAL SECURITY INCOME (SSI)

What can be done if your parents' monthly income, including their Social Security, is inadequate? They can—if they are not doing so already— apply for additional income under the federal Supplemental Security Income program, which provides additional funds for blind, disabled, and aged people with inadequate resources

Your father, at sixty-five or over, is eligible for minimum SSI benefits if his monthly income falls below $354 or if he and your mother together have a monthly income below $532 (1988 figures). They do not have to be destitute in order to apply. Certain personal and household possessions, with a limit of $2,000, will not be counted against them. They may own a house; they may own a car with a retail value of up to $4,500. A car will not be counted at all if it is used for transportation to a job or to regular treatments for a specified medical problem. The cash value of their life insurance policies with face values of $1,000 or less is not counted, nor are burial plots they may have bought for themselves and other members of their immediate family. Your father may retain up to $1,000 in burial funds for himself and up to $1,000 in burial funds for your mother (or his current spouse if he has remarried). Cash resources of

$1,900 for an individual or $2,850 for a couple were permitted in 1988, but have been increased in 1989 to $2,000 for an individual and $3,000 for a couple. The first $20 of their retirement check is not counted. The first $65 of their earnings and half of the remainder are not counted either.

Eligibility requirements for SSI can be checked at your local Social Security office. These requirements are standard across the country. There is variation, however, in the amount of SSI benefits. As of 1988, all but seven states add to the federal minimum with a "state supplement." Those states that do not are: Arkansas, Georgia, Kansas, Mississippi, Tennessee, Texas, and West Virginia. In those states which do add to the minimum, the supplement varies. As of 1988 supplements range from $2 to $393 a month for an individual. Only four states—Alaska, California, Connecticut, and Massachusetts add to the mininum to bring benefits up to the poverty level: $3,770 for an individual.

EXAMPLE: John Doe is sixty-six in 1988. He does not work and lives alone in a small house he owns. He has $1,500 in the bank. He has no pension and no contributions from his children. His only income is his monthly Social Security check.

Social Security check	$230
Less deductible	− 20
Countable income	$210
Supplemental Security Income minimum	$354
Less countable income	−210
	$144
Federal SSI check	$144
Social Security check	+230
TOTAL INCOME:	$374

If John Doe lives in one of the states that does not provide a supplement, his income is $374. If he lives in California, which adds a $221 supplement, his monthly income is $595. If he lives in Oklahoma, which adds $64, his monthly income is $438. If he lives in Maine, which adds $10, his income is $384. The state supplements are January 1988 figures and are, of course, subject to change. Some states decrease their supplements when federal benefits are increased.

A sizable number of older people, however, although eligible for SSI, do not make use of it. Sometimes they are completely unaware of its existence. Sometimes they have modest savings tucked away—just enough to make them ineligible. But many are too proud and independent, unwilling to accept assistance. While SSI was intended to be a supplement to Social Security rather than a welfare program, it does not seem to have been able to shake off the stigma of welfare. Some older people therefore refuse to apply for it.

How are Social Security and SSI similar? Both programs are run by the Social Security Administration of the Department of Health and Human Services of the U.S. government. People can get both if they are eligible for both. Anyone who is dissatisfied with a ruling under either program has a right of appeal through the Office of Hearings and Appeals of the Social Security Administration. (Ask for details at your local office.)

How are they different? Social Security benefits are paid from contributions made by the working population under sixty-five. (Income up to $48,000 a year is taxed as of 1989.) As of 1988, employees and employers must each pay 7.51 percent of the employee's wages into Social Security. Self-employed people must pay 15 percent of their income. The rates include 1.05 percent for hospital insurance under Medicare. Future rate increases can be expected, raising the tax to 7.65 percent in 1990. Similar increases will affect the self-employed. The money for SSI assistance comes from general funds of the U.S. Treasury: personal income taxes, corporation taxes, and other sources.

Social Security is uniform throughout the United States. SSI varies from state to state. Social Security is a program of insurance wherein benefits depend on average earning over a period of years. SSI is a program of *assistance* wherein benefits depend on need.

INDIRECT NONCASH SUPPLEMENTS

Some financial aid is provided for the elderly through programs that offer them not money itself but opportunities to cut down on what they spend. Title III C of the Older Americans Act makes funds available to the states for projects providing meals for the elderly: hot lunches, congregate meals (meals served in a central location—church, synagogue, senior center etc.), and some home-delivered meals for the homebound. (See Chapter 8.) Everyone over sixty is eligible, and the cost is determined by the individual's ability to pay. Unfortunately, there are only a limited number of these projects serving a limited number of meals in a limited number of locations.

Government food stamps and the Commodity Distribution Program (under the U.S. Department of Agriculture) also help to defray food costs, but here again the needs of the elderly far exceed the available supply of stamps, which must be shared by the needy of every age. The federal government also provides rental assistance and, in a few locations, public housing to low-income older people. Once again the need far exceeds the supply.

Taxpayers over age sixty-five are allowed some benefits under the taxation regulations. Three provisions in the federal tax code benefit older people (a fourth, the additional exemption for those over age sixty-five, was eliminated after 1987 by the Tax Reform Act of 1986):

1. The exclusion of veterans' pension income and, for those with less than $25,000 (single) or $32,000 (couple) adjusted gross income, the exclusion of Social Security and railroad retirement benefits from taxation.
2. The one-time exclusion of up to $125,000 in capital gains from sale of a home after age fifty-five.
3. The elderly tax credit for low-income individuals with few or no Social Security benefits.

A number of states and local communities also offer property tax relief, rental assistance, and heating-cost assistance to older homeowners and tenants.

Depending on where they live, the elderly may find a variety of different ways to save money. Some communities give out half-fare or free transportation cards; some supermarkets issue their own food stamps providing a 10 percent reduction on total costs; some movie houses offer half-price tickets at certain hours. Many of these commercial businesses do not make loud public announcements of reduced prices for elderly shoppers. The only way to find out is to ask. There is no overall nationwide policy on these noncash benefits, which vary greatly from location to location. Information about your parents' community can be found through their Area Agency on Aging. (See Appendix A, pages 267–72.)

REVERSE MORTGAGES

When Phil and Donna Rose bought their $20,000 home in 1950, they took out a thirty-year mortgage. Thirty years later they made their last monthly payment and had a mortgage-burning party to celebrate. In 1980 they not only owned their house free and clear but, after years of skyrocketing housing prices, their $20,000 was now worth $175,000. By the time they retired in 1985, they felt they were sitting on a gold mine. But were they?

Their combined retirement income of $25,000 seemed adequate at the time to cover their own needs, but they had not taken into account their house's needs. Over the next few years they had to dip into their modest savings to pay for a new roof, a new septic tank, and repairs to their sagging porch. In addition, their property taxes rose sharply after a recent townwide assessment. When their old heating system broke down and needed to be replaced before another winter, they were stymied. Because of the high value of their house they could easily qualify for a home-equity loan, but they would not be able to cover the loan's monthly installments. Their only options were to sell their treasured family home and move, or to continue to let their house eat up dwindling savings they had hoped would protect them when they were really old. Terrified of losing their financial security blanket, they decided to sell their house and move. Zoning in their town, however, did not permit apartments, so they had to move to a nearby town to find one. It was only three miles away, but Phil and Donna felt cut off from friends, relatives, and patterns of living built up over half a lifetime.

Many older people—single individuals and couples—face Phil and Donna Rose's dilemma: they are house-rich but cash-poor. A surprising number—78 percent—of older homeowners own their homes free and clear, their mortgages having been paid off years ago. But not everyone chooses to hang on to the old homestead. For many, it's "Who needs to rattle around in this empty place with the children gone?" or "Jack can't handle the stairs anymore!" or "It's our last winter with snow and ice— we're off to Florida!" or "This place is worth $250,000—let's take the money and run!" But probably just as many love their homes, seem able to manage normal maintenance, and are determined to live right where they are forever! Sudden, catastrophic household repairs can blight these dreams and force the elderly owners to move.

There is now a third option to add to the two which were available to the Roses: reverse mortgages, or RMs (also called reverse annuity mortgages, or RAMs). RMs vary in design, but all have a similar purpose. They make it possible for older people to tap the resources in their homes rather than in their savings accounts. With an RM or a RAM, a homeowner receives from a bank or other lending institution a lump sum, a line of credit that can be drawn on when needed, or a monthly amount for a certain period or for life. Unlike a regular mortgage—a home-equity or a home-improvement loan, which has to be paid back with interest in monthly installments—an RM imposes no repayment obligations. At the end of a certain period, or when the owner moves or dies, the home is sold; the total amount borrowed plus interest is deducted from the selling price and is returned to the lender. With some RMs the owner must share with the lender some portion of the amount the house may have appreciated over the years since the loan was signed. An RM, of course, means that heirs will receive diminished legacies.

An RM seems like the answer to elderly homeowners' prayers, but like all other sure-fire schemes these reverse mortgages have their own loopholes, limitations, exceptions, and abuses.

The tax situation with reference to the money received from such mortgages has not yet been clarified. Because of all the uncertainties RMs, although introduced quite a few years ago, have been slow to catch on. Bankers, loan institutions, and homeowners themselves have been wary of them. But now enough safeguards to reduce risks have been introduced so that the number of these mortgages is expected to grow rapidly over the next years. In 1987 RMs were available only in Connecticut, New Jersey, Massachusetts, California, and a few pilot counties in other states.

Despite the new safeguards, older people considering a reverse mortgage—and only those over sixty-two can qualify—should go about it cautiously. A first step might be to contact their state's Agency on Aging for advice on various programs available. Once the reverse mortgage and its terms have been selected, experts agree that a lawyer should review all the clauses to be sure the buyer is protected.

WHO PAYS THE MEDICAL BILLS?

Your parents may be hale, hearty, independent, and contented at the moment. You may be amazed at how well they seem to get along, even though you are pretty sure they do not have much money. But that reassuring situation is not likely to continue if either one—or both—develops a chronic condition, a general state of poor health, or a serious illness, and begins to need to see a doctor more frequently, and to spend more on drugs (the largest single medical expenditure) and other health-related items. No other expense is more draining for the elderly and more potentially disastrous than medical expense. Government and private insurance programs, while helping to meet some of the costs, are by no means able to cover all of them. There are always loopholes and gaps in the coverage for acute illness, and there has been almost no insurance for the elderly to offset the calamitous cost of chronic illness requiring ongoing care.

Your parents, like the majority of older Americans, probably rely heavily on one of two government programs which help to defray medical costs: Medicare or Medicaid, both established under the Social Security Administration. They may also carry some additional private medical insurance to fill some gaps left uncovered by Medicare.

MEDICARE

Medicare is a federal health insurance program covering 32 million men and women over sixty-five and some younger people who are physically disabled. The Medicare program, with funds totaling $50 billion in 1988 including fees collected monthly from the Social Security checks of its members, is divided into two sections:

PART A: Hospital insurance helps to pay for medically necessary inpatient hospital care. It also contributes to posthospital care in a skilled nursing home.

PART B: Helps to pay for doctors' services and for inpatient hospital services such as physical and speech therapy, both particularly important following strokes and accidents.

Contrary to popular assumptions, a Medicare card does not arrive on your parents' doorstep along with the birthday cards the day one of them turns sixty-five. They must apply for membership. Medicare is *not* automatic and it is *not* free.

The Medicare program has undergone two major changes in the 1980s: the *Prospective Payment System*, which determines hospital charges, and the *Catastrophic Coverage Act of 1988*. This act provides for a significant expansion of Medicare benefits to members who, in earlier years, often found their assets wiped out by a serious illness. The provisions for the new health care bill will be phased in over the next several years, and benefits will rise annually.

The *Prospective Payment System* was developed by the federal government to help stem hospital costs, which have been escalating steadily. In 1971 total outlays for Medicare were $7.5 billion. This figure rose to $50 billion in 1982 and is expected to reach $116 billion—more than double—in 1992. Hospital costs are responsible for the lion's share of the total expenditure. Under the old system the government paid hospitals for the care given Medicare patients. With the Prospective Payment System, hospital reimbursements by Medicare are based on average costs for specific diagnoses—Diagnostic Related Groups, known as DRGs. As of 1985, there were 470 categories of DRGs. This is how the system works:

Seventy-year-old John Grant is admitted to the hospital for a gall-bladder operation. The surgery goes well; he recuperates quickly and is discharged on the fifth day. Pete Fletcher—also seventy—also undergoes gall-bladder surgery. He recuperates slowly but nevertheless is discharged on the seventh day. His family is furious that the hospital has "kicked out" a frail old man and "dumped" him on his relatives, who are ill-equipped to give him the kind of nursing care he needs.

The Medicare reimbursement for a gall-bladder operation has been determined under DRGs to be $3,000 and the hospital stay to be seven days. If the hospital had kept Pete Fletcher longer, the reimbursement by Medicare would still have been $3,000 and the hospital would have had to carry the extra costs. If a patient is discharged sooner than the DRG's allotted time, thereby lowering the costs, the hospital still gets $3,000 and can keep the difference. When there are serious complications, a patient may be kept in the hospital longer than the time the DRG has set, and Medicare may pick up some of the extra costs, but this does not happen routinely.

DRGs give hospitals the added incentive to function on a cost-efficient basis and also to discharge their patients as quickly as possible. If John Grant had been discharged after five days, the hospital would not have used up the $3,000 allocated for gall-bladder surgery. It would have made money on him. Conversely, it would have lost money on Pete Fletcher if it had kept him longer.

Medical opinion of the DRG system varies. Some doctors feel that the system works for the benefit of patients partly because they are encouraged to get back on their feet quickly and not to linger invalid-style in a hospital bed for an unnecessarily long time. Others feel that too many elderly patients are sent home too quickly when they still need hospital care. A free booklet, *Medicare's Prospective Payment System: Knowing Your Rights*, is available from the American Association of Retired Persons. This booklet explains how DRGs might affect your own parents and how to protect their rights, particularly at the time they are facing discharge from the hospital.

MEDICARE UNDER THE
NEW CATASTROPHIC COVERAGE ACT

Under the new provisions, each eligible individual pays a monthly sum of $27.10 as of January 1989. The new law adds a new "flat" premium of $4.00 a month to the basic monthly premium to help pay for the new expanded benefits provided by the 1988 law. About 60 percent of Medicare beneficiaries will pay only the flat premium, which added to the monthly premium of $27.10 brings their monthly total in 1989 to $31.10.

The new bill provides for a sliding scale of self-insurance. The richer your parents are, the more they will pay. Costs will rise for Medicare beneficiaries according to their federal income tax. In 1989 they have to pay a 15 percent surtax for every $150 they owe in taxes. The amount assessed will rise with income and the largest sums will be paid by those with the highest income. The surcharge does not rise indefinitely but will have a "cap" in 1989 of $800 for a single individual and $1,600 for a couple. Costs will continue to rise over the next years. The flat premium of $4.00 a month, is expected to rise to $10.20 in 1993. The supplemental premiums will also grow each year, and by 1993 are expected to be $42 for every $150 of taxable income (28 percent) with a cap of $1,030 for a single person and $2,100 for a couple. Only single individuals with incomes of $50,000 or more and couples with incomes of $80,000 or more will pay the maximum premium.

THE TIMETABLE FOR EXTENDED BENEFITS:

1989

Free hospital coverage up to 364 days a year after the payment of an annual deductible of $564. Under the old system patients had to pay deductibles for each "spell" of illness and co-insurance after 60 days. The new law requires only one deductible and eliminates the co-insurance.

Coverage of acute care in a skilled nursing home is expanded from 100 to 150 days a year after a co-payment of $211 a day for the first 8 days. (Placement in both hospitals and skilled nursing facilities must be termed "medically necessary" by a physician.)

Hospice benefits are extended beyond the original 210-day period if a physician or hospice director certifies that the beneficiary is still terminally ill.

1990

Under Part B of the old law, Medicare paid only 80 percent of approved charges by physicians after meeting a $75 annual deductible. The patient was responsible for the remaining 20 percent, which in serious or chronic illness could be a staggering amount. The new law provides for 100 percent coverage of physicians' fees after the patients' out-of-pocket payment has reached $1,370. This ceiling is to be adjusted every year.

Drugs, one of the heaviest sources of medical expense for older people, will begin to be phased in. In 1990 only the cost of in-hospital intravenous and immunosuppressive drugs will be covered.

Mammograph screenings for breast cancer will be covered every other year for women over sixty-five. The cost of the test, however, cannot exceed $50.

Annual coverage for home health services will increase from the original Medicare-approved 15 days to 38 days.

Medicare will pay for up to 80 hours of respite care by a homemaker for relatives (caregivers) attending patients at home.

1991

Medicare will begin paying 50 percent of all prescription drug charges after a deductible of $600 has been paid by the individual beneficiary. Sixty percent will be covered in 1992 and 80 percent in 1993. An estimated 5.8 million enrollees are expected to reach the $600 limit in 1991. Millions more will benefit over the next two years. The $600 deductible will increase in 1992 and 1993 to keep up with inflation.

While the Catastrophic Coverage Act does seem to provide expanded benefits for some older people, there are rumblings of discontent among the affluent elderly, who feel they will be carrying the main financial burden and not receiving enough in return. Furthermore, the new surcharges levied against them cannot be taken as medical deductions for income-tax purposes.

The average yearly medical bill for someone over sixty-five is $4,202. Of that sum, even under the new law, Medicare pays only a part. The individual is still responsible for deductibles and co-payments, which can add up, but even after these are paid Medicare does not necessarily pick up the rest of your parents' medical expenses. Medicare regulations contain a series of "nots": Medicare does *not* cover care that is considered "unreasonable and unnecessary." This would apply to procedures such as face-lifts, tummy-tucks, and other forms of elective plastic surgery. Medicare does *not* cover long-term custodial care in a nursing home, which can spell financial disaster. Lack of coverage for long-term illness is still the biggest gap in the Medicare law. Medicare covers some skilled nursing home care but does *not* cover intermediate care in or out of a nursing home. Except for the new limited coverage under the new respite care benefit, Medicare does *not* cover homemaker services, personal care, home-delivered meals, hearing aids or tests, dental care, routine foot care, eyeglasses, or routine refractions (eye tests). This is a long list of "nots" and excludes relief for the very conditions older people are most likely to suffer from. (The one exception in this list of nots is that Medicare allows one new pair of glasses per year to patients who have had cataract surgery.)

Medical bills will be disallowed if your mother or father receives care from persons or organizations whose services are not certified by Medicare. You or your parents can check the Medicare status of any service or physician you consult by asking directly or calling your local Social Security office.

Even though coverage for doctors' fees will be expanded in 1990, it will still take care only of approved amounts which Medicare has fixed as "reasonable charges." Not all doctors and medical services are willing to accept the fees established by Medicare, so it is wise for you or your parents to make it a practice to ask in advance whether the professional consulted accepts Medicare assignments. If so, the doctor will sign the appropriate forms and the patient will not have to pay anything more.

If not, your parents will be expected to cover the bill themselves, then apply for Medicare reimbursement and finally co-insurance payment. The process may be slow, and even when the reimbursements arrive they may not cover the amount paid out. If your parents cannot afford to pay the extra amount above assignment, they may have to find another doctor. Agreeing to accept Medicare fees is purely voluntary on the part of doctors and other health-related professionals. Unfortunately, the rate of agreement has been declining in recent years.

In addition to establishing the ceiling on assignments, Medicare has recently been able to direct how much above that ceiling a doctor may charge for a given procedure. For instance, an internist may charge a patient under sixty-five $50 for a quick office visit. If the same doctor accepts assignment for a patient over sixty-five, he will receive only $37. If he does *not* accept assignment, he will be allowed to charge only $46.

In 1988 Massachusetts enacted legislation guaranteeing health insurance for all. It also is the first state to require physicians to accept Medicare assignments. Other states are considering similar legislation. While some physicians are willing to go along with the new law, others, infuriated, are leaving the state to set up practice elsewhere.

Confusion is rampant about the way Medicare works, about what services are covered, and even about how to fill out a Medicare form correctly. The Medicare carrier in Florida reports that 30 to 40 percent of the claims received for payment from older people are incomplete or incorrectly filled out. The Florida Medicare carrier started conducting seminars on Medicare claim-filing. In Indiana, because of similar confusion, the carrier distributed how-to leaflets on claim-filing procedures. One New England hospital has recently assigned a group of volunteers, trained and supervised by lawyers, to help patients complete their Medicare claim forms.

If you and your parents share this general confusion, you are likely to find some clarification in *Your Medicare Handbook*, a pamphlet describing the details of the entire program and available free at any Social Security office. Here you will find spelled out which services are covered, the range of payments allowed, how to submit insurance claims, and the addresses of all organizations across the country selected by the Social Security Administration to handle claims.

Your parents may be surprised to discover that they have rights. They do not have to accept without protest decisions which they feel are unfair in their own individual circumstances. They have the right to appeal through the Office of Hearings and Appeal under the Social Security Administration. They can find out at their local office how to ask for a review, but anyone starting such a procedure should be forewarned: the process may be time-consuming and it may be months before the outcome is known. The address and phone number of your parents' local Social Security Office can be found in the telephone directory under U.S. Government, Department of Health and Human Services, Social Security Administration.

PRIVATE HEALTH INSURANCE

Because it was originally assumed that Medicare coverage would carry the major burden of medical expense for the elderly, many health insurance policies cease coverage when insured individuals reach sixty-five or become eligible for Medicare. This assumption no longer holds true. In 1988 medical costs far exceeded Medicare reimbursement, which paid less than one-half—48 percent.

The gaps in Medicare coverage have proved to be so costly that whenever possible many older people carry supplementary medical insurance to help defray the costs: medical deductible and coinsurance costs, extra inpatient hospital days, outpatient services, and extra posthospital days in a skilled nursing facility. Supplementary health insurance policies are available to the elderly from a number of insurers to fill the gaps that Medicare leaves open or to pay for services not covered by the program. Such policies go under a variety of names, such as "65-Plus," "Medicare-Tie-In," "Supplemental Coverage," "Medicare Plus," or "Medigap." The policies are usually handled by the same carriers that handle Medicare claims. Their names and addresses can be found in the back of *Your Medicare Handbook*. As of 1984, 72 percent of people sixty-five and over were covered by some form of supplementary private insurance even though these policies were not cheap and averaged $300–400 in 1984. The cost is undoubtedly higher today.

Such "Medigap" policies may cover Part A or Part B of Medicare deductibles or both, and sometimes—but not always—may cover services not covered by Medicare at all. In 1987 Jennie Lienart, a sixty-seven-year-old widow suffering from serious glaucoma, piled up a drug bill of $800 and, knowing that Medicare did not reimburse for drugs, blithely sent her entire bill to her supplementary medical insurance company. The bill was returned very quickly with the notification that anything *not* reimbursable by Medicare was *not* reimbursable by that company. Jennie will start collecting for her drugs from Medicare and her private insurance in 1991. The supplemental policies also have a long list of "uncovered" services and equipment, most of which are the very ones likely to be needed by an older person: dental and foot care, eyeglasses, hearing aids, routine physical examinations, cosmetic and elective surgery and—the most catastrophic health expense—long-term care provided either at home or in a nursing home.

Many people only realize at retirement or shortly before that their company health insurance will end the moment their gold watches are presented. At age sixty-five they may have to start shopping for supplemental coverage, which may not be easy to find or easy to pay for on their retirement income. They may discover that cost is not the only problem. Insurance companies may refuse to cover anyone with "pre-existing conditions" or only allow coverage to go into effect after 60 or 90 or more days.

Because of the Tax Equity and Fiscal Responsibility Act in effect since 1983, Medicare beneficiaries who continue to work after age sixty-five for companies with more than twenty employees have the option to remain with the company health plan. Medicare then becomes the supplementary insurer.

Men and women planning to retire within the next few years would be wise to find out whether they can continue to pay for coverage under their company health plans.

HEALTH MAINTENANCE ORGANIZATIONS (HMOS)

Health maintenance organizations, or HMOs, are one-stop medical shopping centers that offer service through group policies and provide a broad range of health services for a fixed monthly or yearly premium. This premium can be high; the average payment for an HMO in 1988 was $30.15 per month. In many HMOs the premium is much higher. But in return, the subscriber probably gets the greatest depth and breadth of geoprotection there is. However, HMOs are not widely available in all parts of the United States, and some do not accept anyone over sixty-five who is not already a subscriber. A growing number of HMOs are enrolling Medicare members under contracts with the Department of Health and Human Services. In 1980 there were 44 HMOs nationwide with these special contracts; in 1988, this number had grown to 213. The extent of the services covered under the contract varies, however, so it is wise for your parents to find out in advance, from any HMO they are considering, exactly what services and benefits are covered under its Medicare contract.

There is also a demonstration project under way to establish a new type of HMO called a "social health maintenance organization" (S/HMO). This pilot system provides more comprehensive services than today's HMOs, including certain long-term care services. The jury is still out, however, as to whether such extended coverage will be Medicare-reimbursable.

There is an urgent need at present for increased health protection for the elderly (and for all Americans), not only to extend existing coverage but to pay for services that are not yet covered by government programs, such as vision, hearing, and dental care, extended home care, adult day care and long-term care at home or in a nursing home. Private long-term-care insurance is available now, but the coverage is still limited and only the financially affluent can afford to pay for it. (Nursing home insurance is discussed in Chapter 9, pages 215–17.)

The American Association of Retired Persons, Gray Panthers, Older Women's League, National Council on the Aging, and other action groups are pushing for reforms in Medicare and private insurance coverage. (See Appendix A, pages 316–20, for more information about these organizations.)

MEDICAID

This state-administered program for financially needy patients draws on state and federal funds. Each state designs its own individual program within the broad framework of federal regulations, so there is great state-to-state variation. Basically, people qualify for Medicaid in one of two ways. In most states, those who receive Supplemental Security Income are also eligible for Medicaid, but eligibility does not mean automatic coverage. SSI recipients must apply for Medicaid at their local office. Those with unbearably heavy medical bills must "spend down" to whatever dollar amount determines Medicaid eligibility.

In most states, spend-down occurs in two ways. The first type of spend-down applies to people who live at home but have continuing high medically related expenses. If paying these costs depletes their resources enough, older individuals or couples can apply for Medicaid assistance under the "medically needy" program of their state. There is quite a lot of variation state-to-state in the figures used to define "medically needy." If an individual or couple meets the requirements of their state's program, Medicaid will help to pay medical expenses on an as-needed basis—or as long as the illness continues.

The second type of spend-down accepted by all states occurs when nursing home residents have used up all their resources to cover the cost of their care and cannot continue to pay these charges. At this point, elderly residents can apply for Medicaid. If their applications are approved, the residents must contribute all their monthly income (including Social Security checks) toward their nursing home care, except for a small "personal needs allowance." Medicaid will then pick up the balance, which is determined by a set daily rate that the nursing home has agreed to accept from the state for all Medicaid residents. Switching from Medicare to Medicaid involves no change in the patient's care, which continues as before.

Spending down can be tragically humiliating and disruptive to couples when one partner remains at home and the other is in a nursing home or about to enter one. Until recently the state considered almost all of a couple's total income and assets as funds available to pay nursing home costs. Under this system the husband or wife living outside in the community frequently had virtually nothing to live on, as all the joint assets were being used up. The nursing home resident could then apply for Medicaid while the spouse "outside" was forced to apply for welfare. In some tragic instances, couples would go through divorce proceedings in order to preserve some assets.

Some relief is now available to the wives and husbands of nursing home residents covered by Medicaid, thanks to provisions in the Catastrophic Coverage Act of 1988 (described on pages 163–65). Beginning in September 1989, husbands and wives living in the outside community are allowed to retain income up to 122 percent above the poverty line for a couple, with a limit of $786 per month. The amount of income protected will rise to 133 percent above the poverty line on July 1, 1991, and 150 percent on July 1, 1992. Spouses living in the community will also be allowed to keep combined assets of $12,000 or half of the couple's combined assets, whichever is greater, up to a maximum of $60,000. Beginning in 1990, this figure will be increased each year to account for inflation.

Every state Medicaid program receiving federal funds must supply certain basic services: inpatient hospital care, outpatient hospital services, laboratory and X-ray services, physician services, skilled nursing facilities, rural health clinic services, and some home health care. A wide variety of optional services may be available in the state where your parents are living. These optional additions can include clinic services, prescribed drugs, dental services, prosthetic devices, eyeglasses, private-duty nursing, physical and speech therapy, emergency hospital services, ambulance services, and services by an ophthalmologist, podiatrist, or chiropractor. Case management and other home- and community-based services may also be included. (See Chapter 8 for a discussion of these.) In fact, Medicaid is the primary government payer for intermediate care provided in a nursing home. Despite the wide scope of health-related services offered to Medicaid recipients, it should be remembered that all these services, basic or optional, may be limited in scope or availability. There may also be limitations on the number of days of inpatient services or outpatient visits.

The Medicare Catastrophic Coverage law will require most state Medicaid programs to begin paying the Medicare premiums, co-payments, and deductibles for low-income recipients so that they can receive the same benefits as Medicare beneficiaries. From 1989 on, Medicaid programs will have to provide this coverage for people with incomes up to 85 percent of the federal poverty level ($5,770 annually for an individual in 1988) and with resources which do not exceed twice the SSI standard, which was $1,900 in 1988.

Each year, the income cutoff will rise by 5 percent. By 1992, therefore, all elderly or disabled individuals whose incomes are at or below the poverty level will be covered. The only exceptions to this nationwide coverage are Hawaii, Illinois, North Carolina, Ohio, and Utah, where coverage will be phased in over five instead of four years.

The new law also requires states to assist low-income beneficiaries with the costs of prescription drugs. States can either pay Medicare-reimbursable drug charges until the $600 deductible is met, or if the state's Medicaid program has a prescription-drug benefit, provide the same benefit they offer to Medicaid beneficiaries until the deductible is met and Medicare kicks in.

How are Medicare and Medicaid similar? Both programs are designed to help defray hospital and medical bills. Both programs are part of the Social Security Act. An individual may be eligible for both programs.

How are they different? Medicare is a federal program. Medicaid is a federal-state program. Medicare is uniformly administered by the Social Security Administration throughout the United States. Medicaid programs vary from state to state within federal guidelines and are administered by local social service departments. Medicare is an insurance program available to everyone sixty-five and over. Medicaid is an assistance program available to certain needy people of all ages according to standards of eligibility set by each state.

WHAT CAN YOU DO?

In the past, children who had some financial means were held legally responsible for their elderly parents' support by laws of filial responsibility. Heartbreaking stories were reported of entire families wiped out by the illness of one elderly relative. Money set aside for Johnny's education sometimes had to be used to keep Grandma in the nursing home. Federal regulations prohibit relative responsibility as an eligibility condition for Medicaid with the exception of spouses or the parents of individuals under twenty-one. In administering SSI, however, states *may* hold adult children responsible for their parents. That has been difficult to enforce, and there is a right of appeal to the Office of Hearings and Appeals of the Social Security Administration.

Whether "filial responsibility" has a legal hold on you or not, you may feel it anyhow and wonder what you can do to help when your parents are living under financial privation. If you have plenty of assets, you may be able to take over and support them, but even if you have financial problems of your own, there are a number of ways to help.

- Keep them informed. If you inform yourself on available programs, you may be able to show them how they are eligible for greater benefits. (Don't be surprised if they are better informed than you are.)
- Override their pride. The older generation, particularly the current one, is often too proud to apply for assistance that is due them, fearing the hated stigma of welfare. You may be able to convince them that supplements are not "handouts" but returns from their own contributions as taxpayers.
- Encourage them to work. Your father and mother may be forced to retire, but there is no reason to stop them from taking a second job or starting a second career. If they want to try this, instead of dissuading them, explore with them the possibilities of part-time employment which could provide them with a necessary financial boost without overtaxing their energies. Opportunities are limited, but a few communities have employment agencies dealing exclusively with retired applicants, and Title V of the Older Americans Act established the Community Service Employment Program, which makes funds available to projects employing the elderly.
- Make small regular contributions of your own. You may be afraid it will hurt their pride if you offer them financial help. They may refuse it, but you may be able to persuade them to accept small amounts from you and others in the family. Life at the poverty threshold is grim for anyone at any age, and it is especially grim for the aged. A few extra dollars a month contributed by family members could make day-to-day living a little less dismal, but those extra dollars may be considered as income when Medicaid or SSI eligibility is being determined.

WHAT ABOUT YOUR OWN PREPAREDNESS?

You may have been giving serious thought to your parents' old age and anticipating their future needs. But have you at the same time given any thought to your own? You may be in fine shape now at forty or fifty, but your parents may live another ten, even twenty years. How much extra money or energy will you have to share with them then? You may be single or childless now and in a position to do a great deal for them, but what if you were to die young? The current extended life-expectancy of older people creates the serious possibility that they will outlive their own children, a tragic but not uncommon occurrence.

If, when you contemplate your own situation ten or twenty years from now, it seems unlikely you will be able to do much for your parents, it would be better to discuss this openly. If you remain silent, they may

assume they can count on you and make no alternative plans for themselves. Adult children too frequently play games with their parents. They
send out the message that they know their parents want to hear rather
than the one that is true. An inability to send the correct message may
stem from a child's need to be a "good parent" to his own parents, or
from his need to prove that he is a better parent to them than they ever
were to him.

> The Dodsons were a well-to-do couple with an apartment in Boston and va-
> cation homes in Newport and Palm Springs. They suffered financial reverses
> in their later years, so at the time of Mr. Dodson's death, his widow was left
> literally penniless and quite resentful of her dead husband. Her son, however,
> was able to recoup a small part of the family fortune through his own ingenuity,
> and for ten years he was able to support his mother in an elegant apartment
> hotel with a live-in companion-housekeeper. After a time, the son suffered his
> own financial reverses and his health deteriorated. He continued to support
> his mother, although he could barely support himself and his family. Because
> of his own strong need not to seem a failure to his mother as his father had
> been, he never admitted the financial drain she made on him. But eventually
> he was forced to tell her that he was incapable of supporting her any longer.
> His mother was bitter and resentful, feeling, with justification, that if she had
> been told of the problems earlier she could have made better plans for herself.

PREPAREDNESS VERSUS INTERFERENCE

This chapter began with a strong warning against interfering with the
successful lifestyles your parents may have developed. It may seem that
a contradictory position has been taken in suggesting that you help your
parents plan for the future. Actually, there is no contradiction here.
Preparation does not imply that changes must be imposed on older people
against their will.

The preparedness that has been discussed suggests that families can
enter into a kind of partnership with an elderly relative. Children can
help gather information and guidelines, suggest alternatives, raise cautious warnings, and express concern. The older person, of course, will
make the final decision.

It can happen that your own mother and father may view your efforts
at a partnership with distrust and resentment. They may rebuff any
seeming intrusion into their private lives. But they are just as likely to
respond positively—respecting, even welcoming, your opinion—although
even the most receptive may not be ready to start planning at the same
time you are. It may take them more time, but eventually they may be
willing to share the planning process with you, or take it over for them-

selves. If not, if all attempts fail and you make no progress at all, you will at least have the small comfort of knowing that you have thought through some plans of your own and will therefore be better prepared yourself to know what has to be done if the day ever comes when they cannot manage on their own (see Chapter 10).

8

HELPING WHEN
THEY CANNOT MANAGE—
COMMUNITY SOLUTIONS

"Timmy, it's bath time. Did you pick up all your toys?"

"Yup."

"Timmy! You did not! What's all over the floor?"

"Nothing—just a couple of marbles. I picked up my cars."

"Get those marbles, too. Right now! You know Grandma's coming at six o'clock to sit with you. Come on! Hurry!"

"Awright, awright! I'm doing it as fast as I can. What's the big deal about a couple of little marbles?"

One of Timmy's marbles did make a big deal. Grandma stepped on it as she walked in, turned her ankle, lost her balance, and fell. That night, instead of Grandma sitting with Timmy, Timmy's family sat in the hospital while Grandma's broken hip was set. Before the marble she had been a self-sufficient seventy-year-old, ready to help out whenever one of her children needed her. Afterward, the tables were turned, and it was clear to them that she needed their help for the first time. But that was the only thing that was clear. It was unclear how much help she would need, what kind of help, and for how long.

The story of Timmy's grandma is not unusual. A widow or a widower, or an elderly couple, may move along through the years functioning reasonably well and presenting few if any problems to their children, who accept the status quo and give little thought to its impermanence. But one day a crisis can occur with little warning. A stroke can render an older person partially or totally incapacitated in a matter of hours. Even light falls can result in serious fractures.

More often than not, however, an approaching crisis gives off warning signals. Telltale signs appear months, possibly years, in advance, and all too often are ignored or denied by everyone. (As noted in the previous chapter, when the signals are picked up early, some crises can be averted.) Your father may be suffering from a number of diseases which limit rather than incapacitate him, although it is obvious to everyone that his normal resiliency is declining, his social world closing in, and his friends dying off. He may also have hidden clinical conditions that only surface after a serious accident, a physical trauma, or an emotional one. Common crisis-producers are the death of a spouse, an acute illness (pneumonia or a severe bout of flu), a serious fracture, or a frightening experience (a car accident or a mugging), even though no injury is sustained. Crises are frequently overcome and many elderly people return to independent living, but for others the crisis is the last straw. It does irreversible damage, and independence is gone forever.

Diseases are not necessarily crises in themselves. The crisis develops when a disease interferes with an older person's ability to manage. The day that your mother learns she has cancer may be agonizingly painful for everyone, but the real crisis will come when her illness begins to interfere with her normal routine and her ability to manage. An old man can live with his diabetes for years, but one day the disease may develop to the point where amputation of a limb is necessary or blindness occurs. Arthritis may eventually make walking impossible; glaucoma may advance to partial or total blindness. Mental disorders must be evaluated in terms of the disability they produce. Your mother's occasional loss of memory may disturb her and upset you without seriously hindering her ability to take care of herself, but if she becomes increasingly forgetful or disoriented, it may one day become unsafe for her to continue to live alone. The amount of help the elderly need is largely determined by the extent of their physical and mental incapacities.

The extent of permanent disability left after acute illness or accident is equally unpredictable. The recuperative powers of two convalescents may be very different. One may return to semi-autonomous life within a matter of months, while the other may retire into a permanently dependent state.

Disease, disorder, and accident do not always dictate terms for the future; the future depends just as frequently on the physical and emotional resiliency of individual elderly patients as well as the supports available to them within their families and their communities.

PUTTING ALL THE
PIECES TOGETHER: THE ASSESSMENT

Neither the elderly nor their children can look into a crystal ball in times of crisis and see what lies ahead. The safest way to judge the future is to find out as much as possible about what is going on in the present. What does Mother have going for her? What does she have against her?

This is the time to take a deep breath and to slow down even if Mother is in the hospital and her discharge is imminent. Don't rush things. It's particularly hard to make intelligent assessments of the long-term needs of older people while they are in the hospital. Playing for time is critical, since recovery is slow for the elderly. What looks hopeless today may seem hopeful next week. If DRGs, the mechanism for limiting acute hospital stays, force your mother out of the hospital, the family should seek temporary short-term plans until they can get a clear picture of the situation.

While your mother is recuperating from a fractured hip, an important job for you to do, if you are the responsible relative, would be to collect as much relevant information about her overall situation as possible. The process can be compared to putting together a jigsaw puzzle. Her future is made up of a number of separate but related pieces, and when all of them are fitted together a clear picture emerges. The pieces in your mother's case include her hip itself and how it is healing, her general physical condition, her emotional strengths and weaknesses, her personality, her motivation, her finances, and, perhaps most important of all, how and where she lives. Even if there is every reason to believe that she could make a good recovery, she will undoubtedly need some amount of help during the recuperative period. She may never be able to manage completely alone. Her future depends to a great extent, therefore, on the range of help she can find in her community. When the help she needs is not available, her only alternative may be to enter a nursing home. (The variety of vital community services making it possible for older people to avoid institutionalization will be described later in this chapter.)

The best way to understand all the pieces in your mother's situation, and how they fit together in the total picture, is to arrange for a comprehensive assessment of the many aspects of her life. After that, you will have a clearer idea of the care she is likely to need and be better able to plan accordingly. If you and she have done any contingency planning, as discussed in the last chapter, you may now be ready to put some of those plans into action. Others will have to be revised and adapted to meet her current needs. The same kind of comprehensive assessment is helpful for older people who are not in the hospital but are having serious difficulty at home. Although lengthy medical procedures cannot be done in the home, most of the assessment can be made there, and much insight can be gained in that way. When an elderly man is seen in his own home setting, it will be easier to understand how much help he will need if he is to remain there.

THE PHYSICAL PIECES

After an illness, an accident, or a general physical decline, an old man may wonder, "What's happening to me?" and his wife and children may ask themselves, "How much damage has been done?" "Is he getting worse?" "How long can he go on like this?" "What can we do to help him?"

A complete physical examination, including hearing and vision testing, is the first and most crucial step to be taken before any answers can be given. But you may hit a snag right there. Since the medical profession in general has given low priority to the problems of the elderly, it is unsafe to assume that every physician is familiar enough with geriatric medicine to make an accurate diagnosis. The diseases of the elderly, as pointed out earlier, are often so closely intertwined that they can present a confusing picture, difficult to interpret unless a physician has special knowledge and experience.

Illness does not always show the same familiar signs and symptoms in the old as in the young. Diagnosis is often more difficult. Unfortunately, there are doctors who, because of lack of geriatric training in medical school, lack of experience with the elderly, lack of time, or lack of interest, tend to attribute an endless variety of symptoms to one cause—aging— and look no further. It is easy but dangerous to pin the hopeless, catchall term "Alzheimer's" on confused, disoriented, even hallucinating older patients. They may in reality, as Dr. Robert Butler points out, be suffering from a treatable, reversible brain condition resulting from any number of causes.

It may be hard for your mother to stand her ground with a doctor and insist that her questions be answered, her condition explained, and its treatment mapped out. It could be just as hard for you to speak for her if she cannot speak for herself. But there is a growing movement today urging the patient's right to know. If you are dissatisfied with the answers you get—if they seem casual, unconcerned, fatalistic—you may be able to obtain more convincing answers at another consultation. Your mother's doctor may dismiss her deteriorating vision with the comment "Nothing can be done about it!" And he may be right. Perhaps nothing can be done about the disease that is destroying her sight, but a low-vision professional may be able to teach her how to make the most of her remaining eyesight.

Your father may be fortunate enough to have a competent, interested family doctor who has known him for quite some time. A longstanding close relationship with an older patient can be particularly helpful in assessing his overall physical condition. Your own knowledge of your father's medical history can be useful, too, and added into the assessment. You may also be an important source of information when your father sees new doctors. He may forget his symptoms, or give an incomplete history. You may be a more accurate reporter with a clearer memory. But if he does not have a doctor you both trust, and you don't know whom to see, there are better ways to go about finding a competent opinion than searching the Yellow Pages or asking a friend, neighbor, or Aunt Emma. There may be a nearby medical school, a hospital with a medical-school affiliation, or even a reputable local hospital where you can find the names of doctors with geriatric experience. The county medical association or a local social agency may also have names on file (see Appendix A, pages 280–316). A few communities—about thirty in the country—have compiled directories listing cooperating physicians and including information about their training, credentials, fees, office hours, and Medicare and Medicaid participation. By writing to the Health Research Group, 2000 P Street, Washington, D.C. 20005, you can find out if there is such a directory covering your own community.

THE PSYCHOLOGICAL PIECES

The impact of illness and disability on an older person's emotional state is often ignored even though this can sometimes cause as much damage to the patient as the physical condition itself. Some, but not all, physicians are careful to take that vital element into account as part of a general physical examination. The incidence of psychiatric disorders increases greatly with age. If your mother's problem seems clearly a mental one involving any of the extreme reactions discussed in Chapter 4, then obviously a psychiatric examination is necessary, but sometimes it is hard to distinguish between primary and secondary conditions. The elderly may react with severe anxiety or depression to a physical or a mental loss; the anxiety and depression may in turn precipitate further physical deterioration. Unfortunately, there is a great lack of psychiatric services for the elderly in many parts of the country. People over sixty-five have a high incidence of psychological and emotional problems, yet they often can find no one to turn to for help. Very few of the elderly consult private psychiatrists. Many of these professionals stress the urgent need for more research into the mental problems of the elderly—an area quite neglected until recently.

You may have a number of sources to consult in your community.

Psychiatrists, psychiatrically oriented physicians, social workers, and nurses can be helpful in evaluating the significance of emotional factors in your mother's condition. The county medical society and your local hospital, family service agency, and public health or visiting nurse associations are usually good sources for referrals.

THE FUNCTIONING PIECES

Physical and psychological factors fill in only part of the total picture of an older man or woman in a crisis situation, because physicians are interested mainly in diagnosis or treatment. They can tell you what's wrong with your father, what caused his problem, what other conditions contribute to it, and what procedures will modify it, but they may fail to consider carefully enough how the problem is likely to affect your father's own personal life and his day-to-day functioning. "Be sure he keeps to his diet and takes his medication. Call me if you have any problems, and I'd like to see him again in three weeks," a doctor may say pleasantly as you leave the office with your father. You may have no cause for alarm about his physical symptoms, but other considerations may concern you. If he lives alone all or some of the time, will he be able to resume his daily routines—shopping, cooking, dressing, bathing, toileting? Will he be alert or coordinated enough to protect himself from all the potential hazards in his environment? Can he manage the stairs, pay his bills, take his medicine regularly, keep to his diet? Will he call you or someone else if he is in trouble? Even more important is his motivation to regain independence. If he has lost motor skills, will he be willing to relearn them through exercise or physiotherapy? Is he receptive to using compensatory devices, such as wheelchairs or walkers?

Often local community agencies such as your area agency or office on aging, senior center, family service agency, or hospital can arrange for a trained staff member to make a home visit to assess how well your father functions in his daily routines in and out of the house. Without this evaluation, you may too hastily assume during a crisis that your father is permanently disabled, plan accordingly, and make him more helpless than he really needs to be. Or, you may underestimate the extent of his disability, provide inadequate support, and invite a serious accident.

The assessment may be done by a nurse or social worker who may also act as a care (case) manager. A care manager can not only assess your father's needs but help to find services to meet them. He or she may also play an ongoing role, periodically checking on services and finding out whether your father, and you yourself, are satisfied with the care being provided. (See pages 203–4 for private care managers.)

THE SOCIAL PIECES

Some missing pieces in the total picture can be found by evaluating the social environment in which older people are living. Will they be able to remain in familiar surroundings? How much help will they need in order to stay there? Some families set up schedules, take turns, and share the responsibility of caring for a disabled mother or father. One particularly devoted relative may be available or willing to take on the job. Older people who are rich may hire the necessary help, or a wealthy son or daughter may provide it. Friendly neighbors may be willing to pitch in and provide the extra support necessary. Essential help may be found outside the close circle of family and friends through public or private agencies in the community.

Knowledgeable social workers or care managers can be particularly helpful in sorting out the options available in each individual case. That valuable source of information is often rejected hands down by families who are reluctant to turn to outside professionals, preferring to keep family matters within the family itself. But in addition to providing an accurate description of services readily available in a given community, and explaining eligibility rulings and the real costs involved, a professional, in a home visit, may be able to size up the older person. Although many independent-thinking fathers and mothers are suspicious of strangers and refuse to allow any outsiders to invade their privacy, a competent social worker may be able to persuade even the most reluctant to allow such outsiders as homemakers, home health aides, and visiting nurses to enter their homes to help them.

A social worker or care manager can also serve as a middleman when there is a communication problem between the generations in a family. A lack of communication may have a longstanding history in some families, or it may become a problem only in times of crisis. Children may be unable to tell painful truths to their parents, or the parents may refuse to listen. Someone outside the family can often supply the objective viewpoint that is missing and provide supportive counseling to the upset older person.

THE FINANCIAL PIECES

Financial realities must always be included in the total picture, because money—or the lack of it—can be a crucial factor in the recovery process, speeding it up or blocking it completely. When a special or even an adequate diet is called for, elderly convalescents may or may not be able to pay for it. If they cannot, they may then suffer further malnutrition and deterioration. Rehabilitation can often be accelerated by physiotherapy, special retraining procedures, or the use of certain prosthetic devices, but everyone cannot afford such so-called luxuries. So Mrs. Jones, because of her adequate monthly income, may return to semi-independent life, while Mrs. Smith, struggling along at the poverty level, will never be able to leave her wheelchair again. Money also determines whether enough extra household help can be hired to enable a semi-independent older man or woman to remain in the community. When adequate help cannot be provided free by relatives and friends and cannot be paid for, that fact alone may force a family to consider some form of institutional placement.

WHO PUTS ALL THE PIECES TOGETHER?

Even though an overall assessment and care management make sense in principle, they may be close to impossible to obtain in reality. You may have trouble finding any competent help at all. Again, the stumbling block is society's historic lack of concern for the problems of the elderly. The professions are at present ill-equipped to offer the thorough physical, psychological, and social workups needed by millions of older citizens in trouble, even though individual competent professionals know how valuable those workups can be. In some locations across the country, where it may be difficult to find professionals, you may have to be your own father's or mother's evaluator and care manager and put the whole puzzle together yourself from assorted bits of information, insights, and advice. It may be little comfort, when you are forced to settle for makeshift compromises, to know that more concern for the welfare of older people is shown in other parts of the country where, unfortunately, you do not live, or will only be shown in your own community in the future when, unfortunately, it will be too late to help your own parents.

Professional and community interest in the population sixty-five and over has grown in recent years, and promises to keep on growing in years to come as this population continues to increase and cannot be ignored. More community agencies are serving older people, providing assessment and care-management services, home care services, adult day care, and housing. (See "What Does the Community Have to Offer?," pages 192–203.) The goal of these home- and community-based services is to enable older people to keep on living in their own homes as long as possible.

A great deal of attention has been given recently to providing older persons with a single entryway to the community where a thorough assessment can be made of their situation and the services they need pooled from perhaps a variety of sources, coordinated, and managed for them. The assessment is seen as a vital preliminary to good planning by these service providers, just as it should be seen by the family and the older person.

The Older Americans Act amendments of 1978 strengthened the authority and flexibility of local area offices on aging to designate single focal points in communities for information, referral, and service delivery. Some of these programs have developed to such an extent that case-management services including assessment are provided. Most recently the federal government is funding a pilot demonstration program in eleven states to provide coordinated services to the frail elderly with a strong emphasis on assessment.

"Geriatric assessment units" are another important development. Usually sponsored by hospital centers, these units are few in number. Most notable is the service provided by Duke University, including full psychiatric, medical, psychological, functional, and social workups that closely involve the family. Two of New York City's major hospitals have established special facilities which deal exclusively with older people: Health Access, which provides special health services for older adults at Columbia-Presbyterian Medical Center; and the Phyllis and Lee Coffey Geriatric Clinic at Mount Sinai Hospital.

Your own need for an assessment of your mother's condition may come, as it does for many families, while she is still in the hospital recovering from some acute episode. If you are bewildered about what to do when she is discharged, you may be referred to the hospital social service department, where a social worker will help you locate the place where you can find the advice you need. The social worker may also be able to suggest appropriate arrangements to make after the assessment is completed. But things do not always go that smoothly. There may be no competent social service staff at your hospital; it may be difficult to set up the assessment; the general hospital policy may be to recommend institutionalization as the simplest course of action; or your doctor may resent anything he considers outside interference in his private cases.

If you find out, as many people do, that there is nowhere to turn for a thorough professional assessment, the best way to proceed is slowly, deliberately, watchfully. If you do not panic, you yourself may be quite adept at figuring out what is happening, since you have known your parents longer and better than anyone else. Obviously, workable arrangements must be made to care for a disabled person adequately during an emergency, but they should not be solidified too quickly into permanency. They should be subject to revision until the situation stabilizes and its long-term implications become clear.

Jenny Franklin laughs a little sheepishly today when she remembers all the terrible thoughts that galloped through her mind whenever she looked at her crippled father in the early weeks following her mother's sudden death. "I couldn't bear to look at him. He seemed ten years older. All the progress he'd made in getting around after his car accident vanished overnight. Someone had to lift him from the wheelchair to the bed. He hardly spoke, barely listened to anyone. I kept wondering, How can he go on? Not alone here! He'll have to move in with us! I'll have to quit my job to take care of him! But I can't do that! A nursing home, maybe? Never! Not that! But what? I found myself wishing he'd died, too. What was left for him?"

Lucky for Jenny that she did not know which way to turn and therefore did nothing. She took time off from work to help her father through the first devastating effects of her mother's death. Then, slowly, everyone noticed he seemed to be getting stronger, moving around a little better every day, eating more, taking notice, responding. A few months later it became clear that with some additional help—granted, that was a problem to arrange—he would be able to live a somewhat independent existence. When he remarried a few years later, Jenny was a little ashamed that she had predicted such a dire future for him just a short time earlier.

Pessimism may, on the other hand, be warranted. Jenny's father was lucky, but many are not. Emergencies may pass, leaving older people totally incapacitated. Radical changes must be made then, and families will be consoled by the certainty that they had no other alternatives. They will be less likely to torment themselves months later with guilty self-accusations, all beginning with phrases like, "If only we'd realized . . ." or "We never should have . . ." or "Why did we. . . ."

WHAT KIND OF CARE?

Since crises vary in severity, in duration, and in extent, there are several different ways to cope with them. During the acute phase, older people, like younger ones who are seriously ill, need intensive care. But once that phase has passed, other types of care are often more appropriate. It is important to find the right balance in your own situation. Too little care can make your mother overanxious and helpless. Too much care can make her unnecessarily dependent. Either extreme may lead to additional problems. Complicating the question is the fact that her condition will change in time—and not always for the worse. Reassessment is critical in order to determine the right care at the right time.

OFF-AND-ON CARE

This level of care is neither continuous nor intense. It is required when older people cannot really manage alone and need occasional help. It would be ideal if off-and-on care were available to all the elderly, even those in comparatively good health, as part of preventive care, but it is especially important to the numbers who can manage some but not all of the time. Your parents may need outside help only during special periods: minor illnesses or accidents, the death of a loved relative or friend. When an emotional flare-up is triggered by some crisis, they may need occasional periods of support provided by counseling, or individual or group therapy. Temporary care should be available for just the amount of time it is really needed—no longer, no shorter.

Undoubtedly, the best place to find such care today, as in years past, is still within the immediate family. That does not mean that you have to be around your parents all the time; you don't have to take them into your own home or consider nursing-home placement. Simply knowing that you will be available when they need you can be all the reassurance they need in order to manage for themselves the rest of the time.

Sons, daughters, and in-laws, as well as sisters, brothers, nieces, and nephews, are usually quick to respond to a close relative's crisis if they are in any position to respond at all, and not only when that relative lives with them or around the corner. Assuming there is a basically affectionate relationship between the generations, close relatives provide an all-important ingredient often missing in off-and-on care from outsiders: the loving comfort that gives the extra boost to an older person's recovery.

Eighty-year-old Maude Evans had a cardiac condition and high blood pressure, but had managed to live by herself for ten years. When she was feeling well she was able to manage her small apartment, cook for herself, and visit her friends and relatives. Periodically she suffered cardiovascular flare-ups which required close medical supervision and a good deal of rest. At times the flare-ups made her anxious and depressed; at other times they were precipitated by an emotional upset. During those episodes her daughter would visit her daily to take care of the house, prepare meals, and do necessary chores. Occasionally during an acute phase a twenty-four-hour home health aide was hired to stay with her, but as soon as her condition improved, Mrs. Evans was eager to have her house to herself again and ready to return to her former pattern of living. Just knowing she had someone to turn to for help if things went wrong made her able to manage alone when life was going smoothly.

The family is not always in a position to respond even to a temporary emergency, and substitutes may be found to provide temporary care. A close friend or a neighbor may be able to stop in. The necessary care may be arranged, if possible, through social or health agencies, which will be described later in this chapter. If, because of complications in your own life, you sense in advance that you will be unable to provide off-and-on care for one of your parents, you may decide to prepare for that situation in advance and look into the outside help available in your parent's community.

Being prepared in advance will relieve both you and your parents. You will know there is someone they can call when problems arise, and they will feel more secure, too. Self-reliant though many elderly people may be, they are usually willing to give up some portion of their treasured independence. Particularly crucial to off-and-on care are rehabilitation services. Following an illness or accident, some older people can be restored to independent living or semi-independent living if they are provided with physical and occupational therapy services to restore functioning that may not be permanently lost.

When off-and-on care is not available, either from a social network or from some kind of community service, conditions that could have been nipped in the bud often deteriorate into chronic conditions. Or the anxiety of having no one to turn to in case of emergency may be too much for an older person and the family to bear. Unnecessary, radical changes may be made because of these factors, often with traumatic effects on everyone.

SUPPORTIVE ONGOING CARE

This is middle-range, second-level care needed by the elderly who do not alternate between independence and dependence. Many older people have chronic disabilities which permit them to function in some areas but not in others. They are not likely to improve, but they are often able to get along well, despite their handicaps, if ongoing care is provided in specific areas. Your father's heart condition may prevent him from managing his apartment alone, but if someone comes in to prepare at least one meal a day for him, and do the marketing and the heavy cleaning, he can probably remain where he is—and where he may vehemently insist he *wants* to remain.

Supportive care may be required by the elderly who are arthritic, crippled, partially blind, or partially paralyzed, but it may also be necessary for those who have no one specific infirmity but are just generally weakened by advancing age. Although no longer able to manage any physical chores, they may be perfectly capable of thinking clearly, making their own decisions, knowing exactly what they want, and saying so loud and clear. Supportive care may also be necessary for those who are physically sound but, because of minimal mental impairment, need someone to help them manage their routines or their money, or make complicated decisions. Their ability to make decisions for themselves in some areas, however, should never be underestimated. Only when there is evidence that they are endangering themselves or others should their ability to make their own decisions be questioned.

As in the case of temporary care, supportive care can be provided by children and close relatives, but it is long-term, ongoing, and sometimes very demanding. Many families may find it too heavy a burden. Since it is always possible for any machinery to break down when outside help is used—a housekeeper gets sick, a doctor is unreachable, transportation to an essential treatment does not show up—the disabled person should ideally have a permanent contact with someone, either in the family or in the community agency, who will respond to a breakdown in service.

Community agencies who accept responsibility for providing this essential care will, if well run, have back-up services. A case manager assigned to ongoing responsibility will make other arrangements, too.

LONG-TERM INTENSIVE CARE

Eventually, for some older people, the time does come when halfway measures are no longer enough. One day, after a stroke, a heart attack, or severe mental deterioration, your mother may no longer recognize you or anyone else, or she may be permanently invalided. Your father may not know where he is, or he may have lost control of his bodily functions. People in those tragic conditions require twenty-four-hour care. Some, whose overall condition may not be so hopeless, are still disabled enough to require constant medical attention and skilled nursing. That is the point at which many families feel forced to consider institutionalization, which may now become the only solution. But intensive care is also possible either in an older person's home or in a child's home.

> Prior to her stroke, seventy-eight-year-old Gina Tarrant had lived with her daughter and her daughter's family. She had been a good-humored, cooperative person who blended well into the family, helping when needed and rarely interfering. She was an excellent babysitter, and shopped and took care of the house while her daughter and son-in-law went to work every day.
>
> Her stroke left her paralyzed on one side of her body and unable to handle any of the activities of daily living, including bathing, dressing, feeding, and toileting. At times she was incontinent. But following her hospitalization the family decided to bring her home. They bought a hospital bed and other equipment to make nursing care easier and hired a home health aide to come in every day from nine to five. A visiting nurse stopped by regularly to check on Mrs. Tarrant's condition, and a local doctor made occasional house calls. Her daughter and son-in-law took over in the evening and on weekends, but other relatives came in regularly to relieve them when they needed a break.
>
> Fortunately, there happened to be a number of other relatives willing to share the responsibility, and no one individual was seriously overburdened.

Mrs. Tarrant, although partially paralyzed, remained in her familiar setting, aware of her family and the love and concern that surrounded her.

Gina Tarrant was fortunate that outside help was available in her community and that so much "inside" help was offered by her extended family. Intensive care can be provided under less favorable conditions. One family member—a daughter, a daughter-in-law, a niece, a sister—may be willing enough and strong enough and dedicated enough to assume the major responsibility. But no one should volunteer impulsively without a full understanding of the rigorous demands of the job. If you are contemplating caring for your mother or father yourself, you might discuss the case first with a registered nurse at a hospital or a visiting nurse in your community, and find out as much as you can about the necessary routines.

It is essential to realize in advance that when a patient needs intensive care it must be available round-the-clock, seven days a week. You will be able to take time off, of course, but only if the care is provided in your absence by someone else. Beds must be made several times a day, baths and sponge baths given, bedpans emptied, medications administered. Special care must be taken of the skin to avoid bedsores. Any minor skin condition may be aggravated by incontinence. You may have extra laundry duties and kitchen duties. Nutritious meals—sometimes involving special diets—must be served three times a day, as well as periodic snacks. Orders from the doctor are to be followed and reports on the patient's progress turned in to the doctor. Efforts should be made to encourage a patient to take care of himself whenever he can: grooming, shaving, feeding. His morale must be considered, too. The life of a shut-in or a bedridden invalid can be endlessly dreary and lonely. Some kind of recreation and entertainment must be provided—handicrafts, books, music—and visitors encouraged to stop by. Patients can be difficult, discouraged, irritable, demanding, suspicious, or resentful, but care is still expected to be performed with cheerfulness, compassion, understanding, and caring. This is why respite time away from these duties is crucially important (see page 199).

HELPING THE MENTALLY IMPAIRED

When caring for an older person with some degree of mental impairment, it is essential to have some ongoing psychiatric and medical supervision. Medications may be prescribed for some agitated elderly patients, and a calm, structured atmosphere with a regular ordered routine is usually the most effective. Too much stimulation and excitement can be overwhelming and confusing. Sometimes it's the medications themselves which cause added confusion, so these need careful monitoring.

Body language—of the patient and the caregiver—can often transmit clearer messages than spoken language. A confused old man may not be able to verbalize his fears, but his contorted face and thrashing arms may be caused by some real or fancied terror. An intuitive caregiver will pick up this clue. Spoken words of reassurance may do little to calm an agitated patient, but she may quiet down when the caregiver strokes her forehead and gently squeezes her hand, thereby sending an unspoken message of caring and protection.

If intensive care of a physically disabled parent is a rigorous job, the care of a mentally impaired one is equally taxing, even if it is not round-the-clock. You may find it particularly draining because of your close emotional involvement. Dealing with your mother's confusion, disorientation, loss of memory, and possibly delusions day after day can be nerve-racking, and even though you understand that she cannot help the way she behaves, you may still feel hurt and rejected when she does not even recognize you.

The best approach, which involves an almost superhuman effort for many children, is to remove yourself as much as you can from your personal feelings and try to help her hold on to some threads of reality. Although you find the endless repetition agonizing and frustrating day after day, she may be less confused if you quietly repeat simple factual statements: "Yes, you've had your lunch," or "No, it's not morning, it's bedtime," or "Today is Thursday. Tomorrow is Friday," or "This is Jane—your sister." Big calendars, large clocks, even photographs of relatives can be ever-present silent reminders of everyday realities. Other compensations for memory loss and confusion are lists of daily activities in clear view, safety reminders ("Turn off the Gas," "Lock the Door"), color-coded drawers and cupboards, labeling of utensils frequently used. Older people with only partial mental impairment frequently suffer brief periods of disorientation, slipping into confusion and then out again. The more concrete clues they have available, the less likely they will be to lose their grasp of reality.

The same detached calmness can be helpful for the mentally impaired who distort reality. Arguing about what is real or imagined will not help, but will rather make them more anxious and compound their confusions or delusions. There is no advantage to be gained by a pitched battle with your mother when she anxiously insists, "The mailman has a gun!" or "The delivery boy is a thief!" or "The homemaker is poisoning me!" Better results may follow if you can sidestep what she says and pick up the feelings accompanying her words. When your first impulse is to snap back impatiently, "Nonsense! How can you say that nice little Billy Forse is a thief?" try taking a deep breath and saying instead, "You're frightened, aren't you, Mom?" If your father keeps angrily insisting your husband has a girlfriend, and everyone is talking about your own immoral behavior, he'll never believe your denials. But he might respond if you ask him, "You're angry at us, aren't you, Pop?"

Despite its demands and frustrations, the care of the very sick can be quite rewarding if it is provided with devotion and high competence. But regardless of the success you have with your patient, regardless of your ability to handle the routines, it is absolutely essential that you arrange for regular periods of relief—respite time—from a job that goes on round-the-clock and weekends, too. Friends and relatives may be willing to take over for you at regular intervals. Public health and visiting nurses and health aides may also provide some respite and may be invaluable in showing you more effective nursing techniques. Medicare's recent Catastrophic Coverage law has finally recognized the problem of caregiver burnout and has taken a few steps toward alleviating it. But the newly extended respite-time coverage provides only temporary stopgap help and does nothing to ease the relentless burden of long-term care.

Even if you are confident that you can manage the job with all its physical and emotional demands, one final question must be answered before you take it on: What does everyone else in the family feel about it? Is it possible that although you do not resent your demanding job, others will resent it? Their freedom will probably be curtailed in some way, too. You may end up devoting all your energies to one member of your family while neglecting everyone else. Think of the additional burden you may then have to carry—your guilt at neglecting them and your resentment that they make you feel guilty!

If your decision to keep your mother or father at home is predicated on help you expect from others in the family, then their wishes should be considered in advance. If you do not choose to involve them earlier and make a unilateral decision, they may not choose to pitch in and help you later. When the situation has been discussed freely in advance and all individuals have been allowed to say how much responsibility they are willing to accept, family disruption can be avoided, and the resulting family unity can work wonders (see Chapter 10).

In their book *Gramp*, photographers Dan and Mark Jury put together a pictorial record of the last years in their grandfather's life—years during which the old man became seriously deteriorated and incontinent. Nevertheless, he remained in his home, cared for by his loving and devoted family. The Jurys admit that they were able to keep Gramp with them until he died, partly because of the genuine feelings they all had for him and partly because there were enough of these loving people in the family—especially young, strong grandsons—to take the ongoing care in turns. No one person was victimized or martyred. Great satisfaction can be gained by caring for a deteriorating but well-loved relative at home, a satisfaction that often is compensation enough for the heavy investment of time and energy required from everyone. The Jury family and others like them stand as modern examples of the old Iroquois Indian precept, "It is the will of the Great Spirit that you reverence the aged even though they be helpless as infants."

YOU MAY NOT BE QUITE
AS IMPORTANT AS YOU THINK

When off-and-on care or supportive intensive care is necessary for one of your parents, *someone* must be around to provide it, but that someone does *not* have to be exclusively you, or your younger sister, or your older brother. Because society has provided such limited assistance to the elderly, they only turn to their children for lack of anyone else to turn to. Even today, when more services are becoming available, your mother may have no idea where to look for help outside of her family. You may not know either and feel obligated to take the total responsibility for her care yourself.

Finding someone else to share a burden is not buck-passing or shirking, although it may be labeled that by other family members, friends, or neighbors, who may tut-tut when they see a stranger coming in every day to take care of old Mrs. Grenville or an outsider taking old Mr. Packer to have his leg brace adjusted. They may enjoy gossiping about Mrs. Grenville's "unfeeling" daughter or Mr. Packer's "no-good" son. Meanwhile Mrs. Grenville may be quite content that she has someone to take good care of her, and Mr. Packer may be relieved that his brace can be adjusted regularly without bothering his busy son. Both old people may prefer to have their children around when there are fewer chores to do and more time for them to talk and enjoy each other.

It may come as a surprise to learn that someone else might provide *some* services to your parents better than you can. While training programs for families in caregiving are appearing on the scene and proving very helpful, skilled workers less emotionally involved may provide much better care. Caregiving can become a heavy burden on families, and the quality of the care they give may suffer in time. Social workers in England, where a wide variety of community supports are provided to the elderly, believe strongly in a partnership between the old person, the family, and community agencies in maintaining the old person. No one goes it alone. The burden is shared.

Other family members can fulfill a variety of roles in relation to the elderly, roles which in the long run can be as beneficial as a central caregiving role. They can be supervisor or coordinator of services, financial manager, advocate, shopper, transporter, friend, companion, or simply a loving daughter, son, or grandchild who visits. This type of role will be determined by the family member's other abilities, health, obligations to others (family, job, community). It will also be determined by what the older person *wants*.

Modern sons and daughters, so accustomed to feeling guilty about their parents, may overestimate their own roles in their parents' lives. Studies suggest that the older generation, even when it has close ties with its children, sometimes prefers a measure of separation. Why else do so many choose, as one report shows, houses or apartments in retirement villages with no extra bedrooms? This choice may be made not only because of cost or convenience but also to prevent lengthy visits from children and grandchildren.

Your mother may have been "on your back" all your life, but if she was never that way when she was younger and only in her old age burdens you with endless phone calls, requests for rides, and constant attention, it may not be that she is deliberately burdening you, but that she has no one else to call. If she could Dial-a-Ride or Dial-an-Aide when she needs transportation out of the house or help inside it, she might not have to call on you so often.

> "I'd love to come visit you and the children," an elderly aunt living in a one-room apartment in a retirement village said pleasantly when her niece called, "but it will have to be next month. This month I'm too busy. I go for physiotherapy every day, I've promised to read to my neighbor who's blind until her regular reader comes back, and I've found someone to help me get to that concert series I wanted to hear." All those activities were being undertaken by an eighty-year-old who needed a walker to get around. Her niece, who had felt guilty for weeks because she had not made the effort to invite her "poor old aunt" for the weekend, hung up the phone feeling surprisingly unnecessary.

WHAT DOES THE COMMUNITY HAVE TO OFFER?

The ideal community, particularly for the elderly, should be able to offer basic health and social services: family doctors (willing to make house calls on the homebound); specialists, including psychiatrists; twenty-four-hour emergency care; dentists; and a nearby, well-equipped general hospital with provisions for psychiatric emergencies and short-term treatment. Somewhere in the larger community there should also be a psychiatric hospital and some well-run nursing homes, social service agencies and a variety of other helping services offering in-home and out-of-home assistance, as well as housing designed to meet the needs of older residents. But the ideal community does not actually exist. It is probably safe to state that *no* community at present can take care of all the needs of its elderly.

Fortunately, community services are available now in most parts of the country. This growth has been stimulated by a number of federally funded programs, supplemented in many states by state general-revenue funds. Each state has an Office for the Aging, usually located in the capital, and local Area Agencies on Aging (see listing in Appendix A, pages 267–72) established and funded by the Older Americans Act and augmented with state and local funds. These agencies plan and coordinate community services for the aging. Title III of the Older Americans Act funds social services, nutrition programs, and in-home services.

Medicaid is another source of funds for community services in some states. But these are available only to older people who have low incomes and assets or who "spend down" to be eligible. Social service block grants awarded to states to provide community social services for people of all ages may fund some services for the elderly.

For information on what is available in their own community you or your parents can contact the local Area Agency on Aging or senior center. Addresses and phone numbers can be found under the government listing in the Blue Pages, in the Yellow Pages under "Senior Citizens" or "Social Service Organizations," or in the Silver Pages—a directory specially compiled for the elderly in some areas.

The Veterans Administration (VA) also provides services to eligible veterans. Veterans and their families should contact their local VA office for more information on services and eligibility requirements.

A number of services bring help directly into the home and are particularly important to the homebound. The local senior center, Area Agency on Aging, or Family Service Agency can tell you which ones operate in your parents' community. You may even find a directory of services for older residents of the community. These agencies often have professional staff members—social workers or care managers—who can help to determine the appropriate services to meet your parents' needs and to make arrangements for the delivery of these services. You may prefer to make these arrangements yourself or pay a private geriatric-care manager to make them (see pages 203–4).

Despite the growth of services and programs, you and your parents may not be aware of what is available right in your own community. Even if you are well informed, you may not know which service is best for you or how to apply for it. The best way to start is to contact someone who knows the overall community setup, someone who can give you the information you need and refer you to the appropriate service. (Medical services, information, and costs are discussed in Chapter 7.)

INFORMATION AND REFERRAL SERVICES

Some areas have special information and referral services (publicly or privately funded) to guide residents of all ages to appropriate local services. Here you can usually find out exactly what services there are and which ones your own mother or father is eligible to use. When there is no independent information and referral (I & R) office, similar information can be found at local sectarian or nonsectarian family service agencies or senior centers whose staffs of professional social workers are usually well briefed on the community. These professionals may also arrange for an assessment for one of your parents, advise on the type of care necessary, and refer you to other specialized services. You and your parents may also be given the name of one specific social worker to call on when further problems arise. (See Appendix A, pages 280–316.)

It is tremendously helpful and comforting for older people—and their families—to know that they can always turn to the same person when troubles arise. Your mother may speak warmly of "that nice Mrs. Walker down at the agency"—the person she calls when she needs help. Professionals are becoming increasingly aware of the need to provide this continuity. They have come to realize that the fragmentation of services to the elderly and the confusing array of possibilities often make it impossible for families to sort everything out and locate the help they need. It is also a time-consuming process. Case management is viewed as the answer to the confusion: a case management agency will assign one worker to an elderly person—and whatever family is involved—and conduct an assessment, calling on medical and nursing personnel, social workers, and other consultants as needed. This same worker will pull together the necessary services, coordinate them, and then supervise them while they are being used. As the older person's condition changes, the cluster of services being received will be increased or decreased.

Other agencies may provide case management services in addition to a wide variety of other functions. They may serve a small community, a neighborhood, or even a larger area and be staffed by social workers, nurses, home health aides, and homemakers. This is an ideal way to guarantee consistency and continuity of care. Unfortunately, case management and similar agencies are not to be found everywhere, so many families must manage themselves, making do with whatever scattered services they can find.

When no family service organizations are listed in your phone book, you can write to the Family Service Association of America for the agency closest to your parents' community. The personnel of their local Social Security, Medicaid, or welfare offices are usually familiar with the range of services offered and may be particularly reliable in knowing which ones your parents will be financially eligible to use. Physicians and clergymen are also likely to have a general idea of what goes on in the community. Further information can sometimes be found by consulting special groups, such as the American Cancer Society.

Children often feel particularly helpless or overwhelmed when facing the heavy responsibility of caring for their ailing parents, and it can be a tremendous relief to discover that there are other helping people around to shoulder some of the burdens.

When services bring help directly into their homes or make it possible for them to leave their homes, older people usually find that life seems better. The anxiety and depression so many of them feel because of their disabilities may be alleviated. The loneliness and isolation, so much a part of old age in America, can be partially counteracted.

AT-HOME SERVICES—MEDICALLY RELATED

Older people needing nursing or rehabilitative care may receive either one through Medicare's "home health care." Home health care, however, is provided for only a short period of time, and a physician must certify that it is needed. A variety of care is included under "home health."

A few words of caution are necessary here. While similar services may be found in communities across the country, there may be great variations in quality and performance. There may be scandals, mismanagement, inefficiency, incompetence at any point. General, overall standards may be lacking, or there may be no one available to monitor and supervise every local facility.

VISITING NURSES

Most communities have some nursing professionals—registered nurses, public health nurses, and licensed practical nurses. The nursing staffs of these services may be limited and must cover the needs of every age level, so it may be impossible for some of them to meet the needs of the elderly sector adequately. The elderly have so many needs!

Visiting nurses represent to the elderly a crucial link to other community services. They keep up to date on new programs being set up and on the most direct means of making use of old ones. Local visiting nurse groups are usually run by voluntary organizations and have a sliding scale of fees reimbursed by Medicare only after a serious illness or hospitalization and then only for a short time. Visiting nurse fees vary according to the location and the individual's ability to pay.

REHABILITATION SERVICES

These special services are provided by professionals in the home. Physical, speech, and occupational therapy are covered under Medicare only when certified as necessary by a physician. Help for the visually impaired is also provided in the home by vision rehabilitation agencies. Coverage for vision therapy varies state-to-state, although low-vision services are now covered by Medicare.

HOMEMAKER–HOME HEALTH AIDE SERVICES

While the nurse takes care of vital medical problems (along with the physician), the homemaker–home health aide makes everyday life move along more smoothly. When these aides are available, they may make it possible for families to postpone institutionalizing an elderly relative or to avoid this completely. Here again, the supply is limited and the need growing. In 1979 there were 5,000 homemaker services across the country. In 1988, there were 15,000. Families hoping that a homemaker–home health aide will work miracles for them must always be aware that there may be none available when they need one. There are an estimated 197,000 aides to meet an estimated need of well over 300,000. (See Appendix A, pages 272–79, for a selected list of these services.)

Homemaker–home health aides are trained in household and personal care and usually work under the supervision of a nurse, social worker, or other health professional. *Homemakers* are responsible for housekeeping, but in some cases may be specially trained for working with older people. They may offer some amount of personal care—bathing, dressing, toileting, feeding, walking. The *health aide* is trained primarily for patient care, but may assume some household responsibilities. Families must keep in mind that health aides are not professionals (nurses); neither are they servants (maids). Families should also be aware that even if a homemaker–home health aide is available, there is no guarantee that he or she will be competent, kind, or dependable. These aides are not licensed and in some locations have no professional supervision.

AT-HOME SERVICES—NONMEDICAL

A variety of other helping services are available in some, but not all, communities. Many of these are provided by social service agencies which deal with older people, family service agencies, and homemaker–home health aide agencies. Of course, you do not necessarily have to deal with official agencies but can make your own private arrangements for the kind of help your parents need. Services performing supportive tasks within the home include the following:

MEALS ON WHEELS

Although adequate nutrition is a vital ingredient in the overall health of the elderly, malnutrition, which aggravates physical and mental problems, is the fate of too many. Poverty is a major cause of malnutrition, but another is the inability of frail older people to prepare the right kind of diet for themselves, particularly if they live alone and have no one to cook for and eat with. Low-cost or free meals are offered in many locations now, but here again the need far exceeds the supply.

Meals on Wheels was started in 1943 under voluntary auspices. Now some food programs are still fully supported by private donations, but some have a combination of private, community, and federal funding from such sources as sectarian organizations, the United Way, and Title XX of the Social Security Act. Some meal programs, called "Home-Delivered Meals," are funded only by the 1978 amendments to the Older Americans Act. Meals on Wheels, which has private funding, may fix fees, but Home-Delivered Meals, which is federally funded, may not charge. A contribution is suggested, but no payment is required.

When a hot meal is delivered every day, it provides not only nutritional benefits for the elderly recipients but a side benefit as well. The volunteer delivering the meal is sometimes the only daily human contact the homebound have with the world outside. They can look forward every day at mealtime to a friendly chat and a little human concern, which can be as satisfying to the spirit as the nutritious meal is to the body. The volunteers not only serve as social supports but provide a vital link, reporting back to the sponsoring organization on the condition of their homebound elderly clients.

HOMEMAKER AND PERSONAL CARE SERVICES

These men and women may come from the same agency which supplies home health aides. Homemakers are responsible for running a house, shopping, doing laundry, and light cooking. Personal care aides assist a convalescent or a chronically ill individual in bathing, dressing, eating, and walking.

TELEPHONE REASSURANCE PROGRAMS

The telephone represents a lifeline for many of the elderly living alone, but even when there is a phone, they may not be able to get to it to make an outgoing call for help in the event of an accident or acute illness. Both they and their children often worry about those possibilities. A daily phone call by a regular caller at a prearranged time can serve as the best reassurance that all is well, for one more day at least. Children often set up their own systems, calling every day at the same time to say, "Hello, Mother, how are you?" and the elderly themselves sometimes set up "buddy" systems in which two or more friends will call each other. But children may live too far away, making daily long-distance phoning too costly; buddies may vanish or die off. Then a volunteer or commercial telephone checking service charging moderate fees can be used instead. Here again the older person receives an added bonus, the chance to hear the sound of a human voice every day: "Hello, Mrs. Gavin. How are you today?" If Mrs. Gavin does not answer her phone, help will immediately be sent to her home, and if she does not answer her door, a neighbor, friend, or nearby police or fire station is asked to check in person and see if anything has happened to Mrs. Gavin. Lives have often been saved that way.

ESCORT AND TRANSPORTATION SERVICES

Because they are afraid to go out of the house alone—afraid of getting hurt, getting mugged, or getting lost—even semi-independent old people are forced, too soon, to be shut-ins. Little has been done to adapt public transportation to the physical limitations of the elderly. Stairs in subways are too steep, steps into buses and trains too high, curbs too low, signs too confusing or too hard to read. After trying to deal with all the hazards of going out, an older man or woman may just give up. It may be depressing and demoralizing to be isolated inside four walls, but at least it's safe.

The elderly have traditionally depended on their children, close relatives, and friends to accompany them, but escort services sometimes providing transportation can now be found in some, although not many, communities. When your mother leaves her home with an escort, both you and she will have some sense of security that, despite the hazards and complexities of the transportation system, she is likely to arrive safely at her destination.

CHORE SERVICES

Some older people are able to take care of themselves in their own homes, but they are unable to take care of their homes alone. For lack of physical strength or lack of money, they are unable to handle repairs and maintenance. They need someone to come in to fix leaks, put up storm windows and screens, mow lawns, and do other household repairs. Funds are available in some communities for projects which provide necessary assistance at reduced cost. In a number of communities, vigorous and capable older men and women volunteer to act as handymen and chore people for their contemporaries who are incapacitated.

FRIENDLY VISITING

Even when escort help is available, many older people are too incapacitated to leave their homes and therefore have no escape from homebound
life. Friends and relatives can relieve the isolation, boredom and loneliness, but when there are few nearby, friendly visiting, often described
as organized neighborliness, can take their place. Friendly visitors may
be university students, volunteering their services or charging only small
fees. The International Ladies Garment Workers and other unions include
friendly visiting programs among their services for their retired employees. In many places friendly visitors are elderly themselves, but active
and self-sufficient enough to visit and help contemporaries who are shut-
ins or severely handicapped. These visitors stop in on the homebound on
a regular schedule, one or more times a week, and do whatever any other
concerned guest might do: play chess or cards, write letters, help with
mending and picking up around the house, run local errands, make telephone calls, sit and chat, and, perhaps most important of all, *listen*. The
continuing companionship is the best antidote to the loneliness and endless
silence which are so built into the life of a shut-in.

COMPANION SERVICES

Companion Services provide trained men or women to offer company and
supervision to a convalescent or invalid at home. These companions may
be volunteers or be paid on a sliding-fee basis. This is the service which
can sometimes provide the lifesaving respite—or break—for the caregiver.

RESPITE CARE SERVICES

Special attention is being given these days by professionals to the importance of respite services to relieve family members responsible for
ongoing care. It is essential that these caregivers have regular time-off
periods. Here and there, nursing home and hospital beds are set aside
for nonresident elderly men and women who may stay for a night or two,
or a week or two, making it possible for their families to have time off
or even to take a vacation. If no organized respite services exist in a
given area, a companion or a homemaker may be found who can take
over for the caregiver once or twice a week and provide the much-needed
respite. In Birmingham, England, there is a night-watcher service which
gives families a night off or checks on older people living by themselves.

OUT-OF-HOME SERVICES

Some older people are luckier than the shut-ins and are able to leave
their homes more easily, but they often find, once they do go out, that

they have no place to go. Some communities have little to offer, but others have a great variety: educational and religious classes, health services, occupational, physical, and psychological therapy, as well as recreational and social opportunities. Settings for these services include senior centers, churches and synagogues, schools, hospitals, and adult day care centers.

SENIOR CENTERS (FOR THE WELL ELDERLY)

Originally established decades ago to provide social activities for older people, many senior centers now offer a much broader range of activities and services, some of which are designed to help their members cope with the many challenges of old age. In additional to recreational and educational activities, a center may offer information and referral services, care management, home-delivered meal programs, and congregate meals. Members have a chance to enjoy the companionship of contemporaries as well as that of younger volunteers and professional staff members. A number of senior centers offer intergenerational programs for young and old together. There are now 9,000 senior centers across the country.

CONGREGATE MEALS

The Older Americans Act makes funds available to local organizations to provide low-cost, nutritious meals to older people (sixty and over) in central locations—schools, churches, synagogues, community and senior centers. This nutrition program has two aims: to improve the diet of older people and at the same time to offset the isolation so many of them suffer. Too many elderly men and women hardly bother to eat because they have no one to eat with. Meals are served at the various centers five days a week. There are no financial eligibility requirements.

TRANSPORTATION SERVICES

In addition to escort services particularly important to the disabled, safe transportation is crucially important, though sadly neglected, for the elderly who are less handicapped but find the regular services difficult or frightening to use. Volunteer groups under a variety of different names, such as Dial-a-Bus or Dial-a-Car, and often sponsored by religious and social clubs, make convenient transportation available in private cars or buses. Occasionally these groups provide specially equipped buses or vans with ramps for wheelchairs and walkers. Some communities provide half-fare cards to older citizens, and a few offer free transportation. The 1978 amendments to the Older Americans Act have been sponsoring demonstration projects in a limited number of areas. If these projects prove successful they may become more widespread—assuming they can be funded.

ADULT DAY CARE (FOR THE FRAIL OR IMPAIRED)

These centers provide the same protected environment for the old as day care centers do for the young. Adult day care has been set up to meet the needs of older people who need help but not round-the-clock, who are too dependent to manage alone but too independent for nursing home placement. The centers may be located in their own buildings or in senior centers, churches, synagogues, hospitals, nursing homes, mental health centers, or private homes. The programs vary but usually provide some or most of the following services: assessment; counseling; nutrition, including a midday meal; nutritious snacks; special diets and nutritional education; personal care; health services, including blood-pressure monitoring; height and weight checks; medication dispensing; health education; and arrangements for physical, dental, foot, eye, and ear examinations. Many adult day care centers also provide transportation to and from the center, on special outings, and to and from doctors' appointments. These centers, like the at-home services described earlier, make it possible for frail older men and women to continue to live in their own homes or with families. An added benefit provided by these day care programs is extra respite time for caregivers.

> Inoperable cataracts had made eighty-six-year-old Fritz Hoffman almost blind. Nevertheless, he was still alert, well oriented, and able to enjoy his record player, radio, talking books, friends. Unable to shop, prepare his meals, clean his house, or go out alone, he was dependent on others for protection and supportive care. Since he loved getting out of the house, his daughter, who lived an hour away, arranged for him to go to a day care program—funded by Medicaid, for which her father was eligible—at a local nursing home. Every day a bus picked him up early in the morning and delivered him home in the late afternoon. A homemaker–home health aide came in twice a week to help him with household chores and shopping. His evening and weekend meals were delivered by a Meals on Wheels program from a nearby church.
>
> At the day care center, Mr. Hoffman was given rehabilitative help to handle his blindness, medical and nursing care when he needed it, and the opportunity to have a social life he enjoyed. All of this could have been provided for him twenty-four hours a day at the nursing home next door, but it was important for him to preserve some portion of his independence and remain for some part of his life in his own home.

CAREGIVER SUPPORT GROUPS

These support groups may be informal gatherings of men and women who share the same concerns and feel the need to discuss problems and solutions. Many such groups are started by caregivers themselves with little or no professional backup, while others are established by health and social service agencies, or civic and religious organizations. These groups provide an especially therapeutic forum where caregivers can air their fears, frustrations, resentments, guilt feelings, and burdens with a sympathetic, understanding audience eager to air their own problems. One woman, the caregiver for her father, gained enough strength from her support group to stand up against the older man's domineering behavior for the first time in her life. She was seventy-five years old and her father was ninety-eight! To find out about support groups in your area, contact your local senior center or Area Agency on Aging office, or start your own. The National Council on the Aging also has a directory titled *Ideabook on Caregiver Support Groups*.

PAYING FOR COMMUNITY SERVICES

When it comes to paying for community services, the picture is hardly encouraging. There is little available in the way of third-party reimbursement for these services, especially the nonmedical services described earlier. Although the funding sources described on page 193 have helped to increase the supply of community services, the greater part of federal funding still goes for institutional or nursing home care, primarily through Medicaid. Medicare does not pay for community services except for a limited amount of home health care, as described earlier. One of the greatest drawbacks to Medicare, constantly repeated in this book, is its continuing failure to provide coverage for long-term care. (See "Long-Term Health Insurance" on pages 215–17.)

SPECIAL HOUSING
WITH SPECIAL CARE

Many of the services just described can be used by the elderly living in a variety of settings: their own homes, their children's homes, foster homes, and boarding homes. Those who are prosperous may find some of these services in cooperatives, retirement hotels, condominiums, retirement communities, and apartment complexes specially adapted to the needs of older people. Such housing should ideally be built with barrier-free designs, wide doorways for wheelchairs, low shelves, sit-in showers, handrails, and emergency buzzers. In addition to providing some meals and recreational facilities, these living arrangements may also have homemakers, home health aides, and sometimes nursing care available. Without that readily available care, many of the elderly tenants would be forced to enter nursing homes.

The elderly who are partially disabled and with few financial assets beyond their Social Security checks have no such range of living arrangements to choose from. They are forced to rely on either stopgap measures or institutional placement. In increasing numbers of locations throughout the country, special living arrangements are being set up which enable low-income older men and women, although partially disabled, to remain in their communities and to continue to live semi-independent existences. Those living arrangements, sometimes called domiciliary housing, congregate housing, adult homes, foster care homes, or assisted residential living, all provide a number of services as well as food, shelter, companionship, and recreation.

The truth of the matter is that there are tremendous inadequacies in all kinds of specialized housing for the elderly, and in low-cost housing for all ages. In this respect the United States has lagged far behind many Western European countries and Israel. No overall plan by public, private, nonprofit, or private-profit sponsors exists.

WHEN YOU CANNOT HELP ENOUGH

CARE/CASE MANAGEMENT

Gena Worth—a fifty-year-old divorcee—always stopped in on her mother after work to help the eighty-one-year-old diabetic woman: to fix a light supper, supervise medication, and assist her in bathing. When Gena was offered a promotion to senior buyer in her company, she was elated, but then realized that the new job would involve extensive and frequent travel. How could she accept it when her mother needed her on a daily basis?

Even though Gena lived near her mother and wanted to help, she could not continue the daily support without making drastic sacrifices in her own life. Her community may have been rich in supportive services for the elderly, but she had no idea which would be the right ones for her mother or how she would be able to coordinate and supervise them once she had found them.

Some social agency staffs include care managers, or case managers, skilled professionals who can provide client assessment and case planning as well as finding, coordinating, and monitoring necessary services. Care management fees in these agencies are on a sliding scale—low or no-cost for those who cannot pay and higher for those who can. Schedules are usually crowded; there may be a waiting list, or there may be no care managers at all on certain social service staffs.

Professionals have become aware of the need for care managers, and in recent years there has been a rapid increase in private geriatric care managers and management agencies. Gena Worth did *not* have enough time to devote to her mother's care, but she *did* have enough money. She located a private care management agency and paid for the ongoing support her mother required. If you feel that such an arrangement would be helpful to you and your parents, be sure to check the credentials of the care manager you hire. Anyone who assumes this role should have a degree in social work, psychology, counseling, or nursing and be state-certified or licensed. Professional organizations such as the National Association of Social Workers have clinical registers of members in private practice.

Thanks to geriatric care managers, sons and daughters living far away from their parents can find some peace of mind. Nothing is more alarming for children than getting word that a parent who lives far away is in trouble. Whether the trouble is a minor crisis or a major one, it can produce frantic anxiety and family turmoil. If you live on the East Coast and your parents on the West Coast, you may fly out on occasion to help them, but if their difficulties are ongoing, how can you spend your life in the air shuttling back and forth between the coasts? An agency, social service or private, in your own community may be able to put you in touch with a similar agency in your parents' community to find and monitor the necessary help. Although now there are more such agencies nationwide, there is no guarantee that one can be found in every area. When one is available, however, it can help to bridge the painful distance separating concerned children and their parents.

A NEW LEGAL
SPECIALTY—"ELDER LAW"

Your family lawyer, well-trained in wills and estates, may know little about the intricacies of Medicare and Medicaid regulations and even less about the financial problems of aging. Because of the complications involved in arranging the affairs of older people, a new legal specialty—"elder law"—has been growing over the last ten years. A lawyer specializing in the legal problems of the elderly can help clients understand various options open to them under government programs, as well as counseling them on legal steps they can take to protect their assets in the event of serious or chronic illness.

Too many older people receive no legal advice. Not only do they not have a geriatric lawyer, but many cannot afford a lawyer at all to advise them on their rights and to safeguard their assets. When problems needing legal intervention arise, however, help can sometimes be found through legal aid societies, which provide low-cost advice for all age groups. Area Agencies on Aging are good sources of information on where to find legal help.

Your parents may seek legal advice themselves in order to put their affairs in good shape, but some older people, reluctant to think about the future and what may lie ahead, refuse to consider advance planning. If a crisis comes, you may be drawn in to make plans yourself. One day your father may obviously be unable to handle his funds or to pay his bills. He may go off on crazy spending sprees or be threatened with eviction for nonpayment of his rent. He needs some kind of protection. After consulting his lawyer, you may be advised to select one of three procedures most commonly used, which can also be quickly put into action: power of attorney, joint tenancy, or inter vivos trust. All three require that your father be sufficiently alert—and willing—to enter into a contractual agreement.

1. *Power of attorney* is used most frequently. If your father gives you power of attorney, he thereby allows you to manage his funds. Power of attorney will be terminated if your father becomes incompetent, *unless* he has stated in writing, while competent, that the document should remain valid in the event of his incompetency.
2. *Joint tenancy* is also frequently used and does not have the same limitations as power of attorney, because each party has total control over the funds regardless of the competency of the parties involved. If your father is able to enter into a joint tenancy contract with you or another responsible person, and deteriorates thereafter, the joint tenancy continues.
3. An *inter vivos trust* is the most sophisticated of the three and provides the greatest flexibility. Using that procedure, your father may create a trust for himself, naming himself as trustee, but at the same time providing for a successor trustee (you or another person) to take control if he becomes incapacitated.

Each of these legal procedures has its own drawbacks and limitations, all of which should be reviewed with a lawyer. They may also be costly, but the most important problem to be faced is that most old people are reluctant to turn over all or even a portion of personal control of their own financial affairs. You may be caught in the middle of an uncomfortable dilemma if your father is reluctant to accept any help from you. Either you insist on helping him, thereby antagonizing him and making him feel more powerless than ever, or you sit back and do nothing, watching him squander his money or be exploited by others.

THE PAINFUL PROCESS OF INCOMPETENCY PROCEEDINGS

The day may come when your father's mental condition deteriorates to such a point that he is no longer capable of managing his affairs at all. He may be too disabled to enter into any contract, and the only way open to your family may be to have him declared incompetent by the courts. Incompetency proceedings, like many other legal proceedings, vary from state to state, but they usually involve certification by physicians or psychiatrists of the older person involved, and appointment of a guardian to manage his affairs and provide for his needs and well-being.

Many families find the mere idea of incompetency proceedings too painful to consider. There is still much shame and stigma attached to any kind of mental illness in our society. New York State recently enacted a conservatorship law designed to avoid the emotional burden normally involved in incompetency proceedings. That law provides for the appointment of a conservator to take over the financial affairs of anyone who becomes too impaired because of advanced age, illness, infirmity, or mental deterioration to manage alone. If your father is seriously deteriorated mentally and psychiatric hospitalization is necessary, he may refuse to commit himself. You may have to have him committed involuntarily, a procedure usually requiring the endorsement of several physicians.

PROTECTIVE SERVICES

Painful legal proceedings or commitment might be avoided altogether if an adequate array of community services could be provided for the mentally impaired older person. They would include legal, medical, psychiatric, nursing, homemaking, and home health aide services, coordinated by a social worker skilled in helping the often resistant older person. Protective services such as these are sometimes provided by local welfare offices and voluntary agencies.

WHAT IF THEY WON'T BE HELPED— BY YOU OR ANYONE ELSE?

There are legal steps to take in cases of mental incompetence, but in cases of physical incompetence the course of action is less clear. Most older people are willing to ask for help and to accept it when they cannot manage, but some may refuse any help of any kind from anybody. Although it is obvious to everyone else in the family that Mom and Dad are incapable of taking care of themselves, Mom and Dad think they are managing very well and resent any suggestion that they are not.

"I'm perfectly fine. Stop worrying about me!" an eighty-year-old crippled father may shout at his son for the fiftieth time. "I can still manage my own affairs," a half-blind mother may insist. But he's *not* fine, and she *can't* manage. Many older people ask for too much help; others ask for too little. Some won't accept any. They may refuse to accept the limitations imposed by their age, their physical deterioration, and their financial plight. They will not listen to logic and reason, nor will they be coaxed, bribed, or cajoled into changing their lifestyles.

Sometimes both your parents may be in that position—refusing all offers of help, rejecting any alternative living situations, and insisting on staying right where they are even though their house is an unsanitary shambles and full of hazards. If you take matters into your own hands and make arrangements for them, they are legally within their rights to fire summarily any outside help you bring in. There is not much you can do except wait for the day a serious accident or illness incapacitates one or both of them. Surreptitiously helping behind their backs may make you feel better but at best will only postpone, rather than prevent, disaster.

Occasionally, if they will not listen to you or anyone else in the family, they may listen to someone they trust who is not a relative: a minister, a rabbi, a priest, a social worker, a doctor, or even a close friend. But if they will not accept any compromise in their living arrangements, the most you can do is firmly state your own feelings and the limits of your own involvement (see Chapter 10).

Although children are urged to give quiet support to their parents' lifestyles, no child is urged to support a pattern which threatens life and health. Your warning that you may have to withdraw from your close relationship with them may seem cruel, but it may be the only way you can get through to them. It is likely that you carry a more valued weight in their lives than their independence.

Mary and Frank Visconti were not managing. Their daughter knew it, their friends knew it, but they would not admit it. Money was not a serious problem but no outside help was allowed to remain for long. They were both undernourished, their clothes and bodies uncared for, and their apartment littered. Their daughter went back and forth between her town and theirs trying to bring order out of the chaos and hoping each time to persuade them to accept some compromise. Their son-in-law finally stepped in to settle the situation. He did not give orders; he was not dictatorial; he allowed the old people to be involved in future plans. He gave them three choices: all they had to do was select one.

"All right, which will it be? Come and live with us. Go to a nursing home together. Or *stop firing the housekeeper!*"

A REALISTIC AFTERTHOUGHT

This chapter has described the variety of ways children may be able to help their disabled, aging parents and the variety of services that may supplement or replace their help.

In many communities—perhaps in yours—a reassuring number of services are available. But do not relax too quickly if the Yellow Pages of your phone book list homemaker, escort, transportation, and other helpful services. Your reassurance may not last long if all the homemakers are busy just at the moment your parents need one, all the escorts booked, and all the cars spoken for. Visiting nurses may be overworked, social workers may be carrying heavy caseloads, and there may be long waiting lists at the health services.

We hope a greater number and a greater variety of services will continue to develop across the country during the coming years, offering the elderly and their families a wider variety of options and opportunities for support and care. (See Chapter 11.)

9

HELPING WHEN THEY
CANNOT MANAGE—
THE NURSING HOME SOLUTION

The second stroke did not kill eighty-year-old Peter Vorman, but it severely paralyzed him. He lived—but he needed care twenty-four hours a day. Someone had to be there all the time to feed him, bathe him, dress him, take him to the bathroom, and medicate him. Neither his wife, a semi-invalid herself, nor his children, who were married with families of their own, could give him the care he needed. There were only limited community services in the small town where they lived. The family made a careful study of available nursing homes and settled on the one they felt would suit Mr. Vorman best. Once he had moved in and was comfortably settled, his family left feeling relieved.

But Mrs. Vorman could not forgive herself for "abandoning" her husband, and the children never lost the feeling that they had failed their father, "locked him up," "put him away."

The Vorman family is not alone. The very term "nursing home" conjures up a series of unhappy, even terrifying images in the minds of old and young alike. At best, the words suggest coldness, impersonality, and regimentation; at worst, neglect, mistreatment, cruelty, and loneliness. Unfortunately, negative images can legitimately be used in describing some institutions. But they cannot be used broadside. While there are too few excellent nursing homes and too many disgraceful ones, the majority lie somewhere between these two poles.

No nursing home can work miracles. No nursing home can make the old and feeble young and vigorous again. No nursing home menu will ever please all elderly palates—sensitivities vary and taste buds are often duller. No nursing home will solve the various roommate problems or prevent friction between residents—communal living has its built-in stresses. Dissatisfaction is predictable in some areas of nursing home life.

When nursing home placement is necessary for an elderly parent, realistic sons and daughters must face an imperfect situation and at the same time face two other painful realities: the irreversible deterioration of a person they love, and their own inability or unwillingness to care for that person.

Institutionalization, although often a tragic step, is not tantamount to dying. There still may be some gratifying living ahead. Nor does institutionalization necessarily imply family rejection. But those are widely held suppositions often reinforced by the elderly themselves. "No matter what happens," a dying mother may say to her children, "don't ever let your father go into a home," or "Promise me you'll never put me in one of those places."

It is important to note that placement in a nursing home need not necessarily be permanent. Sometimes, elderly persons enter a nursing home for rehabilitation or recuperation after an illness. Such short-term stays are often covered by Medicare. Their homes in the community, however, must be held for them. For the poor older person this is sometimes impossible, although Social Security and SSI payments are beginning to cover such situations.

Elderly residents may change their minds after entering a nursing home and, with help, return to their former homes. Sometimes their condition improves sufficiently to make this possible. But the move back to the community may be impossible without sufficient resources. The family often makes the crucial difference.

The statistics are misleading. While it is true that at any one time less than 5 percent of the nation's elderly are living in institutions, 25 percent of that group at some point in their later years spend time in one, either temporarily, until they recover from a serious illness, or permanently, until they die. It may surprise those who share the prevailing negative assumptions to learn that it's not always the children who "put their parents in nursing homes." A number of older people enter voluntarily; they are not pushed in, cast aside by rejecting relatives, or locked up against their will. Unfortunately, the false assumptions still prevail.

All four of Maria Vincente's children were horrified when their mother, after making a fine recovery from a serious hip fracture, announced her intention to enter a local intermediate care home. Why did she need this? Didn't she believe they all loved her and wanted to take care of her? Hadn't they all helped her after her fall? And the grandchildren, too? Why should strangers take care of her when she had family? But Maria, a feisty, determined eighty-year-old, could not be dissuaded. As a matter of fact, she had already made all the arrangements.

On the day she was to take up residence, her neighbors dropped by her apartment to say good-bye. To each one she whispered with a resigned sigh, "My children are putting me in a nursing home." Her daughter, overhearing, burst out, "Mamma! How can you say that! You know it's not true!" "I know and you know," Maria replied calmly. "But I have to tell them something *they'll* understand."

Maria Vincente did not share the popular belief (or misconception) that institutionalization inevitably signifies the end of it all. There are some, but not many, Marias around. Most families have two obstacles to hurdle prior to accepting a nursing home solution: they must overcome both their own aversion and the opposition of the potential nursing home resident. It is hard to pinpoint the exact moment when institutionalization becomes a necessary move—what provides the tipping point that forces the decision. In cases of severe incapacity, the need for such an action is more obvious. But the tipping point may also come from a combination of factors: partial incapacity, combined with inadequate help in the home, exacerbated by increasing personality conflicts. The tipping point may arrive sooner for an elderly relative who is difficult, demanding, and uncooperative, or in families who are burdened with their own problems. But for most families, whenever the tipping point comes—whether it is early or late—it is painful to accept, for it may represent failure to them and a finality in terms of their parents' lives.

A PLANNED OPTION OR A FORCED DECISION?

The longer people live, the greater is the likelihood that they will develop disabling conditions requiring protective or skilled care. That care can, of course, be provided outside the institutional setting. Some old people can stay right where they are if enough money is available in the family and enough services are available in the community. But often neither money nor services can be found and institutionalization is the only solution. Many families prefer to ignore the future, coasting blithely along as if no such grim possibility lay ahead. Such families may spare themselves anxiety by not dwelling on a disaster that may never happen, but consider the odds: at some point, *one out of every four* older people will enter a nursing home. Those who have investigated nursing homes in advance will be in an infinitely more advantageous position to make a sound choice.

When there is no immediate crisis demanding solution, there is time for a thorough review of all possibilities, as well as a thorough analysis of the preferences and attitudes of the older person involved. Nursing home placements made on the basis of impulsive, frantic decisions usually produce disaster all around. The mother or father in question may feel bewildered, coerced, infantilized, and rejected. In addition, rushed placements allow no time to investigate the quality of an institution or to find the one offering rehabilitative, restorative, and supportive services. "Who's got room for Mom right away?" is the only question there is time to ask, rather than, "Which is the best place for Mom? Where will she be happiest?" An essential ingredient in all of this planning is to make sure that Mom is involved step by step. She, after all, has the ultimate right to make the final choice, if she is still capable mentally.

Deliberate and careful planning for a placement has the further advantage of giving both families and parents sufficient time to prepare themselves emotionally. The feelings stirred up by placement can be so intense that counseling may be invaluable to everyone during this time. Your mother may need someone to whom she can express her anxiety over the separation which placement will bring and her feelings of perhaps being unwanted. Since placement is usually a less socially acceptable solution to a problem than remaining in one's own home, it can create feelings of anger, sadness, and guilt, all of which need to be aired if the transition is to be smooth for all concerned. (A list of counseling services is provided in Appendix A, pages 280–316.)

This chapter will summarize important steps to follow in selecting a nursing home. It will offer guidelines for the actual admission and sketch a brief review of institutional life itself as it affects those inside and the relatives who remain in the outside world.

Not knowing where to start is the quandary shared by many families when they first approach the unexplored territory of nursing homes. "How do we go about the whole thing?" they ask helplessly. There are thousands of nursing homes in the country, varying in capacity from twenty-five to more than one thousand beds. In some geographic locations the choice is limited; in other areas there are dozens to choose from. There are also three different types of sponsorship:

1. Voluntary—nonprofit, sectarian or nonsectarian, governed by a lay board
2. Proprietary—private, profit-making
3. Public (very few)

In the wake of the nursing home scandals, public and private agencies in some locations have drawn up lists of acceptable nursing homes in their particular areas. Local information and referral services, social service agencies, ministers, doctors, and nurses may know if such a list has been compiled for your parents' community. Even if no such list exists, the same sources can usually tell you something about the local nursing homes. A directory of accredited voluntary homes, listed by state, may be obtained from the American Association of Homes for the Aging, the national organization of nonprofit homes and housing for the aging (see Appendix A, p. 316).

But knowing what's available is only the beginning. A series of logical steps must then be taken in order to find the answer to the crucial question "What is the right home for Mother?" or "Which is the best home for Father?"

STEP ONE: UNDERSTANDING THE KINDS OF CARE AVAILABLE

First of all, certain questions must be considered. What kind of care do nursing homes offer? Do they all offer the same kind? How do they differ from hospitals? In choosing a nursing home it is important to remember that all facilities are not alike, that they offer different levels of care, and that under the federal laws regulating Medicare and Medicaid, two types of facilities are recognized: the skilled nursing facility and the intermediate care facility. You may wonder which facility is the right one for your father.

THE SKILLED NURSING FACILITY

A skilled nursing facility is considered necessary for someone requiring intensive care: twenty-four-hour-a-day supervision and treatment by a registered nurse. Some states—New York, for example—have point systems to determine who may be admitted. Utilization review committees keep close tabs on admissions. Residents of skilled nursing facilities, if they qualify, are eligible for Medicaid coverage in all states of the union.

INTERMEDIATE CARE FACILITIES

When round-the-clock nursing by a registered nurse is not considered medically necessary, an older person may be eligible for an intermediate care facility, which provides twenty-four-hour-a-day care under the supervision of a registered nurse. As of 1975, intermediate care was covered by Medicaid in most states at about half the cost of skilled nursing care.

HOMES WITH BOTH LEVELS OF CARE

Many institutions offer both levels—skilled and intermediate. A resident may only need the intermediate level this year, but next year his condition may deteriorate—or his condition may improve, and the nursing home's utilization and review committee may decide that he can be moved to a lower level of care. When both levels are available in the same place, shifting from one level to another can be done smoothly and is less traumatic to both the older person and his family than a move to another institution. If you are uncertain about which level of care is necessary for your father, you can ask for an assessment of his needs from your doctor, an intake team at a hospital or nursing home, or a qualified medical social worker or nurse.

This is the time to make sure that nursing home or intermediate care is really the right solution. If placement is made incorrectly, there is always a danger that your father may be shifted to a different level of care or even back to the community.

SHELTERED CARE HOMES

This is a third type of facility, which provides personal care only, not nursing. Such homes may be independent, or may be located in nursing homes with one or both levels of care.

STEP TWO: UNDERSTANDING HOW MONEY DETERMINES YOUR OPTIONS

Unfortunately, as in every other aspect of the lives of the elderly, dollars and cents must be considered in choosing a nursing home. The financial picture today is not as bleak as it used to be before the establishment of Medicaid, but it is essential to determine before choosing a nursing home whether it is approved for Medicare and Medicaid, assuming your parents are eligible for either. Medicare covers only care in an approved skilled nursing facility for up to one hundred days posthospitalization and for specified conditions. Medicaid covers the cost of care for eligible persons in approved skilled nursing facilities for as long as their condition merits it.

If your parents have no money, several agencies can guide them through the steps that must be taken to apply for Medicaid coverage of nursing home placement (refer to Chapter 7 for Medicaid eligibility): their local Department of Social Services (welfare department), their local Medicaid office, and their local Social Security office. The nursing homes themselves can be helpful, too, and if there is one particular nursing home your parents prefer, they can find out directly from the admissions department there if residents are admitted under Medicaid. If so, the home will help with the necessary applications.

Be prepared to discover, however, that many homes do not accept residents who cannot pay for at least some initial period of time and therefore will not accept anyone who must be admitted on Medicaid funds from the beginning. When your parents have no money at all, their options are limited in every area of their lives—including nursing home selection.

LONG-TERM HEALTH INSURANCE

Despite the expanded benefits becoming available under the new Catastrophic Coverage Act of 1988 (see pages 163–65), a gaping hole still remains in health protection. There are still no provisions for long-term care, either at home or in a nursing home, for anyone except the needy who qualify for Medicaid. The act does add an extra 50 days to the 100 originally allowed by Medicare, but these do little to offset the costs of years of chronic illness. A few do qualify for Medicaid coverage, but the rest of the elderly—from the near-poor all the way to the affluent—have to depend on their own resources to cover chronic disability. Even if these resources appear to be more than adequate, they melt away surprisingly fast. Children of an institutionalized Alzheimer's disease patient are often devastated to discover after just a few years that their father's seemingly ample assets have been eaten up and he is ready to qualify for Medicaid without a need to "spend down." His months in the hospital have spent down for him. The U.S. House of Representatives' Select Committee on Aging found in 1985 that two-thirds of older individuals and one-third of older couples in Massachusetts were impoverished after thirteen weeks in a nursing home. Similar percentages can be found in other states.

Most people are not poor when they enter a nursing home but become poor very quickly. Look at the costs of these institutions: the nationwide average for a year in a nursing home was $20,000 in 1988, and this figure is expected to rise to $55,000 by the year 2018, assuming that inflation remains at a moderate level. In many specific locations the costs of caring for the chronically ill are much higher. New York City's costs in 1988 averaged $50,000 for a nursing home and $25,000 for home care.

The elderly segment of the population is expanding quickly, but the number of individuals needing care for chronic illness is growing even faster as more and more men and women live on into their eighties, nineties, and one hundreds. The federal government, having taken care of the nation's needy with Medicaid, has left the rest of the elderly and disabled to fend for themselves. There is a desperate need for some kind of financial protection against such crippling costs.

Aware of this need, a number of insurance companies have recently begun to offer long-term-care insurance policies. While this innovation was heralded by some as the panacea for a serious national problem, the panacea has turned out to be little more than a good Band-Aid, if that. Such long-term policies are often expensive and therefore out of the reach of the average pocketbook. In 1986 premium costs ranged annually from $100 to $3,500, depending on the beneficiary's age (the older the individual, the higher the premium, naturally), how long the beneficiary must be receiving care before benefits begin, and the amount, duration, and extent of benefits. Furthermore, such policies usually establish at the time of signing the dollar amounts beneficiaries will receive at some future time if they need nursing home care or long-term care at home—if home care is covered at all, which is not the case with many policies. No adjustments are made for inflation. If the policy is signed in 1989 setting a figure of $100 a day for nursing home care, that's what the beneficiary will receive in 1999 even if the daily costs have doubled in ten years.

To add to the confusion, most policies include such an intricate web of disclaimers, waivers, and limitations that many beneficiaries find it almost impossible to cut through the tangle in order to see clearly just what they are buying. Some policies require hospitalization for a prescribed number of days before benefits can go into effect; yet many older people do not require acute care in a hospital before their nursing home care begins. This works a particular hardship on Alzheimer's patients, who usually enter nursing homes directly when taking care of them in their own homes becomes too difficult. Some policies will cover care in a skilled nursing home or perhaps an intermediate home, but will not cover care in a custodial home at all. Here again, Alzheimer's patients may be excluded, as well as stroke victims, who need extended custodial care if they are to recover or permanent custodial care if they do not improve.

No policies pay for time spent in rest homes, old-age homes, mental institutions, and alcohol or drug rehabilitation centers. Most policies limit benefits for existing mental or nervous disorders, which may or may not include Alzheimer's disease—the very one people fear and the reason why they want to buy long-term coverage in the first place. Vague language in a policy may give the carrier the leeway at the moment of crisis to decide whether or not a policyholder who has paid premiums for years in good faith will be allowed to draw benefits.

So many pitfalls lie ahead for prospective buyers of long-term health insurance that the safest protection is to have policies checked over by lawyers or professionals in nonprofit organizations to make sure that all i's are dotted and all t's crossed. If this is not possible, buyers are urged to read every line of their policies—fine print and all—to be sure that what they are buying will be watertight when they need shelter. (The May 1988 issue of *Consumer Reports* gives a careful analysis of the range of long-term health insurance policies.)

RELATIVE RESPONSIBILITY

Adult children formerly had to accept filial responsibility. They were held accountable financially for their parents' nursing home bills. Today under Medicaid regulations they are no longer held legally responsible. But another complicated issue has come up—the transfer of assets. In order to qualify for Medicaid, an elderly person is permitted to have only the minimum assets described in Chapter 7. To reach this minimum, therefore, potential nursing home residents have often attempted to transfer assets to someone else—a son, daughter, grandchild, or spouse. In the past this was seen as a move to defraud the government and was not allowed. Although the situation has changed in recent years—some transfer of funds is now legal—it is still full of confusions, limitations, and restrictions which require legal advice for clarification. A lawyer, preferably one with "elder law" experience, can sometimes help families set up trusts and make other financial arrangements to protect their parents' assets.

So much for filial responsibility and its confusions. Now comes an equally confusing situation concerning spouse responsibility. Until recently husbands and wives were held legally responsible for each other's nursing home payments in every state. This ruling often had disastrous consequences (see page 169). The situation changed in 1988 with the new Medicare Catastrophic Coverage Act. As of September 1989, the spouse remaining in the outside community is permitted to retain a certain amount of the couple's income and assets (see page 170 under "Medicaid"). While this new ruling does keep spouses in the community from destitution and welfare, there is a $60,000 ceiling on the amount they can retain. This may seem like a fortune to some, but not to others who will have to watch sizable assets built up over a lifetime get eaten up by nursing home fees.

Careful financial calculations and projections are essential before any nursing home placement can be made, even when children feel they are in a position to pay for their parents' care. You may feel you do not need to worry about finding a Medicaid-eligible home for your father. Between his assets and your own, you are confident that there will be plenty of money to cover a completely private placement. But will there really be enough? What if he lives another ten years? What if you have a heart attack and must retire early? If your father should outlive you, will

there be money enough to protect him, as well as your widow and your
children?

STEP THREE: EVALUATING QUALITY

A review of the dollars and cents of nursing home finances and the levels
of care offered is the preliminary groundwork preparing the way for a
thorough investigation of individual nursing homes. That investigation is
the most important step in finding the answer to the crucial question,
"Which one will be best for Mother?"

Finding the ultimate answer involves making up a list of possibilities
in the desired geographic area, checking the opinions and judgments of
knowledgeable people, and then inspecting each one in a personal visit.
Whenever possible, it is recommended that the prospective resident be
encouraged to take the initiative, or at least share all the steps including
the inspection tours and the final decision.

A JOURNEY INTO THE UNKNOWN

It is not hard to make up a list of nursing homes or to gather opinions
about them, but visits to nursing homes—particularly the first ones—are
often bewildering, depressing, even terrifying experiences. One visitor
reported, "I felt like a stranger in a foreign land. Nothing looked familiar,
not even the people. It was terrible—all I wanted to do was run!"

That reaction is not unusual, nor is it surprising. The world of the
nursing home is unknown territory to the general public. Unless involved
professionally or because of a relative in residence, the average person
manages to stay blissfully ignorant about these places, almost unaware
of their existence. Until recently there has been little to call public attention to them, and the recent interest has centered mainly on the
scandals involved.

The TV screen takes viewers into submarines, jails, drug centers,
jungles, mountain peaks. Hospitals, thanks to the various media, are as
familiar as neighborhood backyards. Drs. Kildare, Casey, and Welby and
an army of their colleagues have brought examining rooms, therapy
rooms, operating rooms, emergency rooms into the living rooms of the
nation. European writers took their readers into TB sanitaria in the past.
Solzhenitsyn did the same with the cancer ward. But who has opened up
the doors of the nursing homes for the elderly and invited the public in?
The country knows more about life on the moon than it does about life
in those institutions. How ironical it is—only a handful of us are ever
likely to walk on the moon or orbit in space, yet most of us are likely to

grow old. For some reason the media have allowed the nursing home world to remain clothed in mystery. No wonder people find it painful and frightening when they penetrate this mystery for the first time by actually visiting an institution.

That mystery—that not knowing what to expect—accounts for much of the initial shock so frequently reported by visitors. Perhaps the main shock-producer for the novice visitor is the nursing home population itself. This may be the first time old age has ever been encountered en masse. You may know your own mother well, understand her problems, ache for her pains and her losses. Because of your involvement with her you may even consider yourself quite a geriatric expert. But in a nursing home you must face everyone else's elderly parents, and all the range and variety of deterioration that old age has to offer, although residents of intermediate care facilities look much healthier than residents of skilled nursing facilities. On your first visit you may be struck only by negative impressions: people in wheelchairs, in walkers; disoriented old men, weeping old women. Your immediate reaction may be, "My mother doesn't belong here—not with these people." If your mother happens to be with you on the first inspection tour her reaction may be similar: "This is no place for me."

Later on, in subsequent visits to other institutions or even on a return trip to the first one, when the initial impact has lessened you may come to accept the wheelchairs and the walkers and the disorientation—and be able to see beyond them to other residents enjoying a variety of activities and busily participating in the daily routine of "their home." A second visit or even a third may be necessary in order to sort out the bewildering kaleidoscope of impressions and come to a final decision.

YOU CAN LEARN A LOT FROM YOUR RECEPTION

While it is true that first impressions about a given nursing home are sometimes incorrect and need revising, it is usually possible to sense immediately and correctly the attitude of a nursing home's staff toward your visit. Is there a friendly welcome? Are you encouraged to tour freely, ask questions, talk to residents and staff? If the staff seems defensive, reluctant to let you tour, or insists on showing you only what *they* want you to see, you would probably be right in supposing that there is something they want to hide. Openness is usually a clue to quality, and all parts of an institution should be open to you. Potential residents and their relatives are consumers shopping for a way of life. They have a right to know down to the last detail exactly what kind of a life they are buying.

Since the privacy of residents should always be respected, certain specific areas of any nursing home may be in use and closed to you when you visit. If you are particularly interested in seeing those areas, it may be necessary for you to return at another time. Return visits can be time-consuming and exhausting, but they can pay off in terms of additional information gained, which may have a crucial bearing on your parent's future adjustment.

WHAT DO OTHER PEOPLE HAVE TO SAY?

Other people's opinions can be extremely helpful. Some families prefer to gather as much information pro or con on a specific home prior to a first visit, while others decide to visit cold and check out their impressions with informed people afterward. The families of residents already living in a home can tell you about their experiences, and the nursing home staff is usually willing to suggest names for you to contact. Community agencies, physicians, and clergymen are all good sources of information and may even be willing to tell you why they prefer one institution over another. A final source can be the state agency which licenses the homes you are visiting.

It is safer to use more than one source of information. When talking to families of residents, always keep in mind that emotions run high when a relative is institutionalized. Sons and daughters may be ruled by strong personal feelings and prejudices not universally shared; so weigh all violent opinions carefully. If a friend says of an institution you are considering, "That snake pit! They killed my father there!" she may possibly be justified, but you would be wise to check further. Similarly, don't accept blindly a daughter's glowing report of Apple Tree Manor. Her views may be colored by her relief that someone else is finally taking care of her difficult, demanding, troublemaking mother.

If you are completely repelled by your visit to one nursing home, you may decide to reject it without further investigation. But if you are leaning toward another one, it would be safer to check it through several sources and see if your positive feelings are reinforced. No one person or agency is acquainted with, or even interested in, every aspect of good nursing care. All informants have their own personal or professional bias. A nursing home shopper acts like a computer—allowing all relevant information to be fed in and hoping that eventually a definitive answer to the original question, "What's the right nursing home for Mother?" will appear on the print-out.

WHAT TO LOOK FOR WHEN YOU VISIT

Prospective applicants and their families find a checklist helpful on nursing home visits. Because the tours have such emotional undertones, visitors often blank out on many questions they planned to ask and forget essential things they wanted to see. (A sample checklist is provided in Appendix B, pages 321–24, but you may want to draw up your own to cover your specific requirements.) Some queries on the list can be quickly settled by simple observation, others by talking to residents and members of the staff.

You probably will have checked out the home's overall licensing status prior to your visit, but if not, now is the time to review it and to find out whether specific staff members are licensed also. Licensing is crucially important, and if a home is unlicensed, try to avoid it, because you can be sure there is something seriously wrong with it. Some states also require that the administrators be licensed. Always check this qualification, too, because the administrator is the key figure—the one who sets the tone of the entire institution. Other personnel on staff should be licensed or certified whenever possible: physicians, registered nurses, occupational and physical therapists, dieticians, and social workers.

Once the routine items are taken care of, a visitor needs to be concerned with three broad areas in each institution: the quality of the medical, nursing, and other therapeutic services; the quality of the housekeeping and meal services; and finally, the *climate* of the home—its social life and psychological atmosphere.

MEDICAL SERVICE

Every home should have a physician available in case of emergency—on staff or on call. some good homes allow residents to be treated by their own private physicians as often as necessary. Other patients must depend on the home's physicians, and it is important to find out how often they visit. (In some states it is mandatory that all nursing home residents be visited by a physician once a month.) If a resident does not have a private physician and there is none on staff, be sure to find out how the home guarantees regular medical attention.

Other specialized medical consultants should be available—either on staff or within easy call—for psychiatric, dental, eye, and foot care. Those specialties are far from minor or incidental ones, and become more and more essential with age. Even the best nursing home cannot be expected to serve as a fully equipped hospital, but every institution should have an ongoing arrangement with a nearby hospital for acute illnesses. If there is no hospital nearby, it is important to find out how the home functions in emergency situations.

NURSING SERVICE

The competence and humanity of the nursing staff probably affect resident morale more than any other service. Nurses, aides, and orderlies have

more continuing contact with residents than anyone else on staff, and
their attitudes and behavior have great impact. In a skilled nursing facility, one or more registered nurses—depending on the size of the
home—should be on duty at all times, giving medication and directly
supervising the care of residents. Licensed practical nurses with at least
one year of specialized geriatric training should be on duty round-the-
clock on all shifts. In an intermediate care facility, all nursing duties
should be directed by a registered nurse.

SPECIALIZED THERAPEUTIC SERVICES

Highly competent medical and nursing staffs are essential, but they cannot be responsible for all aspects of nursing home care. Other services,
some of which may be required by state health codes, are also essential
if an elderly resident's ability to function is to be restored or even maintained: occupational therapists, physiotherapists, dieticians, social workers with clinical training.

WHAT ABOUT THE MENTALLY IMPAIRED RESIDENT?

The care of the elderly with advanced chronic brain disorder is a fledgling
art that has so far developed only limited therapeutic skills. But the
backward approach to senility is a thing of the past—or it should be. You
have a right to expect that any good nursing home will have a positive
approach to the mentally impaired, shared by staff members in all services. The attitude involves tremendous patience, understanding, and
warmth toward the residents formerly written off as hopeless or impossible to reach. No surefire therapeutic tools have been developed yet to
deal successfully with the problems of mental impairment, but the search
continues, and some measures are effective in offering some structure
and meaning to the lives of the very disoriented.

Some homes are trying out rehabilitation programs: attempts to help
patients recapture a little or some of their cognitive powers lost through
disuse, the traumatic brain damage of a stroke, or the insidious physical
damage to the brain as seen in Alzheimer's disease.

In the past, older people with severe mental impairment were usually
placed in state hospitals, but after the establishment of Medicaid most
states have tended to transfer their elderly patients, except those considered dangerous, out of the hospitals and into nursing homes and dom-
iciliaries. If your father is suffering any serious mental impairment, it is
particularly important to make sure that the home he enters is equipped
to deal with his condition. Psychiatrists and specially trained staff members should be available.

IS IT ALL SHADOW OR SUBSTANCE?

Many nursing homes boast a wide variety of special services. They offer in their brochures an impressive staff of professionals to prospective applicants and their families. But visitors are advised to ascertain by personal observation whether the boasted services are actually making an impact and whether the professionals are in evidence. Are the residents clean and properly dressed during the day? By what time? Are physical and occupational therapy rooms in use or empty, showing little sign of ongoing programs? Are residents involved in activities, or are they lined up in rows against the wall staring into space? Are they responsive to each other and to what is happening around them? Do you feel you've walked into Sleeping Beauty's palace and found a perfectly set scene with all the actors fast asleep? Poor nursing homes rely on sleep as a great problem-solver and often medicate residents heavily in order to avoid trouble. Even when there are high standards of professional staffing, efficiency, and cleanliness, steer clear of homes where residents spend much of their time in bed and asleep.

HOTEL SERVICES: HOW GOOD IS THE HOUSEKEEPING?

Every institution must provide room and board for its residents, but the mere existence of basic requirements is not enough—they should also be provided in an attractive physical plant which includes comfortable rooms, a safe, clean environment, and furnishings appropriate and comfortable for residents with disabilities. An older person can adjust much more quickly to attractive, familiar surroundings than to a hospital atmosphere suggesting coldness, efficiency, and sterility. A homelike effect can be achieved when residents are allowed to furnish their own rooms with personal items. Pleasant living requires more than well-furnished bedrooms. There should also be comfortable public rooms and dining halls, recreation rooms, special-purpose rooms where residents can have some privacy, and ideally some opportunity for fresh air and sunshine outdoors. Even urban institutions can provide terraces and roof gardens.

THE CLIMATE: A HOMELIKE OR
STERILE AND REPRESSIVE ATMOSPHERE?

Judging the climate and making an accurate prediction of the prevailing "weather patterns" can be one of the most challenging parts of any nursing home visit. This may be the major factor determining whether your parent will make a reasonably good adjustment to nursing home life or will slip further into emotional or physical deterioration. Accurate weather prediction is notoriously difficult. Professional facilities and services in one home may meet your highest hopes, but the fine quality may be neutralized by an atmosphere of coldness and repression. An unfortunate climate may not prevent you from selecting a particular home if everything else seems to suit your needs, but it may be enough to warn you that there may be trouble in the future.

A variety of indicators predict quite reliably the social and psychological atmosphere of any home. Some are subtle and difficult to pick up; others are built into the organization of the home. The ideal atmosphere combines friendliness, warmth, and concern. It permits residents to maintain a sense of personal dignity. It respects privacy, allows individuality, and has room for some degree of freedom. This is not easy to achieve, and even though it may appear spontaneous and undirected, it usually is just the opposite and results from explicit expectations percolating down from the top—from the board of directors and administration through the supervisors and professionals.

PERSONAL PREFERENCES
MAY DICTATE CHOICES

In addition to finding a home with high performance in all areas, some families have their own particular needs. Homes can be found which answer a variety of individualized demands. (In California there is even one institution which caters mainly to old, blind, non-English-speaking Japanese men and women.) Your own needs may not be so specific, but you may know that your mother will be happy only in an environment corresponding to her cultural, religious, or ethnic background. It may be crucial for her, if she is an orthodox Jew, that she live in a place where the dietary laws are strictly observed. If she is foreign-born and has difficulty with English, she may need someone around who understands her language. Equally crucial can be the location and setting of the home— whether it is in the country, the suburbs, or the city.

The Farmer family was delighted to find a top-flight home conveniently located in their own suburban town. There were beautiful grounds and a view of rolling hills from every window, and the family fully expected old Mrs. Farmer to make a good adjustment there. She had certainly seemed favorably impressed when she visited before her placement. To her children's great disappointment, however, she remained withdrawn and apathetic, while the nurses reported that she slept badly and ate little. Eventually it was discovered that she hated the country and pined for city sights and sounds. Born in the shadow of the Third Avenue El in New York City, she had lived all her life on a busy main thoroughfare. Fire engines, ambulances, and noisy traffic never disturbed her sleep, but crickets, bullfrogs, early-rising birds, and the wind rustling in the trees outside her window terrified her and kept her sleepless. Neither she nor her children had considered that possibility when they selected the home.

When everything else is equal, proximity can be the deciding factor in selection of one home over another. You may know already that your mother thrives on close contact with you or another of her children. Frequent visits will be crucial to her well-being. If so, it may be better for everyone if she selects a home nearby, even if it is imperfect, where you can visit easily without disrupting your life completely. A more distant place may offer a wider range of services, but those benefits will not serve instead of family visits. You know your own mother best!

WHEN THERE IS NO CHOICE

It is tragic that for many people in many places there is no choice, or only a limited choice. When your mother begins to deteriorate, you may look into all the nursing homes within a wide radius of your community and find nothing available to meet your standards. Because of family finances, the state of your own health, or the absence of workable alternatives, you may be forced to settle for mediocrity or worse. If—after you have obtained a good assessment of your mother's condition, involved her in the search for a nursing home, and inspected them all—you are forced to settle for an institution that falls far below your hopes, you will receive in return for all your efforts the cold comfort that you are not to blame. You can rightfully blame society at large when you see at close range the narrow, limited, inadequate provisions made for the nation's elderly citizens.

MAKING THE FINAL DECISION

Eventually all the relevant data will have been collected, and you may find that several nursing homes emerge as worth considering. In all likelihood no single one will satisfy every one of your hopes, and there will probably be pros and cons in each. But despite the fact that there are several possibilities to choose from, most families find the period leading up to a final decision to be a time of anxiety, insecurity, and guilt.

Regardless of the degree of planning and the excellence of the institution selected, nursing home placement, although providing relief from some difficult problems, symbolizes for many people irrevocable changes in familiar and valued relationships.

This is the moment when families must accept the fact that someone else will be taking care of an ailing parent from now on. For many families it represents the end of a long struggle to maintain their parent in the community. They will have to deal with the guilt they feel when they admit that they are unwilling, incapable, or inadequate to continue providing care themselves. It may also be the time when a daughter who has considered the possibility of taking her father into her own home must realize that she has made her final decision and that she cannot (because of conflicting demands in her life) or will not (because of her conflicted feelings about her father) ever ask him to live with her.

At this time, when family unity is most desirable, family tensions often run high: between husbands and wives—"If you weren't so selfish you'd let my mother live with us"—or between brothers and sisters—"We'd love to take Father, but how can we when we travel so much? Why don't you take him?"

Difficult as this period prior to nursing home placement can be for the relatives, it can be even more painful, more terrifying, for the older person involved. Your father's nursing home placement can represent the ultimate in a series of losses he has suffered: the loss of his household and his role as a householder. All the roles which in combination made up his status in society are now gone. At an advanced age he faces an identity crisis: "Who am I?" and "What am I doing here?" He must now adapt to someone else's routines and regulations because, no matter how small, intimate, or family-like the nursing home, certain basic routines must be carried out. Even the best home requires the surrender of some independence, and that is a cruel loss for men and women who have formerly prided themselves on their self-reliance and self-sufficiency.

BECOMING A
NURSING HOME RESIDENT

WHEN MOVING DAY COMES—
ADMISSION AND EARLY ADJUSTMENT

The transition to nursing home life can be an orderly, carefully maneuvered undertaking, unless the move is made directly from a hospital to the home and a speedy, efficient transfer is necessary. But whether the transition is hectic or leisurely, it is well to remember that the admission itself is a traumatic process for prospective residents and their relatives as well. There must be room for a variety of feelings at that time: irritation, anger, recrimination, depression, and disappointment. Intermingled with all these painful feelings may also be a sense of relief for everyone, both the new resident and the family, that "the worst is over."

To a certain extent a sense of relief is warranted, because the long and often wearying period of uncertainty and indecision is past. But it is certainly too soon to sit back complacently—a long and sometimes equally wearying period of adjustment lies ahead. Now, as the nursing home staff enters into the picture, a relationship which was formerly two-sided, involving children and an elderly parent, becomes three-sided. A delicate balance must be found between a hands-off, no-interference approach and an overly involved one. The best way to achieve this balance is to aim for it from the beginning.

DOING THEIR OWN THING

Whenever possible, the older person should be in charge of his own move, taking the major responsibility even if it slows things up and inconveniences everyone a little. He should discuss the date of his admission and make the arrangements for the closing of his own home, the handling of his finances, and the choice of clothing and furniture he will take with him (assuming the home allows this). If he cannot manage those procedures physically, he should at least direct them and be consulted all along the way. He may want to distribute his belongings to special friends and relatives, a process that is more time-consuming and less efficient than calling someone, such as an auctioneer or the Salvation Army, capable of removing everything in a matter of hours. He may find it more reassuring to think of his treasured possessions remaining with friends rather than going to strangers. If he's indecisive, don't make decisions for him, but help him make a choice for himself. "Your blue coat is pretty shabby— do you want to take that, or your new brown one?" is a better ploy than "I'm packing your new brown coat; that old blue one's not worth taking." Don't be surprised, either, at the unlikely array of items he decides to bring. "Surely you're not taking that mothy old pillow—it's falling apart!" But that mothy old pillow may involve a lifetime of memories. It may be too precious to leave behind and may be just the thing that will add a familiar touch to a strange room in a stranger place.

The more deeply involved he is, the less he will be likely to feel that he has been coerced and treated like a child, and the deeper will be his commitment to his new home. He will be able, if permitted to do his own thing, to link his former life with his new one.

Doing their own thing, however, does not invariably guarantee the desired results, and even the most understanding approach may not succeed with someone who is consistently negative.

The Gordon family was keenly aware of the need to allow old Mrs. Gordon to do her own thing. While she was in traction in the hospital they discussed nursing home placement with her, visited various homes themselves, reported about each one in detail, and let her decide on the one she preferred. Instead of moving her directly to the home from the hospital, they made complicated arrangements to allow her to return to her own house for a week and direct the disposal of her possessions as well as her own packing. The family prided

themselves that never once during the whole difficult period had they told her
what to do. It came as quite a shock to them, therefore, to hear her frequently
refer to that period as "the time you made me give up my house and sent me
to this place."

ONCE THEY ARE IN RESIDENCE

Each home has its own approach to welcoming a new resident, and it is
now that the new three-sided staff-family-resident relationship begins.
Some homes treat the admission process with the greatest consideration,
assigning trained staff members to help the newcomer, remaining close
by his side, and helping to orient him to his new surroundings. This
procedure is particularly helpful for the mildly confused or blind person.

Other homes, which are excellent in different ways, are perfunctory
about the admission process and do little to introduce the new resident
to the new surroundings. If your mother senses a laissez-faire attitude
when she comes in, she may want you to be there with her as much as
possible in the early days. Frequently the home itself will ask relatives
to spend considerable time with a new resident even when the staff is
available and ready to help. Other homes prefer relatives to stay in the
background in the early days, until the new resident has settled in.

New residents must make some dramatic adaptations during their
early days in the home. Already exhausted physically from the strains
of moving and emotionally by the assortment of feelings aroused by the
move, they must now become familiar with new patterns of living: new
daily routines, new rules, and new roommates, unless the resident can
afford a private room. A newcomer may wake up in the night and ask in
bewilderment, "What's that strange person doing in my bedroom?" In
the midst of all these new adjustments, they must continue to adapt to
the physical disabilities which made nursing home placement necessary
in the first place. It's not surprising that it is often a very rocky time.

THERE MAY BE REVERSALS

Many new residents suffer physical and mental reversals during this
adjustment period. Although occasionally severe and devastating, these
may only be temporary setbacks which improve significantly with time.
Residents with Alzheimer's and other dementias may show improvement
in a secure environment.

Your own parent may be in that fortunate group that adjusts quickly
and shows rapid improvement in a few weeks. Speedy changes for the
better are often seen in the malnourished elderly, whose overall condition
improves remarkably with a balanced diet. Sociable people, who felt

cruelly isolated in their own homes or apartments prior to placement, often flourish when they find companionship again, and those who have made the move independently without pressure or persuasion from relatives make the transition more easily.

EVERYONE MAKES MISTAKES

In their eagerness to speed up the adjustment or because of a continuing unresolved sense of guilt, families often make mistakes. It is impossible to catalogue the endless variety of human errors made by relatives whose intentions are good and whose judgment is poor, but two common ones should be avoided.

1. *Beware of early visits home.* Weekends away, overnight visits, or even dinner invitations, instead of making the adjustment process less painful for new residents, usually do the opposite. Adapting to the strange atmosphere involves a slow, steady progression from one stage to the next. Each day that passes helps to erase strangeness. Shuttling back and forth between an old life and a new one is confusing, and the physical travel adds stress at an already stressful time. It will be hard to refuse if your mother begs to visit or pines to have Sunday dinner with the family, but one Sunday dinner might set back her adjustment by several weeks. Residents themselves often sense the potentially harmful effects of visits outside and refuse all invitations.

"Not yet, thank you," said one particularly sprightly old lady, repeatedly refusing her relatives' invitations to dinner. "Not while I'm in training."

"Training for what?" they asked.

"I'm training myself to stand the terrible cooking in this place," was the answer, and she waited four months before accepting an invitation.

2. *Beware of panic.* Nursing home professionals report that it can take as much as six months for an old person to make a reasonable adjustment to institutional life. But the ups and downs of the period are hard to take, and too often families and staffs are quick to panic and to regret the admission or feel that the resident has been placed in an inappropriate part of the home. This may turn out to be true eventually, but it is too early to jump to conclusions. Patience and helpful support can go a long way in helping a resident return to his former self. Jumping the gun, taking drastic measures, insisting that another home would be better and moving him, will only put him under further stress and compound his problems.

WHAT IF THEY DON'T ADJUST?

The adjustment process can take as long as six months. Some residents adjust with a kind of passive acceptance, neither happy nor unhappy, abiding by the daily routines and participating in activities with little enthusiasm. Others are active participants obviously flourishing, deeply involved, ready to take responsibility, full of ideas for changes. But then, sadly, there will always be some who never adjust at all, remaining actively unhappy and finding no redeeming compensations in home life. They may sink irreversibly into mental or physical decline.

Families always hope for a positive adjustment, but it is hard to predict at the outset whether this will happen. Nursing home professionals who have seen hundreds of elderly people and screened dozens of applicants are unable to say who will do well in institutional life and who will not. Even if the outcome could be reliably predicted—even if someone devised a test to prove that Mr. Jenkins will never adjust to nursing home living—there might be no other workable alternative for Mr. Jenkins, and placement would have to be made anyhow.

The children of residents who never adjust have a particularly difficult burden to bear: they must watch their parents' unhappiness and pain, at the same time suffering feelings of guilt and shame for their involvement in the placement. But blaming themselves will not help, nor will it help to blame the staff or the institution. The difficulties of the elderly in our society often go far beyond their children's help and the help of any institution.

In the ideal situation, the staff, the family, and the resident will emerge after the adjustment period with a smoothly working relationship, a three-sided partnership in which each side assumes different responsibilities. The resident does something that no one else can do for him: adjusts and adapts. The staff offers something which the family cannot: twenty-four-hour-a-day skilled protective care. And the family offers something the staff cannot: intimate affection, links with the past, and contact with the community outside. While the ideal situation is hard to reach and all three sides are often in conflict with each other, some kind of workable relationship can usually be developed.

THE ROLE OF THE STAFF

Staff members are responsible for the ongoing functioning of every nursing home—they are the physicians, the nurses, the orderlies, the aides, the therapists, the cooks. But they are human beings, too, with human reactions, and they cannot perform miracles with severely sick or disabled old people. They appreciate praise and gratitude, bristle at unfair criticisms, resent uncalled-for interference with their work. On any institutional staff there may be individuals who are lazy, hostile, sloppy, inefficient, surly, or neurotic, and they deserve to be reported for their faults. But there may be many—one hopes more—individuals who are skillful, sensitive, thoughtful, conscientious, and genuinely devoted to the older people in their care. They deserve to be praised for their work, although that reward is usually forgotten.

FAMILY AND STAFF INTERACTION

When mutual feelings of respect exist between staff and family, when neither feels second-class citizenship, the resident will reap the benefits. The staff will feel free to consult the family, and the family to consult the staff.

But even when free and easy communication is encouraged, families should not forget that every nursing home must run on a schedule and personnel may not always be available. It is wise to check ahead about the most convenient time to talk to a doctor, a nurse, or a social worker. Since most professionals are overworked and busy, it is also wiser to keep your consultations within reasonable limits, and your anxieties in check. When there is no emergency and you have only minor concerns, it would make sense if you took care of all of them in one meeting rather than separate ones—for example, "Doctor, I've noticed quite a few things that worried me about Mother's condition in my last few visits. Could I talk with you about them sometime this week?"

Staff members all the way down the line are likely to be more receptive to families who respect schedules and abide by rules. They have a right to be irritated by people who break rules arbitrarily or ask that unnecessary exceptions be made "just this once." Sneaking in food forbidden medically on a resident's diet, disregarding visiting hours, taking a resident out without notice—all those actions are frustrating to the staff and add extra problems.

Tipping and giving gifts (even on Christmas or special occasions) are frowned on in most reputable homes; in some states they are prohibited by the health code. But relatives and residents quite routinely ignore this prohibition. Families should think twice, however, because tipping staff members at any level is equivalent to treating them like servants, buying their favors, implying that they cannot be trusted to do their jobs without being bribed. It's only human to want to express your gratitude to someone who has been particularly attentive to your mother, but there are other ways to say thank-you. Staff members are always appreciative when grateful families send notes praising their efforts to the administrator or the board of trustees. Translated into more concrete rewards, those notes can lead to promotions, but the appreciation is not always viewed in such crass terms. Nursing home personnel like to be thanked in person for their efforts and to know that the care they have given an elderly resident has been recognized and valued.

THE ROLE OF THE FAMILY

Although not involved in the health and physical well-being of the residents, the family plays an equally important role in nursing home life. It maintains the old bonds of affection, understands its own relative's idiosyncratic needs, and provides the link with the community outside. Frequent visits are very supportive for most old people, but close relationships can also be kept going long-distance. Regular communications— cards, letters, phone calls, photographs, newspaper clippings—can reassure elderly men and women that their close ties are still strong and that those they love are still constantly concerned about their welfare.

Nursing home residents, while they often thrive on family contact, can also manage to get along without it. Close friends can act as substitutes; other residents and sometimes even staff members step in to fill the gaps left by absent or uninterested relatives. Occasionally, residents previously torn by longstanding destructive relationships use their nursing home placement as an opportunity to withdraw from family battles, turning to new relationships within the home.

The extent of your own involvement with your own resident-parent will depend on your old relationship, your own availability, and your parent's needs and receptivity.

There are, of course, self-sufficient, somewhat withdrawn residents who require little emotional nurturing from anyone—family, friends, or staff. They may let it be known that they prefer to be alone, retired into a shell—the form of adaptation to institutional life that suits them best.

KEEPING THE ELDERLY
IN TOUCH WITH THEIR COMMUNITIES

Nursing home residents, although they need twenty-four-hour-a-day care, can still be deeply interested in the world outside. Some residents become recluses, but most are eager to be informed about "what's going on out there," and their families are their best informants. They also usually want to be informed truthfully; just because they are disabled or ill, they do not deserve to be protected from all unpleasant realities. Bad news as well as good news should be shared, although many families try to hide the bad and are particularly reluctant to reveal the death of a close relative, a friend, or even a pet. "Don't let Mother know!" is often the first thought in everyone's mind when tragedy strikes, but Mother, even though she seems confused and disoriented, is usually quick to sense when something is wrong. She may then become more confused, wondering what that "something" is that no one will talk about. It is un-realistic to try to hide the death of a close friend or family member, and the attempt usually leads to more trouble. If Uncle Joe used to visit her regularly, how will she be able to understand why he doesn't come any-more? It may be less painful for her to accept his death than to sit day after day thinking he has forgotten her.

The old can often accept tragedy much better than you think they can—possibly even better than you do. They may even be able to help you if you give them the chance. People living into their seventies, eighties, or nineties have had plenty of time and opportunity to experience tragedy. If you deny them their right to hear painful news, then you also deny them an equally important right: to share in the pain of the people they love. No wonder that kind of treatment leaves them feeling excluded. Although no one should live on a constant diet of bad news, the chance to share in family problems may be the one thing that penetrates the self-involvement shown by so many nursing home residents—and old people in general.

> People used to turn to Mary Philips when they were in trouble. She was valued as a concerned mother and grandmother and a helpful friend, until she became ill and entered a nursing home.
>
> There she seemed to withdraw into herself and showed little interest in anyone else. Visitors were shocked at the change in her and tried to rouse her with reports of family and community activities—but only the pleasant ones. She showed little interest in those and quickly changed the subject back to her favorite one: herself. One day her son, overburdened by his own prob-lems, let slip news of her grandson's arrest on drug charges. Instead of having the adverse effects everyone might have feared, that was the news that finally roused her, and she responded to it with all her former concern and under-standing. Afterward, her family were able to resume their old relationship with her, turning to her with their troubles and thereby reassuring her that she was still part of their lives.

MEETING IDIOSYNCRATIC NEEDS

You and your family, who know your mother best, also know her special needs and interests. One of the dangers of institutional life is that those highly personal details can be overlooked by the staff, which, because of lack of time, may tend to treat everyone in a uniform way. A loving daughter will know what kind of underwear her mother finds most com-fortable, what kind of powder she likes after the bath, which flower is her favorite, and which fruit she enjoys the most. A son may be tuned in to his father's need for a night light and his intense aversion to the only newspaper circulated in the home. All those little needs may seem inconsequential, but when they are added up they can make the difference between happiness and unhappiness in the home.

Families also are aware of the particular talents of their relatives. Those talents often pass unnoticed in the confusion of the adjustment period, and if no one asks directly, "Can you play the piano, Mr. Fisher?" Mr. Fisher may never reveal that talent himself. Creative residents can enrich the entire nursing home environment, as well as their own lives, if they are allowed to put their talents to use.

THE DEMANDING RESIDENT

Some elderly residents make insatiable demands on their families: telephoning constantly, insisting on more visits than anyone can reasonably manage to make, complaining loudly about poor care, and accusing every relative of selfishness and lack of concern. That kind of demanding behavior is sometimes seen right after admission, and if it is out of character and dealt with calmly by the family, it may subside after the difficult period is over. It may also result because a nursing home resident, forced to give up control in so many areas of daily life, may need to assert himself in whatever way he can.

But if people have been demanding, selfish, and resentful prior to admission, they are likely to continue that way, and their families will have to learn how to deal with them. Easier said than done, such families will say; if they haven't learned to say no to a domineering mother in fifty years, it's hard to begin. But some of the fearsome power of a dominant mother may fade in the nursing home setting, and it is possible for her family—even at that late date—to tell her firmly, without becoming rejecting, just how much they can be expected to do for her. They may even learn to say no at last.

Demanding behavior, whatever its causes, is used by elderly residents as a way to trap their relatives. If you spend inordinate amounts of time with your father just because he insists—you are trapped. If you become guilty when your father complains about the "miserable conditions" in the home—you are trapped. Complaints should be considered and checked for validity, of course, but the worst trap of all is allowing yourself to become involved in a power struggle with the staff over your father's care. He'll never give up behavior that produces just the results he thinks he wants until you set limits on your time and energy and involvement. When he realizes that further demands are fruitless, he will gradually— it is hoped—begin to focus less on you and more on his involvement with other residents.

THE DEMANDING FAMILY

Families resort to demanding behavior just as frequently as their resident relatives. They may disguise their demands by being oversolicitous, by incessant visiting, and by constant complaints and interference with the staff, all of which may put an undue emotional strain on their own relatives. There are always reasons for such behavior. A son may be trying to curry his mother's favor, to stay in good with her. A daughter may be continuing a lifetime of sibling rivalry, still competing with her sisters and trying to prove that she's the best one after all. Children may be overly attentive to quiet their guilt or to protect their share of an expected inheritance. Excessive behavior from families is as destructive as excessive behavior by residents and becomes even more destructive if the staff gets drawn in.

> Frances Wilson, a rather simple person herself, had raised three successful professional children, all of whom were very dependent on her and very competitive with each other. When she was seventy-nine she became seriously disoriented and her children arranged for nursing home placement. They did not really accept her mental deterioration, which they aggravated by their demands. She deteriorated further after placement, partly in retribution for their action and partly to withdraw from further conflict.
>
> Her oldest daughter took the leadership among her siblings, as she had always done, and constantly found fault with the staff. She blamed them for not rehabilitating her mother, but at the same time interfered with their efforts to help. Most of her hostility she aimed at nonprofessional personnel—aides and orderlies—whom she snubbed. They reacted with understandable hostility, some of which rubbed off on the old lady. As the three-way battle continued, her condition regressed to the point where she became incontinent and uncomprehending, and deteriorated beyond help.

HELP FOR THE TROUBLED FAMILY AND RESIDENT

Most competent homes have social service staffs capable of helping with troubled family relationships. Psychiatric consultation may also be available. The trouble may be recognized first by a staff member who, hearing that a family's behavior is too demanding on a resident or overly critical of personnel, suggests a consultation. Similarly, families who are being drained by a relative's demands, or are in serious conflict with the nurses, may ask for help themselves. When no services are available or additional ones are needed, help can be found outside the institution from social workers, social agencies, or private psychotherapists.

Self-help groups, organized and run by families themselves, are appearing in many nursing homes. The members have much to offer each other: support, information, and above all the reassurance that they are not alone in their problems.

WHEN THINGS GO WRONG

Things can go seriously wrong with nursing home care even in the best-run institutions. If you have selected your mother's home with great care, you may find it hard to believe that any criticism you feel (or any complaint she makes) could be valid, and you may wonder at first if the trouble lies in your own unreasonable expectations or in your mother's unreasonable demands. But when you are convinced that a complaint is justified, you have a duty to speak up about it, or even to take drastic action. You can call your local department of health if you have a justifiable complaint that is being ignored. The Older Americans Act made funds available for ombudsmen at the state level to "receive, investigate, and act on" complaints made by elderly residents of long-term care facilities. The Area Agency on Aging will know if your state has such ombudsmen and if so, how to contact them.

A move to another institution, disruptive though it can be, may be the only humane way to escape mistreatment. If you find your mother's basic needs are constantly neglected—if she suffers from bedsores (decubiti), is frightened and withdrawn, and the staff is callous to her condition or pooh-poohs your concern—you may be forced to move her. But you have a further responsibility beyond her personal welfare: a responsibility to other residents and an obligation to lodge a detailed complaint with the proper authorities.

In general, however, the situation is neither drastic nor clear-cut. You may find some conditions wanting and others good, neither bad enough to warrant a move nor good enough to reassure you. When things are going reasonably well, you may be tempted to adopt a "don't make waves" or "don't rock the boat" philosophy. But a series of minor incidents added up over time can produce major setbacks. Poorly prepared meals, rudeness or callousness from a staff member, missing clothing, beds still unmade or residents still in night clothes at noon—all should be reported. In nursing homes, as in all institutions, there is a chain of command, and if you do not find satisfaction at the first level, take your complaint on up, from floor nurse to nursing supervisor or administrator. Complaints may be aired through resident councils by residents themselves or through relatives' auxiliaries by the families. Those groups can exert great pressure on the administration to improve general welfare, and therefore general morale, but they are not found in every institution; often they exist in name only.

When no such machinery exists, the proper authority can be alerted in a businesslike way by letter or telephone. You have a right to expect an answer to any complaint. If no answer is received and the problem continues, repeat the process until you see action. If you run into a stone wall but are reluctant to transfer your parent, there are higher authorities for complaints outside the institution. Philanthropic institutions have boards of trustees or are supervised by umbrella philanthropic organizations. All nursing homes are accountable to the state department of health which licenses them, and there are channels through which families can take legal action. Such drastic steps should not be necessary in responsible homes where concerned administrators welcome consumer feedback, aware that a constant dialogue between staff, residents, and families produces the most constructive results.

DON'T BE AFRAID

Families often fear that their complaints will cause the staff to retaliate against their helpless relatives. Actually, experience—in well-run homes—shows that a resident who speaks up for his rights or has a vocal and alert family to speak up for him usually receives better care. Keeping quiet or being afraid allows a bad situation to get worse, and rather than retaliation, responsible consumer feedback usually produces improved services. Pity the timid residents who are afraid to complain and have no families to back them up—they are the more likely victims. There is growing public pressure at present for the appointment of nursing home advocates to protect the rights of such helpless residents. Most states now have ombudsman programs keeping watch on nursing homes.

A REASONABLE GOAL

This chapter has laid out basic steps to nursing home selection. It has reviewed procedures likely to make the transition to institutional life less painful, and supportive behavior to encourage a satisfying adjustment after placement. But steps and procedures, easy enough to describe on paper, are not so easy to follow exactly as directed. Imperfection is predictable at some stage.

Human behavior has its own built-in imperfections, too. When facing nursing home placement with their elderly parents, some children handle the process with total success, while others fail completely. But in general, well-intentioned children will ride a seesaw between success and failure. You may find it difficult to behave according to this book. Some recommendations will run counter to your personality. Patience, understanding, and empathy cannot be produced just because an emergency calls for those qualities, nor can they ever operate consistently. Rather, they are likely to fluctuate according to other pressures in your life. Your most realistic goal may be to help your mother or father in the direction of a *reasonably* satisfying adjustment and, in the process, to achieve a *reasonably* peaceful state of mind for yourself.

10

THE FAMILY
TASK FORCE

Greg and Sandy Pratt prided themselves on their ability to plan ahead. They had never been caught unprepared. "We're a great team," Greg used to say proudly, explaining that whenever they were faced with a decision they'd always done their homework first and were primed with all necessary information. Buying a home, finding a summer camp, changing jobs—their decisions were never impulsive or off the cuff. When it came to guardianships for their children they went all-out. They talked over various possibilities with brothers and sisters, in-laws, lawyers, accountants, even the minister at their church. They not only worked out careful plans but backup plans as well. "Sandy even insisted on backups for the backups," Greg teased.

But when Greg's mother had a stroke, he and Sandy were caught unprepared for the first time. They didn't have the slightest idea what to do next, where to turn for advice, what help she might need in the future. The whole family was hovering around anxiously, but Greg didn't know which of his relatives could be counted on to help. He wasn't even sure how much responsibility he and Sandy would be willing to shoulder. "She's eighty-two years old, for God's sake!" Greg burst out desperately to Sandy one day. "We've had years to prepare for this and we didn't do a thing!"

Americans as individuals tend to think ahead. Just like Sandy and Greg, we spend time and energy planning for future events: vacations, new cars, our children's education, life insurance, long-term career goals. Some of us give more than a passing thought to our own old age. But, like Sandy and Greg, too many of us are caught unprepared when elderly parents begin to fail.

"Taking Action"—Part 2 of this book—has reviewed the wide range of help available to the elderly who cannot manage alone. It has also stressed the importance of the family in locating and making use of this help. The underlying theme of the entire book has been that the family is the major support system for its elderly members but turns to the community when more help is needed than it can provide alone. We've come a long way from the days when the family was accused of neglecting or abandoning its aging relatives. Joseph Califano, former secretary of the Department of Health, Education, and Welfare, admitted in 1978: "Too often in the past we have designed our programs for the elderly with the individual but not the family in mind. We have failed to tap the strengths of the family."

Although these words are undoubtedly true, many families do not know how to tap their strengths or how to be effective. Even though willing, they may be unable to deal with the number of unfamiliar challenges appearing in old age. This chapter, therefore, is not concerned with specific problems but offers families a systematic approach to these problems in general. Many issues raised now have been touched on in earlier sections of the book—they may seem repetitive. But here for the first time they are discussed as essential elements in an overall strategy designed to produce effective—and collective—family action. The strategy to be reviewed may not be of interest to all families. It may not be needed by those who have worked out their own special ways of taking care of their own special problems. Nor does the material that follows have to be taken as an all-or-nothing proposition. Parts of the strategy may seem appropriate to your own family situation and you may want to incorporate them into your own plan of action; other parts may seem inappropriate and you may decide to ignore them.

Many families always work together on shared problems—particularly when these involve the older generation. Over time, they develop cooperative patterns that work for them. When Mother begins to fail or Father has a crisis, an army of concerned relatives rally round. Good, solid solutions may be found. But if all the efforts do not bring reasonable results, it may be because this "army" does not know how to function as a cohesive unit; it may not understand the strategy of collective action.

The mere idea of collective action may seem truly foreign to other families, those who are fragmented by conflicts and whirling forever on a merry-go-round. The members may never have even tried to take collective action about anything in the past. How can they start now just because Mother is sick? Unable to work together on her behalf, they may find it easier to ignore her problems or to argue about them. Is she or isn't she getting worse? Whose suggestions are acceptable and whose are worthless? While the arguments continue, Mother's condition is likely to deteriorate further and the family conflicts intensify because of this. If constructive action is ever going to be taken, the merry-go-round must stop its aimless circling.

GETTING OFF
THE MERRY-GO-ROUND

It probably will not be easy to stop. The crisis in an aging parent's life is likely to accelerate the speed of the merry-go-round and fragment the family still further. The crisis may even precipitate dissension where there never was any—at least on the surface. Families whose relationships have been reasonably smooth over the years may find themselves in serious conflict for the first time. At the very point when it is essential that close relatives work with each other, they may start to work against each other.

Families who realize themselves the value of working together are often able to shelve their conflicts at difficult times—at least for a while— and organize their fragmented members into a new unit, a kind of a task force for action, which instead of circling around problems can attack them directly. Forming this task force sometimes requires new behavior patterns. Many people will be surprised to hear that these patterns can be learned even late in life when longstanding relationships seem to have solidified forever. Even the old power structure in the family can be modified. In most families the power lines were drawn up long ago. Certain members have been recognized by all as the most powerful, others as submissive. The power may be held by one person or by several wielding their power as a team. The most dominant member may be the oldest child or the youngest, the richest, the favorite, or the one with the closest pipelines to the parents. The power may also be held by the aging father himself—or even by the frailest mother.

The less powerful, even though initially willing to try to work collectively, may give up almost before they start, assuming that their opinions will—as usual—count for nothing. "Sam always has to have his own way." "Father won't ever listen to us." "No one can say anything to Mother." But it is a mistake to assume that the power elite will continue to operate forever and that collective action "is not possible in our family." Just because the dominant forces will, naturally, try to exert the most power when collective action is needed, the followers should not assume they have zero power. Actually, the weakest in the group may have the most powerful weapon of all: withdrawal. Once the dominant members realize they are likely to have no followers and may end up carrying all the problems themselves, they may be willing to cede some of their power.

Just as new behavior patterns within the family power structure can be learned, so other new patterns leading to collective action can be learned, too. The learning process can be seen as a series of steps. If the steps are taken successfully, the result can be a family task force prepared to go into action. The steps, to be sure, may not progress in a smooth, straight line. Several may be taken forward, but then one may have to be taken backward—or sideways. There are traps lying in wait along the way that may threaten the success of the entire process. But if families are aware in advance of the possibly rocky road ahead, they will be better prepared to take all steps—forward, backward, and sideways—in their stride.

STEP ONE: PLANNING A FAMILY CONFERENCE

When the family is in an uproar about the situation of an elderly parent, one member may be tempted to take matters into his or her own hands, bring order out of chaos, and settle everything with a dictatorial announcement: "It's all arranged. Mother's going to move into Fairmont Manor a week from Friday. *I've* made all the arrangements." It may seem at the moment like a shortcut to sanity, but dictatorial edicts often produce mutinies among the lower ranks. Furthermore, the elderly parent, feeling railroaded into a new situation, may make a poor adjustment.

A family conference is the alternative to dictatorial rule. When successful, it provides the forum for open communication between all members—including, of course, the aging parent in question. The conference does not have to be a formal affair or even face-to-face. It can be an informal meeting with everyone getting together at sister Betty's house on a Sunday morning. Some of those invited may refuse to come—that's to be expected—but the conference can proceed without them. However, a basic number should attend or the meeting at Betty's house will end up as a waste of a good Sunday morning. While it is more efficient if all involved can meet face-to-face, it is important that family members living far away are brought in, too. Conference phone calls can be arranged whereby relatives, separated by thousands of miles, can talk directly to each other. Once it has been decided to hold a family conference, the next question to be considered is which family members should participate— whom to include, whom to exclude. One person, however, can never be left out, and that is the person most closely involved with the problem: Mother herself, Father himself.

STEP TWO: FINDING OUT
"WHAT DOES MOTHER HAVE TO SAY?"

This probably seems like an unnecessary question. How could Mother be forgotten? Easily! So many problems must be dealt with when crises arise in the lives of the elderly. Sons and daughters frantically search for solutions while still trying to keep their own lives, their business affairs, and their children functioning smoothly. Although all the confusion may be caused by Mother's crisis, and the family conference itself is specially convened in order to figure out "what's best for Mother," Mother herself may be the forgotten woman. No one may remember to tell her what's going on or to ask her what *she* thinks would be best for her. If Father is alive, even though frail himself, he also must be consulted. Excluding one or both of the elderly parents, while understandable, may be the very thing that causes carefully made plans to boomerang. Here again, as in most dealings between the generations, shared decisions are likely to produce the best results. Some semblance of a partnership can continue to operate between the generations even when the older one may plead, "Tell me what to do." Unless totally incapacitated, the elderly have a legal and moral right to share in decisions that affect their own lives. If unable to attend the family conference in person, they should be kept informed of the proceedings.

STEP THREE: DECIDING WHO ELSE IS INVOLVED

All sons and daughters—some with greater, others with less concern—are naturally connected to their parents' problems. Nobody can assume automatically that a sister can be left out because she "never visits Mother" or a brother because he "never lifts a finger for Mom and Dad." Even though your younger brother may have lived far away for years, the rest of the family living nearby should think twice before plunging ahead with their own decisions just because he's called long-distance to say, "Go ahead. Do what you think best." Even if he shows little interest in the plans as they are being made, he may appear months later and tell your mother, "If I'd been around I'd never have let them do this to you," thereby torpedoing any adjustment she may have begun to make in some new situation. A sister who has offered generous financial support should be brought in even if she too lives far away and cannot oversee in person how her money is spent. Her opinion should be considered, or she may feel unappreciated later on and may even withdraw her support. Sons and daughters who live far away are still your parents' children and may even be the very ones to whom your parents always turn for advice—a somewhat bitter pill to swallow for the family on the spot who takes everyday responsibility.

Other family members, such as sons- and daughters-in-law, may be closely concerned. Your parents may still be very close to their own brothers and sisters, or to nieces, nephews, grandchildren, cousins, and all the variety of step-relatives brought into the family by divorce and remarriage. Three criteria can be used to decide who should sit in on the family conference and become members of the family task force once it develops: Who is most concerned? Who is most affected? Who has resources to offer? The family conference may break down at its first session if the wrong people are included and the right ones left out. Just because your brother Jim is difficult and argumentative, he should not be excluded. He may be particularly influential with your mother. Furthermore, once he's blown off steam, he may be willing to play an important role in the task force. Even if it is assumed in advance that your sister Lily will be Mother's caregiver, Lily should be given a chance to discuss the job and how it would affect her life. The title should not be conferred on her in absentia. Cousin Millie, on the other hand, whose main function is giving advice and criticism, should be excluded. She contributes nothing in terms of time and energy. Meaningless plans may result if unconcerned relatives share in decisions that will in no way affect their lives.

STEP FOUR: GIVING THE FLOOR TO ALL

It is essential that all those attending have a chance to speak their minds, to lay their cards on the table, to explain their own personal situations, their own capabilities, intentions, preferences. Suggestions and options from each one should be considered. If the floor is monopolized by the loudest members, the most articulate, the most powerful, then valuable contributions from the meeker participants may never be heard.

While the task force is only in its infancy at this stage and is far from arriving at solutions to the problem at hand, this first go-around lays the groundwork for full family participation. Trial balloons will be floated, a grab bag of ideas shared. Many of these may be discarded later, but some may eventually become part of a workable plan at a later stage.

At this point a new leadership may begin to emerge. The former family dictator is not likely to remain as leader—brother Sam, for instance, who has held the power for years, or sister Mary, who has controlled the purse strings. Rather, the power may shift to brother Jack or sister Peggy, who are trusted and respected by everyone or who have specific skills and understanding. Sam, though unseated, need not feel excluded. He may still give the soundest legal advice or have the best understanding of money. Mary's role cannot be discounted either—her resources are important. The new leadership does not necessarily become another dictatorship; it may be shared, with different leaders taking over different tasks or at different stages.

The early sessions of the family conference—even with a well-chosen membership—may be stormy. This may be the first time these concerned relatives have been forced to communicate with each other in a group rather than on a one-to-one basis. Sparks may fly and old conflicts be rekindled. But a word of warning must be given here: a family conference of this type is not going to resolve these old conflicts surfacing from the past. Nor should it be used for this purpose. It cannot be allowed to develop into a shouting match or a free-for-all which would prevent everyone from tackling the problem at hand. What happened years ago in the nursery is not relevant here. What is relevant is Mother's welfare or Father's disability. Anyone who goes off target should be brought back by one of the new leaders or by anyone with a steadying hand—or with the least involvement in the confrontation.

But even if everyone stays right on target, the participants may discover things about each other—and about themselves—that they never knew before. You may come to see that your friction with your husband over your parents' care was not caused, as you kept insisting, by *his* unreasonable jealousy, *his* hostility or selfishness, but by *your* disregard of his feelings and *your* neglect of the children. If you are the caregiver for your mother, you should be given an opportunity to list your complaints about the burdens you carry alone. The others should listen. But if you are willing to listen to them in return, you may learn that your behavior has seemed autocratic to them and rejecting of their offers to help. It may begin to dawn on you that they have not been doing their share because you have not allowed them to. The stormy sessions may be painful, but they can clear the air by helping to clarify the strengths and weaknesses of each member.

STEP FIVE: IDENTIFYING THE PROBLEM

Before the problem can be identified there's work to be done. More information may need to be gathered about the elderly parent's condition and situation. Professionals—doctors, nurses, psychiatrists, or geriatric specialists—may need to be consulted. Helpful information may be found in books: a review of the earlier chapters of this book might prove useful. Information-gathering is a necessary process because the problems of older people often present a confusing picture.

When a problem arises for a family in its earlier stages—mother, father, and growing children—it is not only easier to define *who* is involved but *what*, precisely, the problem is: Mary is doing badly at school. Johnny has nightmares. Father is drinking too much. Mother is depressed. Each one of these problems, naturally, has deeper ramifications, but each one offers a starting point. With the elderly, the picture can be much less clear. There may be general agreement that Mother is not doing well— although there may be some in the family who continue to deny that anything is wrong. Mother herself may be the loudest in her denials. But even when everyone agrees that Mother needs help there may be complete ignorance about what, specifically, her problem is and what, specifically, can be done about it.

> Eighty-one-year-old Charles Denver was obviously slipping, and his family was concerned. His hearing and eyesight were failing. He was withdrawn, apathetic, forgetful, weak. He was losing weight and had fallen on several occasions. His daughter wanted him to see an eye doctor. His son thought he needed psychiatric help. Luckily, Charles's sister suggested a general checkup with her own internist, who discovered that Charles was severely malnourished and anemic. Although he was not blind, his deteriorating sight made it increasingly difficult for him to cook for himself as he had done since he was widowed a few years before. He cooked less, bought less food, ate less, and therefore grew weaker. He became depressed and his appetite diminished further. Once the basic problem had been identified, Charles's family was able to start working on concrete, specific solutions. Instead of agonizing, "We must do something about Father," they now could move ahead knowing that they "must do something about *Father's diet*."

Families tend to panic and stand still when problems seem overwhelming in scope. Once a specific trouble spot is identified, they know better where to direct their energies to find specific solutions. Charles Denver's family was able to pinpoint his main problem with comparative ease, but it is not always this straightforward. Sometimes the basic problem is buried too deeply. Obvious surface difficulties may become red herrings leading families in the wrong directions. More time and effort and further information may be needed before the true root of the trouble is isolated. This may be the point where outside professionals have to be brought in or consulted—doctors, nurses, social workers.

Once identified, the problem may not be as easy to cope with as Charles Denver's malnutrition. It may have many levels and require more complicated solutions. In such cases it may help to break down the problem into manageable components, taking care of the most urgent first.

> Amanda Heller was eighty-two, widowed, and living alone in a small but comfortable apartment. Her income, though modest, was adequate enough to cover some household help, but she refused to have any. This worried her two sons, but they admitted she seemed to manage well enough until she had a

severe bout of flu. During her illness she allowed her sons to bring in a practical nurse, but as soon as she felt a little better she fired the woman.

After her recovery the family was alarmed by what seemed to be serious changes in her personality and living habits. Formerly methodical and meticulous about her home and her appearance, she gradually lost interest in both. She had once prided herself on her cooking, even when alone, but in a short time she stopped cooking completely and lived on tea and crackers. She became increasingly suspicious of everyone—even of her sons and their wives. Despite her frail condition and formerly frugal spending habits, she started going on buying sprees, piling up large bills for clothing she never wore but left lying around in boxes. Neighbors reported on several occasions that they'd seen her giving money to people she hardly knew. Whenever relatives visited they found personal papers, checkbooks, and bankbooks strewn carelessly around. One day her older son retrieved some uncashed dividend checks from the trash can.

She ignored her sons' concern and refused to allow her daughters-in-law to help her in the apartment. The family felt helpless, overwhelmed by Amanda's steadily deteriorating condition. They seemed incapable of doing anything until a friend, who had been through a similar situation himself, advised against searching for an overall solution. He suggested approaching things one by one, attacking the most pressing problem first.

It was obvious that there was an urgent need to conserve Amanda's dwindling finances, so her sons' first move was to consult a lawyer to learn what legal steps could be taken. While a conservatorship was being arranged, they prevailed on their mother to see a geriatric specialist, who began an overall assessment of her physical and mental condition. *Then*, the family turned to the living situation and hired a homemaker to maintain the apartment and to help Amanda with her daily routines—meals, dressing, and personal hygiene.

The process was time-consuming, but breaking the situation into manageable segments enabled the family, no longer overwhelmed, to take effective action.

STEP SIX: DISCOVERING
WHO WILL MAKE COMMITMENTS

Encouraging progress will seem to have been made when a specific problem or problems are identified. The situation will begin to develop greater clarity. The family now knows what's wrong, and may even have some idea of the necessary solutions. It is probably less clear how these solutions will be put into operation, and by whom. How much responsibility will each family member be willing to take?

This is a kind of zero hour for everyone. All involved are now forced to face squarely how much of an investment they are honestly willing to make as individuals in providing the solutions for a parent's problem. It can be a painful experience. It usually involves admitting personal shortcomings and inadequacies. Charles Denver's daughter, who had always devotedly claimed, "I'd do anything in the world for Father," may now have to ask herself whether she is willing to cook her father's dinner every night to be sure he has a balanced meal. Her claim to devotion may seem less impressive when she is forced to admit to herself and everyone else, "I'd do anything in the world for Father—*except* cook dinner for him every night." Self-confrontation may take place now or later on as the situation continues or deteriorates, but whenever it takes place it can be a disillusioning experience and may account for one or more of the members dropping out of the task force temporarily or even permanently.

Roadblocks to helping may be more objective and realistic. A son obviously cannot take on any daily responsibility in his mother's life if his job requires him to travel constantly during the week. He may, instead, commit himself to taking his mother for her physiotherapy every Saturday morning. A daughter who works full-time cannot take care of her crippled father's housekeeping as well as her own, but she and her aunt may alternate weekend housekeeping while others share responsibility for the weekday chores. A certain amount of trial and error may be necessary before any solutions mesh well and move along smoothly. Even when they seem to be running perfectly they must be open to change and revision according to new developments.

STEP SEVEN: SETTING PRIORITIES

At this point it is necessary for everyone to step away from the extended family and the collective process. All individuals and couples need to move back into their own family units and examine the other commitments in their lives. Helping your father or mother is not likely to be the only commitment you have. There are undoubtedly plenty of others already, and these must be considered. If you take on a new one, how will this affect other people, other activities, even other pleasures that may be important to you? How much are you prepared to give up? It's a difficult choice to make, and it's a rare person who can choose easily without guilt, conflict, or regret. The new commitment may be easier to accept—or to refuse—if you see it in relation to others you have made already. It might help to ask, "If I take on some major responsibility for my mother's care, how will this affect my children? my grandchildren? my husband? my wife? How will it affect my community activities, my work, my health? How will it affect the time I need for myself or with my friends?"

The priority you give to helping your mother may be determined not by other commitments but by the relationship you have had with her all through the years. Your feelings—discussed in Chapter 2—may decide the priority. It will not help to watch with awe and envy as your neighbor, who has as many commitments as you do, still manages to devote part of her life to her mother. Their relationship with each other is probably quite different from yours with your mother. Despite the similarity in your lives, when it comes to mothers there's no similarity at all. You may feel cold-blooded and heartless—"a thankless child," indeed—if it turns out that you cannot give your mother's needs the highest priority in your life. But better to admit this now—out loud—than to make a commitment you cannot sustain. Better to announce in advance the limits of the help you can be counted on to give. At least you can be counted on for something. Others in the task force may refuse to be counted on at all and vanish completely.

STEP EIGHT: REACHING AN AGREEMENT

If the task force has been able to take the first seven steps with a certain amount of success and has not lost too many members along the way, it should be ready for the eighth and last step: to make an agreement. Discussion has been essential all through the seven steps and it is equally essential at the eighth, but at some point here talk must stop. Decisions must be made—an agreement must be reached. Only when the agreement is accepted will the task force be able to take action. The agreement may not be completely satisfactory to everyone. It may require compromise and sacrifice from many members. But once accepted, it will represent a group commitment binding on all individuals.

The final agreement reached at step 8 may surprise everyone and be totally different from anything ever dreamed of at step 1 when the family conference was being planned.

> Even though she had two brothers and several aunts, Sonia Kepple had always taken care of everything for her disabled father. Not only was she in daily touch with him, but, despite having a part-time job, she visited him several times a week and supervised the homemakers who took care of him in his apartment. Every weekend when the homemaker was off she brought the elderly man to her home in the suburbs.
>
> She and her husband never had time alone with each other or their children and felt worn out by their endless routine. Finally, in desperation she called her brothers and her aunts to her house and accused them all of shirking responsibility and leaving everything to her. She was amazed to learn after her outburst that she wasn't the only one who felt ill-used. She found that everyone assumed she enjoyed taking charge of everything and that the others resented her for not allowing anyone else to be close to her father. It dawned on her for the first time that the others had not been doing their share because she had not permitted them to.
>
> When the air cleared, everyone offered to help. The aunts committed them-

selves to supervising the weekday homemaker, while the brothers agreed to rotate weekends with Sonia.

But on the first weekend with the younger son, the eighty-six-year-old man, waking up in a strange place, became confused, turned on all the lights, woke the children, and tried to get out of the house in his pajamas. On the second weekend, the older son started out to pick up his father but on the way skidded on wet leaves and drove his car into a ditch.

The new weekend plan seemed doomed to failure. Sonia's brothers were unable to follow along in the pattern that Sonia had developed. But the family refused to admit defeat. They were stumped for a time. So they stepped back and began to retrace their steps. They reassessed the problem and realized that their elderly father was more confused than they had realized. Too much moving around only increased his confusion. They then revised their original commitments and came up with a different agreement. Rather than moving their father every weekend, the brothers decided that on *their* weekends they would share the cost of a weekend homemaker and would take turns supervising things at their father's apartment on Saturdays and Sundays. Sonia would still continue to take her father to her home when it was her turn because her place was familiar to him.

By not insisting that things had to be done *her* way, by allowing her brothers to try something different, Sonia was able to spend two out of three weekends alone with her family.

BEWARE OF TRAPS ALONG THE WAY

Progress is rarely smooth from step 1 to step 8. It's a lucky family who can take all eight steps in its stride and arrive at the finish line without stumbling along the way. Unpredictable, unavoidable roadblocks may appear at any time and must be dealt with. Other traps are more predictable, and if the task force is aware of these in advance it may be able to avoid them completely. The four that follow are the most common.

KEEPING SECRETS

Honesty is an essential ingredient if the task force is to function efficiently. Members of the task force may be tempted to keep secrets—from each other and from their parents. Some secrets may have been kept for years out of guilt, shame, pride. A sister, for instance, may not want to admit to the rest of her family that her marriage is in trouble and that one of the causes of conflict with her husband has been her close relationship with her mother through the years. Instead of admitting why she cannot be counted on to take her place in the task force, she may keep her secret and agree to participate. When her husband walks out on her several months later and she has to take a job, the task force can no longer function according to its original agreement. It must regroup in order to form a new one.

Families often keep secrets for more altruistic reasons and because facing the truth can be painful.

Margaret Frank's children never came out and told her why it would be impossible for her to remain alone much longer in the big house where they'd all grown up. They knew how much she loved it so they circled around the truth, singing the praises of a small apartment in a retirement complex nearby. They tried to convince her that she'd be happier there, less lonely, have more activities to fill up her time. But Margaret refused to be budged.

What her family did *not* tell her because they did not want to worry her was that her older son Bill had developed a back problem and could no longer take care of his mother's house and garden repairs. Her son-in-law was in line for a promotion that would require relocation to a nearby town, so her daughter, Jess, would not be able to help her mother with the domestic chores as much as she had in the past. Most important of all, Margaret's doctor had told the family that she should no longer be climbing stairs because of a deteriorating heart condition. The family stalemate occurred because one side kept secrets and the other side, therefore, saw no reason to make any changes in her life.

HIDING FEELINGS

This is closely related to keeping secrets and is often intertwined with it. As discussed in Chapter 2, negative feelings about close relatives— particularly about parents—are often uncomfortable, and many people prefer to keep them hidden. Their behavior is predicated on what they think they *ought* to feel rather than on what they *do* feel in reality.

Polly Taylor had always enjoyed her role as "good girl" in the family. Everyone with a problem turned to Polly and knew she could be counted on for help. When Polly's father became blind, the rest of the family automatically assumed that she would act as caregiver. Polly herself dreaded the thought. She'd always been ready to pitch in to help others through a crisis, but the idea of taking ongoing, permanent responsibility terrified her. Furthermore, she secretly felt that she had never been fully appreciated by her father and resented him for this. But Polly could not admit her feelings and with apparent willingness agreed to be caregiver. By refusing, she would have had to give up her role of "good girl." As a result, she took on the responsibilities, performed them badly, and eventually had to give up both roles—caregiver *and* good girl.

Polly was aware of her true feelings and knew she was hiding them from the others, but some people manage to hide their feelings from *themselves*. These feelings may have been buried for so long that they no longer seem to exist. They may only surface again and disrupt carefully laid plans when there must be renewed involvement and close contact with an aging father or mother, or with the family as a whole. When these feelings do surface, plans may have to be completely revised.

PROMISES, PROMISES

One of the most dangerous traps of all is the hastily given promise. While unrealistic promises may be made on the basis of the two previous traps—secrets and hidden feelings—they also may be made out of honest intention prompted by the emotions of the moment. People who make these promises may genuinely believe *at the time* that they expect to keep them. Deathbed promises to a dying parent such as the one mentioned in Chapter 7—"Of course I'll bring Father to live with us"—can produce the greatest problems. Having to back out of such a promise is truly traumatic. It's guilt-producing enough to break a promise to the living; how much more guilt is involved when the promise broken has been made to the dead.

But promises are not always made at the deathbed. The task force can find itself boxed in by a promise made too hastily to a living parent.

"You won't ever go to a nursing home. We promise."

"You'll never have to give up the house. We promise."

"We promise we'll visit you every day."

"If you don't like it in Greenfield Manor you can leave. We promise."

The words "But we promised Mother" can paralyze the entire task force and prevent it from taking further action. Words like *every, never, ever, always,* are equally dangerous. A revised version of the promises made above would keep the future looser and plans more open to revision:

"We know how you feel about nursing homes, Mom, and we feel the same way. Let's see how you get along when you come home from the hospital. We promise to help you as much as we can."

"You and Dad can't go on paying those terrible heating bills. We know how much you want to stay in the house so we've all decided to chip in to help. But with the way oil prices are skyrocketing we can't promise to do it forever."

"Don't worry—we won't let you be lonely. We'll all visit you as often as possible. We promise."

•   •

"It's going to be hard getting used to being in Greenfield Manor but we promise we'll all be around a lot at the beginning until you feel more at home."

JUMPING THE GUN

Although the best plans are usually made through slow, thoughtful analysis, the task force is often forced into speedy action by a crisis: "Mother's going to be discharged from the hospital a week from Tuesday. Who's going to take care of her? Where's she going to go?" No time here to deliberate over these questions—there's a deadline to meet. Some arrangements will obviously have to be made for a week from Tuesday. But here again families tend to overestimate their immediate problem, thinking that the arrangements made for that Tuesday must last a lifetime. That would be an overwhelming challenge. A delaying action allowing for further investigation is likely to produce better results. Instead of trying to deal with the *long-term* future—especially at a time of crisis when no one can think clearly—it's usually possible to make arrangements for the *immediate* future: "Mother's going to a convalescent home for a few months when she leaves the hospital. We'll see how she does there." The task force that takes this route will now have the next months free of pressure. During this time it can watch how things go, consider possible solutions for the future, review them with Mother, and, as the months pass, develop a clearer idea of which options are realistic.

Speedy action, however, is often demanded by an impatient task force—or an impatient member. Each one has an individual life to lead, a family to care for, problems to cope with, work to do. It's understandable why many may be eager to arrive at an agreement that permits them to return to their own affairs again. There's a real danger that the impatient ones may try to hurry up deliberations in order to reach some agreement—any agreement. The elderly parents themselves may be the most impatient, rushing impulsively into arrangements that are unrealistic for the future and likely to lead to further problems. If your parents are intent on giving up their apartment and moving to a retirement complex, you and the rest of the family might admire their independence and quickly support their idea, especially if they had been increasingly demanding of everyone's time and attention recently. You may all breathe a sigh of relief and wish them well. However, it would be wise if one of you were to point out the potential hazards of their move, reminding your father that your mother's arthritis has been getting progressively more severe, and while she could manage now in the retirement community, she might not be able to remain there if she became incapacitated a year from now. Then, where would they go? The quick agreement made by an impatient task force, or railroaded through by an impatient member, is likely to cause further time-consuming problems for everyone in the future.

WHEN THERE'S AN IMPASSE

The task force is likely to come to a dead stop—not once but possibly several times—as it tries to move ahead to an agreement. An impasse is to be expected. It may come about for any one of a number of reasons: The task force may exhaust all its resources without reaching a workable agreement reasonably satisfactory to all. A power struggle may develop in which the question to be answered is not "What's best for Mother?" but "Who's head of the family?" Weaker relatives, after trying and failing to have any real say in the deliberations, may throw up their hands in despair and vanish from the task force—at least temporarily.

But an impasse does not mean failure. The whole process of getting together and trying to form a task force is likely to be a novel experience in many families. Learning how to talk to each other honestly without hiding behind old masks and postures can be an uncomfortable experience—as bewildering as learning a new language. When the impasse is reached, things may stall for a while but can get moving again if the task force realizes all is not lost—that it can step back briefly, take a breather, regroup, and then start again. Landing on the dreaded box "Back to Home Plate" in the old board game Parcheesi does not mean that the game is over, unless some poor sport slams away in a huff. It just means starting over.

The second go-round may be quite different from the first. The power lines may have started to shift. Mother may be getting feebler, less able to assert her authority over herself and everyone else. A powerful brother may be anxious to return to his own affairs and be more receptive to collective rather than unilateral action. The breather may have given everyone a chance to regroup, to gather more information, to consult more experts, and to gain fresh insights. It may also give an opportunity to exert informal pressure on particularly rigid members. The original impasse may have occurred because a younger brother took a strong stand and refused to be budged. He may fear he'll lose face if he gives in to an older brother, his lifetime rival. Continued confrontation by the task force en masse is likely to harden his position still further, thereby creating the impasse. In such a situation, it may turn out that he is more reasonable in private than in public if he is approached informally and diplomatically by someone in the family whom he respects. This chapter has stressed a process made famous by President Woodrow Wilson when drafting the peace treaty of World War I—"open covenants, openly arrived at." But this openness does not preclude some diplomatic behind-the-scenes persuasion. It may be just what's needed to break the impasse and start moving again.

The family who finds it difficult to gather momentum after it has stalled may get the push it needs from an outsider—someone whose ideas are more objective, less emotionally charged. This can be a respected friend, a more distant, uninvolved relative, or a professional trained to cut through tangled feelings and clear the way for further action.

Family therapy originally considered effective mainly for the family in its early years is now proving successful in dealing with troubled families at any age. Instead of working only with the nuclear family—parents and their growing children—therapists now look to the more extended family and bring in any members closely involved with the problem or likely to contribute to the solution. It is particularly important, however, that the family therapist consulted is experienced in dealing with the elderly.

LOOKING TO THE FUTURE

Even when all steps have been taken, all traps avoided, all impasses broken through, and all agreements accepted, the task force cannot assume it will move along smoothly forever. Nor do the members need to fear that they have locked themselves into situations from which there is no escape. Life will go on, and as it does, the problems of the elderly parents are not likely to remain constant. Things may deteriorate—or improve. The task force must be ready to adapt its original agreement accordingly. The composition of the task force membership may change because of death, illness, relocation, divorce, or abdication. Replacements will be needed and responsibilities reallocated.

But if the task force has been able to function smoothly for a time, it will not be destroyed by setbacks. The family will have discovered that working together produces the most effective action. It will then be willing to regroup, revise, readjust, and move on.

11

TAKING A STAND

Kitty Braden dropped out of college before her first child was born and went back to finish after her youngest child reached junior high school. In her first semester her mother died and Kitty, unable to let her nearly blind father live alone, brought him to live with her. Kitty dropped out of college for the second time.

• •

Jack Philips, a science teacher with three children—one in college already and the other two moving up through high school—learned last year that his mother, after a long struggle with cancer, had used up all her health insurance benefits and her money and could no longer pay for the medical and nursing care she needed. Jack and his brothers now share those expenses. Jack moonlights on the evening shift at the Lomax Plant.

• •

Mary Murphy, although sad and lonely in the early days after her father's death, was a little ashamed of the thoughts that kept running through her head: "No more Medicare forms to fill out . . . no more frantic scrambling for homemakers and nurses . . . no more emergency calls in the middle of the night . . . no more visits to that terrible old neighborhood . . . no more canceling our plans because Dad has another attack. . . . Thank God, all that's over."

Those three families—and many others like them—prove false the popular belief, that "children in modern society neglect their old parents." Such families know they do everything they can for their old parents under the circumstances. The only thing they do not do is try to change the circumstances.

If adequate, protected alternative living arrangements had been available for their fathers, Kitty and Mary would not have had to disrupt their own lives. If adequate insurance coverage for chronic illness had been available for his mother, Jack would not have had to moonlight. None of these children would have loved their parents less, but they would have had to sacrifice less of their personal lives. For a long time now society has been calling the younger generations to task for their shortcomings. The message has been, "You are not taking good enough care of your elderly relatives." Perhaps it is finally time for those generations to call society to task for its shortcomings, with the message, "*You* are not taking good enough care of your elderly citizens."

It is now a generally accepted fact that most families with elderly relatives are doing their best to help, some with greater and others with lesser success. And society itself has been trying to "care enough" for its elderly. But if a visitor from another planet were to ask how America treats its older citizens, the answer would depend on the respondent's point of view. The optimist—always seeing the glass half full—might reply, "Life in the eighties is much better for older people than it used to be. Look how far we've come in the fifty years since Social Security began, in the twenty-five years since the passage of the Older Americans Act. Look at the decline in poverty among the elderly, falling from 35 percent in 1959 to 12.6 percent in 1986. Look at Medicare, look at Medicaid, look at SSI! Look at the millions who are being helped to live better." But the pessimist—always seeing the glass half empty—might counter with, "Look how much still needs to be done! Look at the millions who still need help."

Both these statements are true in part. This book has reviewed many of the federal programs which do benefit the elderly: income benefits; financing of health care; protection of rights with laws preventing discrimination against older workers; programs of fundamental research on aging in the National Institute of Aging; federal supports for state and local organizations providing services for older men and women. Indeed, many of these citizens are in fine financial shape thanks to pensions, private investments, and annuity plans in addition to Social Security checks. Current economic statistics reveal that the over-fifty population is better off financially than the under-fifty. A new stereotyping acronym has been added to the familiar yuppies, guppies, and puppies of the eighties: the *Woofs*, standing for Well-Off Older Folks!

But the fact that the elderly today have more support than their parents and grandparents does not mean that they have *enough* support. Some, like the Woofs, live well and are visible (often to the resentment of younger folks). But others live badly and are invisible. Society still too often fails its elderly who are frail, dependent, incapacitated. It frequently fails older people who are independent and determined to stay that way.

How long will independence last for an old man who has a limited income, substandard housing, and little health protection? The poverty figures may show a dramatic decline, but too many millions still live below the poverty threshold and millions more count as near-poor. This latter group includes some who are poor for the first time because their resources have been drained away in their old age by long illnesses.

In *some* places *some* services are being set up, improved, or expanded, but these do not help older people who do not live in those places but one hundred, two hundred, or five hundred miles away. The overall needs of older men and woman across the country are still being inadequately and unevenly met.

Because of lack of services in your own community, you may, like Kitty Braden, feel obligated to reorganize your life in order to take care of your widowed father. Or, if that is not possible, he may be forced to accept institutional placement. That initial placement may not be a final solution either, and you may have to move him to a second institution if the first one is closed down or provides poor care.

There is a general call out today for more support and additional services, although a cynic might paraphrase Mark Twain's comment about the weather—everybody's talking about the needs of the elderly but nobody's doing much about them. At the present time a greater danger comes not from too little addition but from too much subtraction—from moving backward instead of forward. In the current economic pinch there is an ever-present threat of cutbacks in existing benefits and services. Anyone living through the financial crises of the cities is becoming used to nightly news bulletins announcing drastic curtailments of services or the outright closing down of hospitals, clinics, senior centers, and meal programs. Whenever there is a need to save money, the most obvious place to look for cuts is frequently found in the funds for the elderly.

The greatest opposition to cutbacks and the greatest pressure for increments has come, until now, from the elderly themselves, who have become more vocal and better organized to protect their own well-being and state their own demands. Pressure has also come from professionals, young and old, active in the field of aging.

Little pressure has come yet, however, from a potentially powerful group: the families of the elderly, who have merely hovered anxiously on the sidelines, accepting their personal guilt, settling for stopgap measures, complaining to themselves about their problems, but rarely making their voices heard. Perhaps it has happened because private citizens have tended to think of elderly relatives as family, rather than public, responsibilities. As individual sons and daughters, they may have supported measures designed to improve the general welfare of the elderly, but how much more powerful they could be if they raised a collective voice.

Perhaps they remain silent out of ignorance, uncertain how to go about speaking collectively. Perhaps they hesitate to speak out, fearing that by asking society to help their parents they would be asking for charity and therefore be forced to accept the stigma of welfare. Perhaps they feel guiltily aware that they could be doing more themselves, and are not. Perhaps they fear that by demanding greater public support for their parents, they would expose themselves as evading their responsibilities as sons and daughters.

Pressing for social action is another way for sons and daughters to behave responsibly to their parents and, in the long run, a more constructive way. Social action will not separate parents from children. Even if the day ever comes when all elderly men and women are well supported, well fed, well housed, and well nursed, those with close relationships will continue to turn to their children for benefits only the intimate family can provide. Children and close family members are usually tuned in to the idiosyncratic needs of their elderly relatives and offer the special personal understanding and individual affection that is essential and that no one else can provide. Impersonal, large-scale operations can lend basic support, but when public support comes in the door, private relationships will *not* fly out of the window. They will continue to yield their traditional benefits.

The children of the elderly, sandwiched in between older and younger generations must give in two directions at the same time. They receive no compensation for that double burden, and they are usually the most heavily taxed. They have a right to stand up and shout, "We need help, too! Pay attention to us!" They also have a right to hope that someone listens.

ATTENTION, LEGISLATORS, INSURANCE UNDERWRITERS, EMPLOYERS!

The inequalities of the Social Security system, particularly as they affect elderly women, need to be evened out so that becoming a widow does not also usually mean becoming poorer. Regulations that prevent the elderly from working, or penalize them for working, need modification. The rulings at present carry a double penalty: the elderly are denied the right to earn more than a minimal amount of monetary income, and they are simultaneously denied the right to earn the psychic income which comes from feeling useful and productive. Once these regulations are modified, other modifications are necessary, particularly in the attitudes of employers reluctant to take on elderly employees.

The children of the elderly, many of whom are willing and able to care for a disabled father or mother, have a right to financial assistance, in the form of either tax reduction or some type of government subsidy to help to defray their outlays of time and effort. Such small compensation would inevitably cost less in public funds than a nursing home bill covered in full by Medicaid. A subsidy or tax rebate might provide just the necessary balance to offset the tipping point that forces nursing home placement of many elderly people.

When this book first came out in 1976, it stressed the urgent need for major public/private financing of long-term illness. Now, thirteen years later, the need is *still* urgent and *still* unmet. That is a recurring theme in this third edition. Private insurance policies for nursing home care and chronic illness do exist, but so far are expensive and offer only uncertain protection. The new Medicare Catastrophic Coverage Act helps families to pay for acute illness, but it does little to relieve the financial burden of long-term illness and chronic disabling conditions. The irony is that although more men and women are living longer now, they can look forward to slim protection for conditions most likely to develop in the later decades. Fifteen percent of those over sixty-five have Alzheimer's disease, 13 percent have significant vision problems, 25 percent have significant hearing loss, and untold millions have serious dental problems. Medicare makes little provision for these conditions. This lack of government concern is especially ironic in view of the fact that for the last eight years—until 1989—the Man in the White House was a septuagenarian who wears two hearing aids himself.

ATTENTION, PLANNERS, BUILDERS, ARCHITECTS!

Numbers of elderly men and women are trapped at present, because of low incomes, in substandard housing, in decaying neighborhoods, with landlords who have no interest in tenant welfare once the rent is paid. Other aging mothers and fathers, who would prefer independent arrangements, are trapped in stressful living situations in their children's homes for lack of financial resources to pay separate rents.

Government subsidies, now lagging seriously behind, are essential to provide low-cost housing—or special units within larger complexes—to meet the variety of elderly needs. The layout of each individual structure should be geared to safety and comfort, with services built into the overall design, so that tenants have help readily available for meals, housekeeping, and medical attention.

It is unlikely that the need for new special housing will be met in the near future, so only small numbers will benefit for many years. Those who continue, out of choice or out of necessity, as tenants in their previous living quarters could be offered rent reductions or rent subsidies instead, while tax rebates could be available to homeowners. There is a trend in this direction in some communities, but so far no nationwide pattern.

The elderly at all income levels need housing—not only the low-income elderly—and there should be a variety of styles in a variety of locations. Because of the tremendous diversity among the elderly millions, it cannot be assumed that any one type of housing will suit all tastes. Some people may head south to warmer climates, but others, as recent studies show, may head north to colder climates. Retirement does not have to involve uprooting or moving. Many old people want to stay right where they are despite difficult climates. They see no reason, because of advancing age, to trade familiar winter snows for alien sunny beaches, but their own communities may not offer appropriate housing: small enough, cheap enough, manageable enough.

Why should Ellen Vorst—retired after thirty years of teaching in one small affluent community—be forced to move to another town when her house becomes too big for her to manage alone? She would like to stay where she is, but zoning in her own town forbids apartments, so she has no choice. Why should exile be the reward for years of dedicated community service?

Even when they decide voluntarily to move to a retirement community, all the elderly do not have the same requirements. They may all require living arrangements that provide a range of services, but those services can be provided in a variety of settings. The physical environment is important to one couple, while the psychological atmosphere is more important to another. There should be options open: country, urban, or suburban locations; large communities or small clusters; much communal interaction or freedom for independent living. Older people are sometimes only happy in age-segregated communities where contacts are with their elderly contemporaries. Others dread such exclusive ghettos and look instead for age-integrated communities offering ongoing contacts with their own generation and with children, teenagers, and young adults as well.

ATTENTION, PHYSICIANS, PSYCHIATRISTS, NURSES, SOCIAL WORKERS!

Adequate health care, like adequate housing, is predicated on adequate funding, and many older Americans today are going without good health care because of the tremendous expense involved and the many gaps in insurance coverage.

Here again, money is not the only roadblock. The medical professions have had to focus on an awesome number of physiological and psychological ills which threaten human life, and the highest priorities have been assigned to understanding these ills, learning how to treat and cure them. Professionals have not been able to focus as intently on the special problems of the elderly or to give high priority to their care, treatment, and understanding. Perhaps, in addition, the healing professions have been less interested in the care of chronic conditions, which so often are the fate of the elderly and which defy healing. Or perhaps these professions have also incorporated the fears, the denial, and the avoidance of the subject of aging prevalent in the larger society.

The second edition of this book suggested in 1982 that the medical professions were in the process of realigning priorities and recognizing the need to understand better the physical and emotional needs of older people. That optimistic projection of seven years ago has not yet been realized. The elderly segment—less than 13 percent of the total population—accounts for more than 36 percent of physician time and more than 40 percent of acute-care hospital admissions. Despite these realities there is still an inadequate number of geriatric specialists coming out of medical schools. The American Public Health Association reports that only 150 physicians a year complete fellowships in geriatric medicine or geriatric psychiatry, and that 500 physicians in all have completed fellowships in either specialty.

The shortage of physicians trained in geriatrics is not the only shortage in health care specialists for the elderly. There is an urgent need for geriatric nurses, social workers, physical therapists, dieticians, and speech therapists. Public support is needed to assure a greater allocation of funds to underwrite the continuing development in training programs not only in medicine but in allied fields as well. While the shortages in these health care fields may be serious now, they may assume crisis proportions unless solutions are found before the baby boom generation reaches old age early in the next century.

JOIN THE ACTION

Appeals for help, for attention, can be sent out to legislators, planners, architects, physicians, psychiatrists—but who can be sure these appeals will be heard and answered?

A significant influence leading to the enactment of important new federal legislation and appropriations to benefit the elderly in the past decade

has been the organized pressure and vocal demands of the elderly themselves in such groups as the Gray Panthers, the American Association
of Retired Persons, the National Council on the Aging, and the Association of Retired Federal Employees. Whatever success those growing
organizations have achieved may have come from their do-it-yourself
philosophy. Instead of remaining silent until someone else recognized
their needs and passed legislation to benefit them, they have pressured
for legislation on their own behalf, using the same formula developed by
other minority groups—blacks and Indians—and by women. None of the
vocal groups have gained as much as they asked for, but they have gained
something more than they had before.

The hard-pressed generations in the middle can be thought of as a
minority, too, with special problems of its own that have been ignored.
No one talks about that minority and no one hears from it. It does not
have the built-in qualities which make for an easily mobilized pressure
group. It is uncohesive and dispersed, scattered geographically, fragmented socially and economically. Its one shared problem is its only
common bond, but that may become a unifying force when members of
the minority learn that as individual protesters they will not gain what
they want.

If they want tax relief in return for the support and services they
personally offer their elderly parents, they will have to organize and
demand it. If they suffer because their community is poor in services for
the elderly, they are more likely to get those services—and respite from
daily routines—if they work for them together.

Many families, however, although ready and eager to do something,
have little experience in community action. They may never have organized anything before and may have little idea of how to get started. A
good way for such novices to begin could be to take a look at what other
people have been doing in other places and to examine programs that are
already established and working successfully elsewhere. All across the
country, in scattered locations, small effective programs can be found
that benefit only a limited number of older people. Those programs can
be used as models and duplicated again and again, thereby benefiting an
increasing number of older people.

No one individual family can establish a program—original or imita-
tive—alone. But a number of families working in partnership can demonstrate why a program is needed, how it can be put into operation, and
how many people it will benefit. Then they can apply for funds from a
public or private source for a small-scale pilot project. If the pilot project
is successful, it can be expanded with continuing funds over subsequent
years.

There is nothing new in such procedures. They have been used often in the past by families of patients suffering from certain devastating diseases—cystic fibrosis, muscular dystrophy, cerebral palsy. Parents of mentally retarded children met together to develop shelters, workshops, and camps when these facilities were lacking in their communities. Young mothers and fathers, unable to find local nursery schools, joined together to begin their own, even if they started taking turns in each other's playrooms.

Meal services for the elderly, transportation services, companion services, escort services, clubs, homemaker groups, can all be started by small groups in communities where there are few formal programs. A preliminary informal organization can do more than provide needed assistance; it can give families a chance to discuss their common problems, to raise possible solutions, and to begin to discover perhaps for the first time that they are not alone and that the clout of the group is stronger than the clout of the individual—that combined voices carry over greater distances than a single voice.

The same kind of informal family organization can make progress in the nursing home setting as well as in the outside community. Friends and relatives of the elderly are being organized in New York City, under a special grant from the Greater New York Fund, as "watchdog groups" to monitor nursing home operations and push for improved services. Similar family watchdog groups need to be organized for the protection of nursing home residents in every community across the country.

Family watchdog groups to monitor standards and prevent abuses are needed, not only in nursing homes, but in every service offering care for the elderly, because there is the possibility of poor performance in every one. Scandals have already rocked the nursing home "industry." Adult homes, boarding homes, and residences are being exposed every day for providing substandard living conditions. Fires are not uncommon because of inadequate safety systems. Medicare and Medicaid funds have been misused by doctors and health care providers. Similar abuses will creep into any new programs that are established for the elderly in the future unless there is careful monitoring by public agencies and alert family consumer groups. Unless carefully supervised, the home care services may, before long, end up playing a new version of the nursing home scandals.

NEW IMAGES FOR OLD

Images are important in American society, and once a negative image has been projected it has a tendency to cling. Because the term "sixty-five-and-over" has developed a generally negative image, older people are too often brushed aside. Too many valuable resources have been and continue to be wasted, too many skills abandoned, too much knowledge unused, too many talents buried, too much initiative stifled. Many older people, flatly rejecting popular stereotypes, go right ahead and live just the kind of life they want to live or are able to live. Their own personal experience proves that contentment, creativity, understanding, self-reliance, may be intensified rather than diminished in the later decades. They are proud, not ashamed, of their age, and want the world to know it: "What can I do for you today, young lady?" asked the salesman jovially. "First you can stop calling me 'young lady,' " replied his elderly customer, "because I'm an old woman. Then you can show me a nylon hairbrush."

Other aging people are less forthright. They move toward old age with dread. They spend their energies denying their years, afraid to identify themselves as old. Believing that the benefits of life can only be found in the younger years, they never allow themselves to discover the positive benefits of the older years. Still others, while identifying themselves as old, accept the stereotypes and allow themselves to feel useless, dependent, and finished long before it is necessary.

As the baby boom of the 1950s becomes the geriatric boom of the year 2000, the elderly sector of the population is expected to reach 32 million. At some point later in the twenty-first century, one-quarter of the population may be "sixty-five-and-over." Society may have been able to believe that 10 percent of its members were outside the mainstream, but 25 percent will not be so easy to ignore.

Public and private attitudes have been changing, but they will need to change more dramatically. In recent years, as the elderly have become more visible, the focus on that group has been largely on their needs and their problems. To the other negative images of aging, therefore, another image has been added: that of the underdog, always a prime attention-getter. We tend to rally for the underdog. When we finally became aware of the inhuman conditions in certain nursing homes and the victims became real people on our TV screens, we reacted to the nursing home scandals with more public outrage. But as the miseries suffered by some elderly men and women were made so dramatically clear, they inevitably underscored and reinforced the longstanding negative images: To be old is to be helpless. To be old is to be dependent. To be old is to be useless. To be old is to be unhappy.

Just as organized pressure coming from the elderly themselves has influenced legislation, pressure from the same source is also working to modify negative images and stereotypes. The revised image being projected emphasizes diversity. It urges public concern for the old who are sick and helpless and dependent. It does not leave out the old who are cantankerous, difficult, rigid, repetitive, resentful, eccentric, or the old who are useful, creative, imaginative, optimistic, resourceful, involved, adventurous.

The generation in the middle can help to change the negative images if it is willing to take the time to notice how often the images are false. Once it becomes clear that there are endless possibilities available in the years "sixty-five-and-over," just as there are in the years "sixty-five-and-under," there may be less reason to dread the years ahead and less cause to turn away from those who have arrived at old age already. The new image may not take hold in time to help our parents, but it may take hold in time to help someone else's parents—or perhaps ourselves—or our children.

≈≈≈≈≈≈≈≈

WHERE TO FIND HELP

1. STATE AND TERRITORIAL AGENCIES ON AGING

These agencies will provide information about local resources, including Area Agencies on Aging.

ALABAMA

Commission on Aging
502 Washington Avenue
Montgomery 36130
(205) 261-5743

ALASKA

Older Alaskans Commission
Department of Administration
Mail Station 0209, Pouch C
Juneau 99811-0209
(907) 465-3250

AMERICAN SAMOA

Territorial Administration on Aging
Office of the Governor
Pago Pago 96799
011 (684) 633-1252

ARIZONA

Aging and Adult Administration
Department of Economic Security
1400 West Washington Street
Phoenix 85007
(602) 255-3596

ARKANSAS

Division of Aging and Adult Services
Department of Social and
    Rehabilitative Services
Donaghey Building, Suite 1428
Seventh and Main Streets
Little Rock 72201
(501) 371-2441

CALIFORNIA

Department of Aging
1600 K Street
Sacramento 95814
(916) 322-5290

COLORADO

Aging and Adult Services Division
Department of Social Services
717 Seventeenth Street
P.O. Box 181000
Denver 80218-0899
(303) 294-5913

CONNECTICUT

Department on Aging
175 Main Street
Hartford 06106
(203) 566-3238

DELAWARE

Division on Aging
Department of Health and Social
  Services
1901 North DuPont Highway
New Castle 19720
(302) 421-6791

DISTRICT OF COLUMBIA

Office on Aging
1424 K Street Northwest, 2nd Floor
Washington 20011
(202) 724-5626

FLORIDA

Program Office of Aging and Adult
  Service
Department of Health and
  Rehabilitation Services
1317 Winewood Boulevard
Tallahassee 32301
(904) 488-8922

GEORGIA

Office of Aging
878 Peachtree Street Northeast
Room 632
Atlanta 30309
(404) 894-5333

GUAM

Public Health and Social Services
Government of Guam
Agana 96910

HAWAII

Executive Office on Aging
Office of the Governor
335 Merchant Street, Room 241
Honolulu 96813
(808) 548-2593

IDAHO

Office on Aging
Statehouse, Room 114
Boise 83720
(208) 334-3833

ILLINOIS

Department on Aging
421 East Capitol Avenue
Springfield 62701
(217) 785-2870

INDIANA

Department of Aging and Community
  Services
251 North Illinois Street
P.O. Box 7083
Indianapolis 46207-7083
(317) 232-7006

IOWA

Department of Elder Affairs
Jewett Building, Suite 236
914 Grand Avenue
Des Moines 50319
(515) 281-5187

KANSAS

Department on Aging
610 West Tenth Street
Topeka 66612
(913) 296-4986

KENTUCKY

Division for Aging Services
Department of Human Resources
DHR Building, 6th Floor
275 East Main Street
Frankfort 40601
(502) 564-6930

LOUISIANA

Office of Elderly Affairs
P.O. Box 80374
Baton Rouge 70898
(504) 925-1700

MAINE

Bureau of Maine's Elderly
Department of Human Services
State House, Station No. 11
Augusta 04333
(207) 289-2561

MARYLAND

Office on Aging
State Office Building, Room 1004
301 West Preston Street
Baltimore 21201
(301) 225-1100

MASSACHUSETTS

Executive Office of Elder Affairs
38 Chauncy Street
Boston 02111
(617) 727-7750

MICHIGAN

Office of Services to the Aging
P.O. Box 30026
Lansing 48909
(517) 373-8230

MINNESOTA

Board on Aging
Metro Square Building, Room 204
Seventh and Robert Streets
St. Paul 55101
(612) 296-2544

MISSISSIPPI

Council on Aging
301 West Pearl Street
Jackson 39203-3092
(601) 949-2070

MISSOURI

Division on Aging
Department of Social Services
2701 West Main Street
Jefferson City 65102
(314) 751-3082

MONTANA

Community Services Division
P.O. Box 4210
Helena 59604
(406) 444-3865

NEBRASKA

Department on Aging
301 Centennial Mall South
P.O. Box 95044
Lincoln 68509
(402) 471-2306

NEVADA

Division on Aging
Department of Human Resources
Kinkead Building, Room 101
505 East King Street
Carson City 89710
(702) 885-4210

NEW HAMPSHIRE

Council on Aging
Building No. 3
105 Loudon Road
Concord 03301
(603) 271-2751

NEW JERSEY

Division on Aging
Department of Community Affairs
363 West State Street
P.O. Box 2768
Trenton 08625
(609) 292-4833

NEW MEXICO

State Agency on Aging
La Villa Rivera Building, 4th Floor
224 East Palace Avenue
Santa Fe 87501
(505) 827-7640

NEW YORK

Office for the Aging
New York State Executive
   Department
Agency Building No. 2
Empire State Plaza
Albany 12223
(518) 474-5731

NORTH CAROLINA

Division on Aging
Kirby Building
1985 Umpstead Drive
Raleigh 27603
(919) 733-3983

NORTH DAKOTA

Aging Services
Department of Human Services
State Capitol Building
Bismarck 58505
(701) 224-2577

OHIO

Department on Aging
50 West Broad Street, 9th Floor
Columbus 43215
(614) 466-5500

OKLAHOMA

Special Unit on Aging
Department of Human Services
P.O. Box 25352
Oklahoma City 73125
(405) 521-2281

OREGON

Senior Services Division
313 Public Service Building
Salem 97310
(503) 378-4728

PENNSYLVANIA

Department of Aging
231 State Street
Harrisburg 17101-1195
(717) 783-1550

PUERTO RICO

Gericulture Commission
Department of Social Services
P.O. Box 11398
Santurce 00910
(809) 721-3141 or 722-0225

RHODE ISLAND

Department of Elderly Affairs
79 Washington Street
Providence 02903
(401) 277-2858

SOUTH CAROLINA

Commission on Aging
915 Main Street
Columbia 29201
(803) 783-3203

SOUTH DAKOTA

Office of Adult Services and Aging
Kneip Building
700 North Illinois Street
Pierre 57501
(605) 773-3656

TENNESSEE

Commission on Aging
706 Church Street, Suite 201
Nashville 37219-5573
(615) 741-2056

TEXAS

Department on Aging
Capitol Station, P.O. Box 12786
1949 IH 35
South Austin 78741-3702
(512) 444-2727

TRUST TERRITORY OF THE PACIFIC

Office of Elderly Programs
Community Development Division
Government of the Trust Territory of
the Pacific
Saipan 96950
Telephone 9335 or 9336

UTAH

Division of Aging and Adult Services
Department of Social Services
150 West North Temple
Box 45500
Salt Lake City 84145-0500
(801) 533-6422

VERMONT

Office on Aging
103 South Main Street
Waterbury 05676
(802) 241-2400

VIRGINIA

Department on Aging
James Monroe Building, 18th Floor
101 North Fourteenth Street
Richmond 23219
(804) 225-2271

VIRGIN ISLANDS

Commission on Aging
6F Havensight Mall
Charlotte Amalie
St. Thomas 00801
(809) 774-5884

WASHINGTON

Aging and Adult Services
  Administration
Department of Social and Health
  Services
OB-44A
Olympia 98504
(206) 586-3768

WEST VIRGINIA

Commission on Aging
Holly Grove–State Capitol
Charleston 25305
(304) 348-3317

WISCONSIN

Bureau of Aging
Division of Community Services
1 West Wilson Street, Room 480
Madison 53702
(608) 266-2536

WYOMING

Commission on Aging
Hathaway Building, Room 139
Cheyenne 82002-0710
(307) 777-7986

2. HOMEMAKER–HOME HEALTH AIDE SERVICES

There are over five thousand homemaker–home health aide programs in the country, about half of which are in agencies certified for Medicare. Some of these are licensed or certified by the state. Others have received approval from various professional organizations, such as the National League for Nursing. The following list, adapted from the 1988 *Directory of Homemaker–Home Health Aide Services*, contains the names and addresses of programs accredited or approved by the National HomeCaring Council, a Division of the Foundation for Hospice and Homecare, at the end of March 1989.

ALASKA

Anchorage

*Home Health Care
4107 Laurel Street
Anchorage 99508
(907) 561-2162

Juneau

*Alaska Management Technologies
Homemaker–Home Health Aide
  Program
240 Main Street, No. 701
Juneau 99801
(907) 586-3944

* Accredited after a site visit.

ARKANSAS

Little Rock

Pulaski County Council on Aging, Inc.
1700 West Thirteenth Street, Suite 100
Little Rock 72202
(501) 372-7878

CALIFORNIA

Claremont

*Visiting Nurse Association of Pomona-
  West End, Inc.
170 West San Jose, Suite 200
P.O. Box 908
Claremont 91711-0908
(714) 624-3574

CONNECTICUT

Greenwich

*Greenwich Homemaker Service
Department of Social Services
101 Field Point Road
Greenwich 06830
(203) 622-3800

New Britain

Visiting Nurse and Home Care
  Services of Central Connecticut, Inc.
205 West Main Street
P.O. Box 1327
New Britain 06050
(203) 224-7131

Ridgefield

*District Nursing Association of
  Ridgefield, Inc.
304 Main Street
Ridgefield 06877
(203) 438-8214

DISTRICT OF COLUMBIA

*Homemaker—Health Aide Service of
  the National Capital Area, Inc.
1234 Massachusetts Avenue
  Northwest, Suite 1015
Washington 20005
(202) 638-2382

GEORGIA

Athens

Athens Community Council on Aging,
  Inc.
230 South Hull Street
Athens 30605
(404) 549-4850

Savannah

Chatham County Department of
  Family Children Services/
  Homemaker Services
P.O. Box 2566
Savannah 31498
(912) 651-2070

ILLINOIS

Chicago

*Family Care Services of Metropolitan
  Chicago
Homemaker Service Division
234 South Wabash Avenue
Chicago 60604
(312) 427-8790

INDIANA

Liberty

*Union County Council on
  Aging and Aged
P.O. Box 333
Liberty 47353
(317) 458-5500

IOWA

Adel

*HomeCare Services, Inc.
Courthouse, Room 103
Adel 50003
(515) 993-3158

Davenport

*Visiting Nurse and Homemaker
  Service, Inc.
P.O. Box 4346
Davenport 52808
(319) 324-5274

Des Moines

*HomeCare Plus
1111 Ninth Street, Suite 260
Des Moines 50314
(515) 286-3993

Eldora

Hardin County Homemaker
  Health Aide Service
County Office Building
Eldora 50627
(515) 858-2309

MAINE

Auburn

Androscoggin Home Health
  Services, Inc.
1100 Minot Avenue, Box 1660
Auburn 04211-1660
(207) 795-4025

Bangor

*Community Health and Counseling
  Services
43 Illinois Avenue
Bangor 04401
(207) 947-0366

Caribou

*Diocesan Human Relations
  Services, Inc.
Northeastern Maine Homemaker
  Service
15 Vaughn Street
P.O. Box 748
Caribou 04736
(207) 498-2575

Portland

*Diocesan Human Relations
  Services, Inc.
Holy Innocents' Home Care Service
83 Sherman Street
P.O. Box 797
Portland 04104
(207) 871-7431

Waterville

*Diocesan Human Relations
  Services, Inc.
Home Care Services
35 Elm Street
P.O. Box 59
Waterville 04901
(207) 873-1146

MARYLAND

Baltimore

*Homemaker and Casework Services
Associated Catholic Charities
430 South Broadway
Baltimore 21231
(301) 732-5000

MASSACHUSETTS

Boston

Jewish Family & Children's Services
31 New Chardon Street
Boston 02114
(617) 227-6641

Holyoke

*Holyoke Visiting Nurse
  Association, Inc.
317 Maple Street
P.O. Box 246
Holyoke 01040-0246
(413) 534-5691

MICHIGAN

Ann Arbor

Child and Family Service of Washtenaw, Inc.
2301 Platt Road
P.O. Box 7054
Ann Arbor 48107
(313) 971-6520

Detroit

CareGivers
2111 Woodward, Suite 700
Detroit 48201
(313) 964-5070

Branch Office
North District Office
   28 North Saginaw, Suite 810
   Pontiac 48058
   (313) 334-5100

*Renaissance Health Care, Inc.
20700 Greenfield, No. 320
Detroit 48237
(313) 968-5300

MISSISSIPPI

Tupelo

Methodist Senior Services
Outreach Services
2800 West Main Street
Tupelo 38801
(601) 844-3713

MISSOURI

Rolla

Missouri Home Care
600 Pine Street
P.O. Box EE
Rolla 65401
(314) 341-3456

St. Louis

Grace Hill Skilled Home Care
Neighborhood Health Center, Inc.
2500 Hadley Street
St. Louis 63106
(314) 241-2200

Jewish Family and Children's Service
9385 Olive Boulevard
St. Louis 63132
(314) 993-1000

NEW HAMPSHIRE

Ossipee

*Carroll County Health and Home
   Care Services
Carroll County Complex
Ossipee 03864
(603) 539-4171

Portsmouth

*Area Homemaker—Home Health Aide
   Service, Inc.
249 Islington Street
Portsmouth 03801
(603) 436-9059

NEW JERSEY

East Orange

*Midpoint Health Care Services, Inc.
60 Evergreen Place
East Orange 07018
(201) 672-3833

*Personal Touch Home Care of
   New Jersey, Inc.
7 Glenwood Avenue
East Orange 07017
(201) 677-2224

Hackensack

*Norrell Health Care
131 Main Street
Hackensack 07601
(201) 488-6151

Hamilton Square

*Alan Health Care Services
1700 Whitehorse Hamilton
   Square Road, Suite B-4
Hamilton Square 08690
(609) 587-4415

Jersey City

*Visiting Homemaker Service of
   Hudson County
586 Newark Avenue
Jersey City 07306
(201) 656-6001

Branch Offices
   564 Broadway
   Bayonne 07002
   (201) 823-3800

   501 70th Street
   Guttenberg 07093
   (201) 854-3600

Long Branch

*Visiting Homemaker–Home Health
   Aide Service
Family and Children's Service of
   Monmouth
191 Bath Avenue
P.O. Box 505
Long Branch 07740-0505
(201) 222-9100 or 542-6160

Paterson

*Visiting Homemaker Service of
   Passaic County
2 Market Street
Paterson 07501
(201) 523-1224

Toms River

*Visiting Homemaker Service of Ocean
   County, Inc.
105 Sunset Avenue, CN 2010
Toms River 08754
(201) 244-5565

Trenton

*Mercer Street Friends Center
223 North Hermitage Avenue
Trenton 08618
(609) 396-1507

Westfield

*Visiting Homemaker Health Aide
   Service of Central Union County,
   Inc.
526 North Avenue East
P.O. Box 846
Westfield 07090
(201) 233-3113

Woodbury

*Visiting Nurse Custom Care, Inc.
P.O. Box 508
Woodbury 08096
(609) 845-0460

NEW YORK

New York City

*Home Care Services–GHI
330 West 42nd Street, Room 305
New York 10036
(212) 239-6360

Syracuse

*Home Aides of Central New York,
   Inc.
503 East Fayette Street
Syracuse 13202
(315) 476-4295

Yonkers

Family Service Society of Yonkers
Homemaker Service
219 Palisade Avenue
Yonkers 10703
(914) 963-5118

Branch Office
2172 Central Park Avenue
Yonkers 10710
(914) 337-6718

NORTH CAROLINA

Asheboro

Regional Consolidated Services, Inc.
P.O. Box 1883
Asheboro 27204-1883
(919) 629-5141

Brevard

Home Life: Transylvania Community
Hospital
Box 1116
Brevard 28712
(704) 884-3898

Fayetteville

Cumberland County Coordinating
Council on Older Adults, Inc.
824 Branson Street
Fayetteville 28305
(919) 484-0111

Greensboro

Homemaker—Home Health Aide
Services
United Services for Older Adults
P.O. Box 21993
Greensboro 27420
(919) 373-7998

Hayesville

*Good Shepherd Home Health
Agency, Inc.
P.O. Box 465
Hayesville 28904
(704) 389-6311

Hendersonville

Henderson County Department of
Social Services
246 Second Avenue East
Hendersonville 28739
(704) 692-2215

Jacksonville

Onslow Coordinating Council on
Aging
105 Third Street
P.O. Box 982
Jacksonville 28540
(919) 455-2747

Lenoir

Caldwell County Health Department
619 Lower Creek Drive Northeast
P.O. Box 1378
Lenoir 28645
(704) 757-1236

Raleigh

*Homemaker—Home Health Aide
Service of the Council on Aging of
Wake County, Inc.
3800 Barrett Drive, Suite 210
Raleigh 27609
(919) 787-7505

Smithfield

*Johnston County Health Department
618 North Eighth Street
Smithfield 27577
(919) 934-4168

Winston-Salem

Senior Services, Inc.
836 Oak Street, Suite 320
Winston-Salem 27101
(919) 725-0907

OHIO

Batavia

*Clermont Senior Services, Inc.
Home Health Technician Service
2085-A Front Wheel Drive
Batavia 45103
(513) 724-1255

Cincinnati

*United Home Care
2400 Reading Road
Cincinnati 45202
(513) 621-8989

Cleveland

*The Benjamin Rose Institute
Homemaker–Home Health Aide
  Service
1422 Euclid Avenue, Suite 500
Cleveland 44115-1989
(216) 621-7201

Ravenna

*Highland Home Health Care
220 West Highland Avenue
P.O. Box 309
Ravenna 44266
(216) 296-3851

OKLAHOMA

Oklahoma City

Mary Mahoney Memorial Health
  Center
12716 Northeast 36th Street
P.O. Box 30589
Oklahoma City 73140
(405) 769-3301

PENNSYLVANIA

Allentown

Homemaker Health Aide Service
Family and Counseling Services of
  the Lehigh Valley
411 Walnut Street
Allentown, 18102
(215) 435-9651

Altoona

*Home Nursing Agency and VNA
Home Nursing Agency Community
  Services
201 Chestnut Avenue
P.O. Box 352
Altoona 16603
(814) 946-5411 or (800) 445-6262

Ardmore

*Community Home Support Services
104–108 Ardmore Avenue
Ardmore 19003
(215) 642-8425

Bellefonte

*Centre HomeCare, Inc.
221 West High Street
Bellefonte 16823
(814) 355-2273

Bridgewater

*Homemaker-Home Health Aide
  Service of Beaver County
Stone Point Landing
500 Market Street, Suite 104
Bridgewater 15009-2998
(412) 774-4002

Harrisburg

*Homemaker-Home Health
  Aide Services, Inc.
2001 North Front Street
Harrisburg 17102
(717) 232-2547

Norristown

*Visiting Nurse Association/Home
  Health Services of Montgomery
  County and Vicinity
1109 DeKalb Street
Norristown 19401
(215) 272-1160

Philadelphia

*Homemaker Service of the
  Metropolitan Area
801 Arch Street, Ground Floor
Philadelphia 19107
(215) 592-0002

Plymouth Meeting

*Montgomery County Homemaker-
  Home Health Aide Service
531 Plymouth Road, Suite 530
Plymouth Meeting 19462
(215) 941-9555

SOUTH CAROLINA

Aiken

*Aiken Area Council on Aging
159 Morgan Street Northwest
P.O. Box 235
Aiken 29802
(803) 648-5447

TENNESSEE

Memphis

*Mid-South Comprehensive Home
  Health and Hospice
5705 Stage Road, Suite 201
Memphis 38134
(901) 372-2500

TEXAS

Dallas

*Home Health Services of Dallas, Inc.
4313 North Central Expressway
Suite 100
Dallas 75205
(214) 559-4050

VIRGINIA

Martinsville

Piedmont Seniors of Virginia, Inc.
213 East Main Street
Martinsville 24112
(703) 632-6442

Roanoke

*Family Service of Roanoke Valley
3208 Hershberger Road Northwest
P.O. Box 6600
Roanoke 24017
(703) 563-5316

3. FAMILY SERVICE AGENCIES

Counseling and psychotherapeutic services for older persons and their families are provided by some psychiatrists, psychologists, and clinical social workers privately and in a variety of settings: family agencies, outpatient psychiatric clinics, hospitals, and nursing homes. The following list of accredited and provisional member agencies of Family Service America is excerpted from its *1989 Directory of Member Agencies* and is used here with its permission. Included are only those agencies listed as providing "Elder/Supportive Services to Aging."

Accredited Members: UNITED STATES

ALABAMA

Birmingham
35212

Family and Child Services
Administrative Office
5201 Airport Highway
(205) 595-3733
Mary Edna Porter, Executive
    Director
AREA SERVED: Blount, Jefferson,
    Shelby, and Walker counties

Additional Offices
Family and Child Services
    3600 Eighth Avenue South
    Suite 2-102
    Birmingham 35222
    (205) 324-3411
Family Resource Center
    3603 Eighth Avenue South
    Birmingham 35222
    (205) 328-1717

Mobile
36606

Family Counseling Center
6 South Florida Street
(205) 471-3466
Joyce Collier, Executive Director
AREA SERVED: Mobile County and its
    environs

Montgomery
36106

Family Guidance Center
925 Forest Avenue
(205) 262-6669
Walter P. White, Executive Director
AREA SERVED: Autauga, Elmore, and
    Montgomery counties (persons
    who live or work there)

ARIZONA

Phoenix
85006

Jewish Family and Children's Service
2033 North 7th Street
(602) 257-1904
Adrien Shalowitz, Executive Director
AREA SERVED: Maricopa County

Additional Offices
East Valley
    1930 South Alma School Road
    Mesa 85202
    (602) 820-0825
Glendale Office
    5346 West Northern
    Glendale 85302
    (602) 934-4530
Osborn Senior Center
    2942 North Seventh Avenue
    Phoenix 85013
    (602) 274-3398

Scottsdale Offices
 7700 East Roosevelt
  Scottsdale 85257
  (602) 994-2323
 8300 North Hayden Road
  Suite 207
  Scottsdale 85258
  (602) 483-8455
Sun City Office
 9451 North Ninety-ninth Avenue
 Peoria 85345
 (602) 977-1313

Tucson
85716

Family Counseling Agency
209 South Tucson Boulevard
Suite F
(602) 327-4583
Leonard Banes, Executive Director
AREA SERVED: Tucson metropolitan
 area

Additional Office
Branch Office
 3776 North First Avenue
 Tucson 85719
 (602) 742-6380

CALIFORNIA

Burlingame
94010

Family Service Agency of San Mateo
 County
1870 El Camino Real, #107
(415) 692-0555
J. Donald Cameron, Executive
 Director
AREA SERVED: San Mateo County
Burlingame Office serves Burlingame,
 Daly City, Hillsborough, Millbrae,
 San Bruno, San Mateo, and South
 San Francisco

Pacifica Office serves El Granada,
 Half-Moon Bay, Montara, Moss
 Beach, and Pacifica
Redwood City Office serves Atherton,
 Belmont, Menlo Park, Redwood
 City, and San Carlos

Additional Offices
Pacifica Office
 190 Paloma
 Pacifica 94044
 (415) 692-0555
Redwood City Office
 35 Renato Court
 Redwood City 94061
 (415) 365-2284

Glendale
91208

Glendale Family Service Association
3436 North Verdugo Road
(818) 248-2286
Rod Lackey, Executive Director
AREA SERVED: Glendale, La Canada,
 La Crescenta, Montrose,
 Sunland, and Tujunga; other
 residents of Los Angeles County
 if time and staff permit

Los Angeles
90010

Family Service of Los Angeles
Administration
3600 Wilshire Boulevard
Suite 400
(213) 381-3626
Anthony Lufrano, President and
 Chief Executive Officer
AREA SERVED: Metropolitan Los
 Angeles area served by
 metropolitan office. Additional
 offices serve northern, western,
 and southwestern communities of
 the county.

Additional Offices
Dignity Center
  5880 West Pico Boulevard
  Los Angeles 90019
  (213) 933-5586
FSLA Community Center
  17400 Victory Boulevard
  Van Nuys 91406
  (818) 345-8753
Harbor Area Office
  605 South Pacific Avenue
  Suite 201
  San Pedro 90731
  (213) 547-1126
Manchester Center
  1328 West Manchester Boulevard
  Los Angeles 90044
  (213) 778-9593
Metropolitan Office
  3600 Wilshire Boulevard, #400
  Los Angeles 90010
  (213) 381-3626
Project LINC
  17400 Victory Boulevard
  Van Nuys 91406
  (818) 996-8295
San Fernando Valley District Office
  17400 Victory Boulevard
  Van Nuys 91406
  (818) 345-8413
Santa Clarita Valley Office
  23542 209 Lyons Avenue
  Suite 209
  Newhall 91321
  (805) 255-7553
Santa Fe Springs Office
  10016 South Pioneer Boulevard
  Suite 109
  Santa Fe Springs 90670
  (213) 949-9691
Southeast District Office
  11455 Paramount Boulevard
  Suite F
  Downey 90241
  (213) 923-6548

Suicide Prevention Center
  1041 South Menlo Avenue
  Los Angeles 90006
  (213) 386-5111
West Valley Office
  6922 Owensmouth Avenue
  Canoga Park 91303
  (818) 884-5585
Western District Office
  9133 South LaCienega Boulevard
  Suite 220
  Inglewood 90301
  (213) 670-9550
Whittier Office
  7702 Washington Avenue
  Suite C
  Whittier 90602
  (213) 698-7941

Pasadena
91101

Foothill Family Service
118 South Oak Knoll Avenue
(818) 795-6907, (213) 681-5232
David M. Eisenberg, Ph.D.,
    Executive Director
AREA SERVED: Pasadena, plus
    Altadena, Arcadia, Bradbury,
    Duarte, La Canada-Flintridge,
    San Marino, Sierra Madre, South
    Pasadena, and Temple City; and
    other residents of Los Angeles
    County

Additional Office
South Pasadena Office
  1730 Huntington Drive
  No. 203
  South Pasadena 91030
  (818) 795-6907, (213) 681-5232

Riverside
92506

Family Service Association of
Riverside
6927 Brockton Avenue
Suite 1A
(714) 686-3706
Dominick Betro, Executive Director
AREA SERVED: Western Riverside
County, including City of
Riverside, Corona, Norco,
Rubidoux, Moreno Valley,
Perris, Lake Elsinore, Rancho
California, Temecula, March Air
Force Base, Beaumont, Banning,
and Hemet

San Bernardino
92405

Family Service Agency of San
Bernardino
1669 North E Street
(714) 886-6737
Woodrow D. McHarg, Executive
Director
AREA SERVED: San Bernardino, plus
Big Bear Lake, Bloomington,
Colton, Crest Forest, Del Rosa,
Grand Terrace, Highland, Lake
Arrowhead, Loma Linda,
Muscoy, and Rialto. Outpatient
mental health clinic services
available to anyone residing in
San Bernardino County.

Additional Offices
Child Sexual Abuse Treatment and
Prevention Programs
1657 North E Street
San Bernardino 92405
(714) 886-6502
Fontana Branch Office
9161 Sierra Avenue
Fontana 92335
(714) 822-3533

Outreach Counseling Service for
Senior Citizens
1669 North E Street
San Bernardino 92405
(714) 886-6739
Suicide/Crisis Intervention Service
1657 North E Street
San Bernardino 92405
(714) 886-6730

San Diego
92111

Family Service Association of San
Diego County
7645 Family Circle
(619) 279-0400
Stephen J. Carmichael, President and
Chief Executive Officer
AREA SERVED: San Diego and San
Diego County. Metropolitan and
southern areas served by central
office; additional offices serve
northern and eastern
communities.

Additional Offices
East County Office
7373 University Avenue
Suite 222
La Mesa 92041
(619) 698-1601
Escondido Office
1002 East Grand Avenue
Escondido 92025
(619) 745-3811
Fallbrook Office
304 East Mission Street
Suite E
Fallbrook 92028
(619) 723-8181
Mid-City Juvenile Division
6760 University Avenue
Suite 250
San Diego 92115
(619) 583-7511

North Coast Office
  6120 Paseo Del Norte
  Suite N-1
  Carlsbad 92009
  (619) 931-0286
Poway Office
  13422 Community Road
  Poway 92064
  (619) 486-1190
San Dieguito Senior Center
  890B Balour Drive
  Encinitas 92024
  (619) 753-1735
Vista Office
  1070 South Santa Fe
  Suite 27A
  Vista 92083
  (619) 726-0960

San Rafael
94901

Family Service Agency of Marin
  County
1005 A Street
Suite 307
(415) 456-3853
Robert F. Thomas, Executive
  Director
AREA SERVED: Marin County

Additional Offices
Marin City Branch
  Marin City Tenants Council
  101 Drake Avenue
  Marin City 94965
  (415) 456-3853
Novato Branch
  Novato Human Needs Center
  1907 Novato Boulevard
  Novato 94947
  (415) 456-3853

Santa Barbara
93101

Family Service Agency of Santa
  Barbara

123 West Gutierrez Street
(805) 965-1001
Susan Rehm, Executive Director
AREA SERVED: Santa Barbara South
  Coastal Area. Child Guidance
  Clinic serves entire Santa
  Barbara County.

Santa Rosa
95404

Family Service Agency of Sonoma
  County
(Provisional Member Agency)
1212 Fourth Street
Suite O
(707) 545-4551
Cathleen F. Barnier, Executive
  Director
AREA SERVED: Sonoma County

CONNECTICUT

Bridgeport
06605

Family Services—Woodfield
475 Clinton Avenue
(203) 368-4291
Brian J. Langdon, President
AREA SERVED: Bridgeport, Easton,
  Fairfield, Monroe, Stratford, and
  Trumbull. Suburban office serves
  Huntington and Newtown.

Additional Office
Suburban Office Family Services
  500 Purdy Hill Road
  Monroe 06468
  (203) 368-4291

Greenwich
06836

Family Center
40 Arch Street
P.O. Box 7550
(203) 869-4848

Robert M. Arnold, Executive
  Director
AREA SERVED: Greenwich (persons
  who live or work there)

Hartford
06105

Catholic Charities/Catholic Family
  Services—Archdiocese of
  Hartford
896 Asylum Avenue
(203) 522-8241
Patrick J. Johnson, Executive
  Director and Director of Catholic
  Charities
AREA SERVED: Hartford, New Haven,
  and Litchfield counties

Additional Offices
Bristol Office
  225 North Main Street
  Suite 301A
  Bristol 06010
  (203) 589-8662
District Office
  205 Wakeless Avenue
  P.O. Box 364
  Ansonia 06401
  (203) 735-6473
District Office
  200 Colony Street
  Meriden 06450
  (203) 235-2507
District Office
  230 High Street
  P.O. Box 147
  Milford 06460
  (203) 874-6270
District Office
  90 Franklin Square
  New Britain 06051
  (203) 225-3561

District Office
  478 Orange Street
  New Haven 06511
  (203) 787-2207
District Office
  132 Grove Street
  Torrington 06790
  (203) 482-5558
District Office
  56 Church Street
  Waterbury 06702
  (203) 755-1196
Enfield Office
  109 Elm Street
  Lower Level
  Enfield 06082
  (203) 745-1727
Guilford Office
  57 Whitefield Street
  Guilford 06434
  (203) 453-5746
Institute for the Hispanic Family
  160 Main Street
  Hartford 06106
  (203) 527-1124
Institute for the Hispanic Family
Child Guidance Clinic
  95 Park Street
  Hartford 06106
  (203) 524-8974
Mills Pond Group Home C.L.A.
  23 and 25 Tamarack Drive
  Bloomfield 06002
  (203) 243-5536, 243-3778
Refugee Resettlement Office
  125 Market Street
  Hartford 06103
  (203) 548-0059
Simsbury Office
  524 Hopmeadow Street
  Simsbury 06070
  (203) 651-3448
Southington Office
  35 North Main Street
  Southington 06489
  (203) 621-4887

Hartford
06105

Child and Family Services
1680 Albany Avenue
(203) 236-4511
William A. Baker, Executive Director
AREA SERVED: Serves the Capitol
    Region Area.
Northeast Office serves Tolland and
    Windham counties, plus the
    towns in Hartford County east of
    the Connecticut River.

Additional Offices
Dr. Isaiah Clark Family and Youth
    Clinic
  1229 Albany Avenue
  Hartford 06112
  (203) 241-0888
Northeast Office
  110 Main Street
  Manchester 06040
  (203) 643-2761
Valley Family Center
  2 Monteith Drive
  Farmington 06032
  (203) 673-3146

New Haven
06511

Family Counseling of Greater New
    Haven
1 State Street
(203) 865-1125
William F. Mecca, Executive Director
AREA SERVED: New Haven, plus
    Bethany, Branford, East Haven,
    Guilford, Hamden, Madison,
    Middlesex County, North Haven,
    Orange, West Haven,
    Westbrook, and Woodbridge.

Additional Offices
Family Counseling of Guilford
  36 Graves Avenue
  Guilford 06437
  (203) 453-2925

Family Counseling of Madison
  Lee Academy
  Meeting House Lane, Box 1304
  Madison 06443
  (203) 245-4498
Family Counseling of Middletown
  360 Main Street
  Middletown 06457
  (203) 347-9798
Family Counseling of Orange
  380 Boston Post Road
  Orange 06477
  (203) 795-6662
Family Counseling of Woodbridge/
    Bethany
  264 Amity Road
  Woodbridge 06525
  (203) 387-6780

New Haven
06510

Jewish Family Service of New Haven
152 Temple Street
(203) 777-6641
Jared N. Rolsky, Executive Director
AREA SERVED: Greater New Haven,
    plus Ansonia, Bethany, Branford,
    Cheshire, Clinton, Derby, East
    Haven, Guilford, Hamden,
    Kilingworth, Madison, Milford,
    North Branford, North Haven,
    Orange, Seymour, Shelton,
    Wallingford, West Haven, and
    Woodbridge. Service, including
    adoption, provided to anyone
    requesting it.

New London
06320

Family Service Association of
    Southern New London County
11 Granite Street
(203) 442-4319
Jay C. Bloom, Executive Director

AREA SERVED: New London, plus
   Bozrah, Colchester, East Lyme,
   Groton, Ledyard, Lyme,
   Montville, Mystic, North
   Stonington, Norwich, Old Lyme,
   Preston, Salem, Sprague,
   Stonington, and Waterford

Additional Offices
Family Service West
  6 Grand Street
  Niantic 06357
  (203) 739-4290
Montville Office
  1180 Norwich New London
    Turnpike
  Montville 06353
  (203) 848-1917
Stonington Office
  139B Old Stonington Road
  Stonington 06378
  (203) 572-8528

Norwalk
06851

Family and Children's Aid of Greater
   Norwalk
138 Main Street
(203) 846-4203
Florence R. Kraut, Executive
   Director
AREAS SERVED: Darien, New Canaan,
   Norwalk, Weston, Westport, and
   Wilton

Additional Office
Home Care and Parent Aide Services
  181 Main Street
  Norwalk 06851
  (203) 846-4386

Stamford
06902

Family and Children's Services
60 Palmer's Hill Road
(203) 324-3167

Robert J. Short, Executive Director
AREA SERVED: Stamford, plus Darien
   and New Canaan

Additional Offices
Darien Office
  528 Boston Post Road
  Darien 06820
  (203) 655-0547
New Canaan Office
  103 South Avenue
  New Canaan 06840
  (203) 972-0556

West Hartford
06117

Jewish Family Service of Greater
   Hartford
740 N. Main Street
Suite A
(203) 236-1927
Philip Wiener, Executive Director
AREA SERVED: Hartford, East
   Hartford, West Hartford, plus
   Avon, Bloomfield, Farmington,
   Glastonbury, Manchester,
   Newington, Rocky Hill,
   Simsbury, South Windsor,
   Wethersfield, and Windsor.
   Adoption service to residents of
   northern Connecticut, plus New
   London. Service to unmarried
   mothers regardless of residence.

DISTRICT OF COLUMBIA

Washington
20001

Family and Child Services of
   Washington
929 L Street Northwest
(202) 289-1510
John G. Theban, Executive Director
AREA SERVED: District of Columbia.

Additional Offices
Columbia Senior Center
   4121 Thirteenth Street Northwest
   Washington 20011
   (202) 829-4408
Model Cities Senior Center
   4900 Tenth Street Northeast
   Washington 20017
   (202) 635-1900

FLORIDA

Clearwater
34620

Family Service Centers
2960 Roosevelt Boulevard
(813) 536-9427
Richard Murdock, Executive Director
AREA SERVED: Pinellas County

Additional Offices
Palm Harbor Office
   2310 U.S. Highway 19 North
   Suite 525
   Palm Harbor 34684
   (813) 784-7608
St. Petersburg Office
   928 Twenty-second Avenue South
   St. Petersburg 33705
   (813) 822-3961
Seminole Office
   9009 Seminole Boulevard
   Unit 2B
   Seminole 34642
   (813) 393-4090

Miami
33130

Family Counseling Services of
   Greater Miami
75 Southwest Eighth Street
(305) 379-5730
Albert L. Harriett, Executive
   Director
AREA SERVED: Dade County

Additional Offices
North Dade Office
   111 Northwest 183rd Street
   Miami 33169
   (305) 653-9908
South Dade Office
   10720 Caribbean Boulevard
   Miami 33189
   (305) 232-1610
West Dade Office
   9370 Sunset Drive
   Miami 33173
   (305) 279-3322

Miami
33145

Jewish Family Service of Greater
   Miami
1790 Southwest Twenty-seventh
   Avenue
(305) 445-0555
David B. Saltman, Executive
   Director
AREA SERVED: Dade County

Additional Offices
Miami Beach Office
   7455 Collins Avenue
   Miami Beach 33141
   (305) 868-0888
North District Office
   2040 Northeast 163rd Street
   North Miami Beach 33162
   (305) 949-6186
Resettlement Office
   420 Lincoln Road
   No. 208
   Miami Beach 33139
   (305) 532-4137
South District Office
   8905 Southwest Eighty-seventh
   Avenue
   Miami 33173
   (305) 279-6611

GEORGIA

Atlanta
30309

Jewish Family Services
1605 Peachtree Road Northeast
(404) 873-2277
Irving Perlman, Executive Director
AREA SERVED: Metropolitan Atlanta
and Cobb County

Additional Office
Cobb County Branch Office
  1325 Johnson Ferry Road
    Northeast
  Suite 260
  Marietta 30067
  (404) 973-3167
Zaban Park
  (Branch of Atlanta Jewish
    Community Center)
  5342 Tilly Mill Road
  Dunwood 30338
  (404) 396-3250

Augusta
30904

Family Counseling Center/CSRA
1914 Central Avenue
(404) 738-9750
Helen Longley, Executive Director
AREA SERVED: Central Savannah
  River Area

HAWAII

Honolulu
96817

Child and Family Service
200 North Vineyard Boulevard
Building 20
(808) 521-2377
Patti J. Lyons, President and Chief
  Executive Officer
AREA SERVED: State of Hawaii

ILLINOIS

Champaign
61820

Family Service of Champaign County
405 South State Street
(217) 352-0099
Keith Oswald, Executive Director
AREA SERVED: Champaign County

Additional Office
Rantoul Office
  c/o Community Service Center
  1271 East Grove Avenue
  Rantoul 61866
  (217) 893-1530

Chicago
60606

Jewish Family and Community
  Service
1 South Franklin Street
(312) 346-6700, TTY 679-5992
Martin E. Langer, Executive
  Director
AREA SERVED: Cook and Lake
  counties; also Jewish families
  living in communities outside
  counties with no other organized
  resource to meet their needs;
  also, by contractual arrangement
  with Jewish Federation of
  Northwest Indiana, family
  counseling service to persons
  living in East Chicago, Gary,
  Hammond, and neighboring
  communities

Additional Offices
Niles Township Office
  5050 Church Street
  Skokie 60077
  (312) 675-0390
  Hearing Impaired TTY 679-5992

North Suburban District Office
  210 Skokie Valley Road
  Highland Park 60035
  (312) 831-4225
Northern District Office
  2710 West Devon Avenue
  Chicago 60659
  (312) 274-1324
Northwest Suburban Office
  1250 Radcliffe Road
  No. 206
  Buffalo Grove 60089
  (312) 255-4410
South Suburban Office
  3649 West 183rd Street
  Suite 123
  Hazel Crest 60429
  (312) 799-1869
Virginia Frank Child Development
    Center
  3033 West Touhy Avenue
  Chicago 60645
  (312) 761-4550

Chicago
60604

United Charities
14 East Jackson Boulevard
(312) 461-0800
A. Gerald Erickson, President and
    Chief Executive Officer
AREA SERVED: Metropolitan Chicago

Additional Offices
Calumet Center
  235 East 103rd Street
  Chicago 60628
  (312) 264-3010
Case Management Unit
  3157 South Wolcott Avenue
  Chicago 60608
  (312) 247-1290
Edgewater Uptown Senior
    Services
  4753 North Broadway
  Chicago 60640
  (312) 989-7889

Employee Assistance Network
  14 East Jackson Boulevard
  Chicago 60604
  (312) 663-5600
    Northwest Branch
    425 North Martingale Road
    Suite 809
    Schaumburg 60194
    (312) 706-3825
Family and Mental Health Services/
    Southwest
  11220 South Harlem
  Worth 60482
  (312) 448-5700
    Blue Island Branch
    13005 South Western Avenue
    Blue Island 60406
    (312) 371-5170
    Orland Park Branch
    9763 West 143rd Street
    Orland Park 60462
    (312) 460-6122
Family Service Association of DuPage
    County
  402 West Liberty Drive
  Wheaton 60187
  (312) 682-1802
Fox Valley Center at Camp Algonquin
  14 East Jackson Boulevard
  Chicago 60604
  (312) 461-0800
    Camp Algonquin
    Cary Road
    Algonquin 60102
    (312) 658-8212
Loop Center
  14 East Jackson Boulevard
  Chicago 60604
  (312) 939-1300
Midway Center
  3214 West Sixty-third Street
  Chicago 60629
  (312) 436-2400
Murdock Center
  910 West Van Buren Street
  Chicago 60607
  (312) 829-9327

Near North Center
  1500 North Halsted Street
  Chicago 60622
  (312) 266-5411
Parkside Center
  3445 North Central
  Chicago 60634
  (312) 282-9535
South Chicago Center
  3029 East Ninety-first Street
  Chicago 60617
  (312) 221-5141

Elgin
60120

Family Service Association of
Greater Elgin Area
22 South Spring Street
(312) 695-3680
Mark Nelson, Executive Director
AREA SERVED: Elgin, plus Burlington,
  Elgin, Hanover, and Plato
  townships

Additional Offices
Cardunal Area Branch
  211 West Main Street
  Suite 218
  Dundee 60118
  (312) 428-7718
Tri-Village Office
  519 South Bartlett Road
  Streamwood 60107
  (312) 837-8553

INDIANA

Indianapolis
46204

Family Service Association
615 North Alabama Street
Suite 210
(317) 634-6341
James N. Miller, President

AREA SERVED: City of Indianapolis,
  plus Boone, Hamilton, Hancock,
  Hendricks, Marion, and Morgan
  counties

Additional Offices
Boone County Office
  1122 North Lebanon Street
  Room 26
  Lebanon 46052
  (317) 482-6396
Hamilton County Office
  54 South 9th Street
  Noblesville 46060
  (317) 773-6273
Hancock County Office
  Memorial Building
  Greenfield 46140
  (317) 462-3733
Morgan County Office
  89 North Jefferson Street
  P.O. Box 1592
  Martinsville 46151
  (317) 342-0202

Lafayette
47901

Family Services
731 Main Street
(317) 423-5361
Susan Smith, President
AREA SERVED: Tippecanoe County
  (persons who live or work there);
  homemaker service also available
  in Benton, Fountain,
  Montgomery, and White counties;
  8-county regional adult protective
  service program

Additional Office
Homemaker Service
  201 East Pike
  Room 19
  Crawfordsville 47933
  (317) 364-0550

Muncie
47305

Family Services of Delaware County
615 East Washington Street
(317) 284-7789
Fred Koss, Executive Director
A Better Way (shelter for battered
    women)
    (317) 747-9107
Crisis Information Center
    (317) 289-0404
AREA SERVED: Delaware County; also
    areas outside county, especially
    Blackford, Henry, Jay, and
    Randolph counties

Terre Haute
47807

Family Service Association
    in Terre Haute
619 Cherry Street
(812) 232-4349
John Kuchinskas, Executive Director
AREA SERVED: Clay, Greene, Parke,
    Sullivan, Vermillion, and Vigo
    counties; other areas as need
    arises

IOWA

Cedar Rapids
52404

Family Service Agency
1330 First Avenue Northeast
(319) 398-3574
Shirley Stewart, Executive Director
AREA SERVED: Counseling, financial
    management, family life
    education, and employee
    assistance programs available to
    all, regardless of residence.
    Meals on Wheels Service
    available to Cedar Rapids and
    Marion residents.

KANSAS

Kansas City
66102

Heart of America Family Services
8047 Parallel Parkway
(913) 788-5791
Oliver W. Gerland, Jr., President and
    Chief Executive Officer
AREA SERVED: Missouri: Kansas City,
    plus Blue Springs, Buckner,
    Grandview, Independence, Lake
    Lotawana, Lee's Summit, Oak
    Grove, Raytown, and Sugar
    Creek
Northland Office serves Claycomo,
    Gladstone, Kansas City North,
    Liberty, North Kansas City,
    Parkville, Platte City, Pleasant
    Valley, and Riverside
Kansas: Wyandotte County and
    surrounding areas. Johnson
    County, Kansas Office serves
    Overland Park, plus Fairway,
    Leawood, Lenexa, Merriam,
    Mission, Mission Hills, Olathe,
    Prairie Village, Roeland Park,
    Shawnee, South Park, and
    Westwood

Additional Offices
Kansas City, Kansas Office
    5424 State Avenue
    Kansas City 66102
    (913) 287-1300
Johnson County, Kansas Office
    6300 West Ninety-fifth Street
    Suite 101
    Overland Park 66212
    (913) 642-4300

Missouri Offices:
East Jackson County Office
    Crysler Building, Suite 107
    12401 East Forty-third Street
    Independence 64050
    (816) 737-7577

Kansas City, Missouri Office
3217 Broadway
Suite 500
Kansas City 64111
(816) 753-5280
Northland Office
5950 North Oak Trafficway
Gladstone 64119
(816) 454-4819

KENTUCKY

Louisville
40201

Family and Children's Agency
1115 Garvin Place
P.O. Box 3784
(502) 583-1741
Daniel Fox, Executive Director
AREA SERVED: Jefferson, Shelby,
    Hardin, Oldham, and Bullitt
    counties, Kentucky; Floyd
    County, Indiana; also beyond
    these areas as resources permit

MARYLAND

Baltimore
21217

Family and Children's Services
    of Central Maryland
204 West Lanvale Street
(301) 669-9000
Stanley A. Levi, Executive Director
AREA SERVED: Baltimore City, plus
    Anne Arundel, Baltimore,
    Carroll, Harford, and Howard
    counties

Additional Offices
Anne Arundel County—Annapolis
    Office
    934 West Street
    Annapolis 21401
    (301) 263-5743

Anne Arundel County—Brooklyn
    Office
    Arundel Village Medical Center
    5515 Ritchie Highway
    Baltimore 21225
    (301) 636-8280
Anne Arundel County—Fort Meade/
    Pioneer Village
    8319 Pioneer Circle
    Severn 21144
    (301) 551-3484
Anne Arundel County—Pasadena
    Office
    2528 Mountain Road
    Suite 203
    Pasadena 21222
    (301) 360-1244
Baltimore City—Eastern
    Office
    2502 St. Paul Street
    Baltimore 21218
    (301) 366-1430
Baltimore City—Southern Office
    1310 South Charles Street
    Baltimore 21230
    (301) 752-0445
Baltimore City—Western Office
    1301 Park Avenue
    Baltimore 21217
    (301) 669-9000
Baltimore County—Central Office
    303 West Chesapeake Avenue
    Towson 21204
    (301) 825-3705
Baltimore County—East Office
    Eastpoint Office Park, Suite 206
    1107 North Point Boulevard
    Baltimore 21224
    (301) 285-7300
Baltimore County—West Office
    7131 Liberty Road
    Baltimore 21207
    (301) 281-1334
Carroll County Office
    22 North Court Street
    Westminster 21157
    (301) 876-1233

Fort Meade Family Violence Office
Fifth Street
Fort George G. Meade 20755
(301) 677-6895
Harford County Office
125 North Main Street
Bel Air 21014
(301) 838-9000
Howard County Office
8659 Baltimore National Pike
Ellicott City 21122
(301) 461-1277

MASSACHUSETTS

Boston
02108

Family Service of Greater Boston
34½ Beacon Street
(617) 523-6400
Susan T. Vandiver, Executive
Director
AREA SERVED: Boston Office serves
Boston, plus Chelsea, Revere,
and Winthrop
Lexington Office serves Lexington,
plus Bedford, Belmont,
Burlington, Winchester, and
Woburn
Malden Office serves Malden, plus
Everett, Medford, Melrose,
North Reading, Reading,
Stoneham, and Wakefield
Needham Office serves Needham,
plus Canton, Dover, Hyde Park,
Medfield, Millis, Roslindale,
Sharon, West Roxbury, and
Westwood
Quincy Office serves Quincy, plus
Braintree, Hingham, Holbrook,
Hull, Milton, Norwell, Randolph,
Scituate, and Weymouth
Somerville Office serves Somerville,
plus Arlington, Cambridge and
Medford

Additional Offices
Braintree Office
400 Washington Street
Suite 201
Braintree 02184
(617) 849-3012 (By referral only)
Lexington Office
175 Bedford Street
Lexington 02173
(617) 862-2128
Malden Office
389 Main Street
Suites 201 and 202
Malden 02148
(617) 324-8181
Needham Office
475 Hillside Avenue
Needham Heights 02194
(617) 444-9303
Quincy Office
20 Whitney Road
Quincy 02169
(617) 471-0630
Somerville Office
131 Highland Avenue
Somerville 02143
(617) 625-5638

Concord
01742

Concord Family Service Society
Community Agencies Building
(508) 369-4909
William E. G. Batty III, Executive
Director
AREA SERVED: Concord, plus Acton,
Bedford, Boxboro, Carlisle,
Harvard, Lincoln, Littleton,
Maynard, Stow, and Sudbury

Additional Offices
Littleton Office
47 Foster Street
Littleton 01460
(508) 468-0451

Maynard Office
14 Nason Street
Suite 205
Maynard 01754
(508) 897-1800

Dedham
02026

Family Service of Dedham
18 Norfolk Street
(617) 326-0400
Mrs. Barbara P. Kovar, Executive
Director
AREA SERVED: Dedham, Foxboro,
Franklin, Norfolk, Norwood,
Plainville, Walpole, Westwood,
and Wrentham

Fall River
02720

Family Service Association
151 Rock Street
(508) 678-7542
Donald J. Emond, President and
Chief Executive Officer
AREA SERVED: Fall River, plus
Assonet, Somerset, Swansea, and
Westport; also, under some
circumstances, Little Compton
and Tiverton (Rhode Island)

Lawrence
01840

Family Service Association
of Greater Lawrence
430 North Canal Street
(508) 683-9505
Kay Frishman, Executive Director

AREA SERVED: Lawrence, plus
Andover, Methuen, and North
Andover; also southern New
Hampshire

Worcester
01609

Family Services of
Central Massachusetts
31 Harvard Street
(508) 756-4646
Douglas E. Oberreit, Executive
Director
AREA SERVED: Auburn, Barre,
Boylston, Clinton, Douglas, East
Douglas, Grafton, Holden,
Hubbardston, Leicester,
Millbury, New Braintree,
Northboro, Northbridge, North
Grafton, Oakham, Oxford,
Paxton, Princeton, Rutland,
Shrewsbury, Spencer, Sterling,
Sutton, The Brookfields, Upton,
Uxbridge, Westborough, West
Boylston

Worcester
01609

Jewish Family Service of Worcester
646 Salisbury Street
(508) 755-3101
Marvin Najberg, Executive Director
AREA SERVED: Worcester, plus
Auburn, Boylston, Grafton,
Holden, Leicester, Millbury,
North Grafton, Oxford, Paxton,
Shrewsbury, Sterling, West
Boylston, and other towns in the
United Way of Central
Massachusetts area. Families
outside this area but in
Worcester County may be
served, provided full cost of
service is paid.

MICHIGAN

Ann Arbor
48107

Child and Family Service of
  Washtenaw
2301 Platt Road
P.O. Box 7054
(313) 971-6520
William J. Vollano, Executive
  Director
AREA SERVED: Washtenaw County;
  western Wayne County

Additional Offices
Adult Day Care Center
  2309 Packard Road
  Ann Arbor 48104
  (313) 996-0407
Clear House
  704 Spring Street
  Ann Arbor 48103
  (313) 663-2500
Plymouth Adult Day Care Center
  574 South Sheldon Road
  Plymouth 48170
  (313) 451-1455
Plymouth Office
  880 Wing Street
  Plymouth 48170
  (313) 453-0890
Ypsilanti Office
  118 South Washington Avenue
  Ypsilanti 48197
  (313) 483-1418

Detroit
48202

Catholic Social Services
  of Wayne County
9851 Hamilton Avenue
(313) 883-2100
Thomas D. Quinn, President
AREA SERVED: Wayne County

Additional Offices
Eastside Office
  19653 Mack Avenue
  Grosse Pointe Woods 48236
  (313) 881-6645
Northwest Office
  17332 Farmington Road
  Livonia 48152
  (313) 421-3730
Western Wayne Office
  24331 Van Born Road
  Taylor 48180
  (313) 292-5690

Grand Rapids
49503

Family Service Association
  of Kent County
1122 Leonard Northeast
(616) 774-0633
Charles A. Burkholder, Executive
  Director
AREA SERVED: Areawide, primarily
  Kent County

Additional Office
District Office
  3181 Prairie Southwest
  Grandville 49418
  (616) 532-6213

Mount Clemens
48043

Macomb Family Services
57 Church Street
(313) 468-2656
Richard Dobbeck, Executive Director
AREA SERVED: Macomb County

Royal Oak
48067

Catholic Social Services
  of Oakland County
1424 East Eleven Mile Road
(313) 548-4044

Mrs. Margaret A. Huggard,
Executive Director
AREA SERVED: Oakland County

Additional Offices
Farmington Office
26105 Orchard Lake Road
Suite 303
Farmington Hills 48018
(313) 471-4140
Pontiac Office
53 Franklin Boulevard
Pontiac 48053
(313) 334-3595
Sheltering Arms
1658 East Lincoln
Birmingham 48009
(313) 646-1040
Waterford Office
5770 Highland
Pontiac 48054
(313) 674-2203

Southfield
48075

Jewish Family Service
24123 Greenfield Road
(313) 559-1500
Samuel Lerner, Executive Director
AREA SERVED: Detroit and Wayne
County, plus Macomb and
Oakland counties

MINNESOTA

Minneapolis
55404

Lutheran Social Service
of Minnesota
2414 Park Avenue South
(612) 871-0221
Mark Peterson, President
AREA SERVED: Hennepin, St. Louis,
Ramsey, Clay, Goodhue, and
Kandiyohi counties

Additional Offices
Metro East Office
1201 Payne Avenue South
St. Paul 55101
(612) 774-9507
Metro West Office
2414 Park Avenue South
Minneapolis 55404
(612) 871-0221
Northeast Office
600 Ordean Building
424 West Superior Street
Duluth 55802
(218) 726-4767
Northwest Office
American Square West
627 Center Avenue, Suite 3
Moorhead 56560
(218) 236-1494
Southeast Office
5225 West Highway 61
Red Wing 55066
(612) 388-1041
Southwest Office
414 West Becker Avenue
Willmar 56201
(612) 235-5459

St. Paul
55101

Family Service of
Greater Saint Paul
Nalpak Building, Suite 500
333 On-Sibley Street
(612) 222-0311
Ron Reed, President and Chief
Executive Officer
AREA SERVED: Ramsey County, plus
northern Dakota and western
Washington counties

Additional Offices
Family Service at Community Action
Council
14451 County Road 11
Burnsville 55337
(612) 431-7055

Family Service at Martin Luther
  King Center
270 North Kent Street
St. Paul 55102
(612) 224-4601
South Suburban Family Service
  Drovers First American Bank
    Building
  633 South Concord
  South St. Paul 55075
  (612) 451-1434

Stillwater
55082

Family Service of St. Croix Area
(Provisional Member Agency)
216 West Myrtle
(612) 439-4840
Sandra S. Shearer, Executive
  Director
AREA SERVED: Washington County;
  St. Croix County, Wisconsin

MISSOURI

St. Louis
63103

Family and Personal Support Centers
  of Greater St. Louis
2650 Olive Street
(314) 371-6500, 533-8200
Paul K. Reed, President
AREA SERVED: St. Louis City and St.
  Louis County, plus Jefferson and
  St. Charles counties. Illinois
  office serves Belleville and East
  St. Louis, plus Collinsville,
  Edwardsville, Fairview Heights–
  Caseyville Township, Granite
  City, Madison, Venice, and
  adjacent smaller towns and
  villages.

Additional Offices
Clayton Center
  107 South Meramec
  Clayton 63105
  (314) 727-3235
Crestwood Center
  9109 Watson Road
  St. Louis 63126
  (314) 968-2870
Employee Counseling Service
  4455 Duncan Avenue
  St. Louis 63108
  (314) 533-3800
Illinois Center
  3 Executive Woods
  Belleville 62221
  (618) 235-5656, 274-5166
Northwest Center
  9811 West Florissant
  St. Louis 63136
  (314) 521-6464
St. Charles Center
  1360 South Fifth Street
  St. Charles 63301
  (314) 946-6636
West County Center
  443 North New Ballas Road
  St. Louis 63141
  (314) 432-3305

St. Louis
63132

Jewish Family and Children's Service
9385 Olive Boulevard
(314) 993-1000
Harry Rubinstein, Executive Vice
  President
AREA SERVED: St. Louis City and
  County; and all areas served by
  St. Louis Jewish Federation and
  United Way of St. Louis

Additional Office
Annette S. Fox Youth Counseling
    Center
  106 Four Seasons Center
  Suite 101A
  Chesterfield 63017
  (314) 469-3555

NEBRASKA

Omaha
68102

Family Service
2240 Landon Court
(402) 345-9118
F. Peter Tulipana, Executive
    Director
AREA SERVED: Radius of 60 miles—
    Mills and Pottawattamie counties
    in Iowa; Cass, Douglas, and
    Sarpy counties in Nebraska

Additional Offices
Council Bluffs Office
  2 Northcrest Drive
  Council Bluffs, Iowa 51501
  (712) 322-1407
Hilltop-Pleasantview Multi-Service
    Center
  3012 Grant Street
  Omaha 68111
  (402) 451-3483
Little People Day Care Center
  807 Avenue G
  Council Bluffs, Iowa 51501
  (712) 322-3077
Logan-Fontenelle Multi-Service
    Center
  2211 Paul Street
  Omaha 68102
  (402) 341-9186
Mills County Office
  211 North Locust
  P.O. Box 389
  Glenwood, Iowa 51534
  (712) 527-3429

Multi-Service Center at Bellevue
  116 East Mission Avenue
  Bellevue 68005
  (402) 291-6065
Multi-Service Center at Papillion
  117 West Jefferson
  Suites 2 and 3
  Papillion 68046
  (402) 339-2544
Ruth K. Solomon Girls Center
  1601 North Twenty-second Street
  Omaha 68110
  (402) 346-0718
West Office
  2580 South Ninetieth Street
  Omaha 68124
  (402) 397-9098

NEW HAMPSHIRE

For service in southern New
    Hampshire, see Family Service
    Association of Greater Lawrence,
    Lawrence, Massachusetts

NEW JERSEY

Absecon Highlands
08201

Family Service Association
    of Atlantic County
312 East White Horse Pike
P.O. Box 404
(609) 652-2377, 652-4100
Jerome Johnson, President and Chief
    Executive Officer
AREA SERVED: Atlantic County

Additional Offices
Atlantic City Office
  Westside Complex
  Illinois and Marmora Avenues
  Atlantic City 08401
Hammonton Office
  310 Bellevue Avenue
  Hammonton 08037
  (609) 561-9191

School Based Services Office
  400 West Brighton Avenue
  Pleasantville 08232
  (609) 484-3675

Camden
08103

Family Counseling Service
217 South Sixth Street
(609) 964-1990
Dorothy B. Rowe, Executive Director
AREA SERVED: Camden County

Additional Offices
Camden Office
  560 Benson Street
  Camden 08103
  (609) 964-8099
Westmont Office
  212 Haddon Avenue
  Westmont 08108
  (609) 854-0055

Hackensack
07601

Family Services of
    Bergen County
10 Banta Place
(201) 342-9200
Natalie Webb, Executive Director
AREA SERVED: Bergen County and
    employees of business and
    industry participating in Tri-
    State United Way

Highland Park
08904

Family Service Association of
    Middlesex County
901 Raritan Avenue
(201) 572-0300
Joseph Trabucco, Executive Director
AREA SERVED: Highland Park, plus
    Carteret, Cranbury, East
    Brunswick, Edison Township,

Helmetta, Jamesburg, Metuchen,
    Milltown, Monroe Township,
    New Brunswick, North
    Brunswick, Old Bridge
    Township, Perth Amboy,
    Piscataway Township,
    Plainsboro, Sayreville, South
    Amboy, South Brunswick, South
    River, Spotswood, and
    Woodbridge Township

Additional Offices
New Brunswick Office
  75 Paterson Street
  New Brunswick 08901
  (201) 846-6465
Old Bridge Township Office
  18 Throckmorton Lane
  Old Bridge 08857
  (201) 679-2666
Woodbridge Office
  800 St. Georges Avenue
  Woodbridge 07095
  (201) 636-1699

Trenton
08628

Jewish Family Service of
    the Delaware Valley
51 Walter Street
(609) 882-9317, (609) 924-0054 or
    (215) 493-8224
Byron L. Pinsky, Executive Director
AREA SERVED: Mercer County, plus
    Hunterdon and adjacent areas of
    Burlington, Middlesex,
    Monmouth, and Somerset
    counties, New Jersey; also Bucks
    County, Pennsylvania

Additional Offices
Bristol Area Office
  115 Mill Street
  Bristol, Pennsylvania 19007
  (215) 788-9269

Caregivers Center for Families of the
  Aged
The Jewish Center
435 Nassau Street
Princeton 08540
(609) 924-0054 or (609) 921-0100,
  Ext. 3
Makefield-Newtown Office
  Penn Plaza, Suite 206
  3 Penns Trail and Yardley-Newton
  Road
  Newtown, Pennsylvania 18940
  (215) 968-6665
Resident Consultation Service at
  Galilee Village
  Levittown, Pennsylvania 19054
  (215) 547-0138
Windsors Office
  Triple S Plaza
  614 U.S. 130
  East Windsor 08520
  (609) 443-6260

Wayne
07470

Jewish Family Service
  of North Jersey
One Pike Drive
(201) 595-0111, FAX (201) 595-5477
Abraham D. Davis, Executive
  Director
AREA SERVED: Passaic County and
  the following communities in
  Bergen County: Allendale,
  Elmwood Park, Fair Lawn,
  Franklin Lakes, Midland Park,
  Oakland, Rochelle Park, Saddle
  Brook, Waldwick and Wyckoff

Additional Offices
Branch Office
  17-10 River Road
  Fairlawn 07410
  (201) 796-5151, FAX (201) 794-8399

NEW MEXICO

Albuquerque
87112

Jewish Family Service
(Provisional Member Agency)
12800 Lomas Northeast
Suite G
(505) 292-1521
Jane Hertz, Executive Director
AREA SERVED: Greater Albuquerque
  area

NEW YORK

Buffalo
14202

Child and Family Services
330 Delaware Avenue
(716) 842-2750
Eugene Meeks, President
AREA SERVED: Erie County and
  North Tonawanda

Additional Offices
Amherst Regional Office
  5449 Main Street
  Williamsville 14221
  (716) 632-5500
Children's Services Department
  310 Delaware Avenue
  Buffalo 14202
  (716) 856-3802
Conners Children's Center
  824 Delaware Avenue
  Buffalo 14209
  (716) 884-3802
East Regional Office
  45 Anderson Road
  Cheektowaga 14225
  (716) 896-7485
North Regional Office
  3407 Delaware Avenue
  Kenmore 14217
  (716) 876-8174

Reach-Out Kenfield Unit
41 Tower
Buffalo 14215
(716) 835-4571
Reach-Out Masten Unit
1490 Jefferson Avenue
Buffalo 14208
(716) 883-1973
Reach-Out Perry Unit
344 Perry Street
Buffalo 14204
(716) 852-7396
South Regional Office
585 Ridge Road
Lackawanna 14218
(716) 823-2531

Hempstead
11550

Family Service Association
of Nassau County
129 Jackson Street
(516) 485-4600
Salvatore Ambrosino, Ed.D.,
Executive Director
AREA SERVED: Nassau County

Additional Offices
Client Information and Referral
Service (CAIR)
Drug Treatment and Prevention
Service
Alcohol Counseling Service
126 North Franklin Street
Hempstead 11550
(516) 486-7200
Community Organization Services
336 Fulton Street
Hempstead 11550
(516) 538-1310
Link-Age Project
Glen Cove Satellite Office
% Glen Cove Senior Center
130 Glen Street
Glen Cove 11542
(516) 759-9523

Great Neck Satellite Office
% Great Neck Senior Center
80 Grace Avenue
Great Neck 11021
(516) 773-4002
Hempstead Satellite Office
% Jackson Memorial Church
60 Peninsula Boulevard
Hempstead 11550
(516) 485-6128
Herricks Office
% Herricks Community Center
Herricks Road
New Hyde Park 11040
(516) 741-7409
Levittown Satellite Office
% Yours, Ours & Mine
Community Center
Center Lane, Village Green
Levittown 11756
(516) 796-4020
New Hyde Park Satellite Office
Clinton Martin Park
New Hyde Park 11040
(516) 365-7433
Port Washington Satellite Office
% Port Washington Senior
Citizen Center
Flower Hill School, Campus
Drive
Port Washington 11050
(516) 944-6736
Roslyn Satellite Office
% Roslyn Senior Citizen Center
1489 Old Northern Boulevard
Roslyn 11576
(516) 621-7976
Mother-Child Home Program
336 Fulton Street
Hempstead 11550
(516) 485-4600
Mothers' Center
% United Methodist Church
265 Asbury Avenue
Westbury 11590
(516) 338-4477

Mothers' Center Development Project
336 Fulton Street
Hempstead 11550
(800) 645-3828
(in N.Y. State: (516) 486-6614)
Ombudservice Program
98 Cutter Mill Road
Great Neck 11021
(516) 466-9718
Parents and Children Together
336 Fulton Street
Hempstead 11550
(516) 485-1616
Project FRAIL
Clinton Martin Park
New Hyde Park 11040
(516) 365-7433
Young Fathers' Project
336 Fulton Street
Hempstead 11550
(516) 538-1310

New York
10019

Jewish Board of
    Family and Children's Services
120 West Fifty-seventh Street
(212) 582-9100
Jerome M. Goldsmith, Ed.D.,
    Executive Vice-President
AREA SERVED: Counseling, legal, and
    volunteer services for residents
    of Manhattan, Bronx, Brooklyn,
    and Staten Island, plus
    Westchester, Nassau, and Suffolk
    counties
    Court services available for
    metropolitan area

Additional Offices
MADELEINE BORG COMMUNITY
    OFFICES
Counseling Service to Jewish
    Battered Women and Abused
    Children

Sexual Assault Victims Counseling
    Program
26 Court Street
Brooklyn 11201
(718) 237-1337
Refugee Assistance Services
1113 Avenue J
Brooklyn 11230
(718) 692-1122
Services to the Homeless
235 Park Avenue South
New York 10003
(212) 460-0900

BRONX OFFICES
J. W. Beatman-Riverdale Office
4049 Henry Hudson Parkway
Riverdale 10471
(212) 549-6900
Co-op City Office
135 Einstein Loop
Bronx 10475
(212) 671-1876
The Learning Center
4049 Henry Hudson Parkway
Riverdale 10471
(212) 796-8700
Pelham Office
990 Pelham Parkway South
Bronx 10461
(212) 931-2600

BROOKLYN OFFICES
Boro Park Office
1276 47th Street
Brooklyn 11219
(718) 435-5700
Brighton Family Services
2915 Brighton Sixth Street
Brooklyn 11235
(718) 891-5970
Canarsie Office
1943 Rockaway Parkway
Brooklyn 11236
(718) 241-9600

Carey Gardens Early Childhood
    Programs
2964 West Twenty-third Street
Brooklyn 11224
(718) 372-4044
Coney Island Family Center
30001 West Thirty-seventh Street
Brooklyn 11224
(718) 266-3322
Coney Island Office
    2857 West Eighth Street
    Brooklyn 11224
    (718) 266-5300
Counseling Service for Senior
    Citizens and Their Families
    Kings Bay YM-YWHA
    3495 Nostrand Avenue
    Brooklyn 11229
    (718) 648-7703
Mid-Brooklyn Office
    1113 Avenue J
    Brooklyn 11230
    (718) 258-7700
Southern Brooklyn Family Services
    1592 Flatbush Avenue
    Brooklyn 11210
    (718) 258-1714
Starrett City Office
    1201 Pennsylvania Avenue
    Brooklyn 11239
    (718) 642-8955

LONG ISLAND OFFICE
Nassau Suffolk Liaison and Aftercare
    Program
175 Jericho Turnpike
Suite 216
Syosset 11791
(516) 921-5864

MANHATTAN OFFICES
Corporate Health Systems
    120 West Fifty-seventh Street
    New York 10019
    (212) 245-8178

Jewish Conciliation Board of America
235 Park Avenue South
New York 10003
(212) 777-9034
Manhattan East Office
    1651 Third Avenue
    New York 10028
    (212) 860-3500
Manhattan North Office
    84 Sherman Avenue
    New York 10040
    (212) 304-1900
Preventive Services Project
    201 West Ninety-third Street
    New York 10025
    (212) 222-5313

STATEN ISLAND OFFICES
Staten Island Office
    2795 Richmond Avenue
    Staten Island 10314
    (718) 761-9800

Niagara Falls
14301

Family and Children's
        Service of Niagara
826 Chilton Avenue
(716) 285-6984
Gerald J. Kozak, President
AREA SERVED: Niagara County

Additional Office
Lockport Branch Office
    39 East Avenue
    Lockport 14094
    (716) 433-6019

Rochester
14604

Catholic Family Center
50 Chestnut Street
(716) 546-7220
William H. Privett, Executive
        Director
AREA SERVED: Diocese of Rochester

Additional Offices
Area I
  Woodward Health Center
  480 Genesee Street
  Rochester 14619
  (716) 436-3040
Area II
  877 North Clinton Avenue
  Rochester 14605
  (716) 232-2050
Area III
  120 Ontario Street
  Rochester 14605
  (716) 454-7691
Chili Counseling Center
  3161 Union Street
  North Chili 14514
  (716) 594-9454
Counseling Service of the Southern
    Tier
  162 East First Street
  Corning 14830
  (607) 936-4695
Inter Faith Center
  11 Franklin Street
  Geneseo 14454
  (716) 243-0275
Liberty Manor
  Restart Substance Abuse Services
  55 Troup Street
  Rochester 14608
  (716) 546-3046
Restart Drug Office
  55 Troup Street
  Rochester 14608
  (716) 546-3046
Wayne County Office
  Newark Medical Center
  201 Church Street
  Newark 14513
  (315) 331-4867

Family Service of Rochester
30 North Clinton Avenue
(716) 232-1840, TTY 232-1237
James Reed, President

AREA SERVED: Livingston, Monroe,
    Ontario, Orleans, and Wayne
    counties

Additional Offices
Avon Office
  10 Park Place
  Box 206
  Avon 14414
  (716) 226-2360
Greece Office
  550 Latona Road
  Building C
  Rochester 14626
Henrietta Office
  2025 Lehigh Station Road
  Henrietta 14467
Irondequoit Office
  1151 Titus Avenue
  Rochester 14617
Perinton Office
  6780 Pittsford/Palmyra Road
  Fairport 14450
Webster Office
  2112 Empire Boulevard
  Webster 14680

Scarsdale
10583

Scarsdale Family Counseling Service
(Provisional Member Agency)
403 Harwood Building
(914) 723-3281
Geraldine Greene, Executive Director
AREA SERVED: Scarsdale-Edgemont

White Plains
10605

Family Service of Westchester
470 Mamaroneck Avenue
(914) 948-8004
Anne M. Eglinton, Executive
    Director
AREA SERVED: Westchester County

Additional Offices
Mount Kisco Office
  344 East Main Street
  Mount Kisco 10549
  (914) 666-8075
Mount Vernon Office
  10 Fiske Place
  Mount Vernon 10550
  (914) 668-9124
Port Chester Office
  225 Westchester Avenue
  Port Chester 10573
  (914) 937-2320
Tarrytown Office
  54 Main Street
  Tarrytown 10591
  (914) 631-2022
Services to the Elderly
  Mount Kisco Office
  344 East Main Street
  Mount Kisco 10549
  (914) 241-0770

OHIO

Akron
44313

Jewish Family Service
3085 West Market Street, No. 102
(216) 867-3388
Cathy Weiss, Executive Director
AREA SERVED: Akron, plus Canton,
  Cuyahoga Falls, Hudson, Kent,
  Medina, Ravenna, Silver Lake,
  Stow, and Wadsworth

Canton
44703

Family Counseling Services
  of Central Stark County
618 Second Street Northwest
(216) 454-7066
Eve S. Brown, Executive Director

AREA SERVED: Canton United Way
  area, which includes eastern
  three-quarters of Stark County,
  except cities of Alliance and
  Massillon

Cincinnati
45222

Jewish Family Service
1710 Section Road
P.O. Box 37904
(513) 351-3680
Morton R. Startz, Executive Director
AREA SERVED: Jewish residents of
  United Appeal five-county area:
  Butler and Hamilton counties,
  Ohio; and Boone, Campbell, and
  Kenton counties, Kentucky

Additional Office
Cincinnati Office
  7770 Cooper Road
  Cincinnati 45242
  (513) 891-6565

Cleveland
44118

Jewish Family Service Association
  of Cleveland, Ohio
2060 South Taylor Road
(216) 371-2600
Burton S. Rubin, Executive Director
AREA SERVED: Cuyahoga County

Additional Office
Chagrin Office
  28790 Chagrin Boulevard
  Cleveland 44122
  (216) 292-3999

Cuyahoga Falls
44221

Northeast Summit Family Service
2100 Front Street
(216) 928-1159

John Rush, Executive Director
AREA SERVED: Cuyahoga Falls,
Hudson, Munroe Falls, Silver
Lake, Stow, and neighboring
townships upon request

Hamilton
45011

Family Service of Butler County
111 Buckeye Street
(513) 868-3245
Rebecca Gresham, Executive
Director
AREA SERVED: Butler County

Additional Office
Branch Office
3603 Hamilton-Middletown Road
Hamilton 45011
(513) 868-6300, ext. 400

Massillon
44646

Family Counseling Services
of Western Stark County
51 North Avenue Northeast
(216) 832-5043
Edna M. Elliott, Executive Director
AREA SERVED: Massillon, plus
western Stark County

Toledo
43604

Family Service of Northwest Ohio
1 Stranahan Square
Suite 414
(419) 244-5511
Kathleen E. Buescher, President and
Chief Executive Officer
AREA SERVED: Eastern Fulton,
Lucas, Ottawa, and Wood
counties

Additional Offices
Family Service of Ottawa County
127 West Perry Street
Suite 104
Port Clinton 43452
(419) 732-3569
Family Service of Wood County
306 Huntington Bank Building
130 South Main Street
Bowling Green 43402
(419) 352-4624

OKLAHOMA

Oklahoma City
73103

Sunbeam Family Services
616 Northwest Twenty-first Street
(405) 528-7721
Philip A. Holmberg, Interim
Executive Director
AREA SERVED: Oklahoma County and
immediately adjacent areas

Additional Offices
Sunbeam East Center
2001 Martin Luther King Avenue
Oklahoma City 73111
Sunbeam South Center
2662 Southwest Forty-first
Oklahoma City 73119

Tulsa
74120

Family and Children's Service
650 South Peoria
(918) 587-9471
Gail Lapidus, Executive Director
AREA SERVED: Persons who live or
work in Tulsa County and
surrounding areas

Additional Offices
East Tulsa Family and Children's
   Services
   11740 East Twenty-first
   Suite E
   Tulsa 71129
   (918) 437-9495
Westside Family & Children's
   Services
   4965 South Union
   Tulsa 74107
   (918) 446-4549

OREGON

Portland
97210

Metropolitan Family Service
2281 Northwest Everett Street
(503) 228-7238
Ronald Yoder, President
AREA SERVED: Clackamas,
   Multnomah, and Washington
   counties

Additional Office
Senior Opportunities
   2200 Northeast Twenty-fourth
   Portland 97212
   (503) 249-8215
South Metro Office
   4040 Douglas Way
   Lake Oswego 97035
   (503) 635-9429
Washington County Office
   1049 Southwest Baseline
   Suite 450
   Hillsboro 97123
   (503) 648-0753

PENNSYLVANIA

Lancaster
17601

Family Service
630 Janet Avenue
(717) 397-5241

Peter J. Scheenstra, Executive
   Director
AREA SERVED: Lancaster County

Additional Offices
Columbia Office
   430 Locust Street
   Columbia 17512
   (717) 684-5525
Elizabethtown Office
   12 South Market Street
   Elizabethtown 17022
   (717) 367-3320
Ephrata Office
   Ephrata Hospital
   Ephrata 17522
   (717) 738-6185
New Holland Office
   676 East Main Street
   New Holland 17557
   (717) 354-4671
Quarryville Office
   138 East State Street
   Quarryville 17566
   (717) 786-4661
Welsh Mountain Office
   RD 1
   New Holland 17557
   (717) 354-4711

Langhorne
19047

Family Service Association
   of Bucks County
1 Oxford Valley
Suite 717
(215) 757-6916
Audrey Tucker, Executive Director
AREA SERVED: Bucks County;
   Langhorne Office serves lower
   county area; Doylestown Office
   serves central county area; and
   Quakerstown Office serves upper
   county area

Additional Offices
Bucks County Office Center
  Route 413
  Bristol 19007
  (215) 781-3999
Doylestown Office
  20 West Oakland Avenue
  Doylestown 18901
  (215) 345-0550
Quakerstown Office
  136 South Tenth Street
  P.O. Box 471
  Quakerstown 18951
  (215) 538-1616

Norristown
19401

Family Service of
  Montgomery County, Pa.
801 West Main Street
(215) 272-1520
Matthew J. Crowe, Executive
  Director
AREA SERVED: Norristown Office
  serves central Montgomery
  County; Eastern Montgomery
  Branch serves northeastern
  Montgomery County; Main Line
  Branch serves Upper and Lower
  Main Line areas; North Penn
  Branch serves greater Lansdale
  area; Pottstown Branch serves
  southwestern Montgomery
  County; Upper Perkiomen
  Branch serves northwestern
  Montgomery County.

Additional Offices
Eastern Montgomery Branch
  104 Terwood Road
  Willow Grove 19090
  (215) 657-7141
Main Line Branch
  18 Simpson Road
  Ardmore 19003
  (215) 642-5354

North Penn Branch
  713 West Main Street
  Lansdale 19446
  (215) 368-0985
Pottstown Branch
  933 North Charlotte Street
  Pottstown 19464
  (215) 326-1610
Upper Perkiomen Branch
  307 Main Street
  East Greenville 18041
  (215) 679-6635

Philadelphia
19106

Episcopal Community Services
225 South Third Street
(215) 351-1400
Gilbert S. Avery III, Executive
  Director
AREA SERVED: Philadelphia, plus
  Bucks, Chester, Delaware, and
  Montgomery counties

Philadelphia
19107

Family Service of Philadelphia
311 South Juniper Street
(215) 875-3300
Thomas F. Martin, Executive
  Director
AREA SERVED: Philadelphia

Additional Offices
North District Office
  5700 North Broad Street
  Philadelphia 19141
  (215) 549-8600
Northeast District Office
  4932 Penn Street
  Philadelphia 19124
  (215) 744-4700
Southern Division Office
  311 South Juniper Street
  Room 807
  Philadelphia 19107
  (215) 875-3300

West Office
   4534 Baltimore Avenue
   Philadelphia 19143
   (215) 875-3300

**Philadelphia
19103**

Jewish Family and Children's
   Service of Philadelphia
1610 Spruce Street
(215) 545-3290
Harold Goldman, J.D., Ph.D.,
   Executive Director
AREA SERVED: Philadelphia, plus
   Abington, Ambler, Ardmore,
   Bala-Cynwyd, Berwyn, Broomall,
   Bryn Mawr, Devon, Drexel Hill,
   Elkins Park, Flourtown,
   Gladwyne, Glenside, Havertown,
   Jenkintown, Manoa, Melrose
   Park, Merion, Narbeth,
   Overbrook Park, Paoli, Penn
   Valley, Penn Wynne, Plymouth
   Meeting, Radnor, Roslyn,
   Springfield, Upper Darby,
   Wyncote, and Wynnewood

Additional Offices
Allegheny Valley Mental Health and
   Mental Retardation Center
   Mellon Bank Building
   Fifth Avenue and Ninth Street, 4th
   Floor
   New Kensington 15068
   (412) 337-8855
Allegheny Valley Mental Health
   and Mental Retardation
   Center
   335 Fourth Avenue
   Tarentum 15084
   (412) 224-3201
Braddock Office
   500 Sixth Street
   Braddock 15104
   (412) 271-1588

Bustleton Avenue Office
   8253 Bustleton Avenue
   Philadelphia 19152
   (215) 342-6200
Hill Office
   2507 Bedford Avenue
   Pittsburgh 15219
   (412) 682-7302
Main Line Office
   9 East Athens Avenue
   Ardmore 19004
   (215) 896-8181
Northeast District Office
   8900 Roosevelt Boulevard
   Philadelphia 19115
   (215) 673-0100
Northwest District Office
   (Carol Gerstley Center for Family
   Living)
   Foxcroft Pavilion
   Jenkintown 19046
   (215) 884-0285
Southeastern Office
   Executive Building, Suite 312
   332 Fifth Avenue
   McKeesport 15132
   (412) 678-8674
Walk-In Service for Elderly
   6445 Castor Avenue
   Philadelphia 19149
   (215) 533-0102

**Pittsburgh
15213**

Jewish Family and Children's Service
234 McKee Place
(412) 683-4900
Ronald Kottler, Executive Director
AREA SERVED: Greater Pittsburgh
   area

Additional Offices
Anathan House
   1620 Murray Avenue
   Pittsburgh 15217
   (412) 521-1703

Career Development Center
2629 Murray Avenue
Pittsburgh 15217
(412) 422-5627

West Chester
19380

Family Service of Chester County
310 North Matlack Street
(215) 696-4900
Curtis L. Clapham, Executive
  Director
AREA SERVED: Chester County

Additional Offices
Coatesville Office
  423 East Lincoln Highway
  Coatesville 19320
  (215) 384-1926
Kennett Square Office
  209 East State Street
  Kennett Square 19348
  (215) 444-5652
Oxford Neighborhood Center
  35 North Third Street
  Oxford 19363
  (215) 932-8557

RHODE ISLAND

Newport
02840

Child and Family Services
    of Newport County
24 School Street
(401) 849-2300
Peter M. DiBari, Executive Director
AREA SERVED: Newport County

Additional Offices
Middletown Office
  45 Valley Road
  Middletown 02840
  (401) 849-2300

Newport Office
  135 Pelham Street
  Newport 02840
  (401) 847-6845
Portsmouth Office
  81 Bristol Ferry Road
  Portsmouth 02871
  (401) 683-1669

Providence
02906

Jewish Family Service
229 Waterman Street
(401) 331-1244
Paul L. Segal, Executive Director
AREA SERVED: State of Rhode Island

SOUTH CAROLINA

Charleston
29401

Family Service of Charleston County
Community Services Building
30 Lockwood Boulevard
(803) 723-4566
H. B. Free, Executive Director
AREA SERVED: Berkely, Charleston,
    and Dorchester counties

Columbia
29202

Family Service Center
1800 Main Street
P.O. Box 7876
(803) 733-5450
L. Russell Rawls, Jr., President and
    Chief Executive Officer
AREA SERVED: Fairfield, Lexington,
    Newberry, and Richland counties

TENNESSEE

Chattanooga
37403

Family and Children's Services
of Chattanooga
Administrative Office
300 East Eighth Street
(615) 755-2822
Tommy R. Perkins, Executive
Director
AREA SERVED: Hamilton County and
surrounding counties in
Tennessee, Georgia, and
Alabama

Additional Offices
Family Counseling Offices
323 High Street
Chattanooga 37403
(615) 755-2800
Geriatric and Special Services
1100 Gateway Avenue
Chattanooga 37402
(615) 755-2870
Youth Services
317 Oak Street
Chattanooga 37403
(615) 755-2725

Knoxville
37917

Child and Family Services
of Knox County
114 Dameron Avenue
(615) 524-7483
Charles E. Gentry, Executive
Director
AREA SERVED: Knox and other middle
east Tennessee counties

Additional Offices
Blount County Office
309 Court Street
Box 226
Maryville 37801
(615) 983-9390

Family Crisis Center and Runaway
Shelter
2535 Magnolia Avenue
Knoxville 37917
(615) 637-8000
Independent Living
2445 Magnolia Avenue
Knoxville 37917
(615) 637-3060
Project Against Sexual Abuse of
Appalachian Children (PASAAC)
and Knoxville Institute for
Sexual Abuse Treatment
Training
2602 Fifth Avenue
Knoxville 37914
(615) 524-2653
Protective Services Counseling
2455 Magnolia Avenue
Knoxville 37917
(615) 522-6213

TEXAS

Houston
77007

Family Service Center
4625 Lillian Street
(713) 861-4849
E. F. Christman, Jr., Executive
Director
AREA SERVED: Harris, Brazoria, Fort
Bend, and Montgomery counties
Bay Area Service Center serves
southern Harris County, plus
mainland part of Galveston
County

Additional Offices
Bay Area Social Services Center
18301-A Egret Bay Boulevard
Houston 77508
(713) 333-9700

Baystown Office
  Lone Star Bank Building
  1501 I-10 East, Suite 209
  Baytown 77521
  (713) 421-1665
Brazoria County District Office
  215 Flag Lake Drive
  Clute 77531
  (409) 297-3066
El Centro Familiar
  6001 Gulf Freeway, No. B-119
  Houston 77023
  (713) 921-8176
Fort Bend Service Center
  10435 Greenbough
  Building 2, Suite 200
  Stafford 77477
  (713) 499-5681
Montgomery County Social Services
    Center
  25211 Grogan's Mill Road, No. 260
  The Woodlands 77380
  (713) 367-8003
North Office
  330 Meadowfern Drive
  Suite 150
  Houston 77067
  (713) 872-3453
Northeast Office
  14950 Heathrow Forest Parkway,
    No. 270
  Houston 77032
  (713) 987-7791
Pasadena Office
  1149 Ellsworth Drive
  Suite 352
  Pasadena 77504
  (713) 472-2344

Houston
77225

Jewish Family Service
4131 South Braeswood Boulevard
P.O. Box 20548
(713) 667-9336

Solomon M. Brownstein, Executive
    Director
AREA SERVED: Harris, Fort Bend,
    and Montgomery counties

San Antonio
78216

Jewish Family Service
8438 Ahern Drive
(512) 349-5481
Richard Ney, Executive Director
AREA SERVED: City of San Antonio,
    Bexar County, and surrounding
    area

Additional Office
San Antonio Office
  14555 Blanco Road
  Suite 102
  San Antonio 78216
  (512) 493-5376

VIRGINIA

Norfolk
23517

Family Services of Tidewater
222 Nineteenth Street West
(804) 622-7017
Thomas J. Ledwith, Ph.D., Executive
    Director
AREA SERVED: Cities of Norfolk,
    Chesapeake, Franklin, Suffolk,
    and Virginia Beach

Additional Offices
Chesapeake Office
  1015 C Eden Way North
  Chesapeake 23320
  (804) 436-3131
Franklin Office
  300 North Main Street
  Franklin 23851
  (804) 562-3306

Lynnhaven Office
  120 South Lynnhaven Road
  Virginia Beach 23452
  (804) 498-1840
Suffolk Office
  National Bank Building, 7th Floor
  Suffolk 23434
United Way Family Center Office
  4441 South Boulevard
  Virginia Beach 23452
  (804) 671-1119

Richmond
23230

Family and Children's Service
1518 Willow Lawn Drive
(804) 282-4255
Richard J. Lung, President and Chief
  Executive Officer
AREA SERVED: Richmond, plus
  Chesterfield, Hanover, and
  Henrico counties

Additional Offices
Independent Living Program
  3900 West Broad Street
  Building No. 7
  Richmond 23230
  (804) 358-0865
Oasis House (For Runaways)
  2918 Chamberlayne Avenue
  Richmond 23222
  (804) 329-0079
Southside Office
  300 Turner Road
  Suite B
  Richmond 23235
  (804) 276-8166

WASHINGTON

Seattle
98104

Family Services
500 Lowman Building
107 Cherry Street
(206) 461-3883

Robert A. Watt, President
AREA SERVED: King County

Additional Offices
Child and Family Resource Center
  2410 East Cherry
  Seattle 98122
  (206) 684-4739
Eastside Office
  2122–112th Avenue Northeast
  Suite B
  Bellevue 98004
  (206) 451-2869
East Valley Office
  305 South Forty-third Street
  Renton 98055
  (206) 226-1253
Evergreen Stroke Association/ARISE
  Center
  9423 Southeast Thirty-sixth
  Mercer Island 98040
  (206) 461-7839
Greenlake Office
  7601 Aurora Avenue North
  Seattle 98103
  (206) 461-3870
High Point Office
  6536 Thirty-second Avenue
  Southwest
  Seattle 98126
  (206) 938-1314
Rainier Valley Office
  4422 Tamarack Drive South
  Building 483
  Seattle 98108
  (206) 461-3880
South King County Office
  1851 South Central Place
  Suite 212
  Kent 98031
  (206) 854-8705
Widowed Information and
  Consultation Services
  15417 First Avenue South
  Suite D
  Seattle 98148
  (206) 246-6142

WEST VIRGINIA

Wheeling
26003

Family Service—Upper Ohio Valley
51 Eleventh Street
(304) 233-2350, 232-6730
Manuel J. Viola, President and Chief
Executive Officer
AREA SERVED: Brooke, Hancock,
Marshall, Ohio, and Wetzel
counties, West Virginia; and
Belmont, Jefferson, and Monroe
counties, Ohio

Additional Offices
District Office—Senior Services
948 Main Street
Follansbee 26037
(304) 527-4635
District Office—Senior Services
805 Fifth Street
Moundsville 26041
(304) 845-8200

WISCONSIN

Beloit
53511

Family Service Association of Beloit
423 Bluff Street
(608) 365-1244
James E. Jones, Executive Director
AREA SERVED: Beloit and Clinton,
Wisconsin; plus Rockton, Roscoe,
and South Beloit, Illinois

Additional Office
Northern Winnebago County Office
222 West Main Street
Rockton, Illinois 61072

Green Bay
54301

Family Service Association
of Brown County

131 South Madison Street
(414) 437-7071
Thomas Martin, Executive Director
AREA SERVED: Northeastern
Wisconsin

Additional Office
Westside Office
1546 Dousman Street
Green Bay 54303
(414) 499-8768

Manitowoc
54220

Manitowoc Family Service
Association
(Provisional Member Agency)
820 Washington Street
(414) 682-8869
Cynthia Thomas-Dyer, Executive
Director
AREA SERVED: Manitowoc County and
surrounding areas

Milwaukee
53208

Family Service of Milwaukee
2819 West Highland Boulevard
P.O. Box 08434
(414) 342-4560
David L. Hoffman, President and
Chief Executive Officer
AREA SERVED: Greater Milwaukee
area

Additional Offices
Consumer Budget Counseling Service
1225 West Mitchell Street
Milwaukee 53204
(414) 643-4477
Marriage and Family Therapy Clinic
Bay Shore Shopping Center
5900 North Port Washington Road,
Room 114
Glendale 53217
(414) 342-4561

Marriage and Family Therapy Clinic
Edgewood Bank Building
4811 South 76th Street
Greenfield 53220
(414) 342-4561

Milwaukee
53202

Jewish Family Services
1360 North Prospect Avenue
(414) 273-6515
Ralph Sherman, Executive Director
AREA SERVED: Greater Milwaukee
County

Accredited Members
CANADA

ALBERTA

Calgary
T2G 2R7

Jewish Family Service
#200, 4014 Macleod Trail South
(403) 287-3510
Hope Kahane, Executive Director

AREA SERVED: Calgary and Southern
Alberta

BRITISH COLUMBIA

Vancouver
V6B 2A7

Catholic Family Service
(Provisional Member Agency)
150 Robson Street
(604) 683-0281
Thomas Farrell, Interim Executive
Director
AREA SERVED: The Roman Catholic
Archdiocese of Vancouver, the
boundaries of which are from the
International Boundary
northward through the coastal
area to Powell River; from the
coast eastward through Fraser
Valley to Hope and into the
Fraser Canyon; Mission to
Boston Bar and North Bend

Additional Office
Surrey Office
113-14914 104th Avenue
Surrey V3R 1M7
(604) 589-2728

4. NATIONAL AGING ORGANIZATIONS

American Association of Homes for the Aging (AAHA)
1129 Twentieth Street Northwest
Suite 400
Washington, D.C. 20036
(202) 296-5960
Association of not-for-profit housing, continuing-care communities, nursing homes, and community services for the aging. Provides information to consumers and professionals on not-for-profit homes and services.

American Association of Retired Persons (AARP)
1909 K Street Northwest
Washington, D.C. 20049
(202) 872-4700

Consumer organization composed of members age fifty and older, with local chapters around the country. Provides information to consumers on all aspects of aging, influences public policy, and offers travel, insurance, pharmaceutical, and other programs to members.

American Society on Aging (ASA)
833 Market Street
Suite 516
San Francisco, California 94103
(415) 543-2617

Membership organization of professionals in the field of aging and other interested individuals and organizations. Provides information, education, publications, and other resources on aging.

Asociación Nacional Por Personas Mayores (National Association for Hispanic Elderly)
2727 West Sixth Street
Suite 270
Los Angeles, California 90057
(213) 487-1922

Provides information and resources concerning the Hispanic elderly.

The Gerontological Society of America (GSA)
1275 K Street Northwest
Suite 350
Washington, D.C. 20005
(202) 842-1275

Interdisciplinary scientific membership organization of professionals and scholars in the field of aging. Provides information, education, publications, and other resources on aging.

Gray Panthers
311 South Juniper Street
Philadelphia, Pennsylvania 19107
(215) 545-6555

Grassroots advocacy organization of people of all ages, with local chapters around the country. Provides information and advocates for the right of all Americans to decent, affordable health care, housing, and services.

National Association of Area Agencies on Aging (NAAAA)
600 Maryland Avenue Southwest
Suite 208
Washington, D.C. 20024
(202) 484-7520

Association of local area agencies on aging which provide information and referral, and plan and coordinate services, for older people in communities across the country. Provides information and resources on aging services.

National Association of State Units on Aging (NASUA)
2033 K Street Northwest
Suite 304
Washington, D.C. 20006
(202) 785-0707

Association of state agencies on aging responsible for planning and coordinating services for the aging in their respective states. Provides information and resources on aging services.

National Center and Caucus on Black Aged (NCBA)
1424 K Street Northwest
Suite 500
Washington, D.C. 20005
(202) 637-8400

Provides information, resources, training, and housing for older black Americans.

National Citizens Coalition for Nursing Home Reform
1424 Sixteenth Street Northwest
Suite L2
Washington, D.C. 20036
(202) 797-0657

A coalition of over 300 groups and 500 individuals across the nation organized to improve care for nursing home residents. Publishes a newsletter and provides information on legislative and regulatory developments and issues of concern to nursing home residents and their families.

National Council of Senior Citizens
925 Fifteenth Street Northwest
Washington, D.C. 20005
(202) 347-8800

Membership organization of 4,800 senior citizens' clubs around the country. Advocates for decent, affordable health care, housing services, and programs for older people and for people of all ages.

National Council on the Aging
600 Maryland Avenue Southwest
West Wing 100
Washington, D.C. 20024
(202) 479-1200

Membership organization of professionals in the field of aging and other interested individuals and organizations. Provides information, technical assistance and consultation, education, advocacy, and resources on all aspects of aging.

National Indian Council on Aging
P.O. Box 2088
Albuquerque, New Mexico 87103
(505) 766-2276

Provides information and resources concerning older Native Americans.

National Pacific/Asian Resource Center on Aging
United Airlines Building, Suite 410
2033 Sixth Avenue
Seattle, Washington 98121
(206) 448-0313
Provides information, training, and resources concerning the Pacific/Asian elderly.

Older Women's League
730 Eleventh Street Northwest
Suite 300
Washington, D.C. 20001
(202) 783-6686
National membership organization with local chapters around the country focusing on women as they age. Provides information, education, resources, and advocates for policies which will improve the image, status, and quality of life of midlife and older women.

Disease/Condition-Specific Organizations

Alzheimer's Association (Alzheimer's Disease and Related Disorders Association)
70 Lake Street
Chicago, Illinois 60601
(800) 621-0379 or (800) 572-6037 (in Illinois)
Provides information and resources for people with Alzheimer's disease and other dementias and their families. Local chapters around the country sponsor support groups and other programs and services.

American Diabetes Association
Diabetes Information Service Center
1660 Duke Street
Alexandria, Virginia 22314
(800) ADA-DISC; (703) 549-1500 (in Virginia and Washington, D.C. metropolitan area)
Voluntary health organization concerned with diabetes and its complications, with affiliates and chapters around the country. Funds research and provides education and other resources to people with diabetes, their families, health care professionals, and the public.

American Heart Association
7320 Greenville Avenue
Dallas, Texas 75231
(214) 750-5300
Provides information on the prevention and treatment of heart disease.

American Speech-Language-Hearing Association
10801 Rockville Pike
Rockville, Maryland 20852
(301) 897-5700

Membership organization of speech, language, and hearing professionals. Publishes a journal and provides information on treatment of speech, language, and hearing problems.

Lighthouse National Center for Vision and Aging
111 East Fifty-ninth Street
New York, New York 10022
(800) 334-5497; (212) 355-2200; (212) 980-7832 (TDD for deaf and hearing-impaired individuals)

Provides information and resources on vision and again to consumers and professionals. Services include training, technical assistance and consultation, and dissemination of educational materials.

Society for the Right to Die
250 West Fifty-seventh Street
New York, New York 10107
(212) 246-6973

Provides information and education on ethical, legal, and policy issues related to the right to die with dignity. Provides sample living wills and other advanced directives upon request.

Organizations for Family Caregivers

Aging Network Services
4400 East-West Highway
Suite 907
Bethesda, Maryland 20814
(301) 657-4329

Provides consultation and referrals to long-distance caregivers of aging parents or relatives.

Family Caregivers of the Aging
National Council on the Aging
600 Maryland Avenue Southwest
Washington, D.C. 20024
(202) 479-1200

Membership group which provides information and resoures to family caregivers.

National Association of Private Geriatric Care Managers
Yorkville Station
Box 6920
New York, New York 10128

Association of professionals in private practice who provide care management to families of older people needing assistance.

CHECKLISTS FOR
EVALUATING SERVICES

1. NURSING HOMES

I. Where to start
    A. Get a list of nursing homes in your area from
        1. Hospital social service departments
        2. Local Department of Health and Department of Social Services
        3. State Department of Health and Department of Social Services
        4. County medical society
        5. Social Security district office
        6. State and local Office of the Aging
        7. Your physician, clergyman, relatives, friends
    B. Visit several before making a decision.

II. What to notice about the general atmosphere
    A. Are visitors welcome?
        1. Are you encouraged to tour freely?
        2. Do staff members answer questions willingly?
    B. Is the home clean and odor-free?
    C. Is the staff pleasant, friendly, cheerful, affectionate?
    D. Are lounges available for socializing?

III. Is attention paid to the patients' morale?
    A. Are they called patronizingly by their first names or addressed with dignity as "Mr.," "Mrs.," "Miss———"?
    B. Are they dressed in nightclothes or street clothes?
    C. Do many of them appear oversedated?
    D. Are they allowed to have some of their own possessions?

E. Are they given sufficient privacy?
    1. Are married couples kept together?
    2. Are "sweethearts" given a place to visit with each other in complete privacy?
F. Is good grooming encouraged?
    1. Beautician and barber available?
G. Is tipping necessary to obtain services?

IV. **What licensing to look for**
A. State Nursing Home License
B. Nursing Home Administrator License
C. Joint Committee on Accreditation of Hospital Certificate
D. American Association of Homes for the Aging
E. American Nursing Home Association

V. **Location**
A. Is it convenient for visiting?
B. Is the neighborhood safe for ambulatory residents?
C. Is there an outdoor garden with benches?

VI. **Safety considerations**
A. Does the home meet federal and state fire codes?
    1. Ask to see the latest inspection report.
    2. Are regular fire drills scheduled?
B. Is the home accident-proof?
    1. Good lighting?
    2. Handrails and grab bars in halls and bathrooms?
    3. No obstructions in corridors?
    4. No scatter rugs or easily tipped chairs?
    5. Stairway doors kept closed?

VII. **Living arrangements**
A. Are the bedrooms comfortable and spacious?
B. Is the furniture appropriate?
    1. Enough drawer and closet space?
    2. Doors and drawers easy to open?
    3. Can residents furnish their rooms with personal times?
C. Can closets and drawers be locked?
D. Is there enough space between beds, through doorways, and in corridors for wheelchairs?
E. Are there enough elevators for the number of patients?
    1. Are elevators large enough for wheelchairs?

VIII. **Food services**
A. Is there a qualified dietician in charge?
    1. Are special therapeutic diets followed?
    2. Are individual food preferences considered?
B. Are you welcome to inspect the kitchen?
C. Are menus posted?
    1. Do the menus reflect what is actually served?
D. Are dining rooms cheerful?

1. Are patients encouraged to eat in the dining room rather than at the bedside?
2. Is there room between the tables for the passage of wheelchairs?

E. Are bedridden patients fed when necessary?
1. Is food left uneaten on trays?

F. Are snacks available between meals and at bedtime?
1. Are snacks scheduled too close to meals in order to accommodate staff shifts?
2. Is there too long a period between supper and breakfast the next morning?

IX. Medical services

A. Is there a medical director qualified in geriatic medicine?
B. Are patients allowed to have private doctors?
C. If there are staff physicians, what are their qualifications?
1. Is a doctor available twenty-four hours a day?
2. How often is each patient seen by a doctor?
D. Does each patient get a complete physical examination before or upon admission?
E. Does the home have a hospital affiliation or a transfer agreement with a hospital?
F. Does each patient have an individual treatment plan?
G. Is a psychiatrist available?
H. Is provision made for dental, eye, and foot care as well as other specialized services?
I. Are there adequate medical records?

X. Nursing services

A. Is the nursing director fully qualified?
B. Is there a registered nurse on duty at all times?
C. Are licensed practical nurses graduates of approved schools?
D. Is there adequate nursing staff for the number of patients?
E. Is there an in-service training program for nurse's aides and orderlies?

XI. Rehabilitation services

A. Is there a registered physiotherapist on staff?
1. Good equipment?
2. How often are patients scheduled?
B. Is there a registered occupational therapist on staff?
1. Is functional therapy prescribed in addition to diversionary activities?
C. Is a speech therapist available for poststroke patients?
D. Is the staff trained in reality orientation, remotivation, and bladder training for the mentally impaired?

XII. Group activities

A. Is the activities director professionally trained?
B. Are a variety of programs offered?
1. Ask to see a calendar of activities.

    C. Are there trips to theaters, concerts, museums for those who can go out?

    D. Are wheelchair patients transported to group activities?

    E. Is there a library for patients?

    F. Is there an opportunity to take adult education courses or participate in discussion groups?

XIII. Social services

    A. Is a professional social worker involved in admission procedures?

        1. Are both the applicant and family interviewed?

        2. Are alternatives to institutionalization explored?

    B. Is a professional, trained social worker available to discuss personal problems and help with adjustment of patient and family?

    C. Are social and psychological needs of patients included in treatment plans?

    D. Is a professional, trained social worker available to the staff for consultation?

        1. On social and psychological problems of patients?

        2. On roommate choices and tablemates?

XIV. Religious observances

    A. Is there a chapel on the grounds?

    B. Are religious services held regularly for those who wish to attend?

    C. If the home is run under sectarian auspices, are clergy of other faiths permitted to see patients when requested?

XV. Citizen participation

    A. Is the Patient Bill of Rights prominently displayed and understood?

    B. Is there a resident council?

        1. How often does it meet?

        2. Does it have access to the administrator and department heads?

    C. Is there a family organization?

        1. How often does it meet?

        2. Does it have access to the administrator and department heads?

    D. Do the patients vote in local, state, and federal elections?

        1. Are they taken to the polls?

        2. Do they apply for absentee ballots?

XVI. Financial questions

    A. What are the basic costs?

        1. Are itemized bills available?

        2. Are there any extra charges?

    B. Is the home eligible for Medicare and Medicaid reimbursement?

        1. Is a staff member available to assist in making application for these funds?

        2. Is assistance available for questions about veterans' pensions? Union benefits?

    C. What provision is made for patients' spending money?

2. HOMEMAKER–HOME HEALTH AIDE SERVICES

Adapted from the "Basic National Standards for Homemaker–Home Health Aide Services" established by the National HomeCaring Council, 1981.

1. Does the agency from which you are seeking services have legal authorization to operate? Is it licensed or certified?
2. Is the agency accountable to a regulatory body (government agency, national council, or board of directors) that monitors the quality of the services?
3. Does the agency have written personnel policies, job descriptions, and a wage scale established for each job category?
4. Does the agency provide you with both the services of a homemaker–home health aide and a supervisor who makes periodic visits to check on the care given?
5. Is a professional person (registered nurse or trained social worker) responsible for a plan of care?
6. Does the agency provide in-service training for the homemaker–home health aide?
7. Is this training provided by qualified professionals?
8. Is the agency eligible for Medicare and Medicaid reimbursement?
9. Does the agency make regular reports to the community and to certifying bodies?

COMMON DISEASES AND
SYMPTOMS OF THE ELDERLY

1. DISEASES AND CONDITIONS

Some diseases, although they may also occur earlier in life, are much more likely to appear in the later years. Listed below are a number of common diseases that afflict the elderly and some ways in which they may be treated. *All patients should, of course, consult their physicians for diagnosis and treatment of their own individual conditions.*

Alzheimer's Disease

Alzheimer's disease is the best-known and most common of the dementias that afflict older people. It is a neurological disease affecting the cerebral cortex, the outer layer of the brain. At the outset there are only minor symptoms—forgetfulness is one of the most noticeable. As the disease progresses, memory loss increases. Some personality and behavior changes appear: confusion, irritability, restlessness. Judgement, concentration, orientation, and speech may be affected. In severe cases, patients may eventually become incapable of caring for themselves.

The causes of Alzheimer's disease are not known, nor is there yet a cure, but all patients should be under the care of a physician who can carefully monitor their progress and suggest supportive measures as well as routines that will help make life easier for both the patients and their families. Self-help groups for families of Alzheimer's disease patients, under the auspices of the Alzheimer's Disease and Related Disorders Association, can be found in many parts of the country.

Arteriosclerosis (Atherosclerosis)

Arteriosclerosis is a general term for hardening of the arteries. *Atherosclerosis*, one type of arteriosclerosis, causes the narrowing and closing of a blood vessel due to accumulation of fats, complex carbohydrates, blood and blood products, fibers, tissues, and calcium deposits in its inner wall. Other types of arteriosclerosis are uncommon and will not be discussed.

Arteriosclerosis is also related to hypertension (high blood pressure) and diabetes. The extent of arterial involvement in arteriosclerosis increases with age and can affect all the arteries of the body, especially those of the brain, heart, and lower extremities. When the blood supply to the brain is reduced by narrowing of the arteries supplying the brain, disturbances in behavior and cognition may result.

Arteriosclerosis in the aged is treated by attempting to lower the blood fats by diet when they are significantly elevated. Elevated blood pressure should be treated with a low-salt diet and, when necessary, the milder antihypertensive drugs. Cigarette smoking should be discontinued. A program of supervised physical activity is helpful, as is the control of obesity and diabetes. Surgical procedures to relieve or bypass obstructed blood vessels in the chest, neck, heart, and extremities may be of value after careful workup and evaluation of the benefits and risks involved.

Arthritis

Arthritis is a general term referring to any degeneration or inflammation of the joints. It is classified according to its acuteness or its chronicity and also according to the joints involved and specific laboratory and X-ray findings. Many older persons suffer from arthritis, some to a mild degree and others severely.

The most common form, called *osteoarthritis*, involves primarily the weight-bearing joints and is due to the wear-and-tear process that accompanies aging. Inflammatory involvement of the joints, *rheumatoid arthritis*, is less common in the aged. *Gout*, a metabolic disease of the joints accompanied by severe pain and signs of inflammation, may also be seen in the aged. Treatment of arthritis varies with the cause and includes physiotherapy, use of certain anti-inflammatory medications, and orthopedic devices. There are specific drugs for treating gout.

Bronchitis and Lung Diseases

Bronchitis is an inflammation of the cells that line the bronchial air tubes. It may be caused by infection, or by chronic irritation from cigarette smoke or following the inhalation of some harmful substance. Infectious bronchitis may be treated with antibiotics. In the case of chronic bronchitis, cessation of smoking is, of course, imperative. If untreated, chronic bronhitis may progress gradually to pulmonary emphysema.

Pulmonary emphysema, which results when the air sacs in the lungs are distended and damaged, is often found in heavy smokers. The patient suffers from shortness of breath and a cough. Treatment centers around relief of chronic bronchial obstruction by use of devices that help the emphysema patient to breathe. A variety of drugs and exercises are of value.

Cancer

Cancer (malignant neoplasm or tumor) is an uncontrolled growth of a tissue or portion of an organ that can spread (metastasize) to another part of the body. Cancer can occur in the throat, larynx, mouth, gastrointestinal tract, skin, bones, thyroid, bladder, kidney, and so forth. Because cancer symptoms in the aged may be atypical, or may be ignored by the aged patient afflicted with other symptoms and often with a poor memory, comprehensive annual examinations are vital for early detection and treatment.

Cancer may be treated with surgery, radiotherapy (X-ray), chemotherapy (medication), or by any combination of the three modalities. Because life expectancy is limited and the growth of many cancers is slow in the aged, there should be careful consideration of the value and potential side effects of potent methods of therapy before they are undertaken.

Congestive Heart Failure

Congestive heart failure occurs when the heart muscle has been so weakened that its pumping performance is impaired and it cannot provide sufficient circulation to body tissues. This condition may result from many years of untreated high blood pressure, heart attacks, or rheumatic heart disease. It may also be produced by diseases such as chronic lung diseases, anemia, infection, and alcoholism.

Treatment for congestive heart failure is directed at improving the heart's pumping efficiency and eliminating excess fluids. Digitalis derivatives are often used to strengthen the heart muscle, and diuretics and salt-restriction to remove excess fluid from the body. Treatment of a precipitating disease, such as hypertension, overactivity of the thyroid gland, or anemia, may also be necessary.

Coronary Artery Heart Disease

This disease, which is present in almost all individuals over the age of seventy in the United States, involves atherosclerosis of the arteries that supply blood to the heart muscle. In older persons coronary heart disease is superimposed on a heart where there may be a general decrease in muscle-cell size and efficiency.

A heart attack (*myocardial infarction*) happens when a portion of the blood supply to the heart muscle is cut off. In the elderly it is not unusual for there to be hardly any symptoms accompanying an infarction, in contrast to the crushing pain experienced by younger persons. Subtitution symptoms are also common in the elderly. For example, when the elderly heart fails because of a heart attack, blood may back up behind the left side of the heart into the blood vessels of the lungs, causing shortness of breath instead of chest pain. In other cases, the flow of blood from the weakened heart to the brain is diminished, with resultant dizziness or fainting rather than chest pain.

Modern treatment of the complications of acute myocardial infarction (which include irregular heartbeat and heart failure) with drugs, oxygen, and electrical equipment is saving many lives and enabling the period of bed rest to be shortened. Patients with uncomplicated cases now get up out of bed and into a chair much earlier than before, and cardiac rehabilitation is begun early with good results. Cardiac shock (intractable heart failure), however, remains a difficult problem with a high mortality rate.

Common in individuals with coronary heart disease is *angina pectoris*. This condition results from a temporary inadequacy in the blood supply to the heart muscle. Angina is characterized by severe but brief pain over the mid-chest region; the pain may radiate to either or both arms, the back, neck, or jaw. Angina is treated commonly and safely with nitroglycerin.

Depression

Depression, as a clinical problem, is the most common manifestation of mental illness in the elderly. Its symptoms can include feelings of hopelessness, anxiety, and self-deprecation, insomnia, anorexia, weight loss, apathy, and withdrawal. At its most severe, it can include suicidal thoughts. At its mildest, it can be confused with normal mourning following a serious loss. Its symptoms also resemble those of the early stages of dementia. For the elderly, there is a close relationship between poor physical health and depression. Depression can also be a reaction to inter- or intrapersonal conflicts. Psychotherapeutic intervention is often helpful. In the case of severe depression, the use of psychotropic drugs is advisable.

Diabetes Mellitus

Diabetes mellitus occurs commonly in elderly people, and the usual form is Type II. Although is is called non-insulin-dependent diabetes, insulin may be required in certain instances, such as surgery, infection, or trauma. While inheritance is an important factor in Type II diabetes, environmental factors, such as obesity and decreased physical activity, are also involved.

The elderly diabetic may present few or no clinical symptoms of the disease. In fact, complications arising from diabetes may be the first signs of this disease in the elderly. These complications include retinopathy (which can be mild to severe), cataracts, glaucoma, strokes, heart diseases, neuropathy (nerve damage, which can occur in different parts of the body), kidney disease, and impotence.

The prevalence of diabetic retinopathy increases with advancing age from 10 percent at age fifty-five to over 30 percent by the age of eighty. Therefore, regular visits to an ophthalmologist are essential. Foot care should be managed by a podiatrist, since nerve damage or poor circulation can lead to trauma, infection, and possibly amputation. Since exercise improves glucose control and can contribute to weight loss, a prudent exercise program should be discussed with the person's internist and ophthalmologist.

Drug Misuse

Drug misuse causes widespread problems among the elderly. It results from misdiagnoses by doctors, faulty prescriptions, and improper use by patients. Fifty-one percent of deaths from drug reactions involve those over sixty, who comprise only 17 percent of the population. A particular problem for the elderly, who often seek treatment for multiple conditions, is the adverse effect of combining drugs. Alcoholism and dependence on hypnotic drugs to induce sleep are the most frequent types of drug misuse.

Helpful steps include consultation with a physician who is knowledgeable about geriatric medicine and appropriate drug dosages for older people, and who can coordinate multiple drug use. Self-medication even with nonprescription drugs should be avoided.

Ear Diseases

The ear consists of the external, the middle, and the inner ear. Problems in each of these parts may affect hearing. Any condition that prevents sound from reaching the eardrum can cause a hearing loss. Common problems affecting the external ear include impacted ear wax and swelling of the tissues lining the canal caused by inflammation. Problems that frequently affect the middle ear include fluid accumulation and infection within the inner-ear cavity. Hearing losses caused by conditions of the external or middle ear are known as *conductive* losses, since they affect the pathway by which sound is conducted to the inner ear.

Conductive hearing losses are frequently treatable by a physician. Hearing problems involving the middle ear in the aged are similar to those occurring earlier in life. The most common cause is infection. Hearing loss in the middle ear that is not due to infection can often be corrected by surgery. Lesions of the inner ear, if not too extensive, can be helped by the proper use of hearing aids.

Another type of hearing loss results from damage to the inner ear. That is *sensorineural* hearing loss, often called *nerve deafness*. The inner ear houses the nerve structures that receive the sound waves and begin to transmit them to the brain. In most instances, sensorineural losses are irreversible and are not likely to be helped by hearing aids.

Eye Diseases

Cataracts, glaucoma, macular degeneration, and diabetic retinopathy are the four leading causes of vision loss in the elderly. *Cataracts* are cloudy or opaque areas in part or all of the lens of the eye through which light cannot pass. Often cataracts present no problems, but when they do, surgery is usually very successful. The implantation of intraocular lenses is an outpatient procedure at present, well tolerated by most older persons.

Glaucoma is a disease in which too much fluid accumulates inside the eyeball, causing increased pressure and at times internal damage. Best treated by medication in its early stages, glaucoma is an insidious, nondetectable disease. Therefore, regular checkups for glaucoma are important.

The retinal disorders, including *macular degeneration* and *diabetic retinopathy*, increase sharply with old age. The retina is the thin lining on the back of the eye made up of nerves that receive visual images and pass them on to the brain. Macular degeneration adversely affects the part of the retina that permits the perception of fine detail. Diabetic retinopathy, one of the possible consequences of diabetes mellitus, occurs when the small blood vessels that nourish the retina leak fluid or release blood, thereby damaging the retina. In the early stages of these retinal diseases laser treatment can be prevented through control of diabetes. There is no known cure for macular degeneration, which accounts for 70 percent of cases of low vision in the elderly. Rehabilitative low-vision care, therefore, is an important intervention to maximize residual vision.

Hypertension

Hypertension, otherwise known as high blood pressure, when present over long periods of time can lead to arterial disease and eventually to heart failure, stroke, or kidney failure. In the elderly, high blood pressure is unlikely to be of recent origin, and much of the damage to the arterial system has already been done.

Hypertension in the aged should be treated by moderate dietary salt restriction and, if necessary, by drugs. Only the milder drugs should be used in the aged, since the more powerful ones can cause sudden and severe lowering of blood pressure, which may lead to fainting spells or even strokes or heart attacks—the very complications such drugs are used to prevent.

Malnutrition

Malnutrition can mean either overnourishment or undernourishment. In cases of obesity, drastic caloric reduction is not recommended for older persons. Those with high blood pressure and diabetes mellitus can benefit from gradual weight reduction while maintaining a balanced diet.

Undernourishment is a not uncommon problem for the elderly and is often due to a decline in activity or to loneliness, depression, or disability. Severe cases of malnutrition can result in illness and acute mental disorders. The maintenance of a balanced diet is important for all older persons, who are particularly susceptible to nutritional deficiencies.

Neuritis

Neuritis is a disease of the peripheral and cranial nerves characterized by inflammation and degeneration of the nerve fibers. It can lead to loss of conduction of nerve impulses and consequently to varying degrees of paralysis, loss of feeling, and loss of reflexes. Although the term *neuritis* implies inflammation, this is not invariably present. Neuritis may affect a single nerve or involve several nerve trunks.

Diagnostic workup by a neurologist is indicated. Treatment of specific causes, such as diabetes, pernicious anemia, or alcoholism, may be helpful.

Osteoporosis

Osteoporosis is an age-related condition which predisposes bones to fracture with little or no trauma. Four times more prevalent in women than in men, it is characterized by a marked reduction in bone mass. A total of 24 million Americans suffer from all forms of osteoporosis, including the kinds that lead to crippling hip and wrist fractures.

The causes of osteoporosis are unknown, but the condition is associated with a deficiency of dietary calcium and with metabolic imbalance. Interventions found to reduce bone loss in some cases include maintenance of calcium balance, estrogen therapy, and exercise. Treatment to partially restore bone loss in the case of spinal osteoporosis, the disease that can cause a curved spine and stooped posture, has been recently discovered and may be approved by the Food and Drug Administration for general use by 1990.

Stroke

Stroke is a cerebrovascular disorder due to thrombosis, hemorrhage, or an embolism. Eighty percent of those who suffer a stroke survive, but most have residual impairment. The most common impairment is paralysis affecting one side of the body. Speech, perception, and vision can also be affected, and aphasia is often present. The patient's ability to think, however, may not be impaired. Early and ongoing rehabilitation is important to prevent secondary complications and to restore functional abilities.

2 . SYMPTOMS AND COMPLAINTS

The following are some of the more common symptoms and complaints of the elderly. Wrongly regarded by many older patients as being the natural consequences of aging and therefore not worth mentioning to a busy doctor, these symptoms—and indeed, all others—should be reported to a physician by the older person or his family.

Breathlessness

Breathlessness, known as *dyspnea*, is common in the aged and may reflect heart failure, disease of the lungs, or anemia. It is exaggerated by obesity.

Confusion and Memory Loss

Confusion and memory loss as well as disorientation and poor judgment represent changes in intellectual functioning that can stem from a variety of conditions. Abrupt changes in any older person from his or her customary state of functioning should be investigated for a possible physical disorder. These "acute brain syndromes" may result from almost any physical ailment or drug problem. The symptoms are often transient and reversible if the underlying condition is diagnosed and treated. However, these symptoms are also the hallmarks of dementia, which can be diagnosed only through ruling out other underlying disorders and observing gradual deterioration of intellectual functioning over time.

Constipation

Perhaps no part of the body is as misunderstood as the lower digestive tract, which is involved in absorption of nutrients and elimination of solid waste matter. Many people still believe that a daily bowel movement is needed for good health. This belief is false. Not everyone functions on a once-a-day schedule—or needs to. It is common to find people in perfect health who defecate regularly twice a day and others who have a bowel movement only once every two or three days without the slightest ill effects. There are some people who have regular bowel movements at still longer intervals without any health problems.

Constipation cannot be defined in terms of a daily bowel movement, but must be related to each person's overall pattern of defecation. Missing one or two bowel movements should not cause alarm. After a few days, bowel function usually returns to normal and the routine is re-established.

Difficulty in Swallowing

Dysphagia, or difficulty in swallowing, is a common complaint of elderly persons which cannot be ignored. Its onset in old age calls for examination to rule out cancer of the esophagus. Dysphagia may indicate the need for a change in diet to soft, minced, or liquid foods. Bedridden or wheelchair-bound aged persons with marked dysphagia should be fed only by properly trained personnel, to avoid possible aspiration of food into the lungs, which may cause a secondary severe pneumonia or even death by suffocation.

Fainting

Fainting, or *syncope*, may result from a variety of circulatory, neurological, or surgical causes in the aged, as well as from anemia. A careful neurological workup is indicated. Transitory disturbances of the circulation to the brain may be overlooked unless special testing is done. Major injury may result from falls accompanying fainting spells in the aged.

Falls

Accidents are an increasingly important cause of death and disability in the elderly, with one-half of accident fatalities occurring in the home. The most frequent accidents are falls due to poor vision or visibility, vertigo, sedation, mental confusion, or the adverse use of drugs. In addition to medical and rehabilitation care, helpful interventions include sufficient lighting (particularly on stairs), installation of handrails, and proper carpeting.

Fatigue

Fatigue is sometimes a symptom of boredom. If it is coupled with marked inactivity and negativism, it may strongly suggest depression. However, fatigue may also be a symptom of organic disease. It is a particularly prominent symptom of heart disease, anemia, and malnutrition. Persistent fatigue should therefore be checked into by a physician.

Giddiness or Dizziness

Dizziness, or *vertigo*, may occur even in old people who are well, but there are innumerable possible causes, and this condition should always be looked into. Even when it is not a symptom of illness, vertigo is a common cause of falls, with consequent injuries such as the too-frequent, disabling fracture of the hip.

Headaches

Headaches seem to be less common in later life, and it follows that when severe headaches do occur in an older person, they are not to be ignored. They may be due to muscle strain resulting from poor posture, or to infection of the sinuses. Some severe headaches may be caused by lesions within the skull or by inflammation of the walls of blood vessels in the head.

Hearing Loss

Impaired hearing is not inevitable in old age, although some degree of hearing loss is common, especially for high-pitched sounds. Every effort should be made to determine the cause of hearing loss in the aged. Careful examination by an ear specialist should be followed, if necessary, by audiometry and the painstaking process of being fitted for a hearing aid. Loss of hearing may lead to physical danger—for instance, from an unnoticed approaching car. Hearing loss may also lead to isolation and even to paranoid behavior, as those who are not able to understand others will feel cut off from them and may even mistake what they are saying as being of a hostile nature.

Inability to Sleep

The inability to sleep, or *insomnia*, may be a consequence of various discomforts, or else it may be evidence of a psychiatric upset. Persons suffering from anxiety often experience some difficulty in falling asleep, and those who are depressed tend to wake early and toss and turn. Both anxiety and depression are common in the elderly. Some older people are convinced that they must, above all things, have a great deal of extra repose. Others, because of loneliness or boredom, tend to go to bed early at night after having slept during the afternoon as well, and cannot understand why they wake early and cannot get back to sleep. They do not appreciate the lessened need for sleep that accompanies aging.

Lack of Appetite

Although there are wide variations in older persons' eating habits, just as in those of the young, a sudden change in appetite should be considered a symptom to be reported. Lack of appetite, or *anorexia* is a symptom of physical or mental difficulty. A thorough medical workup is needed, followed by a psychiatric evaluation.

Seizures

Seizures, or convulsions, may involve the entire body, or only a part. Whatever the extent, there are involuntary twitchings of the muscles and usually unconsciousness. Seizures may have their onset in old age. Since they may be a symptom of some underlying disease or abnormal condition, they call for a careful examination by a neurologist. Seizures are often unsuccessfully treated with appropriate medication.

Vision Loss

Normal age-related vision changes include a decline in visual acuity; a decline in the ability to adapt to the dark and to function in low level of light; increased difficulty in judging distances and focusing on objects at various distances; and a decline in color discrimination. These changes do not typically result in major functional limitations if appropriate correction is made through regular prescription lenses. However, increasing numbers of older people are experiencing visual impairments that result from age-associated eye diseases. Medical, surgical, and rehabilitative low-vision interventions can be very effective in preventing and correcting these diseases or sustaining and improving visual functioning.

SUGGESTED READINGS

COMPREHENSIVE REFERENCE WORKS

Binstock, Robert H., and Shanas, Ethel, eds. *Handbook of Aging and the Social Sciences.* 2nd ed. New York: Van Nostrand Reinhold, 1985.

Birren, James E., and Schaie, K. Warner, eds. *Handbook of the Psychology of Aging.* 2nd ed. New York: Van Nostrand Reinhold, 1985.

Birren, James E., and Sloane, R. Bruce, eds. *Handbook of Mental Health and Aging.* Englewood Cliffs, N.J.: Prentice-Hall, 1980.

Butler, Robert N. *Why Survive? Being Old in America.* New York: Harper & Row, 1975; Harper Torchbooks, 1985.

Finch, Caleb E., and Schneider, Edward L., eds. *Handbook of the Biology of Aging.* 2nd ed. New York: Van Nostrand Reinhold, 1985.

Lesnoff-Caravagila, Gari, ed. *Handbook of Applied Gerontology.* New York: Human Sciences Press, 1987.

Maddox, George L., et al., eds. *Encyclopedia of Aging,* New York: Springer, 1987.

Palmore, Erdman B., ed. *Handbook on the Aged in the United States.* Westport, Conn.: Greenwood Press, 1984.

Palmore, Erdman B., et al., eds. *Normal Aging III: Reports from the Duke Longitudinal Studies, 1975–1984.* Durham, N.C.: Duke University Press, 1985.

Riley, Matilda White, et al., eds. *Aging from Birth to Death: Vol. 1, Interdisciplinary Perspectives; Vol. 2, Sociotemporal Perspectives.* Boulder, Colo.: Westview Press, 1979, 1982.

Rossman, Isadore, ed. *Clinical Geriatrics.* 3rd ed. Philadelphia: J. B. Lippincott, 1986.

Schick, Frank L., ed. *Statistical Handbook on Aging Americans.* Phoenix, Ariz.: Oryx Press, 1986.

Woodruff, Diana S., and Birren, James E., eds. *Aging: Scientific Perspectives and Social Issues*. 2nd ed. Monterey, Calif.: Brooks/Cole, 1983.

ADDITIONAL REFERENCES AND OTHER READINGS

Gelfand, Donald E. *Aging Network: Programs and Services*. New York: Springer, 1988.

Harris, Louis, and Associates, *Aging in the Eighties: America in Transition*. Washington, D.C.: National Council on the Aging, 1981.

Hendricks, Jon, and Hendricks, C. David. *Aging in Mass Society: Myths and Realities*. Boston: Little, Brown, 1986.

Hess, Beth B., and Markson, Elizabeth W., eds. *Growing Old in America: New Perspectives on Old Age*. 3rd ed. New Brunswick, N.J.: Transaction Books, 1985.

Neugarten, Bernice L. *Age or Need? Public Policies for Older People*. Beverly Hills, Calif.: Sage Publications, 1982.

On Lok Senior Health Services. *Directory of Adult Day Care in America*. Washington, D.C.: National Council on the Aging, 1987.

Rapin, David L., and Stockton, Patricia. *Long-Term Care for the Elderly: A Factbook*. New York: Oxford University Press, 1987.

Troll, Lillian E., ed. *Family Issues in Current Gerontology*. New York: Springer, 1986.

U.S. Department of Commerce, Bureau of the Census. *Demographic and Socioeconomic Aspects of Aging in the United States*. Population Reports, Special Studies, ser. P-23, no. 138 (August 1984).

U.S. Senate Special Committee on Aging. *America in Transition: An Aging Society*. 1984–85 ed. Washington, D.C.: Government Printing Office, 1985.

U.S. Senate Special Committee on Aging. *Crisis in Home Health Care: Greater Need, Less Care: A Staff Report*. Washington, D.C.: The Committee.

White House Conference on Aging, 1981. *Final Report, The 1981 White House Conference on Aging*, vols. 1, 2, and 3.

REFERENCES TO SELECTED PROBLEMS

The Aging Process

Henig, Robin Marantz, and Editors of Esquire. *How a Woman Ages*. New York: Ballantine Books, 1985.

Pesmen, Curtis, and Editors of Esquire. *How a Man Ages*. New York: Ballantine Books, 1984.

Alzheimer's Disease and Dementia

Aronson, Miriam K., ed. *Understanding Alzheimer's Disease*. New York: Charles Scribner's Sons, 1988.

French, Carolyn J., King, Nancy Long, and Levine, Eve B. *Understanding and Caring for the Person with Alzheimer's Disease: A Practical Guide*. Atlanta, Ga.: Alzheimer's Disease Association, 1985.

Mace, Nancy L., and Rabins, Peter V. *The 36-Hour Day: A Family Guide to Caring for Persons with Alzheimer's Disease, Related Dementing Illnesses, and Memory Loss in Later Life*. Baltimore, Md.: Johns Hopkins University Press, 1981.

Caregiving and Home Health Care

Crichton, Jean. *Age Care Sourcebook: A Resource Guide for the Aging and Their Families*. New York: Simon & Schuster, 1987.

Golden, Susan. *Nursing a Loved One at Home: A Caregiver's Guide*. Philadelphia: Running Press, 1988.

Halpern, James. *Helping Your Aging Parents: A Practical Guide for Adult Children*. New York: McGraw-Hill, 1987.

Hogstel, Mildred O., ed. *Home Nursing Care for the Elderly*. Bowie, Md.: Brady Communications, 1985.

McLean, Helene. *Caring for Your Parents: A Sourcebook of Options and Solutions for Both Generations*. Garden City, N.Y.: Doubleday, 1987.

Nassif, Janet Zhun. *Home Health Care Solution: A Complete Consumer Guide*. New York: Harper & Row, 1985.

Shelley, Florence D. *When Your Parents Grow Old*. 2nd ed. New York: Harper & Row, 1988.

Crime and Law

American Bar Association, Commission on Legal Problems of the Elderly. *Law and Aging Resource Guide*. Washington, D.C: The Association, 1987.

Gerry, Prue, and Payne, Barbara P. "Victims of Crime." In Erdman B. Palmore, ed. *Handbook on the Aged in the United States*, pp. 391–410. Westport, Conn.: Greenwood Press, 1984.

Persico, Joseph E., and Sunderland, George. *Keeping Out of Crime's Way: The Practical Guide for People Over 50*. Glenview, Ill.: Scott, Foresman, 1985.

Death, Bereavement, and Widowhood

Boyle, Joan M., and Morriss, James E. *Mirror of Time: Images of Aging and Dying*. Westport, Conn.: Greenwood Press, 1987.

Kalish, Richard A. "Young, Middle, and Late Adulthood." In *Death, Grief, and Caring Relationships*. 2nd ed. Monterey: Calif.: Brooks/Cole, 1985.

Silverman, Phyllis R. *Widow-to-Widow*. New York: Springer, 1986.

Thornton, James E., and Winkler, Earl R., eds. *Ethics and Aging: The Right to Live, the Right to Die*. Vancouver: University of British Columbia Press, 1988.

Weizman, Savine G., and Kamm, Phyllis. *About Mourning: Support and Guidance for the Bereaved.* New York: Human Sciences Press, 1984.

Family Relationships
Brody, Elaine M. "The Etiquette of Filial Behavior." *Aging and Human Development* 1 (1970): 87–94.

Cherlin, Andrew J., and Furstenberg, Frank F., Jr. *New American Grandparent: A Place in the Family, a Life Apart.* New York: Basic Books, 1986.

Cohen, Stephen Z., and Gans, Bruce Michael. *Other Generation Gap: The Middle-Aged and Their Aging Parents.* New York: Dodd, Mead, 1988.

Edinberg, Mark A. *Talking with Your Aging Parents.* Boston: Shambhala Publications, 1987.

Kirschner, Charlotte. "The Aging Family in Crisis—a Problem in Family Living." *Social Casework* 60 (April 1979): 209–16.

Minority Aging
Gelfand, Donald E., and Barresi, Charles M., eds. *Ethnic Dimensions of Aging.* New York: Springer, 1987.

Manuel, Ron C., ed. *Minority Aging: Sociological and Social Psychological Issues.* Westport, Conn.: Greenwood Press, 1982.

Services and Resources
Carlin, Vivian F., and Mansberg Ruth. *Where Can Mom Live? A Family Guide to Living Arrangements for Elderly Parents.* Lexington, Mass.: Lexington Books, 1987.

Gold, Margaret. *Guide to Housing Alternatives for Older Citizens.* Mount Vernon, N.Y.: Consumers' Union, 1985.

Matthews, Joseph L., and Berman, Dorothy Matthews, *Sourcebook for Older Americans*, 2nd ed. Berkeley, Calif.: Nolo Press, 1984.

Rubin, Leona G. *Your 1987/88 Guide to Social Security Benefits.* Rev. ed. New York: Facts on File Publications, 1987.

Wilson, Albert J. E., III. *Social Services for the Elderly.* Boston: Little, Brown, 1984.

Sexuality
Brecher, Edward M., and Editors of Consumer Reports Books. *Love, Sex, and Aging: A Consumers Union Report.* Boston: Little, Brown, 1984.

Butler, Robert N., and Lewis, Myrna. *Midlife Love Life.* New York: Harper & Row, 1988.

Butler, Robert N., and Lewis, Myrna. *Sex After Sixty.* New York: Harper & Row, 1976.

Weg, Ruth B., ed. *Sexuality in the Later Years: Roles and Behavior.* New York: Academic Press, 1983.

HELPFUL ARTICLES, BOOKS, AND PAMPHLETS

American Association of Homes for the Aging.
  Choosing a Nursing Home: A Guide to Quality Care
  Community Services for Older People Living at Home
  Continuing Care Retirement Community: A Guidebook for Consumers
    Available from the American Association of Homes for the Aging, 1050 Seventeenth Street Northwest, Suite 770, Washington, D.C. 20036.

American Association of Retired Persons.
  Checklist of Concerns/Resources for Caregivers. Order number D12957.
  Coping and Caring: Living with Alzheimer's Disease. Order number D12441.
  Growing Old Together: An Intergenerational Sourcebook. Order number D12342.
  Handbook About Care in the Home. Order number D955.
  Miles Away and Still Caring—A Guide for Long Distance Caregivers. Order number D12748.
  On Being Alone: AARP Guide for Widowed Persons. Order number D150.
  Portrait of Older Minorities. Order number D12404.
  Profile of Older Americans. Order number D996.
    Available free from AARP Publications, Program Resources, Department/BV, 1909 K Street Northwest, Washington, D.C. 20049.
American Health Care Association.
  Guide to Nursing Home Living. Order number 00024.
  Thinking About a Nursing Home? A Consumer's Guide to Long Term Care.
    Available from American Health Care Association, P.O. Box 35050, Washington, D.C. 20013.

Bern, Mercedes. *Guide to Choosing Medicare Supplemental Insurance*.
    Available from United Seniors Health Cooperative, 1334 G Street Northwest, Suite 500, Washington, D.C. 20005.

Consumer Information Center.
  Diet and the Elderly. Order number 516T.
  Guide to Health Insurance for People with Medicare. Order number 529T.
  Health Care and Finances: A Guide for Adult Children and Their Parents. Order number 459T.
  Safety for Older Consumers. Order number 425T.
  Turning Home Equity into Income for Older Americans. Order number 137T.
  Your Social Security. Order number 514T.
    Available from Consumer Information Center, P.O. Box 100, Pueblo, Colo. 81002.

Consumers Union. "Who Can Afford a Nursing Home?" *Consumer Reports* 53, no. 5 (May 1988): 300–11.

Goode, Nancy. "New Stand-In Service: How to Keep Close to Out-of-State Parents." *Mature Outlook* 2, no. 5 (September–October 1985): 66.

Johnson, Michael. *I'd Rather Be Home: A Practical Guide for Individuals, Families, and Professionals.*
   Available from Consulting Opinion, 375 Northeast 163rd Street, Seattle, Washington 98155.

Loewinsohn, Ruth Jean. *Survival Handbook for Widows (and for Relatives and Friends).* Glenview, Ill.: AARP Books, Scott, Foresman, 1984.

National Council on the Aging.
   Caregiver Tips. Set of eight booklets. Order number 2032.
   Facts and Myths About Aging. Order number 121.
   Family Home Caring Guides. Set of eight guides. Order number 2023.
   Ideabook on Caregiver Support Groups. Includes directory of 300 caregiver groups in the United States. Order number 2010.
   Memory Retention Course for the Aged. Order number 4160.
   Available from the National Council on the Aging, Family Caregiver Program, Department 5087, 600 Maryland Avenue Southwest, Washington, D.C. 20024.

Public Affairs Committee.
   Home Health Care: When a Patient Leaves the Hospital. Order number 560.
   Protecting Yourself Against Crime. Order number 564.
   Right to Die with Dignity. Order number 587A.
   Available from Public Affairs Committee, Inc., 381 Park Avenue South, New York, N.Y. 10016.

Richards, Marty, et. al. *Choosing a Nursing Home: A Guidebook for Families.* Seattle: University of Washington Press, 1985.
   Available from University of Washington Press, P.O. Box C50096, Seattle, Wash. 98145.

U.S. Department of Health and Human Services, Health Care Financing Administration.
   Your Medicare Handbook, 1989. Order number HCFA 10050.
   Medicaid: HCFA Fact Sheet.
   Available from U.S. Department of Health and Human Services, Health Care Financing Administration, 6325 Security Boulevard, Baltimore, Md. 21207.

U.S. Department of Health and Human Services, National Institute on Aging.
   Age Pages. Collection of fact sheets on disorders and diseases, sexuality, hearing, incontinence, foot care, accidents, nutrition, crime prevention, etc.
   Self-Care and Self-Help Groups for the Elderly: A Directory.
   Available from NIA Information Center/PL, 2209 Distribution Circle, Silver Spring, Md. 20910.

U.S. Department of Health and Human Services, National Institute on Drug Abuse. *Using Your Medicines Wisely: A Guide for the Elderly*.
>   Available from Elder-ED, P.O. Box 416, Kensington, Md. 20740.

U.S. Department of Health and Human Services, National Institute of Mental Health. *Maintenance of Family Ties of Long-Term Care Patients*. Order number ADM 81-400.
>   Available from National Clearinghouse for Mental Health Administration, Public Inquiries Section, Room 11A-21, 5600 Fishers Lane, Rockville, Md. 20857.

U.S. Department of Health and Human Services, Social Security Administration. *Social Security Handbook*. 9th ed. Washington, D.C.: Government Printing Office, 1986.

U.S. Congress, House Select Committee on Aging. *Where to Turn for Help for Older Persons: A Brochure*.
>   Available from U.S. Government Printing Office, Superintendent of Documents, Washington, D.C. 20402, or from Administration on Aging, 330 Independence Avenue Southwest, Washington, D.C. 20201.

U.S. Congress, House Select Committee on Aging, Subcommittee on Human Services. *Exploding the Myths: Caregiving in America*.
>   Available from U.S. Government Printing Office, Superintendent of Documents, Washington, D.C. 20402, Order number 99-611.

Weizman, Savine G., and Kamm, Phyllis. *About Mourning: Support and Guidance for the Bereaved*. New York: Human Sciences Press, 1984.

INDEX

accidents, 65, 68, 175, 176, 333
adolescence, 35–36
adult children. *See* children of the elderly
adult day care, 201
age. *See* aging parent(s); old age and the aging process
aging parent(s): adaptability of, 69–70, 73–74; assessing, 133–35, 177–84; behavior patterns, 81–85, 136–37; communicating with, 181, 232–33; conflicting feelings about, 15–37; death of, 115–29; decision-making role, 186, 242–43, 253–54; family dynamics and, 38–58, 239–55; financial contributions to, 51–52; as grandparents, 53–55; incapacitated, 175–209; independence of, 77–78, 83, 84, 135–37, 226, 227–28, 257–58; individuality of, 233–34; in-laws and, 40–41, 52–53; legal rights, 204–6, 207, 243; life-styles of, 136–37, 207; living with, 148–51; as manipulators, 55–59, 84, 138–41; national organizations for, 316–19; as pawns in sibling battles, 48; personality changes, 78–79, 88;

pride of, 172–73; promises to, 147, 252–53; pseudo-helpless, 138–41; refusal of care, 206–7; remarriage of, 107–9; saying no to, 139–41; as scapegoats, 35–36; widowed, 99–107. *See also* children of the elderly; family and family dynamics; old age and the aging process
Alabama, 267, 280
Alaska, 157, 267, 272
alcoholism, 328, 330
Alzheimer's disease (AD), 66, 85, 87, 178, 215, 216, 222, 228, 260, 326
Alzheimer's Disease and Related Disorders Association (Alzheimer's Association), 88, 319
American Association of Homes for the Aging (AAHA), 213, 316
American Association of Retired Persons (AARP), 9, 98, 147, 163, 169, 263, 316–17
American Cancer Society, 195
American Samoa, 267
anger, 116, 212; extreme, 85; at loss, 80–81, 86; masks for, 43; at parents, 21–22, 34–35, 43

ABOUT THE AUTHORS

Dr. Barbara Silverstone is Executive Director of the Lighthouse, the New York Association for the Blind, which recently established a National Center for Vision and Aging. She is a member of the National Association of Social Workers, a Fellow of the Gerontological Society of America and the American Orthopsychiatric Association, and a former member of the House of Delegates of the American Association of Homes for the Aging. Her most recent activities include serving as president of the Gerontological Society of America in 1988, and chairing the Task Force on Standards and Guidelines for Social Work Case Management issued by the National Association of Social Workers, and the Task Force on Aging and Sensory Change for the Research, Education, and Practice Committee of the Gerontological Society of America.

Dr. Silverstone has addressed national audiences on topics such as family relations of the elderly, long-term care for the frail elderly, the psychosocial implications of aging, and age-related vision loss. Her professional experience has encompassed a wide variety of settings from private practice to psychiatric and rehabilitation services, and has included individual and group psychotherapy with children, young adults, and the elderly and their families. Her other publications include a textbook, *Social Work Practice with the Frail Elderly and Their Families*, co-authored with Ann Burack-Weiss; and the chapters "Social Aspects of Rehabilitation" in *Rehabilitation in the Aged*, and "Issues for the Middle Generation: Responsibility, Adjustment, and Growth" in *Aging Parents*.

Helen Kandel Hyman graduated from Barnard College in 1942 and was a staff writer for CBS for eight years before changing to a career as free-lance writer and editor. In her work, she has concentrated on the two opposite ends of the life-cycle, writing mainly for or about the young and the elderly. She has also written extensively on mental health, medical, and family subjects, including over a hundred radio and television scripts, documentaries, and pamphlets for CBS, NBC, UNICEF, the Family Service Society, the American Hospital Association, and the public health department of the Equitable Life Assurance Society. Her translation from the Italian of *A Treasury of the World's Greatest Fairy Tales* appeared shortly before she began work on the first edition of *You and Your Aging Parent*. Since then she has written and lectured on various aspects of intergenerational relationships.